CHALLENGES IN INFORMATION TECHNOLOGY MANAGEMENT

CHALLENGES IN INFORMATION TECHNOLOGY MANAGEMENT

Editors

Man-Chung Chan | Ronnie Cheung | James N K Liu

Hong Kong Polytechnic University, Hong Kong

World Scientific

NEW JERSEY • LONDON • SINGAPORE • BEIJING • SHANGHAI • HONG KONG • TAIPEI • CHENNAI

Published by

World Scientific Publishing Co. Pte. Ltd.
5 Toh Tuck Link, Singapore 596224
USA office: 27 Warren Street, Suite 401-402, Hackensack, NJ 07601
UK office: 57 Shelton Street, Covent Garden, London WC2H 9HE

British Library Cataloguing-in-Publication Data
A catalogue record for this book is available from the British Library.

CHALLENGES IN INFORMATION TECHNOLOGY MANAGEMENT
Proceedings of the International Conference

ISBN-13 978-981-281-906-2
ISBN-10 981-281-906-1

Printed in Singapore by World Scientific Printers

Challenges in Information Technology Management

The Institute of Systems Management

Sponsored by

The Jiangyin Municipal Government

The Hong Kong Polytechnic University

PREFACE

This book represents part of the improved research output from the International Conference of Information Management (ICITM2007) organized in January 2007 Hong Kong by the Hong Kong Polytechnic University, in conjunction with its own Institute of Systems Management (ISM); the Department of Computing, Taiwan Chung Cheng University; and supported by the Jiangyin Municipal Government of China. The aim of the conference, and so of the book, in this era of rapid development and the proliferation of information, is to stimulate the further application of IT in industry and management. We all know that IT has multiple and growing roles in modern society: it is present at the core of the software and outsourcing industries; it provides vital infrastructure for the service sector, including finance, in cities such as Hong Kong. And in Jiangyin IT is now a primary driver of a fast-developing, technology-based economy. The continued development of this process relies on synergistic co-operation between universities, government, and industry. This conference and this volume have sought to contribute to and encourage this ongoing cooperation.

Our fellow researchers and professionals, from more than 20 countries and 50 universities and institutions, submitted a total of 175 papers to this conference. From these, the reviewers were limited to selecting just 66 regular papers and 10 poster papers and then, for this post conference publication, further papers were invited in addition to the selection of about 50% of the extended conference papers. Further review finally confirmed 30 papers in the following three categories:

(1)Development of Enabling Technologies;

(2)Electronic & Management;

(3)IT Systems & Applications.

These papers feature the results of the latest research in the areas of information systems, enabling technologies, business management, as well as potential applications in industries including education, finance, logistics, medical, tourism, and IT services.

The editors are grateful to all reviewers for their advice in reviewing the many submissions. Thanks also go to our technical writer, Mr Martin Kyle, Mr Denis Guo, and our Publisher, for their tireless efforts in helping to finalize the book. We also thank the School of Professional Education and Executive Development (SPEED) of PolyU for its support for our theme of applied technology in management and e-Learning. The support of these individuals and groups is greatly appreciated.

Man-chung Chan, Ronnie Cheung, James Liu

CONTENTS

PART A

Development of Enabling Technologies

MULTI-AGENT-BASED SYSTEM FOR LOGISTICS SERVICE PROCESS*

FENG HE†
School of Computer Science, North University for Nationalities
Yinchuan, Ningxia 750021, P.R.China

QI XU
School of Business & Management, Donghua University
Shanghai, 200051, P.R.China

In recognition of the increasing importance of rapidly changing needs and opportunities, today's global markets require interoperability to integrate diverse logistics processes to share information and collaborate among logistics partners. The multi-agents system provides a promising computing paradigm for efficient logistics service response and integration of logistics service processes. This paper discusses an approach to designing an integrated logistic system based on multi-agents. A framework of an integrated logistics process is proposed. A prototype based on the proposed framework is implemented using ZEUS toolkit. It presents how the proposed integrated architecture can be used to establish collaborative logistics business environment by providing dynamic processes services.

1. Introduction

It is always a challenge for logistics service providers to deliver products to customers as quickly as possible. Logistics is concerned with the flow of materials in the supply chain, from source through the industrial process to the customer, and then on to re-use/re-cycle or disposal [1] A broad view of logistics management then includes the supervision and control of procurement, production, transportation, warehousing, and inventory stocking across enterprises. Accordingly logistics management should support and plan the return and processing of unused products so as to make more efficient use of available resources. By coordinating all resources, logistics have to ensure that service levels agreements with customers are honored. It becomes a trend that automating logistics processes considers the planning and controlling of material flow within and between companies from suppliers to customers, as well as the management and controlling of used product, potential recyclable and solid waste flows. In other words, automating logistics processes will provide an integrated, end-to-end fulfillment and supply chain management services to the providers of logistics processes [2].

With an adequate coordination and integration of logistics processes, in an economic and environmental context, organizations will be able to get a double effect in their business operations. Recent advances of the multi-agents technologies help the effort of tackling integrated issue in the logistic system [3,4]. The notion of heterogeneous autonomous agents collaborating is a powerful metaphor for distributed and interoperable information systems. The agent-based approach can realize knowledge level cooperation between autonomous systems, which results in the enhancement of distributed systems interoperability, scalability and re-configurability [5,7,8].

In this paper, we discuss an agent-based approach for automated negotiation and coordinated processes among integrated logistics process. The distributed system of autonomous agents functions as an organization, gathering and analyzing information,

* This work is supported by "National Science Foundation of China" (NO:70772073).
† Work partially supported by "Ningxia National Science Foundation " (NZ:0692) and the Foundations of Ningxia key subject for computer application technology.

formulating strategies based on various conditions, and publishing processes information of products to managers. A multi-agents prototype system for logistics processes is developed through the conduct of a concept-proof project and use of a toolkit called ZEUS which is an integrated environment for the rapid development of collaborative agent application.

2. Logistics Service Process

The typical logistics processes include request for customer services, material supply, product storage, product shipping, information tracking, and recycling for used product. Compared with the supply chain business process, logistics business process has fewer and more stable customers. Obviously, integrated services are the core competition ability of a logistics business. It can help its customers to optimize their logistics management strategies, build up and operate their logistics systems and even manage their whole distribution systems [2]. By providing integrated logistics services to various customers, logistics providers could respond their customers quickly and deli ever service or product timely and cost effectively.

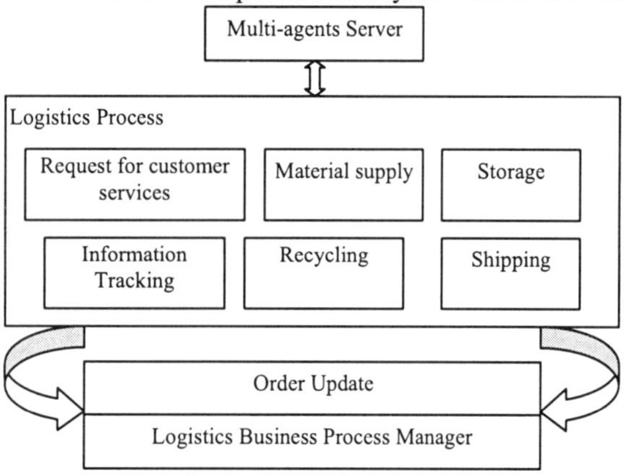

Figure 1: View of Integrated Logistics Processes.

We propose that an integrated logistics processes system involving multiple agents can autonomously perform tasks through exchanging information across enterprises. As shown in Figure 1, logistics interacts with the business process manager in a multi-agents server. Building an integrated logistics system tends to involve the acquisition and integration of many components from different participants, for simplicity, we assume there are 6 participants in this investigation.

The first participant performed task is called request for logistics services (RFLS). The second participant is material supplier (MS), which supplies all the materials needed. We call this task SupplyMaterials. The third participant is product storage provider, called PS. It supplies warehouse to customer through a task called ProvideStorage. The next participant is a transporter, a representative of shipping. It ships products to customers. This task is called Shipping. The fifth participant is R, the recycler of used products. Recycling includes recycling wastes, disassembly, remanufacturing, reusing, and final disposal. It did not possesses initial resources. The final participant is tracking. It monitors analyzes activities information related to the logistics processes.

In this simplified integrated logistics system, each participant (i.e. supplier, warehouse, and recycler, etc.) will be represented by a software agent. Agents have to be designed as such that they can be configured to be used to simulate and control all the coordinative activities among participants.

3. Multi-agent System Design

3.1. *Role Modeling in Integrated Logistics Service Processes*

As indicated in Fig.1, it will be very challenging to ensure that the production and transfer of resources meet the on demand need while managing and monitoring activities throughout the logistics processes lifecycle. By using trade-off relationships between the logistics flow and corresponding information flow, we manage to coordinate activities among all the logistics chain participants in an integrated fashion in order to achieve the common business goals. We utilize the role modeling to address the needs. The role models in this investigation are grouped based on their business domains.

In this work, several agents based on the role model to fulfill the needed roles can be defined (Table 1). Here describes a typical working scenario.

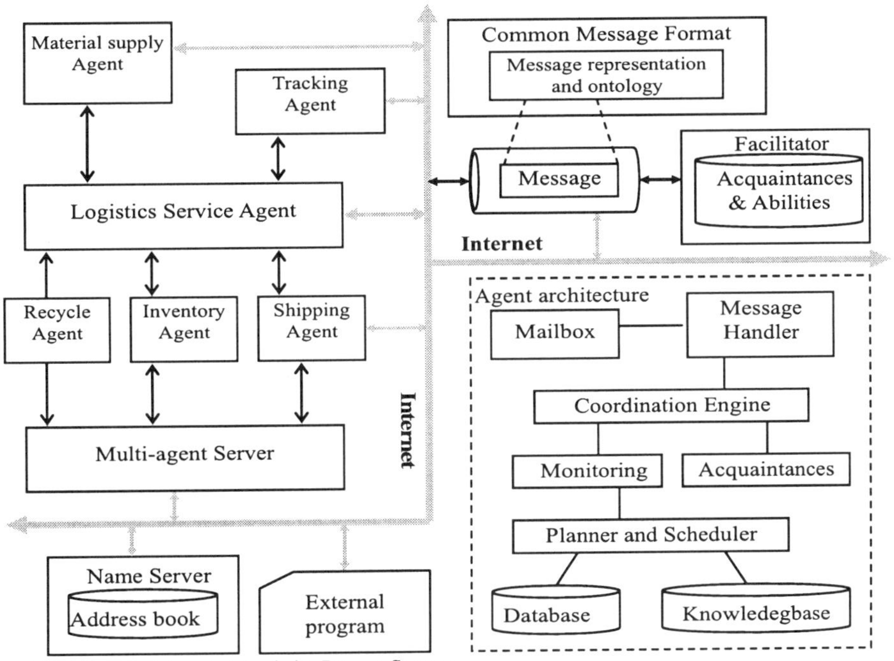

Figure 2: A framework of Multi-agents Integrated Logistics Process System.

Table 1. Agent roles in integrated logistics processes.

Agent Name	Roles Played
Inventory agent (IA)	As a participant role to negotiate with partners, customer and recycler
Shipping agent (SA)	As a participant to negotiate with Other partners
Material supply agent (MSA)	As a participant role to negotiate between Raw material supplier and manufacturers
Logistics service agent (LSA)	As a core-business to respond logistics processes specification.
Recycle agent (RA)	As a participant role to negotiate among partners.
Tracking agent (TA)	As a participant role to track and Monitor information
ANS agent	As an agent name server
Facilitator agent	As facilities to determine the agent's acquaintances and abilities

All task agents (i.e., IA, SA, MSA, LSA, RA, and TA) advertise their abilities, knowledge in the acquaintance database. They use facilitator agent to identify agents with the required abilities and knowledge. They also use an ANS agent to determine the addresses of the identified agents. It is mandatory to have an agent in the Agent Name Server to ensure the realization of agent location independence in this framework. Note that ZEUS [6-9] is an agent development toolkit developed by British Telecom for building agent-based applications. We use ZEUS as the development tool to define and develop agents, their interactions and living environment.

3.2. *ZEUS Tool*

The ZEUS tool-kit is an integrated environment for the rapid development of collaborative agent application. ZEUS consists of a host of editors which an agent developer uses to specify the information required to define a ZEUS agent. The editors mainly include the following [6]:

An Ontology Editor: for defining the ontology of the domain.

A Task Description Editor: a visual editor for describing primitive tasks that the agent can perform.

An Agent Definition Editor: for describing agents logically, their abilities and initial resources.

An Organization Editor: a visual tool for defining the organizational relationships between agents.

A Coordination Editor: for allowing the user select coordination protocols s/he wants to imbue an agent with or for describing new ones.

Above editors facilitate the identification and description of a set of agents, selecting agent functionality and inputting task and domain related data.

3.3. *Agent-based Framework*

According to ZEUS agent architecture [3], we designed an agent-based framework for integrated logistics processes (see Fig.2) to provide an appropriate syntheses and effective coordination mechanism by taking into consideration the agent roles and system characteristics. In this framework, when agent needs to perform a complex task, it is required to collaborate with other agents. To do so, it uses the Facilitator to discover the agents with the required abilities, and the Agent Name Server to determine the addresses of these agents. A common ontology is also required for a shared representation and understanding of common domain concepts. An acquaintance describes the agent's relationships with other agents in the society, and its beliefs about the capabilities of different agents.

The communication between agents is realized using message mechanisms. A message from another agent is received by the agent's Mailbox, which passes the message to the Message Handler for processing. Then, the message is forwarded to the coordination engine to determine whether to achieve the goal and if so, to devise and coordinate an appropriate plan of action. The Planner creates a plan for the goal, utilizing and reserving the resources that are required by the plan. The monitoring agent starts, stops, and monitors system scheduled activities. It also informs the coordination engine of success or exceptional termination conditions of the tasks it is monitoring.

4. Implementation of Multi-agent Logistics Process System

4.1. *Ontology Definition*

Ontology is used to provide a hierarchically structured set of causes and effects for understanding a domain, which is an effective means to explicitly describe knowledge in a knowledge base. Ontology is meant as a collection of names of resource types, their attributes, and functions. It includes a vocabulary for referring to a subject area, and a set of logical statements expressing the constraints existing in the domain and restricting the interpretation of the vocabulary.

Before implementing any agents the developer should define the application ontology. In ZEUS, an individual domain concept is described by using the term "fact". A Fact represents something that an agent believes to be true, either about itself or its external environment. The type of a Fact determines whether it is consumed by a precondition of a Task, or merely referred to. ZEUS provides two kinds of fact: abstract and entity. Here, all the concepts refer to the entity. By ZEUS ontology definition, the designed agents have a complete knowledge of the entire ontology.

4.2. *Agent creation*

We use ZEUS Agent Generator to creating a new agent. This stage consists of four sub-processes that are agent definition, task definition agent organization, and agent coordination, which are repeated for each different task agent in the application.

4.2.1 Agent definition

Agent definition describes the agent's abilities and knowledge (which will change with time, as the agent discovers more about its environment). We need to specify the attributes of each agent, i.e., its social and domain responsibilities – what tasks it can perform, the initial resources of the agents, and the agent planning abilities. ZEUS provides a form-based interface for modeling the ZEUS agents. All the details such as task-name, fact type, attributes and its values can be entered.

4.2.2 Task definition

Agent tasks consume resources to produce their products, with each task lasting for a finite time period. This phase defines tasks in terms of their costs, constraints, demand prerequisites, preconditions, etc. Constraints are special requirements which build a link between a task's pre- and post-conditions. Preconditions may be based on knowledge in the form of facts retrieved from a database. For example, in ZEUS, requesting logistics service specification fact can enter a precondition of logistics service task. Then, a variable that will refer to a specific service instance used when this task is invoked has been created. Next the constraints relevant to this service consumption are entered. In this application we assume that per service contains inventory and shipping time that will impact and restrict the type of SKU and its customer service level. The number of items present after task execution must equal the number available before task execution

4.2.3 Agent Organization

Agent organization illustrates the relationship between the own agent and other agents and acquaintance abilities from other agents [7]. An agent can be ordered by another agent to perform some task, or can collaborate with others to achieve common goals. An agent may be known a priority to other potential collaborators, or may be discovered on an 'as needed' basis via a directory service. Through organization of agents, the relations between agents can be clearly illustrated.

• *Logistics services agent organization*

Specify that IA, SA, MSA RA and TA are its acquaintances, with a relationship of subordinate. Materials supply, inventory, shipping and used-product are their abilities, respectively. By information provided by those tracking agents, the LSA can know what logistics service can be supplied by IA, SA, MSA, and RA. And what used-products can be recycled by RA.

• *Recycle agent organization*

For the sake of brevity we assume that the recycle agent has two acquaintances, MSA and IA, which provide their relevant information to recycle agent. Each acquaintance should be specified by its agent's capabilities. In an integrated system, LSA's ability is service. RA's ability is used-products. By providing this information, the RA knows what service the LSA, IA, SA can perform. It can also know the type and number of used-products by RA. Without that information the Recycle agent would have to discover these capabilities through a Facilitator agent.

4.2.4 Agent Coordination

Agent coordination includes the interaction protocols and negotiation strategies between agents. The interaction protocol is an agent conversation model that describes when an agent is expected to communicate, what messages will be exchanged, and the effect of receiving particular messages. Negotiation strategies are to explain why agents interact. This arises from each agent's intentions and motivations, which are encoded into interaction strategies [7, 8]. The applicability of these strategies is dependent on the status and role of the agent.

Take for an example, when an LSA wants to perform some specification, it needs to negotiate with MSA regarding different attributes of solutions, such as lead time, cost, quality, and number based on the overall utility. It begins in the Initialization state and formulates a message containing its requirements, then broadcasts to all potentially interested MSA, and then the agent moves into the Negotiation state to wait for responses. If an MSA decides to reply it will move into its Negotiation state and use its strategy to formulate a proposal message to send back to the LSA. Then, the MSA waits for a response. When the MSA receives a proposal it analyzes this proposal using its own strategy to evaluate whether the proposal is acceptable or not. Accordingly, it takes a corresponding action, either ending the conversation or sending a new message to the LSA.

Whereas for RA, the coordination is characterized by asymmetrical possession of information; i.e. some entities (e.g., MSA, IA, etc.) will possess information related to the waste or used products that recycling agent does not. As a result, the agents must communicate to share information necessary to their continual operations. In one case, the MSA or IA can be regarded as a publisher to maintain some repository of information, and the recycling agent can be regarded as a subscriber to require the information owned by those agents. The interaction between the publisher and the subscriber involves registration and asking and response to queries. Through this interaction, the recycle agent can timely acquire relevant information and take a recycle action.

In another case, as a monitor role, on one hand, the recycle agent can know the material components of products and analyze their resource efficiency according to the product information that comes from MSA; on the other hand, in terms of environment data of product and production process, the recycling agent can know environment impact degree. By comparing the relevant regulator and policy of environment, the recycle agent simulates the decision-making process to negotiate with a LSA using its own evaluation strategy, and present its proposal message to logistics service agent and decision makers.

4.3. *Service Agent Configuration*

In this paper, service agents include ANS and facilitator agent. The configuration of service agents decides what service agents will be created, and how they will be configured. Usually, an agent society must possess at least one Agent Name Server (ANS). The ANS maintains a registry of known agents, enabling them to map agent identities to a logical network location. In ZEUS, the developer can design an Agent Name Server through a well-developed graphical user interface (GUI). The GUI displays the information on the server's activity, and also provides some control functions. A facilitator typically first retrieves a list of known agents from an ANS; secondly send a message to each of the agents by asking them to reply with details of the abilities they are currently able to perform. If all agent acquaintances and abilities have been determined at design-time and will not change, a facilitator agent might not be needed. However, this situation is unlikely, so most applications will possess at least one facilitator, which can be created and configured using the 'Facilitators' panel in ZEUS [7-9].

4.4. *Task Agent Configuration*

This stage enables the runtime parameters of the specified task agents. This involves supplying information such as the host machines the agents will run on, and the external resources and programs to which the agents will be linked [9]. In ZEUS, this process is performed as follows:

First, the DNS file should be configured. Let the DNS file field contain the same contents as the Name Server's Address File field.

Secondly, link an agent to an external resource. A task agent can obtain the resources it needs to perform its tasks from one of three sources: from its resource database, from other agents, or from an external data source. The latter can be connected to the task agent through a Java class. For instance, a manufacture agent requires a means of capturing the demand that will initiate the material flow; this should be implemented in a separate class and identified in the External Program.

Thirdly, link an agent to an external program. A task agent can be linked to external programs that enable it to send or receive information from the outside world. This external program will typically be a user interface from which instructions are received and to which the agent sends results. In ZEUS, external program is linked by a java class (i.e., an executing agent program). Thus, external program can utilize the agent's public methods to query or modify the agent's internal state. In our ILM system, each task agent can be linked to an external program. Each external program provides a GUI, by which the users can input their decision information as integrated logistics process system operates.

4.5. *Agent Implementation*

Once the task and service agents have been appropriately configured, the agent source code should be generated. All external actions, of which tasks or database accesses are the best examples, are created by the ZEUS tool-kit in the form of callback functions.

5. Conclusion

Integrated logistics process is an emerging paradigm with supply chain management philosophy. Its support system can be developed by new information technology. One of the supports for designing thus system is agent technology. Intelligent agents seem to be an appropriate approach for modeling distributed behavior to coordinate and integrate logistics processes throughout the logistic supply chain. This paper presents the concept and the framework of an integrated logistics process system for logistics service collaboration or collaborative intelligent business in general. It is able to integrate both the forward and reverse logistics and enable appropriate coordination using the multi-agents technology. A prototype system presented in this paper to show how such a multi-agents system can be implemented using the ZEUS toolkit tool, and supports sophisticated dynamic and automatic services collaboration for logistics process service.

Acknowledgments

The work was supported by "National Science Foundation of China" （NO:70772073） and partially supported by. "Ningxia Natural Science Foundation" (NO: NZ0692) and the Foundations of Ningxia key subject for computer application technology.

References

1. J.B.Sheu, Y.H.Chou and C.C.Hu, An integrated logistics operational model for green-supply chain management, Transportation Research Part E, (2004).
2. Ying Wang and Dayong Sang, Multi-agent framework for third party logistics in E-commerce, *Expert Systems with Applications* **29**, 431–436 (2005).
3. P.Romano, Coordination and integration mechanisms to manage logistics processes across

supply networks, *Journal of Purchasing & Supply Management* **9**, 111-134 (2003).

4. H.Baumgarten, C.Butz, A.Fritsch, et al, Supply Chain Management and Reverse Logistics-Integration of Reverse Logistics Processes into Supply Chain Management Approaches, 79-85.
5. Hyacinth S. Nwana, Divine T. Ndumu, Lyndon C. Lee and Jaron C. Collis, ZEUS: A Toolkit for Building Distributed Multi-Agent Systems, http://www.labs.bt.com/projects/agents.html.
6. Xiaolong Xue, Xiaodong Li, Qiping Shen, et al, An agent-based framework for supply chain coordination in construction, *Automation in Construction* **14**, 43-430 (2005).
7. S.N. Hyacinth, D Ndumu and C. Lyndon, "ZEUS: An advanced Tool-kit for Engineering Distributed Multi-Agent Systems, http://agent.aitiaai/download.
8. J. Collis and D. Ndumu, The ZEUS Agent Building Toolkit, Intelligent Systems Research Group,BT Labs, Relases 1.04, British Telecommunication plc., (2000).
9. ZEUS REALISTION GUIDE, http://www.labs.bt.com/projects/agents.html.
10. S.D.Pathak, G.Nordstrom and S.Kurokawa, Modeling of supply chain: a multi-agent approach, White paper.
11. J.Li, Z.Gao and H.C.Zhang, Plug and play information Sharing Architecture and its Application In Green Supply Chain Management, *IEEE International Symposium on Electronics and the Environment*, 157 – 162 (2002).
12. S.Anderson, J.Allen, M.Browne, Urban logistics—how can it meet policy makers sustainability objectives, *Journal of Transport Geography* **13,** 71-81 (2005).
13. R.Anane, M.Younas and C.F Tsai, Agent-based Transactional Framework for the Supply Chain, *Proceedings of Machine Learning and Cybernetics* **4(4-5)**, 1956 - 1961 (2002).
14. A Smirnov., M Pashkin., and N. Chilov, Ontology Management in Multi-agent System for Knowledge Logistics, *Proceedings of Info-tech and Info-net*, **3(29)** , 231 – 236 (2001).

IMPROVED DATA MINING ALGORITHMS FOR FREQUENT PATTERNS WITH COMPOSITE ITEMS

KE WANG
School of Economics and Management, Beihang University
Beijing, P.R. China

JAMES N. K. LIU
Department of Computing, Hong Kong Polytechnic University
Hong Kong, P.R. China

WEI-MIN MA
School of Economics and Management, Tongji University,
Shanghai, P. R. China

Mining association rules are used to analyze the data in a database to discover interesting rules. The algorithms for mining association rules with composite items have the potential to discover rules which cannot be found out by algorithms without composite items. Algorithms for finding large composite items should scan the database for every candidate composite item to determine whether it is large. In this paper, we design some improved algorithms for finding large composite items which only need to scan the database one time to find all the large composite items. This algorithm also allows the reduction of many more redundant candidate composite items.

1. Introduction

Mining association rules are used to analyze the data in a database to discover interesting rules and provide concise statements about potentially useful information. An association rule [1] is a probabilistic relationship expressed in the form $X \Rightarrow Y$ between sets of database attributes. Rules are inferred based on an empirical examination of records in a database, where *X* and *Y* are sets of items, that is, *itemsets*.

The *support* for *X*, denoted as $S(X)$, is the number of transactions that contain all items in *X* (often expressed as a proportion of the total number of records). The support for an association rule $X \Rightarrow Y$ is $S(X \cup Y)$. The *confidence* of the association rule $X \Rightarrow Y$ is the ratio: $\frac{S(X \cup Y)}{S(X)}$. Support and confidence provide the empirical basis for the derivation of the inference expressed in the rule as well as a measure of the interestingness of the rule. The support for a rule expresses the number of records within which the association may be observed, while the confidence expresses this as a proportion of the instances of the antecedent of the rule. In practical investigations, it is usual to regard these rules as interesting only if the support and confidence exceed some threshold values. Hence the problem may be formulated as a search for all association rules within the database for which the required support and confidence levels are attained. Subsets which the support exceeds the required threshold are referred to as *large*, *frequent*, or *interesting* sets [2]. That is to say given a *minimum support* δ, an itemset *X* is *large* or is referred to as a *large itemset* if $S(X) > \delta$. Rules are useful if their confidence is above a *minimum confidence* value specified by users.

The issue of mining association rules with composite items was proposed several years ago. In paper [3], introduces the concept of *composite items* and describes algorithms for mining association rules using composite items. The algorithms allow large itemsets to contain composite items. This enables them to discover certain useful rules which cannot be found out by other existing algorithms without composite items [4-7]. The algorithm for finding large composite items described in [3] should scan the database for every candidate composite item to determine whether it is large. When a database is very large, the efficiency of this algorithm may be affected. In this paper, we design some improved algorithms which need scan the database once in order to find all the large composite items. The algorithms described in this paper are based on a Novel Frequent-Pattern tree (NFP-tree for short). It is similar to the MFP-tree which was first proposed in [8]. The NFP-tree and MFP-tree are both tree structures analogous to Frequent-Pattern tree (FP-tree) [9]. For a given database, the algorithm first scans the database to construct an NFP-tree and then finds large composite items using the NFP-tree. The compositions which do not contain any elements (items) we are interested in are ignored in the NFP-tree. Then the second step that finding large composite items using the NFP-tree is much simple.

The rest of paper is organized as follows. In Section 2, the concept of composite item is introduced and an example is also presented. In Section 3, we formulate how to design and construct an NFP-tree. In Section 4 we describe the algorithm for finding large composite items using the NFP-tree. Section 5 discusses the performance of these algorithms. Section 6 offers our Conclusion and a discussion of future work.

2. Composite Items

In this section, we introduce the concept of composite items with particular reference to [3, 10] and then present an example using the supermarket shopping-basket analysis [11].

Let $I = a_1, \cdots, a_m$ be the set of literals called *atomic items*. A *composite item* is formed by combining several atomic items. The general form of a composite item is $a_1 \vee \cdots \vee a_n$, where $a_j \in I$ for $1 \le j \le n$ and $a_i \ne a_j$ for $i \ne j$. A database consists of transactions where each transaction is a set of atomic items. A transaction contains a composite item if the transaction contains at least one of the atomic items which form the composite item. Atomic items and composite items will be referred to as items in general. An item is *large* if the number of transactions containing the item exceeds the minimum support.

For a composite item consisting of i atomic items, e.g. $a_1 \vee a_2 \vee \cdots \vee a_i$, the ($i-1$)-subitem of $a_1 \vee a_2 \vee \cdots \vee a_i$ is a composite item formed by selecting $i-1$ atomic items from $\{a_1, a_2, \cdots, a_i\}$. For example, $A \vee B \vee C$ has three distinct 2-subitems. They are $A \vee B$, $A \vee C$ and $B \vee C$.

An itemset is a set of items such that none of the items in the set has common items. For example, $\{A, B \vee C\}$ is a valid itemset. However, $\{A, A \vee B, C \vee D\}$ is not a valid itemset as A and $A \vee B$ have common item A.

An *association rule* is an implication of the form $X \Rightarrow Y$ where X, Y and $X \cup Y$ are itemsets, $X \ne \varnothing$, $Y \ne \varnothing$ and $X \cap Y = \varnothing$.

An itemset consisting of i items is called an i-itemset. The ($i-1$)-subset of an i-itemset is an ($i-1$)-itemset which is formed by selecting $i-1$ items from the i-itemset. An i-itemset has i distinct ($i-1$)-subsets. For example, a 3-itemset $\{A, B, C\}$ has three 2-subsets, i.e. $\{A, B\}$, $\{A, C\}$ and $\{B, C\}$.

Tthe shopping-basket example is useful to illustrate both the principal characteristics of the approach and its usefulness. A database is shown in Table 1. In this case, each record in the database is a representation of a single shopping transaction, recording the set of all items purchased in that transaction. It is assumed that

(1) The minimum support is 4.

(2) The users are interested in the composite items generated from set $\{A, B, C\}$

The large items are shown in Table 2 and Table 3. The large itemsets which will be used to generate rules are shown in Table 4. From Table 4, we can get the association rule $A \vee B \Rightarrow C$. It suggests that shoppers who purchase items A or B are also likely to purchase items C at the same time. However, without the composite items, the rule $A \Rightarrow C$ or $B \Rightarrow C$ can't be discovered. In the following discussion, we focus on how to find out all large composite items.

Table 1. Database

ID	Items Bought
1	A C E
2	D E
3	A C D
4	B C
5	B C E

Table 2. Large Composite Items

Composite Items	Support
$A \vee B \vee C$	4
$A \vee B$	4
$A \vee C$	4
$B \vee C$	4

Table 3. Large Atomic Items

Atomic Items	Support
C	4

Table 4. Large Itemsets

Itemsets	Support
$\{A \vee B, C\}$	4

3. NFP-Tree

The algorithms described in this paper are based on the NFP-tree. The NFP-tree is a tree structure defined below.

(1) It consists of one root labeled as "null", a set of item-prefix subtrees as the children of the root and a header table which links to the root node.

(2) Each node in the item-prefix subtree consists of three fields: *item-name*, *count* and *node-link*, where *item-name* registers which item this node represents, *count* registers the number of transactions represented by the portion of the path reaching this node, and *node-link* links to the next nodes or null if there is none.

Considering the user's interest, we construct an NFP-tree as follows.

Algorithm 1 (NFP-tree construction).

Input: A transaction database *DB* and a set *INT* which contains all items that users are interested in.

Output: The NFP-tree of *DB*

(1) Create the root of an NFP-tree, and label it as "null".

(2) For every transaction of *DB*, do:

Check that whether the transaction contains one or more items which belong to *INT*. If it is false, deal with the next transaction. Or else insert the transaction into NFP-tree as follows.

(a) Take out the first item of the transaction.

(b) If the root has a child node whose *item-name* is same as the item then the node's *count*=*count*+1, else create a new node next to the root and let the new node's *count*=1.

(c) Take the current node as the root.

(d) Take out the next item and go back to (b) until all the items are inserted into the NFP-tree.

Taking Table 1 for example, we can construct an NFP-tree as shown in Figure.1. It is assumed that users are interested in the items of set $\{A,B,C\}$; therefore the second transaction in *DB* is ignored in the NFP-tree.

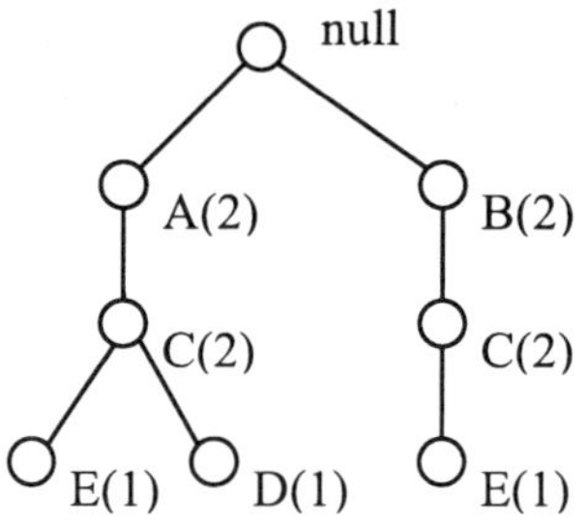

Figure 1. NFP-tree

4. Finding Large Items

Once the NFP-tree is constructed, Algorithm 2 is used to find large items. There are two facts which can easily be obtained from the description in Section 2 and used in the algorithm.

Fact 1.[3] If composite item $a_1 \vee a_2 \vee \cdots \vee a_n$ is not large, then none of the composite items generated from $\{a_1, a_2, \cdots, a_n\}$ is large.

Fact 2. If composite item $a_1 \vee a_2 \vee \cdots \vee a_n$ is large, then a composite item which contains all atomic items in $\{a_1, a_2, \cdots, a_n\}$ is large.

The two facts are used to reduce the candidate composite items in the following algorithm. Therefore, the efficiency of the algorithm is much improved. It is assumed that *LAI* represents the set of large atomic items. Then any composite item which contains the atomic items in set *LAI* is large. *LCI* denotes the set of large composite items and *CC* denotes the candidate set (which consists of composite items) generated by Algorithm 4.

Algorithm 2 (Finding large items).

Input: The NFP-tree, minimum support δ and set *INT*.

Output: All large items.

(1) Scan the NFP-tree to find out all the large atomic items which belong to *INT*, and store them into set *LAI*.

(2) If $LAI \neq \varnothing$, use the items in *LAI* to generate large composite items and store them into set *LCI*. For example, if $INT = \{A,B,C\}$ and $LAI = \{A,B\}$, then $A \vee C$, $B \vee C$, $A \vee B$ and $A \vee B \vee C$ are generated and all of them are large.

(3) $M = INT - LAI$

(4) If M has more than two items, then use all the atomic items in M to form a single composite item N, or else go to (9).

(5) Check that whether N is large using Algorithm 3.

True $\rightarrow$ (6); False $\rightarrow$ (9).

(6) Add N into *LCI.*

(7) Use Algorithm 4 to generate candidate set *CC*.

(8) If $CC = \varnothing$ then go to (9), or else using Algorithm 3 to check every composite item, store the large ones into *LCI*. Then go back to (7).

(9) $LI = LAI + LCI$ is the set of all large items.

Algorithm 2 shows how to find large items with the NFP-tree. In step (1), the algorithm scans the NFP-tree to find out all the large atomic items which users are interested in. After finding out large atomic items, we know all composite items containing a large atomic item which is found in (1) are large from Fact 2. Therefore, step (3) removes the large atomic items from the set *INT*. This operation reduces the candidate composite items which need to be checked in the following. For example, it is assumed that C is a large atomic item found in (1). Then any composite items containing C are large. Thus, the composite items containing C should not be checked again and C is removed from *INT* in the next step. If M is null or has only one atomic item, the algorithm terminates. Otherwise, it should continue to check whether the composite items generated from the set M are large or not. Step (4) uses all the atomic items in M to form a single composite item N. If N is not large, from Fact 1 we know none of the composite items generated from the atomic items in N is large, so the algorithm terminates. If N is large, then the algorithm employs algorithm 4 to generate candidate set and check all composite items in the candidate set whether they are large or not using Algorithm 3 until $CC = \varnothing$, i.e. there is no candidate to be checked.

Algorithm 4 generates a candidate set whose composite items might be large. Fact 1 is used to reduce the candidate composite items in the algorithm. It is same as the algorithm presented in [3]. More details can be obtained from [3]. Algorithm 3 checks a composite item whether it is large or not as follows.

Algorithm 3 (Check).

Input: The NFP-tree, minimum support δ and the composite item (denoted as I).

Output: *True* or *False*.

(1) Let *I.count*=0.

(2) Read one of the child nodes of the root.

(3) Comparing the node with I, if it is same as one of the atomic items in I, go to (5).

(4) If the current node is a leaf node then go to (6), or else take the current node as the new root and go back to (2).

(5) $I.count = I.count +$ the current node's *count*.

(6) Read another child node of the root and go back to (3) until all the child nodes have been read.

(7) If the current root is the NFP-tree's root, the scanning has finished and go to (8). Or else take the father node of the current root as the new root and go back to (2).

(8) If $I.count \geq \delta$ return "*True*", or else return "*False*".

Algorithm 3 scans the NFP-tree to check that whether a composite item is large or not. It scans the NFP-tree with Depth-First Search. While reading a node same as one of the atomic items in I (the composite item needs to be checked), add the current node's *count* up to *I.count*. And then read the other child node of the current root until all subtrees of the NFP-tree have been scanned. Finally, compare *I.count* with the minimum support δ. If $I.count \geq \delta$, the composite item is large and return "*True*", or else return "*False*".

Taking the NFP-tree in Figure.1 for example, the algorithms described above find large items as follows. It is assumed that the minimum support δ is 4 and users are interested in the composite items generated from set $\{A,B,C\}$, i.e. $INT = \{A,B,C\}$.

Firstly, scan the NFP-tree to find out all the large atomic items which belong to *INT*. As shown in Figure.1, there is only one large atomic item, namely C. Therefore, $LAI = \{C\}$. C is large, then $A \vee C$, $B \vee C$ and $A \vee B \vee C$ are large and store them into *LCI*. We have $LCI = \{A \vee C, B \vee C, A \vee B \vee C\}$. The following processing only needs to check the composite items generated from the set $M = INT - LAI = \{A,B\}$.

Secondly, a composite item $A \vee B$ is generated. Then check whether $A \vee B$ is large as follows. Read one child node of the root, say A. It is one of the atomic items in $A \vee B$, so the *count* of $A \vee B$ is up to 2. Then read the other child node of the root. It is B, and is also one of the atomic items in $A \vee B$, so the *count* of $A \vee B$ is up to 4.

Comparing the *count* of $A \vee B$ with the minimum support δ, we know $A \vee B$ is large and then add it into *LCI*.

Finally, $LAI = \{C\}$ and

$LCI = \{A \vee B, A \vee C, B \vee C, A \vee B \vee C\}$. The results are same as those of Table 2 and Table 3. $LI = LAI + LCI = \{C, A \vee B, A \vee C, B \vee C, A \vee B \vee C\}$ is the set of all large items.

5. Performance of the Algorithms

The algorithms designed above construct an NFP-tree firstly. And then scans the NFP-tree to find out all large composite items. In this section, the performance of these algorithms is discussed.

It is obvious that if there is not any large composite item, the algorithms described in this paper are worse than algorithms proposed in paper [3] because of the cost of constructing an NFP-tree. When there is not any large composite item, none of the atomic items is large too. Therefore, no interesting rules will be found. However, such a case is less probable, which is of little significance to the problem discussed in this paper.

For every candidate composite item, the cost of algorithm 3 to check whether it is large or not is less than the algorithm in paper [3]. The algorithm in paper [3] scans the database one time for every candidate composite item. Generally, the quantity of records in a database is much more than the number of items in all records. Algorithm 3 scans the NFP-tree with Depth-First Search. The worst case is that all items in the database are present in the NFP-tree and all the items which users are interested in are far from the root. An example is shown in Figure 2.

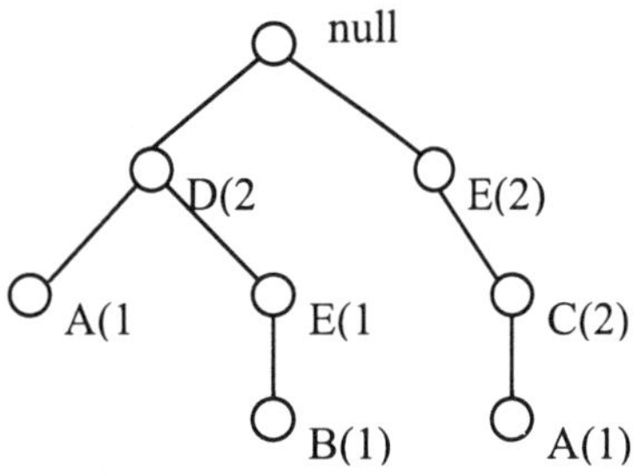

Figure 2. NFP-tree (the worst case)

It is assumed that the set $INT = \{A, B, C\}$. In Figure 2, all the atomic items which users are interested in (i.e. *A*, *B* and *C*) are far from the root. If $\{A \vee B\}$ should be checked, Algorithm 3 will read all nodes in the tree. While it reads the first leaf node (i.e. *A*), the *count* of this item is up to 1. And then while it reads the second leaf node (i.e. *B*), the *count* is up to 2. Finally, the last leaf node of the tree is read and the *count* of this item is up to 3. The process of scanning is finished.

From the NFP-tree, we can get the information of all records which contain items in *INT*. It is shown in Table 5 as follows. The records which do not contain any items in *INT* are ignored in the NFP-tree. Thus, Table 5 does not contain these records.

Table 5. Records from Figure 2

ID	Items Bought
1	D A
2	D E B
3	E C
4	E C A

However, if the users are only interested in the items *A*, *B* and *C*, the NFP-trees shown in Figure 1 and Figure 2 still contain some redundant information (say, *D* and *E*) for finding large composite items. So there are still some improvements that can be considered in algorithm 1 to optimize the configuration of the NFP-tree. Before constructing an NFP-tree, a certain sequence which consists of the atomic items in *INT* is defined. While adding a record into the tree, the items are inserted according to this sequence and the rest of items which are not in *INT* are not inserted into the tree.

Taking Table 5 for example, when $INT = \{A, B, C\}$, we insert the items in a record according to the sequence *A, B, C*. After taking out the first record in Table 5, compare its items (say, *D* and *A*) with the set *INT*. *A* is in *INT* while *D* is not, therefore insert *A* into the tree and ignore *D*. Then read the second and third records, and insert the items *B* and *C* into the tree. The operations are same as the first record. The fourth record has two items in *INT* (say, *C* and *A*). According to the defined sequence, *A* is inserted firstly. There has a node *A* in the tree as a child node of the root already, therefore increase the *count* of *A* by 1. And then insert *C* into the tree as a child node of *A*. Now an NFP-tree with improved configuration of Figure 2 is formed and shown in Figure 3.

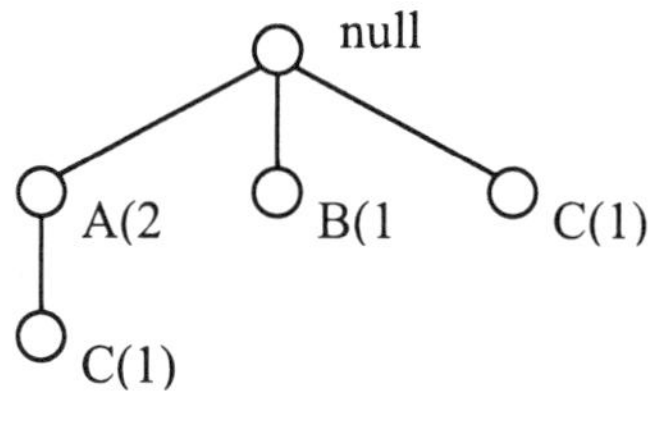

Figure 3. Improved NFP-tree

Comparing Figure 3 with Figure 2, it is obvious to see that the items which users are not interested in are removed in the improved NFP-tree. The configuration of the improved NFP-tree is much simple, thus finding large composite items from the tree will be more efficient.

For an improved NFP-tree, we have the following theorem.

Theorem 1. If there are m items in the set *INT* (which users are interested in), the improved NFP-tree has 2^m nodes at most.

Proof. An example is shown firstly. When $INT = \{A,B,C,D\}$, the case of an improved NFP-tree with the most nodes is shown in Figure 4. It has 16 nodes. Because the items in *INT* are inserted with a certain sequence and other items which are not in *INT* are ignored, two records with the same atomic items in *INT* are reflected in the improved NFP-tree without differences. For example, records (E,B,A,C) and (A,F,C,B) should be both added in the tree same as record (A,B,C).

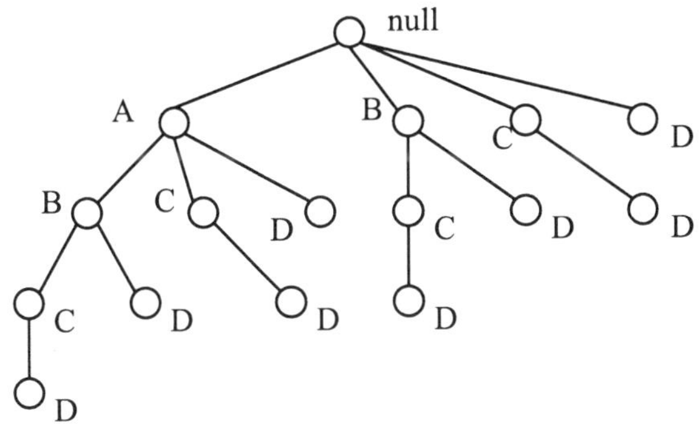

Figure 4. Improved NFP-tree (with most nodes)

In the improved NFP-tree, the paths from the root to every node denote the relevant combinations with the items in *INT*. For instance, the paths from the root to nodes at the first layer denote all the atomic items in *INT*. The paths from the root to nodes at the second layer denote all the combinations with two items in *INT*. If there are m items in the set *INT*, we can obtain $2^m - 1$ different combinations with the items in *INT*. Thus, there must be at most $2^m - 1$ nodes in the tree except the root. So there are at most 2^m nodes in total.

From Theorem 1, it is easy to see that while m is small, the configuration of the NFP-tree would be much simpler. As a result, the algorithms described above will be more efficient.

What is more, if there are some large atomic items, the performance of the algorithms proposed in this paper is much better. Algorithm 2 uses Fact 2 to reduce the candidate composite items. It is assumed that there are m atomic items which users are interested in (i.e. there are m items in set *INT*), and there are n items in *INT* are large where $n \le m$. Then we can obtain the following conclusion.

Theorem 2. By using Fact 2, algorithm 2 can reduce at least $2^m - 2^{m-n} - n$ candidate composite items which should be checked in the algorithm proposed in paper [3].

Proof. There are $2^m - 1$ different combinations with the m items in *INT*. The $2^m - 1$ different combinations contain m atomic items. Thus $2^m - m - 1$ composite items can be generated from the set *INT*. If n atomic items in *INT* are large, then the rest $m - n$ atomic items are not large. There are $2^{m-n} - 1$ different combinations with these $m - n$ items. Thus $2^{m-n} - (m-n) - 1$ composite items can be generated from the $m - n$ atomic items which are not large. None of these $2^{m-n} - (m-n) - 1$ composite items contains a large atomic item. Therefore, the number of the composite items which contain at least one large atomic item is

$$(2^m - m - 1) - [2^{m-n} - (m-n) - 1] = 2^m - 2^{m-n} - n$$

From Fact 2 it is easy to see that all these $2^m - 2^{m-n} - n$ composite items are large. So these composite items do not need to be checked. However, in the algorithm proposed in paper [3], all of them should be checked by scanning the database. Therefore, the performance of the algorithms in this paper is much improved by removing redundant composite items from the candidate set.

6. Conclusion

In this paper, improved algorithms for finding large composite items are designed and the performance of these algorithms is also discussed in the end. After that all the large composite items are found, existing algorithms can be used to find interesting rules easily. As described above, the algorithms only need to scan the database one time to find out all the large composite items. When a database is very large and the set of items which users are interested in is small, the algorithms will be more efficient.

When there is a need to handle a large number of itemsets, we shall consider dividing all the frequent intemsets into frequent equivalence classes and prune all the redundant itemsets accordingly [12]. We can also make use of an initial preprocessing of the data into some tree structure which incorporates a partial count of support totals [13]. This is particular useful in cases that require the data to be partitioned for primary memory use. Distributed data mining algorithms (e.g. [14]) shall be used to help collect frequent itemsets from different partitions.

On the other hand, we trust that the proposed algorithms can be extended to address other problem domains including our investigation on mining forecasting rules from observational meteorological data [15]. For example, we have applied association rule concept to studying related data, with each record listing various atmospheric observations including wind direction, wind speed, temperature, relative humidity, rainfall, and mean sea level pressure taken at a certain time in a certain area, we can find association rules like, "If the humidity is medium wet, then there is no rain in the same area at the same time". When we extend the classical association concept from intra-transactional associations to inter-transactional associations, we can explore the correlative relations of items from different transactions along certain dimensions, giving further room for prediction purpose. For instance, in a meteorological database whose records are organized by transaction time, inter-transactional association rules can represent associations of atmospheric phenomena along the time dimension. The proposed algorithms in this paper can facilitate the discovery of all the largest composite items in the database. This will be the subject of our future work.

Acknowledgments

The work was partly supported by the National Natural Science Foundation of China (70401006, 70671004, 70501015 and 70521001) and CRG grant G-U186 of the Hong Kong Polytechnic University.

References

1. R. Agrawal, T. Imielinski and A. Swami, Mining association rules between sets of items in large databases, *Proceedings of the 1993 ACM SIGMOD Conference on Management of Data,* 207-216 (1993).
2. F. Coenen, G. Goulbourne and P. Leng, Tree Structures for Mining Association Rules, *Data Mining and Knowledge Discovery* **8**, 25-51 (2004).
3. X. Ye and J. A. Keane, Mining Composite Items in Association Rules, *Proceedings of the 1997 IEEE International Conference on Systems, Man and Cybernetics*, 1367-1372 (1997).
4. R. Agrawal and R. Srikant, Fast algorithms for mining associations rules, *Proceedings of the 20th International Conference on Very Large Data Bases*, 487-499 (1994).
5. R. Agrawal and R. Srikant, Mining sequential patterns, *Proceedings of the 11th International Conference on Data Engineering* 3-14, (1995).
6. R. Agrawal and J. Shafer, Parallel mining of association rules, *IBM Research Report RJ10004*, (1996).
7. Y. Aumann, R. Feldman, O. Lipsttat and H. Manilla, Borders: An Efficient Algorithm for Association Generation in Dynamic Databases, *Journal of Intelligent Information Systems* **12**, 61-73 (1999).
8. Jun. Gao and Bai-Le Shi, Research on Fast Association Rule Mining Algorithm, *Computer Science (in Chinese)* **32(3)**, 200-201 (2005).
9. J. Han, J. Pei, Y. Yin and R. Mao, Mining frequent patterns without candidate generation: a frequent-pattern tree approach, *Data Mining and Knowledge Discovery* **8(1)**, 53-87 (2004).
10. X. Ye, and J. A. Keane, Mining Association Rules in Temporal Databases, *Proceedings of the 1998 IEEE International Conference on Systems, Man, and Cybernetics*, 2803-2808 (1998).
11. Ke Wang, James N.K. Liu and Wei-min Ma, Improved Algorithms for Data Mining with Composite Items, *Proceedings of ICITM2007*, 1-6 (2007).
12. Z. J. Xie, Chen Hong and C. P. Li, An efficient algorithm for frequent itemset mining on data streams, P. Perner (Ed.): *ICDM 2006*, LNAI 4085, 474-491 (2006).
13. S. Ahmed, F. Coenen and P. Leng, Tree-based partitioning of data for association rule mining, *Knowledge and Information Systems* **10(3)**, 315-331 (2006).
14. C. Silvestri and S. Orlando, Distributed approximate mining of frequent patterns, *Proceedings of the 2005 ACM Symposium on Applied Computing, SAC 2005, Special Track on Data Mining*, 529-536 (2005).
15. L. Feng, T. Dillon, and J. Liu, Inter-transactional association rules for prediction and their application to studying meteorological data, *Data and Knowledge Engineering* **37**, 85-115 (2001).

ONTOLOGY MATCHING APPROACH BASED ON TRIANGLE FUZZY EXPRESSION*

PENGFEI QIAN
Computer Science Department, Shanghai Jiaotong University, 800 Dong Chuan Rd
Shanghai, 200240, China

YINGLIN WANG
Computer Science Department, Shanghai Jiaotong University, 800 Dong Chuan Rd
Shanghai, 200240, China

This paper introduces an ontology mapping approach based on triangle fuzzy expression. This approach imports several kinds of similarity fuzzy expressions based on concept feature information. These similarity fuzzy expressions can be used to extend traditional mapping based on name and instance to composite mapping based on name, instance, attribute, taxonomy, dependence and axiom etc. To implement this approach, two questions should be answered: the first is the unification of all kinds of similarity fuzzy expressions and the second is how to realize the composite mapping based on the unified similarity fuzzy expression. The triangle fuzzy expression is regarded as the criterion of the other similarity fuzzy expressions. After the transformation from the other similarity fuzzy expressions to the triangle fuzzy expression, the unified similarity fuzzy expression is realized. Simultaneously, a mapping computation tree is also introduced to finish the whole composite mapping through a series of weight configuration, unification and synthesis. Finally, associated with traditional non-fuzzy mapping approach, the mapping accuracy of this approach will be evaluated through an application example.

1. Introduction

How to implement the automatic matching between the similar ontologies of different domains? The first problem is how to realize the automatic matching among the different concepts. A concept is composed of several kinds of feature information (Name, Instance, attribute and taxonomy etc), and 'probability inference' based on the name and instance has already been widely used in computing the similarity between 2 different concepts (for instance, GLUE, and LSD system [1][2][7]), but the other feature information still has not been used or only been used as verification and adjusting [3] in the existing ontology mapping approach. In fact, in the real ontology mapping process, there are several similar features between the ontology mapping concept-pair except the similar probability [3] based on the name and instance (for example: 1.the approximate number of same data attributes between the concept A [having k1 attributes] and the concept B [having k2 attributes] is k; 2.the approximate number of same children between the concept A [having r1 children] and the concept B [having r2 children] is r; (3) The similarity between the two ontology concepts falls into the area [m, n], <0<m<n<1> etc).

The traditional 'probability inference' approach can not been used to compute the similarity based on the above features. Consequently, a kind of fuzzy-based similarity expression is put forward in this paper, which can be used to represent the concept-pair similarity based on certain kind of irregular concept feature (such as taxonomy and dependence relation). Fuzzy-based similarity is not a value locating in [0, 1], but a certain kind of fuzzy expression [4]. Considering the ad-hoc of ontology concept feature information, the fuzzy similarity based on the different feature information between the ontology concept-pair will follow the different similarity fuzzy expression (see the section 2).

To unify different kinds of similarity fuzzy expressions and get a composite mapping result based different features, the triangle fuzzy expression [5] is adopted as the criterion of the other similarity fuzzy expressions, just because the triangle fuzzy expression

* This work is supported by the 973 Natural Key Basis Research and Development Plan (973: 2003CB316905).

has the powerful computation capability [5] and the convenient non-fuzzy processing. After the unification and synthesis, different kinds of similarity fuzzy expressions can be transformed to the unified triangle fuzzy expression and united as the composite mapping similarity using the mapping computation tree (see the section 3). Accordingly, the composite mapping similarity following triangle fuzzy expression can be transformed to the traditional mapping similarity locating in [0, 1] through the non-fuzzy processing.

The remained part of this paper is structured as following: section 2 mainly introduces different kinds of similarity fuzzy expressions, section 3 mainly introduces the ontology mapping approach based on unified similarity fuzzy expression, performance evaluation will be introduced in section 4 and section 5 is a conclusion.

2. Similarity Fuzzy Expression

In this section, we will introduce four kinds of similarity fuzzy expressions: (1) Area similarity fuzzy expression; (2) Structural similarity fuzzy expression; (3) Whether similarity fuzzy expression; (4) Value similarity fuzzy expression.

The triangle fuzzy expression like (l,m,r) is the criterion fuzzy expression (l stands for the left value of the triangle fuzzy number, m stands for the middle value, r stands for the right value). All kinds of triangle fuzzy similarity can be synthesized to form the compound triangle fuzzy similarity through a series of weight, unification and synthesis, the compound triangle fuzzy similarity can also be transformed to a traditional similarity value (locating in [0,1]) through non-fuzzy operation [9].

2.1. *Area Similarity Fuzzy Expression*

'Bayesian' Learner based on case inference [1, 3] is widely used in the ontology mapping approaches. The keystone of the 'Bayesian' Learner is as following: the instances of a concept are regarded as the training data, and the instances of another concept are regarded as reasoning data. Learner is trained to create an inference model that is applied to classify another concept's instances. Considering the single direction mapping characteristic of the 'Bayesian' learner, the sample space overlapping is often used in the existing mapping approach [2, 8]. The core of the sample space overlapping is that the positive and negative instances of a concept are used to train a learner which is applied to partition the sample space of another concept and vice versa. But a hypothesis of the sample space overlapping is that the learner trained by the instances of certain concept can always classify every instances of another concept (positive or negative instance). It is right only in the ideal condition, but in fact, the classification result is frequently uncertain and fuzzy. To resolve this problem and improve the mapping accuracy, area similarity fuzzy expression replaces the value similarity locating in [0, 1].

Because of the random characteristic of sample space, the area similarity fuzzy expression between A and B will follow a brief normal distribution in the area $[sim_{left}(A,B),\ sim_{right}(A,B)]$. The middle value of the normal distribution is $(sim_{left}+sim_{right})/2$, the normal distribution area is equal to the believed area $[\mu-3\sigma,\mu+3\sigma]$ with the probability of 99.7%.(see the fig 1) [9, 10] Then the imitation between normal fuzzy distribution and triangle fuzzy distribution will be the core problem in the transformation from area similarity fuzzy expression to the triangle fuzzy expression.

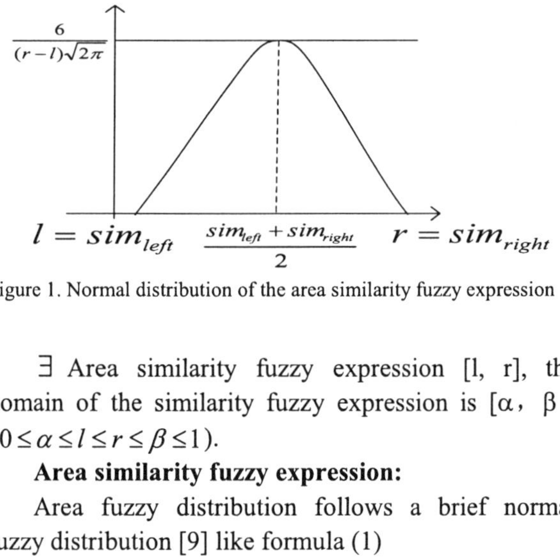

Figure 1. Normal distribution of the area similarity fuzzy expression

∃ Area similarity fuzzy expression [l, r], the domain of the similarity fuzzy expression is [α, β] $(0\le\alpha\le l\le r\le\beta\le 1)$.

Area similarity fuzzy expression:

Area fuzzy distribution follows a brief normal fuzzy distribution [9] like formula (1)

$$f(x)_{\text{area}}=\begin{cases}0 & x\in(\alpha,l)\\ \dfrac{1}{\sigma\sqrt{2\pi}}e^{\frac{(x-\mu)^2}{2\sigma^2}} & x\in(l,r)\\ 0 & x\in(r,\beta)\end{cases} \quad (1)$$

The believed area with 99.7% is $(\mu-3\sigma,\mu+3\sigma)$, and is equal to fuzzy area [l, r], and $l=\mu-3\sigma$, $r=\mu+3\sigma$ $\mu=(l+r)/2$, $\sigma=(r-l)/6$

Triangle fuzzy expression:

$$f(x)_{\text{triangle}} = \begin{cases} 0 & x \in (\alpha, L) \\ (x-L)\dfrac{1}{\sigma\sqrt{2\pi}(M-L)} & x \in (L, M) \\ (x-R)\dfrac{1}{\sigma\sqrt{2\pi}(M-R)} & x \in (M, R) \\ 0 & x \in (R, \beta) \end{cases} \quad (2)$$

Triangle fuzzy expression is based on the three points of the triangle, (L, 0), $(M, 1/(\sigma\sqrt{2\pi}))$, (R, 0), and ($0 \le \alpha \le L \le M \le R \le \beta \le 1$). The formula (2) is the analytical formula [9] of triangle fuzzy expression. According to the Hamming distance [10] computation approach, the imitation between the area fuzzy distribution and the triangle fuzzy distribution can be represented as the formula (3).

$$\rho(f(x)_{area}, f(x)_{triangle}) = \frac{1}{\beta-\alpha}\int_{\alpha}^{\beta} | f(x)_{area} - f(x)_{triangle} | dx \quad (3)$$

Area fuzzy distribution follows a brief normal distribution which is symmetrical. In order to improve the degree in imitation between these 2 distributions, triangle fuzzy distribution for area similarity fuzzy expression will also be symmetrical and has the same top point with the area fuzzy distribution, then $M = \mu = (l+r)/2$, $L = \mu - T$, $R = \mu + T$ (2T is the length of the triangle hemline). The formula (3) can be simplified to the formula (4) for the sake of symmetrical characteristic.

$$\rho(f(x)_{area}, f(x)_{triangle}) = \frac{2}{\beta-\alpha}\int_{\alpha}^{\mu} | f(x)_{area} - f(x)_{triangle} | dx \quad (4)$$

When $T > (r-l)/2$:

$$\rho(f(x)_{area}, f(x)_{triangle}) = \frac{2}{\beta-\alpha}\left(\int_{\alpha}^{\mu-T} 0dx + \int_{\mu-T}^{l} | f(x)_{triangle} | dx + \int_{l}^{\mu} | f(x)_{area} - f(x)_{triangle} | dx\right) \quad (5)$$

When $T < (r-l)/2$:

$$\rho(f(x)_{Segment}, f(x)_{Triangle}) = \frac{2}{\beta-\alpha}\left(\int_{\alpha}^{l} 0dx + \int_{l}^{\mu-T} | f(x)_{area} | dx + \int_{\mu-T}^{\mu} | f(x)_{area} - f(x)_{triangle} | dx\right) \quad (6)$$

When $T = (r-l)/2$:

$$\rho(f(x)_{area}, f(x)_{triangle}) = \frac{2}{\beta-\alpha}\left(\int_{\alpha}^{l} 0dx + \int_{l}^{\mu} | f(x)_{area} - f(x)_{triangle} | dx\right) \quad (7)$$

From the above formula (5, 6 and 7), we can learn:

(1) When $T >> \frac{r-l}{2}$, $\int_{\mu-T}^{l} | f(x)_{triangle} | dx$ (an item of formula (5)) >>0;

(2) When $T << \frac{r-l}{2}$, $\int_{l}^{\mu-T} | f(x)_{area} | dx$ (an item of formula (6)) >>0;

(3) When $T \approx \frac{r-l}{2}$, formula (5, 6, 7) →0.

For the brevity of computation, T is set to $(r-l)/2$ and then $M=\mu=(l+r)/2$, $L=\mu-T=(l+r)/2-(r-l)/2=l$, $R = \mu + T = (l+r)/2 + (r-l)/2 = r$.

Considering the domain of similarity fuzzy expression is $[\alpha, \beta]$ and $0 \le \alpha \le l \le r \le \beta \le 1$, the formula of transformation from area similarity fuzzy expression to triangle fuzzy expression can be expressed as ($(l-\alpha)/(\beta-\alpha)$, $(l+r-2\alpha)/2\times(\beta-\alpha)$, $(r-\alpha)/(\beta-\alpha)$). (See the figure 2)

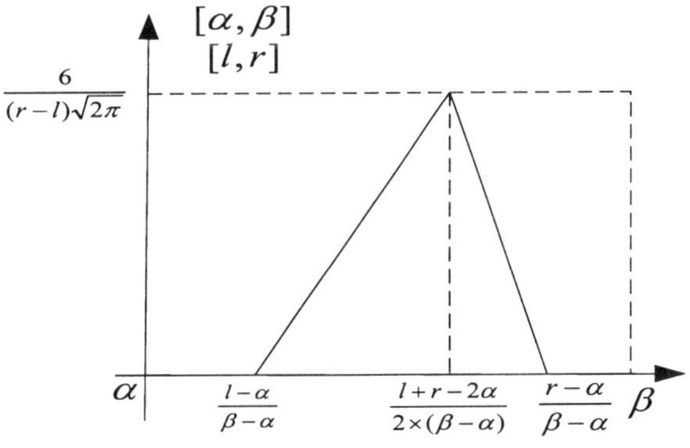

Figure 2. Unification of the area similarity fuzzy expression

2.2. *Structural Similarity Fuzzy Expression*

Structural similarity fuzzy expression is the fuzzy-based result expressional of ontology mapping based on the structural feature information (such as data attribute, object attribute and taxonomy relation etc), structural similarity fuzzy expression is not numerical value locating in [0, 1], but a series of discrete structural fuzzy number (like 1,2,3…etc).

For example, an ontology mapping based on data and object attribute, ∃ concept $A \in O_1$ (the number of attribute is P_A), concept $B \in O_1$ (the number of attribute is P_B), through the computation, the number of same attribute between concept A and B is g_i ($g_i \le P_A$, $g_i \le P_B$). Structural similarity fuzzy expression based on attribute mapping between A and B can be represented as $similarity_{attribute} = g_i$ (g_i is a series of discrete structural fuzzy number such as 1, 2…, g_m $g_m = Max\ (P_A, P_B)$).

Structural similarity fuzzy expression can be quantified as g_i ($g_i \in (0,1,...,g_m)$) [11, 12], which stands for the number of same structural elements between concept pair, g_m is the maximum number of related structural elements in a single concept. The elementary triangle fuzzy similarity for structural similarity fuzzy expression will be represented as the following formula (8):

$$\begin{cases} (\frac{g_i - 1}{g_m}, \frac{g_i}{g_m}, \frac{g_i + 1}{g_m}), 0 < g_i < g_m \\ (\frac{g_i - 1}{g_m}, \frac{g_i}{g_m}, \frac{g_i}{g_m}), g_i = g_m \\ (\frac{g_i}{g_m}, \frac{g_i}{g_m}, \frac{g_i + 1}{g_m}), g_i = 0 \end{cases} \quad (8)$$

For instance, $\exists$ concept pair $< A \in O_1 \leftrightarrow B \in O_2 >$, P_A =5 , P_B =4 , g_m = 5, g_i = 3, the triangle fuzzy expression of structural similarity fuzzy expression (g_i =3) will be expressed as $((3-1)/5, 3/5, (3+1)/5)$ (see the fig 3).

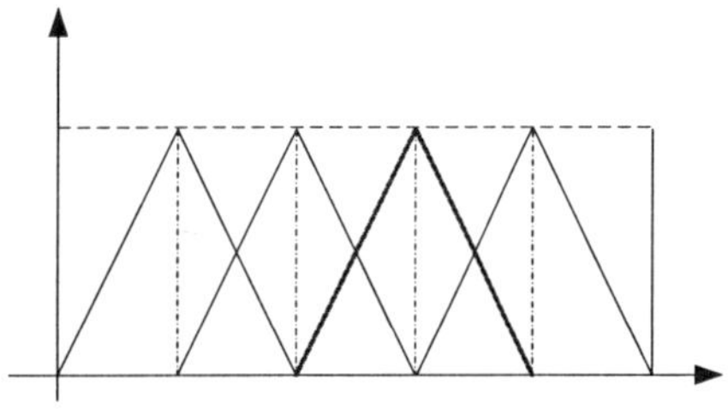

Figure 3 unification of the structural similarity fuzzy expression

2.3. *Whether and Value Similarity Fuzzy Expression*

If the similarity value based on certain feature mapping is true or false (not other values), this kind of expressional form is called 'whether' similarity fuzzy expression. When the similar value is false, the corresponding triangle fuzzy number is [0, 0, 0], and when the similar value is true, the corresponding triangle fuzzy number is [1, 1, 1] (see the fig 4)

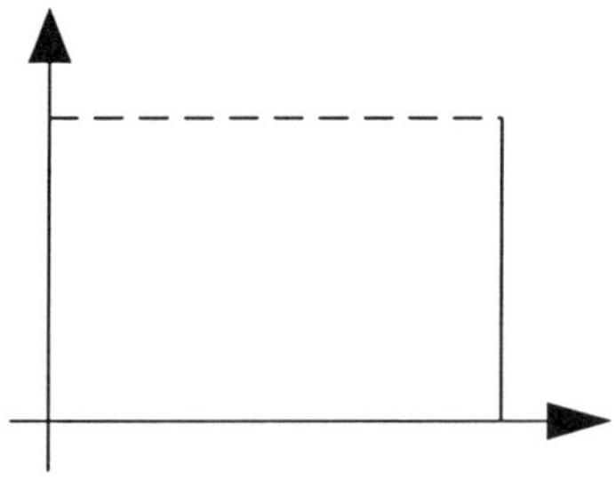

Figure 4. Unification of the whether similarity fuzzy expression

To realize unification, the traditional mapping similarity m (locating in [0, 1]) is called value similarity fuzzy expression, and the corresponding triangle fuzzy number is [m, m, m]. (See the fig 5).

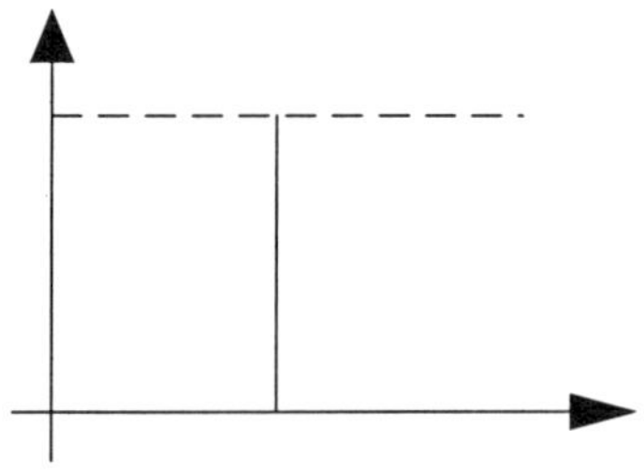

Figure 5. Unification of the value similarity fuzzy expression

3. Ontology Mapping Based On Triangle Fuzzy Expression

The keystone of the mapping approach based on triangle fuzzy expression is an ontology mapping computation tree which is composed of a series of hierarchical ontology mapping nodes, each mapping node corresponds a kind or several kinds ontology mapping features (such as name, instance, attribute, taxonomy etc). According to the position of the mapping nodes in the computation tree, the mapping nodes in the computation tree can be classified as two kinds: Leaf mapping node and Composite mapping node.

(1) Leaf mapping node

Leaf mapping node is the most basic mapping node in the ontology mapping computation tree. Each leaf mapping node corresponds a kind of special mapping feature which is used in the mapping similarity fuzzy expression computation, such as area, structural, whether and value similarity fuzzy expressions (see the section 2). Simultaneously all of these similarity fuzzy expressions also can be transformed to the unified similarity fuzzy expression: triangle fuzzy expression.

(2) Composite mapping node

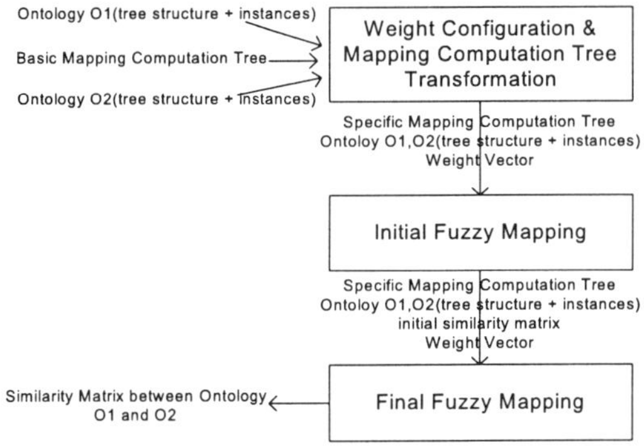

Figure 6. Step 1 → Step 2 → Step 3

Composite mapping node is the synthesis of the other leaf or composite mapping nodes. Because the output results of all kinds of leaf mapping node follow triangle fuzzy expression, the result of composite mapping node also follows triangle fuzzy expression.

The composite ontology mapping approach is composed of three steps: step1, step2, step3 (See the figure 6).

Step1: Weight Configuration of Mapping Node and Mapping Computation Tree Transformation

All nodes in the basic mapping computation tree will be set weight in the step1, if the node together with the sub nodes is not used in the computation, the weight of the node and all the sub nodes will be set to zero. After the weight configuration, the basic mapping computation tree will be transformed to the special mapping computation tree based on a certain application domain.

Step2: Initial Fuzzy Mapping

Because the object attribute, taxonomy and dependence relation similarity computation depend on the similarity of the nearby concept-pairs. To finish the mapping, the near-by concept-pair similarity will be computed in advance without considering the above semantic features. The initial similarity between the concept-pair will be computed based on the name, instance, and data attribute information.

Step3: Final Fuzzy Mapping

According to the special mapping computation tree and initial similarity matrix, the composite mapping computation based on triangle fuzzy expression will be executed in this step. The composite similarity matrix will be achieved after the unification, synthesis and non-fuzzy processing.

4. Performance Evaluation

Here we discuss a very typical example to evaluate the performance of the mapping approach based on triangle fuzzy expression.

Let us assume that there are two UML formatted ontology slices [14] [15] [16]: A (Slice of the Ontology 'HR' in the Enterprise Management Information System) and B (Slice of the Ontology 'Organization' in the Organization Management Information System). The mapping relation between these two ontology slices has been set up.

The detailed information (such as concept name, concept instance number, concept attribute number etc) about these 2 ontology slices: A and B can listed in the table 1.

Table 1. Information of ontology slice A and B

A: Ontology 'HR' in the Enterprise Management Information System							
Name	Em	Job	Co	Loca	C(H)	Cle	Bos
Instance	107	19	27	23	25	81	26
Attri (D)	10	6	6	2	2	7	9
Attri (O)	2	0	3	1	0	0	0
Parent	1	0	0	0	0	0	0
Child	0	0	0	0	0	1	0
B: Ontology 'Organization' in the Organization Management Information System							
Name	Pers	Posi	Cor	Reg	C(O)	Staf	Dire
Instance	120	18	25	20	25	91	18
Attri (D)	9	5	6	2	2	6	8
Attri (O)	2	0	3	1	0	0	0
Parent	1	0	0	0	0	0	0
Child	0	0	0	0	0	1	0

The mapping relation between these two Ontology slice (A and B) can be represented as <Employee: Personnel, Job: Position, Company: Corporation, Location: Region, Country (H): Country (O), Clerk: Staffer, Boss: Director>

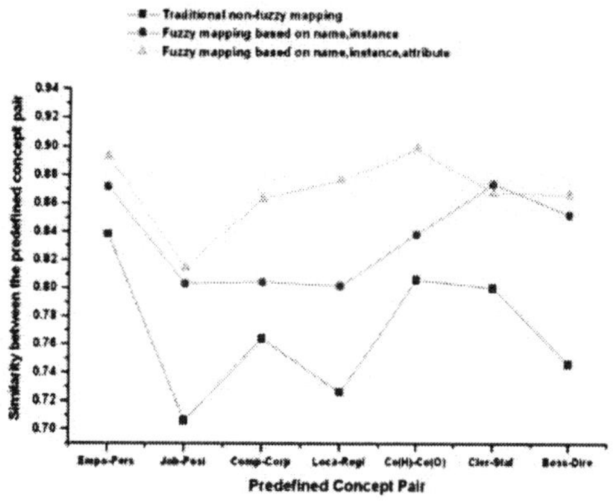

Figure 7. Matching accuracy of three kinds of different ontology mapping approaches

In order to compare the mapping approach based on triangle fuzzy expression to the traditional non-fuzzy mapping approach, 3 kinds of related ontology mapping approaches will be used to finish the above mapping. One belongs to traditional non-fuzzy mapping approach, the other two belong to the mapping approach based on triangle fuzzy expression. (1: Traditional non-fuzzy mapping, 2: Fuzzy mapping based on name, instance, 3: Fuzzy mapping based on name, instance, attribute).

Figure 7 is the mapping accuracy of these 3 kinds of ontology mapping approaches.

From the figure 7, we can learn that the mapping approach based on triangle fuzzy expression has higher accuracy than the traditional non-fuzzy mapping approach, but it is not always right that the more feature information is utilized, the higher mapping accuracy is. Whether a kind of feature is utilized depends on the ontology structure and the special application environment.

5. Conclusion

'Name' and 'instance' are the elementary features of the concept, but there are a lot of discrete and irregular features except 'name' and 'instance' (such as taxonomy relation, dependence relation etc). These features can not be directly used in the 'probability inference'. Therefore, many existing ontology mapping approaches [3] are only based on the 'name' and 'instance', other discrete and irregular similar features between concept-pair are ignored. Accordingly the accuracy is reduced.

To resolve this problem, a kind of ontology mapping approach based on 'triangle fuzzy expression' is produced. The core of this approach is the similarity fuzzy expressions based on different kinds of concept features, which make sure that all kinds of concept features can be used in one mapping computation. After a series of unification and synthesis processing in the mapping computation tree and the non-fuzzy processing, the composite mapping similarities based on elementary and irregular features are produced, which have the higher accuracy than the similarities produced by the traditional non-fuzzy ontology mapping approach.

In the end, we have done a lot of mapping accuracy experiments about this approach, and found that the accuracy of fuzzy mapping approach is higher than the accuracy of non-fuzzy mapping approach.

References

1. A.Doan, J.Madhavan and P.Domingos, Learning to Map between Ontologies on the Semantic Web, WWW 2002, (2002).
2. A.Doan, Learning to Map between Structured Representations of Data, Ph.D. Dissertation, Univ. of Washington-Seattle, (2002).
3. E.Rahm, Philip and A.Bernstein, A survey of approaches to automatic matching, *The VLDB Journal*, 334-350 (2001).
4. A.Li and D.Wu, Elementary Fuzzy Math and Application, The People Publishing House of Xinjiang, (1986)
5. Q.Chen, Fuzzy Values and Their Applications to Fuzzy Reasoning, The Publishing House of Beijing Normal University, (2000).
6. Y.Liu, J.Cao and S.Zhang, Research on Configurable Fuzzy Synthesized Evaluation System and Key Technologies, *Computer Integrated Manufacturing Systems* **10(10)**, 1291-1295 (2004).
7. A. Doan, J. Madhavan, R. Dhamankar, P. Domingos and A. Halevy, Learning to Match Ontologies on the Semantic Web VLDB Journal, *Special Issue on the Semantic Web*, (2003).
8. V.Rijsbergen, Information Retrieval, London: Butterworths, Second Edition, (1979).
9. Z. He. Fuzzy math and Application, The Tianjing Publishing House of Sci & Tech., (1983).
10. L. Han and P.Wang, Application Fuzzy Math. Capital University of Economics and Business Publishing House, (1998).
11. Y.Liu, J.Cao and S.Zhang, Integrated fuzzy synthesized evaluation system, *Computer Integrated Manufacturing Systems* **9**, 149-155 (2003).

12. Y.Liu, Research and Realization of Configurable Fuzzy Synthesized Evaluation System, M.S. Thesis, Shanghai Jiao Tong University, (2004).
13. Y.Wang, Agent-based Method in Handling Conflictive Ontologies for Reusing Legacy Systems, High Technology Letters, (2004).
14. S.Cranefield, S.Haustein and M.Purvis, UML-Based Ontology Modeling for Software Agents. *Proc. of Ontologies in Agent Systems Workshop*, 21-28 (2001).
15. The Object Management Group (OMG), Ontology Definition Meta-model Preliminary Revised Submission to OMG RFP ad/2003-03-40[M], (2004).
16. The Object Management Group (OMG), Ontology Definition Meta-model Revised Submission to OMG RFP ad/2003-03-40[M], (2005).

TOWARDS BUILDING SEMANTIC DECISION TABLES WITH DOMAIN ONTOLOGIES

YAN TANG

Semantics Technology and Applications Research Laboratory (STARLab)
Department of Science, Vrije Universiteit Brussel,
Pleinlaan 2, B-1050 BRUSSEL, Belgium

ROBERT MEERSMAN

Semantics Technology and Applications Research Laboratory (STARLab)
Department of Science , Vrije Universiteit Brussel,
Pleinlaan 2, B-1050 BRUSSEL, Belgium

Decision tables are a simple yet important and powerful tool to help implement the complex logic of many domains. However, the definition of concepts, variables and rules that underlie a decision table often are or become implicit. As the decision tables grow, ambiguities, inconsistencies and conceptual reasoning difficulties arise and building them becomes a time-consuming and difficult task. In order to address the problems, we use ontologies to represent, store and maintain the domain concepts. A decision table annotated with domain ontologies is called *Semantic Decision Table* (SDT). The rules that are generated from the formal commitment, together with the existing domain ontologies constitute the knowledge kernel of SDT. SDT is modeled in the DOGMA framework. It contains plausible binary facts called *SDT lexons*, and the *SDT commitments*, which the agents use to constrain and use the lexons. To facilitate reasoning, we encode the SDT commitments in Prolog prototype. In this paper, we focus on how to write SDT commitments in Prolog. Furthermore, we illustrate the design of the tool and its implementation.

1. Introduction

As decision tables provide reasoning in a compact form, they are used widely in many application domains, such as software engineering, system analysis/evaluation and business decision supporting systems. However, decision tables diverge widely in their representation and supporting algorithms. Drawing a large decision table with a considerable number of conditions and actions can in general become quite a time-consuming and difficult task. *Ambiguity*, *inconsistency* and *misunderstanding* arise when a decision table becomes large. The situation gets naturally worse when many designers are involved.

We argue that the lack of *semantics* is the key cause for such a collaborative decision supporting system. *Ontologies* [5, 6, 7] were proposed to store the semantics of decision tables. A decision table annotated properly with the domain ontologies was defined as a *Semantic Decision Table* (SDT). In our paper [15], we discussed how to construct SDTs. The issue on how to reason such an SDT has not yet been covered.

Seeing that Prolog (Programming in Logic, e.g. in [1]) is an excellent language for providing reasoning facilities, we recently adopted it to encode the SDT commitments. In this paper, we focus on how to write SDT commitments in a Prolog prototype and its tool.

We organize the paper as follows: Section 2 recalls a brief definition of decision tables and their design problems. In Section 3 we discusses the SDT and the Prolog approach to the SDT commitments. Section 4 illsutrates a use case. In Section 5 we design and demonstrate an SDT tool. In Section 6 we compare our work with others'. Section 7 offers our conclusion.

2. Decision Table and Its Design Problem

Following the *de facto* international standard [3], a decision table contains three basic elements: the *conditions*, the *actions*, and the *rules* that describe which actions to be taken based on the combination of the conditions. A *condition stub* contains a statement of a condition and each *condition entry* indicates the relationship between the various conditions in the condition stubs. Each *action stub* has a statement of each action to be taken and the *action entries* specify whether (or in what order) the action is to be performed for the combination of the conditions that are actually met in the rule column.

Table 1 for example is a simple decision table with three conditions: "Bad weather", "It's far from home" and "Money in pocket"; and two actions: "Take a taxi back home" and "Walk back home". The condition "Bad weather" has two condition entries - "Yes (The weather is bad now)" and "No (The weather is not bad now)". The rule column with ID '1' explains the decision rule as "If the weather is bad, it's far from home, and, there is money in pocket, then the decision is to take a taxi back home".

Table 1. A simple decision table example

	1	2	3
Condition			
Bad weather	Yes	Yes	No
It's far from home	Yes	No	Yes
Money in pocket	Yes	Yes	Yes
Action			
Take a taxi back home	*		*
Walk back home		*	

In most situations, the condition entries have value ranges (e.g. cost <= 100) or fuzzy descriptions (e.g. manual work is 'not very heavy'). Here arises the problem of *ambiguity*: what does "cost" mean? Is it associated with the money cost (e.g. €100) or the man work (e.g. 100 months man work)? What is the exact meaning of "manual work is *not very heavy*"? In order to solve this last mentioned problem, decision table makers may clarify the item *value range*. For example, "<= 2 hours" can be applied to the decision item "manual work is not very heavy". The decision makers need to provide the relevant information as much as possible. This solution seems to solve the problem. However, in practice, we observe that massive ill-structured information is hard to reason about by different machines.

Another problem is *conceptual duplication*, which happens during the phase of building a *large* decision table in a *collaborative* environment. For instance, the conditions, such as "stormy - Yes", "temperature - <-5°C", "rain volume - High", can be considered as the *conceptually duplicate* of (or *conceptually similar* to) "bad weather - Yes" in Table 1. When the decision table gets very large, e.g. a table with hundreds of conditions, it is almost impossible for a decision maker to check such duplications.

In the *collaborative* settings, one decision maker might misunderstand (or have his own comprehension of) the meaning of a decision item designated by others. For example, the condition "It's far from home - Yes" in Table 1 can have different measures of distance. Does it mean that the distance is more than 1 km, or more than 3 km?

We argue that the lack of *semantics* is the main cause. Ontologies [5, 6, 7] solve the problem by storing in an information resource a common understanding of a specific domain. Note that an ontology in principle not only transfers human *tacit knowledge* into machine understandable *explicit knowledge* but also captures the *highest-value knowledge* of the domain experts. We argue that experience, insight and expertise may be considered as the *highest-value knowledge* in Knowledge Management.

A decision table needs to be annotated with domain ontologies in order 'to arrive at its formal semantics' [15]. It results in a set of Semantic Decision Tables (SDT), which we discuss in the next section.

3. Semantic Decision Table

DOGMA (Developing Ontology-Grounded Methods and Applications, [11, 12]) approach to ontology engineering was designed as a methodological framework inspired by the conceptual database modelling.

In the DOGMA framework one constructs ontologies by the principle of *double articulation* into two layers: 1) the *lexon base layer* that contains a vocabulary of simple facts called *lexons*; and 2) the *commitment layer* that formally defines the annotation of an application (or "agent") with lexons, and the rules and constraints on these lexons.

A lexon (a plausible, context-specific binary fact) is a quintuple $< \gamma, t_1, r_1, r_2, t_2 >$ where γ is a context identifier pointing to a resource where required concepts are defined. t_1 and t_2 are two terms (the head term and the tail term). Within the context γ, t_1 may have a relation with t_2 in which it plays a role r_1, and conversely, t_2 plays a corresponding co-role r_2. E.g. the lexon <*γ, driver, has, is issued to, drivers license*> means: a driver has drivers license(s); and a driver's license is issued to a driver.

The commitments are expressed in a *commitment language* that can be modelled and easily interpreted, thereby providing reasoning about the ontology. ORM [9], Ω-RIDL [4] and description logic are the examples of commitment language.

SDT modelling is based on the DOGMA framework. The SDT commitment layer communicates with the domain ontology base and the decision supporting applications. It consists of two sub-layers: the *common decision rule layer* and the *ontological commitment layer*. We call the rules at the common decision rule layer "common" because they can be reused by many applications just as an ontology does.

One difference between these two sub-layers is the use range and the restrictions. The ontological commitment layer provides rules for *all* the applications *in a domain* [7]. The common application rule layer provides common rules for those applications but it does not guarantee that those rules are axioms; in other words, they are dynamic and can be changed or overridden by any other applications. The other difference is that the common application rule layer contains instances while an ontology does not.

In this paper we express the SDT commitments with a prototype written in Prolog. Prolog (Programming in Logic, e.g. in [1]) is based on the mathematical notions of relations and logical inferences. It is a mainly declarative language that consists of a data base of facts and axioms (also called *rules*). Several Prolog *facts* together with the Prolog *rules* are used to define a DOGMA *lexon* – a *binary relationship fact type*. Prolog is used for several purposes in this paper, such as 1) to constrain a lexon; 2) to constraint a set of lexons; 3) to provide reasoning facility which includes tracing the *declarative meaning* and the *procedural meaning* of the commitments.

In the next subsections, we classify the SDT commitments into six categories from the methodological aspect: lexon selection, lexon initialization, lexon set construction/manipulation, other constraints used for modelling information, the CSA policies (as the principles of designing a decision table) and the user specific decision rules.

3.1. *Lexon selection*

We demonstrate a lexon selection example in Prolog as:

```
% Example 1: lexon selection
lexon1:-context(society), head_term(person),
role(hasName),corole(isNameOf),
tail_term(person_name).

lexon2:-context(society), head_term(person),
role(has), corole(isOf), tail_term(mother).

selection1:-lexon1, lexon2.
```

We present here the lexon with ID 1 as *<society, person, hasName, isNameOf, person_name>*, 2 as *<society, person, has, isOf, mother>* and the selection of these lexons – selection 1. The Prolog rules *context()*, *term1()*, *term2()*, *role()* and *corole()*, together with the other rules that will appear in the other subsections, are predefined in the library.

We define *context()* to specify the resource where two terms are defined. The Prolog rules *term1()* and *term2()* are defined for the mapping between the lexical tokens and the concepts. The rules *role()* and *corole()* are specified based on the practice. For instance, SDT based decision supporting systems may make use of the hierarchical structure when the role and the co-role are specified as "is-a" or "subtype".

3.2. *Lexon initialization*

An application initializes a lexon through a lexon initialization phase by applying the commitment constraints, such as to define the lexon term value range. The value range, in DB theory, is also considered as *value constraints*. An example is shown as:

```
% Example 2: a value candidate example
lexon3:-context(office), head_term(paper),
role(has), corole(isOf),tail_term( colour).

colour:- [red, green, yellow, gray, white].
```

Example 2 shows the lexon *<office, paper, has, isOf, colour>* and the value candidates of *colour*. The value candidates are collected in a Prolog *list*. This kind of initialization is constrained at the ontological level.

At the application level, a variable can be specified, the example of which is shown as:

```
% Example 3: value initialization
lexon4:-context(weatherContext),
head_term(bad_weather), role(hasValue),
corole(isValueOf),
tail_term(bad_weather_value).

rule1:-tail_term_value(lexon4, yes).
```

The tail term of the lexon *<weatherContext, bad_weather, hasValue, isValueOf, bad_weather_value>* is initialized with the value *yes*.

3.3. *Lexon set construction and manipulation*

These commitments describe how to construct a set of lexons and the relations between sets of lexons. There are five basic set operators used: *set member definition*, *set intersection*, *complementation*, *union* and *subset*. We illustrate here the lexon set exclusion manipulation rule as:

```
%Example 4: set3 = set1-set2.
set3:-intersection(set1, set2).
set1 :- [lexon1, lexon2, lexon3].
set2 :- [lexon3].
```

Other set operators can be found on our website[1].

3.4. *Uniqueness, mandatory and other ORM constraints*

Including the value constraint, there are some other constraints in ORM [9] that can be adopted in ontology

1 All the PROLOG examples can be downloaded at: http://www.starlab.vub.ac.be/website/PrologHRM

engineering. They are: *uniqueness*, *mandatory*, *equality*, *subtype* and *occurrence frequency*. For example, the uniqueness constraint is written as:

```
%Example 5:uniqueness constraint example
lexon5:-context(society), head_term(person),
role(has), corole(isOf), tail_term(mother).

uniqueness(lexon5).
```

In this example, the lexon <society, person, has, isOf, mother> is constrained as "in the context of society, *one* person can have *at most one* mother". The Prolog rule *uniqueness()* is used. In practice, the Prolog rule engine checks if all the instances satisfy the uniqueness constraint. It gives an error message when a "person" has more than one "mother".

Mandatory constraint is applied when a role is played by every member of the population of the object type that is lexically represented by term1 or term2. We define *mandatory()* as the Prolog rule.

Equality constraint is used when two sets have the same members. According to Halpin, the equality constraint is equivalent to two subset constraint [9, page 239]. Two sets are equivalent when one set is the subset of the other and vice versa. The Prolog rule *equality()* is thus defined.

Subtype constraint defined as *subtype()* in Prolog is applied when the population of one type (e.g. the type of term1) is a subset of the other type (e.g. the type of term2). Readers may have a question: why don't we use subset instead? We hereby refer to [9, section 6.5] for the details.

Occurrence frequency constraint ensures a type that is recorded a certain number of times. Or, the type plays the role for a certain number of times. Let's look at the example:

```
occurrence_frequency(lexon1, 2).
```

The occurrence frequency constraint is applied on lexon1 - *<society, person, hasName, isNameOf, person_name>*. A person should have two person names. The Prolog rule *occurrence_frequency()* is used to ensure the occurrence of the role "hasName".

We have discussed several ORM constraints adopted in our approach. In the next subsection, two specific kinds of rules are discussed: 1) the CSA policies, which are defined as the decision table standardizations; and, 2) user defined decision rules.

3.5. *CSA policies*

These rules, which are defined in [3], are the guidelines of making a decision table, intended to determine its legality. For instance, one policy is: zero number of conditions is allowed in a decision table. In another word, the condition number of a decision table is equal to or more than zero.

```
% Example 6
policy1 :- condtionSet(ConditionNbr),
ConditionNbr>=0.
```

The Prolog rule *conditionSet()* in Example 6 is further defined as to automatically retrieve the condition stub number of a decision table.

3.6. *User defined decision rules*

The decision makers can define their desired application rules. They can use the *logical operators and connectives*, such as *negation*, *conjunction*, *disjunction*, *implication* and *equivalence*. Moreover, the *procedural controls*, such as *sequence*, *dependence*, *precedence* and *loop* can be used. We refer the explanation and its expertise of these rules to our recent work (ORM$^+$ modelling approach, [17]).

In this section, we discuss how an SDT can be modeled in DOGMA framework and how to write SDT commitments in Prolog. We demonstrate with a use case in the next section.

4. A Use Case

We use the example in Section 2 to demonstrate the SDT commitments in Prolog.

As discussed, different decision makers may have diverse comprehension of a concept. The following code designed by a decision group, contains the commitments of "weather" and "bad weather".

```
% SDT commitments on "weather"
lexon3:-context(weatherContext),
head_term(bad_weather), role(hasValue),
corole(isValueOf),
tail_term(bad_weather_value).
bad_weather_value:-[yes, no].

lexon4:-context(weatherContext),
head_term(stormy), role(hasValue),
corole(isValueOf), tail_term(stormy_value).
stormy_value:-[yes, no].

lexon5:-context(weatherContext),
head_term(rain_ volume), role(hasValue),
corole(isValueOf),
tail_term(rain_ volume _value).
rain_volume_value:-[low, medium, high].
```

```
lexon6:-context(weatherContext),
head_term(temperature), role(hasValue),
corole(isValueOf),
tail_term(temperature_value).

% SDT commitments on "bad weather"
rule1:-tail_term_value(lexon3,yes).
rule2:-tail_term_value(lexon4,yes).
rule3:-tail_term_value(lexon5,high).
rule4:-tail_term_value(lexon6, V),V<-5.
```

The above commitments[2] define the concept "weather" and "bad weather". The item "bad weather" is indicated by one or any combinations of the following conditions: bad weather value is yes, stormy value is yes, rain volume value is high, or temperature value is less than -5°. We use these conditions to check the *conceptual similarity* of "bad weather".

We have by now discussed how SDT is modelled, coded and reasoned. In the next section, we illustrate the SDT tool design and implementation.

5. System Design and Demonstration

We design an SDT tool to support the decision making process by studying three main components: 1) the decision table lexon extractor, which extracts the lexons from both the users and the tables; 2) the DOGMA lexon converter, which maps available domain ontologies into lexons; 3) the Prolog rule editor, with which users edit and store SDT commitments (Figure 1).

End users may provide their domain specific ontologies in OWL[3] or RDF(S)[4]. For example, our weather ontologies used in this paper are built in OWL. The *DOGMA converter* converts it into domain lexons and commitments. The *Decision Table Lexon Extractor* takes the decision table (e.g.Table 1) as the input and generates the SDT lexons as the output(Figure 2). We use the Prolog Rule Editor to edit, store and browse the SDT commitments.

A common user scenario is: first, the users store a new decision table and generate SDT lexons automatically. Second, the users provide more lexons and the SDT commitments. Third, the users search the relevant commitments and group them. Forth, the tool analyses the stored rules in order to assist group decision making.

[2] How to guide a decision group to write the SDT commitments are out the paper focus; more details can be found in [16].

[3] http://www.w3.org/TR/owl-features/

[4] http://www.w3.org/TR/rdf-schema/

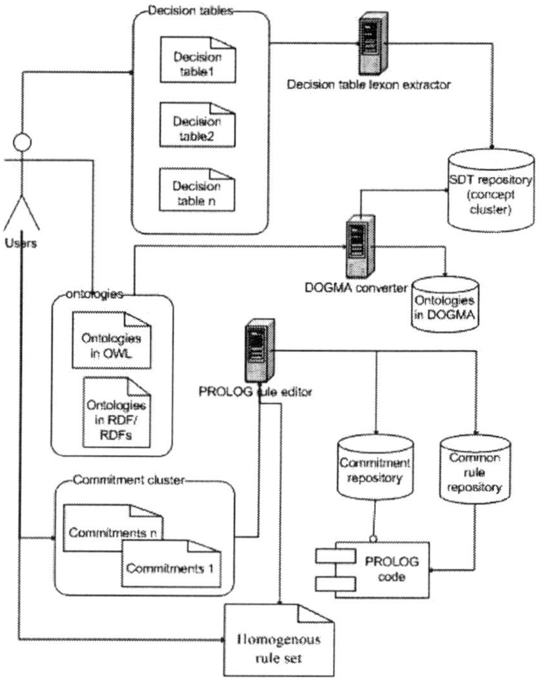

Figure 1. SDT system design

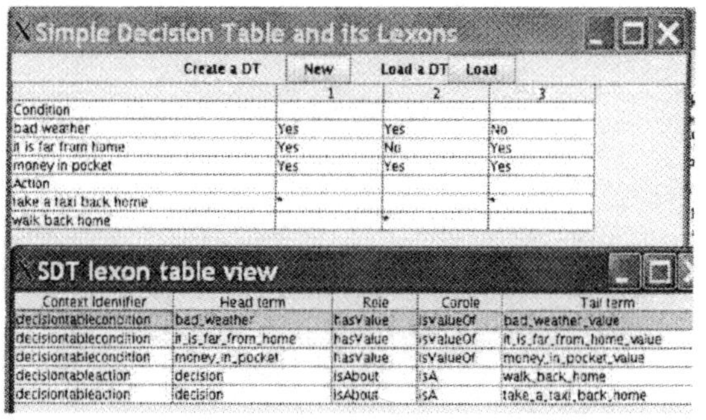

Figure 2. SDT lexons automatically generated

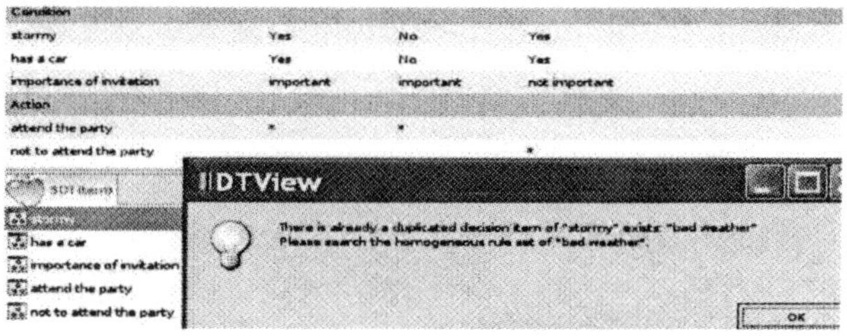

Figure 3. A screenshot of checking the validity - conceptual duplication is detected.

Figure 3 demonstrates a screenshot of an illegal decision table while we check its validity. Suppose that we already have a table with the condition stub of "bad weather", we will get a warn message if we try to add a condition with the condition name of "stormy".

This section demonstrates the SDT tool. We will discuss the related work in the next section.

6. Related Work

As one of the very useful and important decision objects of the decision supporting systems, decision tables have already been studied during many years. Many researchers already tried to combine semantics with decision tables in several application domains.

Goedertier et al. [8] rather focus on the rules and the semantics of the case data and activity flows in business process models, which we shall place at the application layer, i.e. as part of the use of an ontology; they do not discuss the decision table's content (conditions and decisions) and the semantics of the content. We made the semantic analysis on both the decision table itself and its content. And we expect that some of their ideas can be adopted in the future to derive a richer annotation model for our semantic decision tables.

Shiffman et al. in [14] present decision tables as a technique to reduce the complexity of using a medical knowledgebase. They demonstrate how (medical domain) semantics may be exploited ad hoc to simplify these decision tables, thereby indeed turning these tables also, in our terminology, into specific applications committed to such ontologies. In our paper we are instead interested rather in the general knowledge engineering and Knowledge Management principles underlying this process.

Colomb [2] mainly treats decision table related ontologies as "task ontologies" in a domain [13]. They are applied in a medical application context, but his results are general, albeit that the notion of DT used in [2] is restricted compared to the decision table standards CSA Z243.1-1970. The main idea of decision objects in Colomb's paper indeed is that adoption of the correct paradigm aids expert system developers in reducing the size of the problem space. His task ontology on the other hand could be made part of (medical) decision support ontologies in our approach, i.e. SDT + medical domain knowledge + task descriptions.

7. Conclusion, Discussion and Future Work

In order to be able to cope with the limitations of traditional decision tables, we bring ontologies to store the semantics. The process results in a set of SDTs. In this paper, we focus on how to write SDT commitments in Prolog. We then discuss the design and the implementation of the tool.

In the future, we will focus more on the *consistency* and *validation* issues while reasoning about SDT commitments. A more professional version of the SDT tool will be developed. Furthermore, we will investigate on some real applications of SDT.

Acknowledgements

The research is partly supported by the EU Prolix (**PR**ocess-**O**riented **L**earning and **I**nformation E**x**change, http://www.prolixproject.org/, FP6-IST-027905) project and European ITEA AmIE (**Am**bient **I**ntelligence for the **E**lderly, ITEA 2 - 06002) project. It's the authors' pleasure to thank our colleagues Damien Trog and Dr. Jeroen Hoppenbrouwers for reviewing the paper.

References

1. I. Bratko, Prolog Programming for Artificial Intelligence, Addison Wesley Publisher, 3rd edition, (2000).
2. R. M. Colomb, Representation of propositional expert systems as partial functions, *Artificial Intelligence* **109(1-2)**, (1999).
3. CSA, Z243.1-1970 for Decision Tables, Canadian Standards Association, (1970).
4. D. Trog, Y. Tang and R. Meersman, Towards Ontological Commitments with O-RIDL Markpu Language, *Proc. of RuleML'07*, A. Paschke and Y. Biletskiy (eds.), LNCS 4824, (2007).
5. T. R. Gruber, Toward principles for the design of ontologies used for knowledge sharing, *Workshop on Formal Ontology*, (1992).
6. T. R. Gruber, A translation approach to portable ontologies, *Knowledge Acquisition* **5(2)**, 199-220 (1993).
7. N. Guarino, Formal Ontology and Information Systems, *Proceedings of FOIS'98*, 3-15 (1998).
8. S. Goedertier and J. Vanthienen, Rule-based Business Process Modeling and Execution, *Proceedings of the IEEE EDOC Workshop on Vocabularies Ontologies and Rules for The Enterprise (VORTE 2005), CTIT Workshop Proceeding Series (ISSN 0929-0672)*, Enschede, (2005).
9. T. A. Halpin, Information Modeling and Relational Databases: From Conceptual Analysis to Logical Design, San Francisco, California, Morgan Kaufman Publishers, (2001).
10. R. Meersman, The RIDL Conceptual Language, Control Data DMRL research memorandum, (1982).
11. R. Meersman, Can Ontology Theory Learn from Database Semantics? *Proceedings of the Dagstuhl Seminar 0121 'Semantics on the Web'*, (2000).

12. R. Meersman, Ontologies and Databases: More than a Fleeting Resemblance, A.D'Atri and M. Missikoff,(eds.), *OES/SEO 2001 Rome Workshop*, (2001).
13. R. Mizoguchi and M. Ikeada, Towards Ontology Engineering, Technical Report AI-TR-96-1, I.S.I.R, Osaka University, (1996).
14. R. N. Shiffman and R. A. Greenes, Rule set reduction using augmented decision table and semantic subsumption techniques: application to cholesterol guidelines, *Proceedings of Annual Symp. Computer and Application Medical Care*, 339-43 (1992).
15. Y. Tang and R. Meersman, On Constructing Semantic Decision Tables, *Proc. of 18th International Conference on Database and Expert Systems Applications (DEXA'2007),* R. Wagner, N. Revell, and G. Pernul (Eds.), LNCS 4653,34-44 (2007).
16. Y. Tang, On Conducting a Decision Group to Construction Semantic Decision Tables, *OntoContent workshop, Proc. of 9th On The Move to Meaningful Internet Systems and Ubiquitous Computing Federated Conferences and Workshops (OTM'2007)*, 4805-4806 (2007).
17. Y. Tang, P. Spyns and R. Meersman, Towards Semantically Grounded Decision Rules Using ORM+, *Proc. of RuleML'07*, Adrian Paschke and Yevgen Biletskiy (eds.), LNCS 4824, (2007).

PARALLEL LOCAL SEARCH TO IMPROVE THE PERFORMANCE OF GENETIC ALGORITHMS*

YOUZHI ZHENG
Department of Computer Science and Technology, Tsinghua University
Beijing, China

ZHENG QIN
Department of Computer Science and Technology, Tsinghua University
Beijing, China

JUNLIANG CHEN
School of Software, Tsinghua University
Beijing, China

Genetic algorithms are promising search techniques dealing with the combinatorial optimization problems. The main disadvantage of GA is the slow convergence rate of the search. In order to improve convergence rate of the search, the former researchers put forward two common strategies, one is local search methods and the other is parallelization. This paper tries to combine the two strategies and design the architecture of parallel hybrid GA. We propose three parallel hybrid GAs: (1) GA holds the shared population, (2) local search holds the shared population, and (3) independent shared population. This paper selects message passing interface (MPI) to implement the parallel hybrid GAs program. We compare our parallel hybrid GA with the pure GA and the pipelining hybrid GA, and the results of the simulation show that parallel hybrid GAs can combine the merits of the local search approach and the parallel mechanism.

1. Introduction

Genetic algorithms (GAs) can be succinctly characterized as computational models of evolutionary processes. They have been applied to a wide range of applications and have been shown to be a promising search and optimization technique for managing combinatorial optimization problems [1], [2], [3].

One of the main disadvantages of applying GAs to complex problems is the high computational cost associated with their slow convergence rate. The convergence rate of a GA is typically slower than that of local search techniques because it uses little local information to determine the most promising search direction. There are two common strategies dealing with the GA's high computational cost. One is to combine a GA with a complementary local search technique [4], [5], and the other is to parallel the GAs [6], [7], [8].

Because of the diversity of the GA's operators, a hybrid approach which combines a GA and a given local search technique is less likely to be trapped in a local optimum than a pure local search technique is. And local searching will also often mean a faster convergence than would be found using a pure GA. In order to design the efficient algorithm, many researchers and engineers use the parallel mechanism to perform the application. There has been much research into either the hybrid approach or the parallel mechanism but there has been less research into both of them.

* This work is supported by the National High-Tech Research and Development Plan of China under Grant No.2003AA412020 (863), and National Nature Science Foundation Project under Grant No. 60542004.

In this paper we propose parallel local search architecture to improve GA's performance which combines the merits of the local search approach and the parallel mechanism. Our motivation for designing a parallel architecture is to make the hybrid approach easy to be parallelized.

2. Background

In this section we first we briefly review the basic idea and procedures of GAs. We then define the neighborhood structure of the individuals (we call individuals rather than solutions). Finally, we describe some local search methods. These start from some initial individual and iteratively try to replace the current individual by a better individual in a defined neighborhood of the current individual.

2.1. *Genetic Algorithms (GAs)*

GA is a stochastic algorithm that mimics natural evolution, maintaining a set of solutions (called individuals or chromosomes) in a population. To simulate the process of evolution, the selected parent individuals undergo genetic operations to produce new individuals, such as crossover and mutation operators. As in the case of biological evolution, it has a mechanism for selecting fitter chromosomes at each generation. The driving force in genetic algorithms is the selection of individuals based on their fitness which can be the value of an objective function. Individuals with a higher fitness have a higher probability to be chosen as members of the population of the next generation (or as parents for the generation of new individuals). This corresponds to the principle of survival of the fittest in natural evolution.

An important issue in designing a GA is the procedure used to control the genetic operations. There are two alternative procedures: the steady-state and generational.

The most important difference between these two procedures lies in the method used to update the population. The steady-state procedure generally updates one individual in each generation, whereas the generational procedure updates the whole or most of the population. The steady-state procedure normally maintains a population set, whereas the generational procedure maintains two population sets. One population set is the master population set which likes the population set in steady-state procedure, and the other population set is offspring population set.

2.2. *Local search methods*

Local search methods start from some initial solution and iteratively try to replace the current solution by a better solution in an appropriately defined neighborhood of the current solution, where the neighborhood is formally defined as follows:

Definition 1: A neighborhood structure is a function that mappings the every solution $s \in S$ to a set of neighbors $N(s) \subseteq S$. Where S is called the solution space and N(s) is called the neighborhood of s.

Local search methods always stop at the local optimal solution [3]. The definition of a neighborhood structure enables us to define the concept of local optimal solution.

Definition 2: Local optimal solution (or local optimum) with respect to a neighborhood structure N is a solution s^ such that among the set of neighbor N(s^), the objective function (or fitness) of s^ is optimal.

The local search is also called iterative improvement, since each replacement is only performed if the resulting solution is better than the current solution. The local search tries to find a better solution in the neighborhood N(s) of current solution. The methods of the search can be either a first better solution or the best solution of the neighborhood N(s). The former scans the neighborhood N(s) and chooses the first solution that is better than s, the latter exhaustively explores the neighborhoods and returns the solutions with the best fitness.

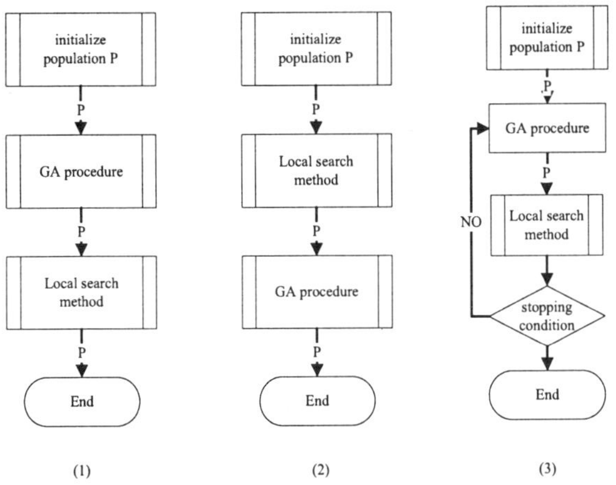

Figure 1. Three pipelining hybrid GAs: (1) GA first, (2) GA last, and (3) staged hybrid

3. The Architecture of Parallel Hybrid GAs

In this section we first describe the architecture for pipelining hybrids and then propose three architectures for parallel hybrid GAs.

3.1. *Pipelining hybrids*

Probably the simplest and most commonly used hybrids before are the pipelining hybrids, in which the genetic algorithm and some other local search are applied sequentially. Typically, pipelining hybrids use the first search algorithm to prune or bias the initial search space such that the second algorithm will either converge more quickly or more accurately. There are three basic types of pipelining hybrid GA, as shown below: 1) the GA is applied first, the local search method is applied last; 2) the local search method is applied first and the GA is applied last; and 3) the GA interleaves with the local search method. See the Fig 1.

3.2. *Parallel hybrids*

Parallel hybrid architecture uses a shared population to allow a GA and local search method to proceed and cooperate paralleling. Each process may work on the problem by itself for one or several iterations before accessing the shared population again. If its findings are better than those in the shared population, it updates the shared population. There are also tree basic types of parallel hybrid GA: 1) GA holds the shared population, local search gets the population (or part of population) through communication; 2) local search holds the shared population, GA gets the population through communication; 3) independent shared population, local search and the GA all get the population through communication. The Fig 2 shows the structure of tree parallel hybrid GAs.

The most advantage of the three parallel hybrid GAs is easy to be parallelized. GAs have very good cooperation with local search methods, and the hybrid algorithms converge to the optimal solutions (or near optimal solution) quickly. GAs mainly explore the search space based on the multiple points (shared population), while local search methods exploit the search space worked on a single solution.

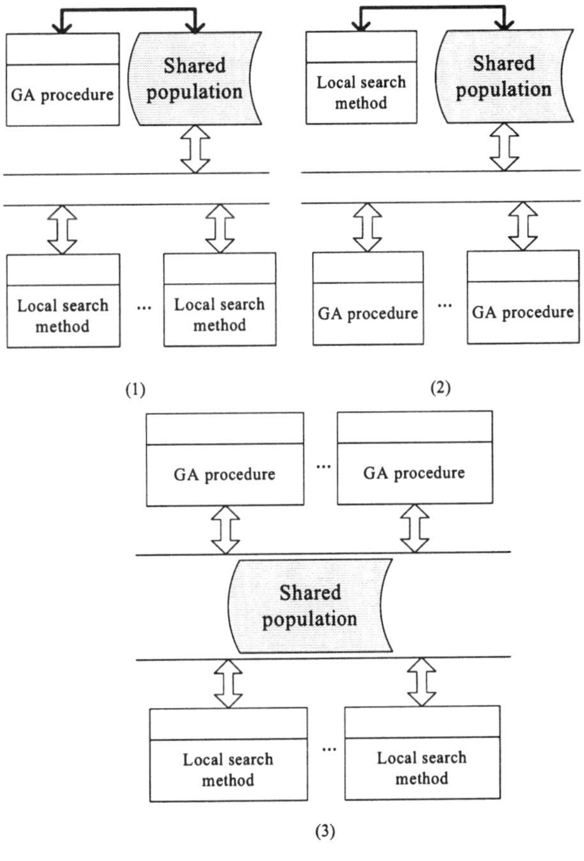

Figure 2. Three parallel hybrid GAs: (1) GA holds the shared population, (2) local search holds the shared population, and (3) independent shared population

4. Integrate Parallel Genetic Algorithms and The Local Search

In this section we introduce how to integrate parallel genetic algorithms and the local search. In other words, we focus on implementing a practical parallel application hybridizing a GA and a local search method.

There are three main steps for implementing a parallel hybrid GAs: 1) Select an appropriate architecture of parallel hybrid GAs; 2) Determine the feasible processes of programming the GA and the local search methods; 3) Choose a communication tool for implementing the parallel hybrid algorithm.

We have described our three parallel hybrid GAs. For a given problem, probably a parallel architecture performs better than the others. In order to build a hybrid GA, we have to perform a serial processes: design a representation, decide how to initialize a population, design a way of evaluating an individual, design suitable operators, design the neighborhood of an individual, and decide when to stop the algorithm and so on. There are several communication tools for parallelizing, such as parallel virtual machine (PVM), message passing interface (MPI)[9], Java, common object request broker architecture (CORBA) etc. Considering the speed of the scientific computations, process migration between clusters, and fault tolerance, we think MPI is currently the better choice for implementing the parallel hybrid GAs.

In order to describe the implementing of the parallel hybrid GAs in detail, we give an example based on the third parallel architecture: independent shared population. There are at least three different application processes: the application process manages shared population (Population Process), the application process runs genetic algorithm (GA Process), and the application process runs local search method (LS Process). Population Process initializes population P (generate random population of n Individuals), then repeatly receives and deals with the message from the other processes until the stopping condition is satisfied. Finally Population Process prints the result and sends the quit message to the other processes. GA Process first initializes MPI then enters four main cycled steps: the step 1 process sends message to Population Process for getting the population; the step 2 process receives message from the Population Process; the step 3 process uses the selector operator, the crossover operator and the mutation operator on the population for one or several times; the last step process sends the worked population back to Population Process. The Population Process does not end until receives the quit message. LS Process runs similar with the GA Process, it sends message to Population Process for getting a solution, applies the local search method on the solution to get the local optimal. Finally LS Process sends back the local optimal back to Population Process and also does not end until receives the quit message. The Fig 3 shows the three processes.

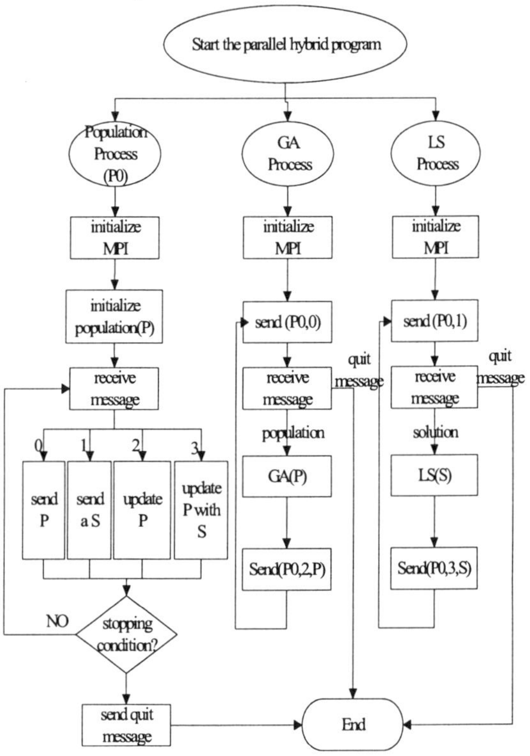

Figure3. A example of parallel hybrid GA program

5. Simulation and Results

We compare our parallel hybrid GA with the pure GA and the pipelining hybrid GA. The type of GA is the generational procedure, and pipelining hybrid GA belongs to the staged hybrid. Our hybrid GA implements as the processes of Fig. 3 based on independent shared population and the application runs parallelly on three computers with the same configuration. The local search method is like G-bit improvement, it defines a value (Δ) to sweep. The parameters of the simulation are defined as follows: probability of the crossover is 0.9, probability of the mutation is 0.01, value of Δ is 0.01, and population size is 200. We simulate two object functions:

The object function 1:

$$\text{Min } f(x, y) = (x^2 + y - 11)^2 + (x + y^2 - 7)^2 + 10$$

$$-6 < x < 6 \text{ and } -6 < y < 6$$

The object function 2:

$$\text{Min } f(x, y) = \sin(x \bullet y) + \sqrt{x+2} + \sqrt{y+2}$$
$$-2 < x < 2 \text{ and } -2 < y < 2$$

The optimal value of object function 1 is 10 when the variable x is 3 and the variable y is 2. Firstly we simulate three programs with the same generation (150). During the simulation, the convergence rate of the pipelining hybrid GA is almost the same as the rate of the parallel hybrid GA, and the pure GA gets the slowest convergence rate. The results also prove that local search techniques converge faster than the pure GA does, and the hybrid GA can improve the algorithms efficiently. Secondly we simulate three programs in the same limited time which is about 3s. This results show that the parallel hybrid GA evolves faster than the pipelining hybrid GA does (150 versus 123), and the pure GA is the fastest one (198). It attributes to two aspects: the local search methods cost some CPU time, and the parallel hybrid GA can run GA and local search process parallelly. Comparing with the object results, the parallel hybrid GA performs better than the other algorithms. We simulate the same processes with the object function 2, and the experiment shows that the simulation gets the same results.

Table 1. First five normalized natural frequencies of a clamped beam with internal hinge at 4 different locations.

	Pure GA		
	result	generation	time(s)
f1	10.213	150	2.3
	10.182	198	3.0
f2	-0.719	500	15.2
	-0.749	988	30.0
	Pipelining hybrid GA		
	result	generation	time(s)
f1	10.011	150	3.7
	10.042	123	3.0
f2	-0.757	500	32.3
	-0.756	462	30.0
	Parallel hybrid GA		
	result	generation	time(s)
f1	10.008	150	3.0
	10.008	150	3.0
f2	-0.756	500	22.1
	-0.757	678	30.0

The results of simulation show that the convergence rate of the parallel hybrid GA is good as the pipelining hybrid GA, and in a certain time span the parallel hybrid GA generates better result than the pipelining hybrid GA does. It is implied that our parallel hybrid GA outperforms the pure GA and the pipelining hybrid GA.

6. Conclusion

In this paper we propose parallel hybrid GAs to improve GA's performance. We design three parallel hybrid GA's architectures for implementing program. From the point of view of practice, the architectures can be easy to be parallelized. We also simulate the parallel hybrid GAs, and the results show that parallel hybrid GAs can combine the merits of the local search approach and the parallel mechanism.

Although we discuss how to parallelize GA and the local search method, we seldom relate the parallelization of GA itself. An open question remains as to how to parallelize the GA itself and the hybrid mechanism. We are exploring this issue as part of future work. We are also concerned about performance of practical combinatorial optimization, because we should consider how many GAs processes and local search processes consist of system is efficient.

References

1. C. A. Coello Coello and A. D. Christiansen, Multiobjective optimization of trusses using genetic algorithms, *Comput. and Struct.* **75(6)**, 647–660 (2000).
2. K. Paramasivam, K. Gunavathi and P. Sathishkumar, Algorithm for low power combinational circuit testing, *TENCON IEEE Region 10 Conference*, 336 – 339 (2004).
3. Christian Blum and Andrea Roli, Metaheuristics in Combinatorial Optimization: Overview and Conceptual Comparison, *ACM Computing Surveys* **35(3)**, 268–308 (2003).
4. Il-Seok Oh, Jin-Seon Lee and Byung-Ro Moon, Hybrid genetic algorithms for feature selection, *Pattern Analysis and Machine Intelligence, IEEE Transactions* **26(11)**, 1424 - 1437 (2004).
5. Y. Hanada, T. Hiroyasu and M. Miki, Tabu: local search mechanism for mega process genetic algorithm, *Cybernetics and Intelligent Systems, IEEE Conference* **1**, 590 – 595 (2004).

6. E. Alba and M Tomassini, Parallelism and evolutionary algorithms, *Evolutionary Computation, IEEE Transactions* **6(5)**, 443 – 462 (2002).
7. A. Mendiburu, J.A. Lozano and J. Miguel-Alonso, Parallel Implementation of EDAs Based on Probabilistic Graphical Models, *Evolutionary Computation, IEEE Transactions* **9(4)**, 406 – 423 (2005).
8. Gexiang Zhang, Weidong Jin and Laizhao Hu, A novel parallel quantum genetic algorithm. Parallel and Distributed Computing, Applications and Technologies, *Proceedings of the Fourth International Conference*, 693 – 697 (2003).
9. Message Passing Interface Forum, "MPI: A message-passing interface standard," *Int. J. Supercomput. Applic.* **8(3)**, 165 – 414 (1994).

A MARKET ACCEPTANCE FRAMEWORK FOR HIGH-TECH FIRMS ACCEPTING THE INNOVATIVE ULTRASONIC CLEANING EQUIPMENT BY DELPHI METHOD AND AHP METHOD

JUNG HUANG

Department of Accounting, National Taichung Institute of Technology
129, Sanmin Road., Taichung, 403 Taiwan, R.O.C.

CHIH-HUNG WU

Department of Digital Content and Technology, National Taichung University
140, Min-Shen Road, Taichung, 403 Taiwan, R.O.C.

WEN-TA HSU

Institute of Management of Technology, Chung Hua University
707, Sec.2, WuFu Rd., HsinChu, Taiwan 300, R.O.C.

TAO HUANG

Department of Business Administration, National Yunline University of Science and Technology
123 University Road, Section 3, Douliou, Yunlin 64002, Taiwan, R.O.C.

The purpose of this study is to introduce the innovated technology of ultrasonic cleaning equipment with the mechanism of the cooperation between the academic circles and businesses. The study focuses on the identification of the local businesses with the equipment and a survey was made to investigate how the equipment is accepted in the market. We target local hi-tech businesses having clean rooms (class ≦ 10000) and extract the constructs influencing the acceptance in the market by Delphi Method and through Analytic Hierarchy Process (AHP), we calculate the relative weighting of each construct and principles to explore the future development of ultrasonic cleaning equipment. From our research, we found that two elements—government policies and publicity are the keys for local hi-tech businesses in selecting the ultrasonic cleaning equipment. Therefore it is suggested that manufacturers, when promoting the ultrasonic cleaning equipment, combine with the government publicity and regulations while enhancing the stability and quality of the equipment so that consumers can identify with the cleaning level after using the equipment. In the meantime, the study also predicts the future requirements and trend of the ultrasonic cleaning equipment and we believe there will be great market requirements with business opportunities.

1. Introduction

In hi-tech industries, the cost of filter nets used in clean rooms is disproportionately low when comparing to the total operating costs. Filter nets, however, play a crucial role in determining whether the plant can bring off a successful process and in affecting the defective rate. IC Fabs of the semiconductor industry, for example, demands highly the capacity of filter nets in clean rooms to rid themselves of contamination particles, to the purpose that the clean rooms can achieve a prescribed standard and attain a high-quality process control. In Taiwan, the filter nets of clean rooms are now all of disposable type, discarded and replaced by new ones after being used. Although this practice assures the quality of the products, the ever increasing waste filter nets cannot be decomposed in landfills on one hand, and they, when incinerated, block fire grids and generate dioxin on the other hand, consequentially increasing social costs. Owing to the raging tide of environment protection, green consumption becomes the norm. Enterprises make the goal of sustainable development attainable by both decreasing the devastation of environment and taking on an image of a green enterprise. A Japan company, of late, utilizing the ultrasound technique, devised cleaning equipment for filter nets which can be applied to the recycling processes of clean-room filter nets in hi-tech plants. Cleansed by this ultrasound cleaning equipment, filter net can restore its function without sacrificing the requirement of the clean room. Accordingly, in addition to reducing the procurement costs, this equipment lessens the amount of waste as well as social costs, making it environment-friendly and cost-effective. This research probes principally the acceptability of ultrasound cleaning device in Taiwan's hi-tech industries; in the meanwhile, by employing Analytic Hierarchy Process to assess the relative weighting of each principle, the future development of such instruments in Taiwan will also be scrutinized. With hi-tech industries having clean rooms (class ≦10000) as its subjects, this research explores the acceptability of ultrasound cleaning device in Taiwan. Extracting the constructs influencing the acceptance in the market by Delphi Method and calculating the relative weighting of each construct and principle through Analytic Hierarchy Process (AHP), we make clear the potential development of ultrasonic cleaning equipment.

This research has three aims: (1) to extract the factors that influence the acceptability of the market by having interview with experts and Delphi Method, as well as setting up the hierarchy structure of this research (2) to appraise the key factors that impact on the acceptability by using Analytic Hierarchy Process to assess the relative weighting of each construct and principle (3) to present conclusions for reference about importing ultrasound cleaning devices, popularizing them, and even undertaking the local enterprise or transferring the relevant techniques.

2. Literature Review

For starters, a bibliography correlating with the techniques of ultrasound cleaning device would be advanced as a sketchy introduction. In general, among methods of cleaning surface pollutants, chemical cleaning and physical cleaning are two principal ones. The former applies detergents directly to the object's surface, either bringing pollutants away from the surface by dissolving them, or separating them from the surface under different cohesion of detergents and pollutants. The latter employs energy generated through the vibration of the cleaning instruments to rid pollutants out of the surface. As a physical cleaning scheme, ultrasound cleaning method nonetheless makes use of cavitation to produce bubbles in liquid and bombard surface with them to free surface of pollutants. Based on the principles of compression and rarefaction, ultrasound cleaning device generates positive pressure and negative pressure and undergoes high-speed undulation in liquid medium, making the pressure among liquid molecules alternate. Vacuum bubbles are thus produced because of the tearing phenomena stemming from pressure difference; as the pressure rises, bubbles grow larger, therefore generating compression and cavitation. When vacuum bubbles crack owing to the applied force of the undulation, the resulting high impact has a local pressure of several thousand atmospheric pressure, which has the ability to clean up the filter net's pollutants. There are two major schemes of ultrasound cleaning: one is to use the impact generated by the burst of vacuum bubbles to bump into the polluted materials and get rid of the pollutants; the other is to wedge tiny bubbles into the interstices between pollutants and object's surface, and then push pollutants away from the surface by taking advantage of the alternative expansion and compression of the bubbles when they are subjected to pressure changes. Detergents are sometimes added in the cleaning process to dissolve pollutants, which, in conjunction with cavitation, should improve the cleaning effect. Fast cleaning speed, excellent cleaning results, accompanying sterilization effect—all these explain why, aside from not hurting the filter nets, ultrasound cleaning process, when compared with other physical or chemical cleaning methods, can achieve superior cleaning quality, thus an appropriate method for high-precision and brittle elements. Figure 2 shows the filter nets before and after cleaning. According to the results of experiment, filter nets cleansed by ultrasound cleaning are qualified for the criteria set by the factory users. Furthermore, Table 1 lists the criteria of clean rooms in various industries.

Table 1. The criteria of clean rooms in various industries

Industry	Criteria of clean rooms
Epitaxial Si、IC Fab、TFT、DRAM	Class ≦100
Optronics、LCD	Class 1~1000
Laser discs	Class 100~10000
LED、PCB、Packaging、Wafer Probe	Class 1000~10000

3. Research Design

3.1. *Subjects of the research*

Four questionnaires are included in this research. At first, an open questionnaire designed specifically for experts of this technique is used to formulate key constructs and elements that would affect the acceptability. The second and third questionnaires, both of Delphi type, take cleaning product manufacturers and experts as subjects to establish a hierarchical structure with factors affecting the acceptability. The subjects of the final AHP questionnaire are those public companies that equip their factories with clean rooms and these rooms must meet the criteria of American Federal Standard 209E[7] of class ≦10000.

3.2. *Research Methods*

This research combines Delphi Method and AHP to set up models and design relevant questionnaires. The introduction of these two methods is presented as follows.Delphi method, originally developed by Olaf Helmer et al., of Rand Corporation in 1948 under a project named "Project Delphi" financed by American Air Force, is now employed in various institutions from government departments to academic facilities. The subjects of this method fill the first questionnaire anonymously. All the questionnaires are collected to perform analysis; the second questionnaire is then designed and sent to every subject with the results of the first questionnaire. The second questionnaire is collected and the whole process is repeated several times until a coherent result is obtained. When it is necessary to forecast new technology with the help of experts, Delphi method would be a good analyzing tool. Analytic Hierarchy Process is a decision-making method proposed by professor Thomas Saaty of University of Pittsburgh, Pennsylvania in 1971 [8][9], which simplifies complicated proposals to concise hierarchical structures, primarily used in problems involving uncertain situations and multiple decision criteria [5]. The main mechanism takes into account factors' influence in every hierarchical level to weighting of factors in their respective upper level. Through comparison between paired factors, the characteristic vectors can be derived to make clear the relative priorities among various factors.

The factors of each construct first undergo comparison to access the relative weighting among factors; then the appraisals focused on (1) marketing factors, (2) environment factors, (3) manufacturer factors, and (4) consumer factors are taken. The 222 public companies equipped with clean rooms that satisfy the American Federal Standard 209-E of class ≦ 10000 compose the body of subjects of the questionnaire. Through calling by phone, mailing and personal interview, the questionnaire are thus presented to stewards or staff in charge of renovation, who decide whether or not to purchase filter nets, to fill out. The returned questionnaires are analyzed by the software Expert Choice. The judging scale is divided into 9 levels, proposed by Saaty and Vargas [10], lest the respondents become confused in answering questions. According to Saaty [5], the number of factors in every hierarchy is limited to below 7, the factors being independent to each other as well, to avoid both complication due to too many factors and incoherent decision making.

Furthermore, some inconsistent questionnaires must be excluded. Satty [11] suggested that Consistency Ratio (C.R.) of every hierarchy and Consistency Ratio of Hierarchy (C.R.H.) must both be less than 01. Those questionnaires that exceed this criterion must therefore be rejected. The average value of each question in the remaining effective questionnaires is then calculated by using weighting average; relative weightings among factors are computed through the average values of them.

4. Data Analysis

4.1. *Analysis of Delphi Method*

To understand the key factors influencing the desire of possessing ultrasound cleaning equipment in hi-tech manufacturers owning clean rooms, we issued 10 questionnaires in each of the two surveys: 2 to experts, 5 to industries and 3 to environment protection agencies. Returned rates are 100% in both surveys. The scoring scale is set to 1~100; the higher the scores the more important the factor is in the eyes of experts and manufacturers, and vice versa. If a factor has a score lower than 60, then it is so inconsequential that it should be ruled out. Moreover, according to the standard recommended by Chang et al. [6], the consistence among specialists is high when variant is less than 0.3, acceptable when less than 0.5. Accordingly, this research performs a descriptive statistic analysis with data of averages and variants coming from the two surveys. Open questions of the first Delphi questionnaire elicit from hi-tech manufacturers totally 23 factors of 4 constructs that would exercise influence in whether ultrasound cleaning equipment would be accepted: Marketing factors: a. product information, b. price, c. outlet, d. promotion. Environment factors: a. government campaign, b. government policy, c.

awareness of environment protection, d. culture, e. cost, f. reference groups, g. enterprise image. Manufacturer factors: a. technician, b. service manner c. service, d. test results, e. brand image, f. technical capacity. Consumer psychology factors: a. quality, b. experience, c. warranty of damages, d. recognition, e. risk, f. intention of recycling.

Table 2. Average scores and variation coefficients of Delphi method

Construct	Factor	The first questionnaire		The second questionnaire	
		average	var. coeff.	average	var. coeff.
Marketing Factors	product information	90	0.07	86.9	0.05
	price	93	0.06	87.5	0.04
	outlet	84	0.12	84.1	0.04
	promotion	74	0.11	72.6	0.06
Environment Factors	government campaign	94	0.03	92	0.02
	Government policy	91	0.05	93.5	0.02
	awareness of environment protection	89	0.06	88.9	0.04
	culture	78	0.09	76.5	0.05
	cost	84	0.08	83.7	0.04
	reference groups	76	0.09	76.6	0.06
	enterprise image	75	0.11	75.6	0.07
Manufacturer factors	enterprise image	58	0.21		
	service manner	60	0.15	62.7	0.14
	service	81	0.09	83	0.03
	test results	90	0.06	89.3	0.04
	brand image	74	0.07	77.1	0.04
	technical capacity	81	0.09	82.2	0.03
	waste water recycling (new)	90		83.3	0.1
Consumer psychology factors	quality	91	0.04	90.4	0.03
	experience	80	0.1	82.3	0.05
	warranty of damages	74	0.14	72.7	0.1
	recognition	77	0.15	77	0.09
	risk	85	0.08	85.1	0.04
	intention of recycling	90	0.05	90	0.03
	durability of filter net (new)	70		74.5	0.09

Note: The grids with gray background color are those of highest scores in their relative construct; with underline, those eliminated from the first questionnaire

From table 2, it is clear that the highest score made by the item "price" in the construct of marketing factors reveals specialists' thinking that consumers are more concerned with the rationality of filter net's price. In the construct of environment, items "government campaign" and "government policy" receive the highest score, showing that in order to popularize this kind of device in Taiwan, government's campaign for reducing waste and recycling, as well as legislation to enforce the regulation, is essential to increase the acceptability of industries. The item "test result" of manufacturer construct indicates that, in experts' opinion, consumers pay much attention in the test result of the filter nets after being cleaned. This concern is also reflected in consumer construct: the high score of item "quality" denotes consumers' laying great emphasis on cleanliness of filter nets when cleaned. It is reasonable to deduct, from data showed in Table 2, that the second Delphi questionnaire has completed the mission of integrating experts' subjective recognition and opinions, so a hierarchical structure consisting of 4 constructs and 24 factors, which would to some extent influence hi-tech industries' acceptance of ultrasound equipment, is thus formulated.

Two factors are appended by specialists to the first Delphi questionnaire: recycling of waste water added to manufacturer factors, durability of filter nets to consumer psychology factors. Table 1 shows the result of the first questionnaire, in which all but the technician factor of manufacturer construct, eliminated with a score lower than 60, are preserved. In the second questionnaire, scores of all factors are greater than 60 and variation coefficients are lower than 0.15, which satisfies the criteria proffered by Chang et al. Because this questionnaire has a more convergent result than that of the first, denoting that the gap of subjective divergence of respondents is narrowed and achieves convergence, so we conclude the Delphi questionnaire, establishing the hierarchical structure of acceptability of ultrasound cleaning device, as is showed in Figure 1.

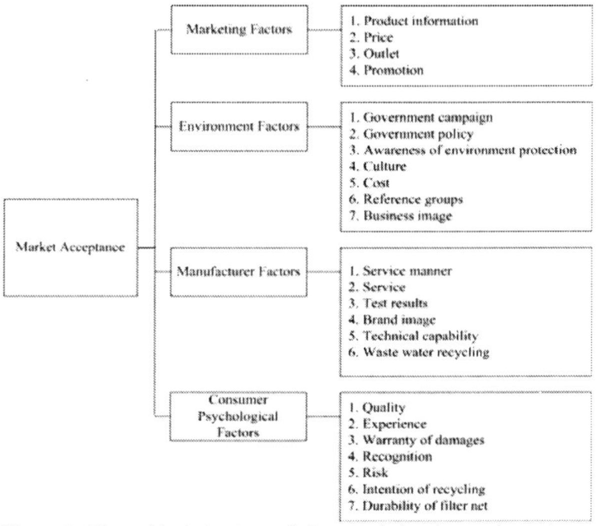

Figure 1. Hierarchical structure of ultrasound cleaning equipment

4.2. *Results of AHP Method*

Exactly 147 AHP questionnaires are issued, among which 56 (38%) are returned and analyzed later with the software Expert choice. To check whether all those questionnaires satisfy the requirement of preferences among the constructs and transitivity, we perform the consistency test to inspect whether there is any judgment error or contradiction, by which both Consistency Ratio and Consistency Ratio of Hierarchy would be ensured. The remaining 43 questionnaires (13 questionnaires have been ruled out) have a C.R.H. value of 0.007<0.1, up to the standard set by Satty. Therefore, geometric average is applied to these questionnaires to find out the average values of the items, through which the relative weightings are thus derived. A thorough list of weightings and their relative priority are showed as follows. The weightings and C.R. values of factors in marketing construct are listed in Table 3: a. product information (13.5%); b. price (40.4%); c. outlet (40.1%); d. promotion (6%); C.R. = 0.02 < 0.1 (up to the standard).

According to the analysis, price (40.4%) and outlet (40.1%) are the most important factors in the eyes of the consumers, denoting that, in marketing construct, consumers take into account the price of filter net first to determine whether to use the technology. At the same time, the service network of recycling filter nets and product delivery are of importance as well, suggesting that a higher degree of convenience and customer value are pursued by customers when they purchase a certain kind of technology.

Table 3. The weightings and priority order of factors in marketing construct (C.R. value=0.02)

Factor	Product information	Price	Outlet	Promotion
Weighting	0.135	0.404	0.401	0.06
Rank	3	1	2	4

The weightings and C.R. values of factors in environment construct are listed in Table 4: a. government campaign (28.7%); b. government policy (32%); c. awareness of environment protection (17.5%); d. culture (6.9%); e. cost (8.5%); f. reference groups; g. enterprise image (3.5%); C.R. =0.07<0.1 (up to the standard). Government policy (32%) and government campaign (28.7%) are among the essential factors, meaning that, in environment construct, government must enact regulations and further advocate the reduction of waste and the importance of recycling before industries could take environment protection seriously and use innovative green equipment with both environmental and economical benefits.

Among regulations issued by the ROC Environmental Protection Administration [1], Article 6 of Resource Recycling Act states that "Priority consideration shall be given to the use of substances that reduce waste production to achieve resource sustainability insofar as is economically and technologically feasible. Priority consideration shall be given to the reuse, recycling, energy recovering, and appropriate disposal, in that order, of substances that have lost their original utility". Article 9: "Enterprises shall comply with the following principles when engaging in industrial activities to reduce resource consumption, control waste production, and promote resource recycling and reuse: 1. Employ clean production technology. 2. Adopt necessary measures to reduce waste production when using raw materials. 3. Implement recycling and reuse of raw materials after they lose their original utility or provide said materials for recycling and reuse, and bear responsibility for the appropriate disposal of materials that cannot be recycled or reused. 4. To prevent goods and containers from becoming waste, enterprises engaged in the manufacture and sale of goods or containers are responsible for increasing the useable life of such goods and containers and implementing the repair and maintenance thereof. Said enterprises shall also endeavor to perform product research, development, and design so as to facilitate recycling and reuse and shall indicate the types of materials used." All this shows that the government has actively promoted the use of green products and strongly inhibited behavior damaging the environment.

Aside from the government's preach of environment protection, that the awareness of environment protection (17.5%) ranks third shows the rising awareness among industries: they think about not only profits but also environment issues like environment damage and ecological pollution.

Table 4. The weightings and order of priority of factors in environment construct (C.R. value=0.07)

Factor	Government campaign	Government policy	Awareness of environment protection	Culture	Cost	Reference group	Business image
Weighting	0.287	0.32	0.175	0.069	0.085	0.028	0.035
Rank	2	1	3	5	4	7	6

The weightings and C.R. values of factors in manufacturer construct are listed in Table 5: service manner (3.1%); b. service (7.8%); c. test results (47.4%); d. brand image (19%); e. technology capacity (18.6%); f. waste water recycling (4.2%); C.R. =0.06<0.1 (up to the standard). The test results of filter nets after being cleaned is the most significant factor to consumers, revealing that consumers place great emphasis on the test results; in other words, filter net's cleanliness after washed must be guaranteed by authority. Because of the high cost of hi-tech industries, if the cleanliness cannot achieve the requirement of quality, the industries will suffer a great loss. In order to reduce the risk and apprehension of hi-tech industries, it is preferable that manufacturers provide test results issued by authoritative agencies to raise the confidence of consumers. Moreover, manufacturer's past brand image (19%) and ability to develop new products are among factors consumers think of less importance.

Table 5. The weightings and order of priority of factors in manufacturer construct (C.R. value=0.06)

Factor	Service manner	Service	Test results	Brand image	Technological capacity	Waste water recycling
Weighting	0.031	0.078	0.474	0.19	0.186	0.042
Rank	6	4	1	2	3	5

The weightings and C.R. values of factors in consumer psychology construct are listed in Table 6: a. quality (34.5%); b. experience (20.2%); c. warranty of damages (3.7%); d. recognition (2.8%); e. risk (22.5%); f. intention of recycling (11.5%); g. durability of filter net (4.8%); C.R. =0.06<0.1 (up to the standard).

As far as consumers are concerned, quality is the most crucial factor, which coincides with consumers' demand of technology. The cleanliness of filter net after being washed is of extreme importance for industries, in that they may suffer operating losses stemming from poor quality of filter nets; therefore, only and stable quality can ensure industries from risk. What's more, risk due to using product (22.5%) and an earlier satisfactory experience in using the product are lesser factors that consumers pay attention to.

Table 6. The weightings and order of priority of factors in consumer psychology construct (C.R. value=0.06)

Factor	Quality	Experience	Warranty of damages	Recognition	Risk	Intention of recycling	Durability of filter net
Weighting	0.345	0.202	0.037	0.028	0.225	0.115	0.048
Rank	1	3	6	7	2	4	5

At last, the weighting and C.R. values of the four constructs are listed in Table 7: (1) marketing factors (5.7%), (2) environment factors (54.8%), (3) manufacturer factors (18.5%), (4) consumer psychology factors (21%); C.R. =0.05<0.1 (up to the standard). From the analysis, environment construct (54.8%) plays a highly decisive role in influencing consumers' purchasing ultrasound cleaning equipment.

Table 7. The weightings and order of priority of the four construct (C.R. value=0.06)

Construct	Marketing factors	Environment factors	Manufacturer factors	Consumer psychological factors
Weighting	0.057	0.548	0.185	0.21
Rank	5	1	4	3

The relative weightings and order of priority of the 24 factors in 4 constructs are listed in Figure 2, in which weightings of are calculated on the basis of acceptability of industries; values in parentheses are weightings of the respective items; numbers following the parentheses are the order the items. In descending order, the priorities of all the evaluation principles are shown as follows: 1.government policy (0.17536); 2. government campaign (0.157276); 3. awareness of environment protection (0.0959); 4. test results(0.087695); 5. quality (0.07245); 6. risk (0.04725); 7. cost (0.04658); 8.experience (0.04242); 9. culture (0.037812); 10. brand image (0.03515); 11. technological capacity (0.03441); 12. intention of recycling (0.02415); 13. price (0.023028); 14. outlet (0.022857); 15. enterprise image (0.01918); 16. reference group (0.015344); 17. service (0.01443); 18. durability of filter net (0.01008); 19. waste water recycling (0.00777); 19. warranty of damages (0.00777); 20. product information (0.007695); 21. recognition (0.00588); 22. service manner (0.005735); 23. promotion (0.00342).

5. Conclusions

In compliance with the ever increasing call for environment protection, green products and resource recycling technology progressively enter the mainstream of research for future enterprises. The ultrasound cleaning technology is one of those green creations. To explore the acceptability of the device, this research designs questionnaires by applying Delphi method, formulates hierarchical structure of factors that would dispose hi-tech industries equipped with clean rooms to accept this equipment, integrates Analytic Hierarchy Process (AHP) into the questionnaire, and reckons up the relative weightings of all constructs and factors from consumers' perspective, finally making a clear recommendation concerning "the acceptability of ultrasound cleaning equipment" as follows. (1) By employing expert questionnaire, the hierarchical structure of "the acceptability of ultrasound cleaning equipment" is thus composed: marketing factors, environment factors, manufacturer factors, and consumer psychology factors, among which environment construct is of paramount importance. Besides, key factors in the order of priority are government policy, government campaign, awareness of environment protection, test results, and quality. (2) The research suggests that manufacturers of ultrasound cleaning device, when making public this product, had better abide by the government campaign and regulations, append test results to filter nets to guarantee the nets to be qualified, strengthen technological stability and quality to elevates consumers' confidence, lessen the risk and worry of hi-tech industries to increase the acceptance of ultrasound cleaning device. Owing to the unfamiliarity with this kind of equipment in hi-tech industries, government agencies, and environment protection institutions, we hope that through systematic discussion and research, this report can serve as an imperative reference in importing ultrasound cleaning devices, popularizing them, and even undertaking the local enterprise or transferring the relevant techniques, as well as in legislation.

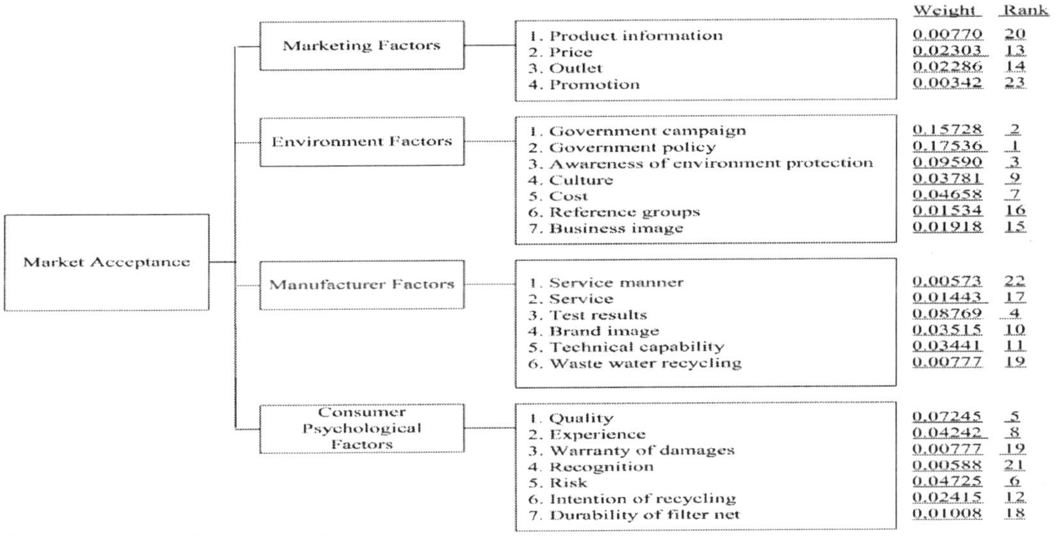

Figure 2. Weighting and order of importance of factors influencing market acceptance

References

1. Law of Environmental Protection Administration Executive Yuan, http://w3.epa.gov.tw/epalaw/index.htm.
2. C. J. Yu, C. Y. Hsu and J. Y. Chen, Introduction to Technology Management: Technology Forecasting and Planning, Wunan Bookstore, (1998).
3. TOENEC, Ultrasonic Cleaning Equipment Lecture (2003).
4. Morida Katumi, Ultrasonic Cleaning, Kindai Henshu Sha, (1989). (in Japanese)
5. Z. Y. Dang and G. H. Tzeng, The Analytic Hierarchy Process Features and Applications, *The Journal of the Chinese Statistical Association* **27(6)**, 13707-13786 (1989).
6. P.C. Chang, N.T. Tsou, B.J.C. Yuan and C.C. Huang, Development Trends in Taiwan's Opto-electronics Industy, *Technovation* **22**, 161-173 (2002).
7. Revised by the Institute of Environmental Sciences 940 E, FEDERAL STANDARD 209E Airborne Particulate Cleanliness Classes in Cleanrooms and Clean Zones, Northwest Highway Mount Prospect, Illinois, (1992).
8. T. L. Saaty, A Scaling Method for Priorities in the Hierarchical Structures, *Journal of Mathematical Psychology* **15**, 234-281(1997).
9. T. L. Saaty, The Analytic Hierarchy Process：Planning,Priority Setting, Resource Allocation, McGraw-Hill, (1980).
10. T.L. Saaty and L.G. Vargas, The Logic of Priorities, Boston, Massachusetts, (1982).
11. T. L. Satty and L.G.Vargas, Models, Methods, Concepts & Applications of the Analytic Hierarchy Process, Kluwer Academic Publishers, (2001).
12. T. G. Leighton, The Acoustic Bubble, Harcourt Brance & Company, (1994).

DETERMINING BATCH SIZE IN A SUPPLY CHAIN

RUEDEE MASUCHUN

Faculty of Engineering, King Mongkut's Institute of Technology Ladkrabang
Ladkrabang, Bangkok 10520, Thailand

WIBOON MASUCHUN

Business Integration, CPF IT Center CO., LTD.
C.P. Tower, 16th Floor, Silom Rd., Bangrak, Bangkok 10500, Thailand

In a supply chain environment, determining batch size at each stage is of importance. Using large batch size can save costs but time is wasted as trade-off. Small batch size can speed up the process but costs are increasing. To represent both aspects, this paper proposes the nonlinear integer mathematical model with the objective function of minimizing both costs and time simultaneously. This model can be used to determine (production) batch size to match up the flow of production at manufacturer with the demand at retailers and means of shipment (transfer batch size). Since the nature of this problem is NP-hard, at each stage of supply chain, the acceptable production and transfer batch sizes are obtained using the advantage of genetic algorithm approach. The numerical illustration and results show that it is not necessary to use the same batch size when manufacturing and transferring.

1. Introduction

In a supply chain environment, it is not straightforward to determine batch size when manufacturing and transferring. Using large production batch size can save costs such as setup costs; however, in large-sized production stage where more than one type of product are produced, other products have to wait longer until all items in current production batch are completed. On the contrary, using small production batch size requires the production to run several setups at the same time as costs are increasing. Nevertheless, the production is flexible in that other type(s) of products can be produced when necessary. For example, rushing order comes. The impact of batch size is also considerable when transferring items to other stages in supply chain. Small transfer batch size can speed up the production process but it must be trade-off with the increased costs. With the large transfer batch size, items have to wait until the pallet/truck is fulfilled. Though, transfer costs are not high compared to those when transferring with small batch size.

To determine batch size either for production or transferring, both aspects, costs and time, must be simultaneously considered. This paper proposes the nonlinear integer mathematical model with the objective function of minimizing both costs and time simultaneously. This model can be used to determine batch sizes at each stage to match up the flow of production at manufacturer with the demand at retailers and means of shipment.

Since this is an NP-hard problem which means that the optimal solution cannot be easily obtained or even it cannot be obtained in a reasonable time. Genetic algorithm (GA) has been widely used to solve the optimization problem because it can provide good-enough solution rapidly. At each stage of supply chain, the acceptable production and transfer batch sizes are obtained using the advantage of genetic algorithm. The numerical illustration is demonstrated and results show that it is not necessary to use the same batch size when manufacturing and transferring.

2. Literature Review

Many researchers have extensively studied about a variety of batch-processing problems which can be classified into a constant batch-processing time and a varying batch-processing time [1]. Using constant batch-processing time, processing times are independent of jobs constituting the batch while in varying batching-processing time problems, processing times depend on the batch constituent. For an overview of both constant and varying batch-processing time problems, we refer to [2]-[13]. This paper studies the varying batch-processing time case.

Several methods have been proposed to solve a variety of batch-processing time problems including 1) dynamic programming based algorithm [14], 2) branch-and-bound algorithm [2], [15]-[16], 3) some heuristics [3]-[4], [8], [11], and lastly 4) approximation algorithms [7]. Since some methods would require an indefinitely long run time but couldn't guarantee an optimal solution, this research applies a genetic algorithm approach.

3. Mathematical Model

To construct the mathematical model, one assumption is made that finished products at any stages will be moved to next stage immediately. Therefore, the inventory will be considered at the beginning of any stages as shown in Figure 1.

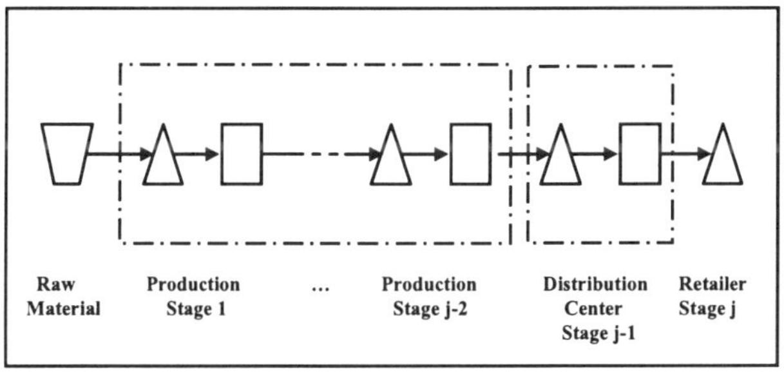

Figure 1. Problem overview

From Figure 1, there are j stages in supply chain, and products are produced by up to j-2 production stages at manufacturer according to the demand from retailers. Finished products are transferred to distribution center which is stage j-1 before distributed to stage j which is retailer.

Given that a planning horizon time covers t periods, using the notation presented in Table 1, the model to match up the flow of production at manufacturer with the demand at retailers and means of shipment is developed. The objective is to meet demand while minimizing the costs including inventory costs, setup costs, and transfer costs as well as the waiting time which will differ according to the assigned value of both production and transfer batch sizes. The conversion factor, α, is required to equate the costs and time and must be thoroughly further investigated since it will affect the results of study.

Table 1. Notation

Problem Parameters		
$Inv_{i,j}$	=	Inventory costs of keeping product i at stage j for one period (\$/unit)
$SUC_{i,j}$	=	Setup costs of producing product i at stage j (\$/minute)
$SUT_{i,j}$	=	Setup time of producing product i at stage j (minutes)
$PT_{i,j}$	=	Production time required to produce product i at stage j (minutes/unit)
$C_{j,t}$	=	Capacity available in period t at stage j (minutes)
$D_{i,t}$	=	Demand from retailers for product i during period t (units)
$TR_{i,j}$	=	Transfer costs when transferring product i from stage j to j+1 (\$/batch)
PC	=	Set of production centers
D	=	Distribution center
R	=	Retailer
J	=	Set of stages in supply chain PC + D + R
α	=	Conversion factor
Decision Variables		
$I_{i,j,t}$	=	Inventory level of product i at stage j at the end of period t (units)
$p_{i,j,t}$	=	Number of production batches of product i at stage j during period t (batch)
$k_{i,j}$	=	Integer ratio of production batch size over transfer batch size of product i at stage j
$PB_{i,j}$	=	Size of production batch of product i at stage j (units/batch)
$TB_{i,j}$	=	Size of transfer batch of product i from stage j to j + 1 (units/batch)

3.1. *Costs*

Inventory costs are costs of keeping product at production center which can be written as $\sum_{i,j} Inv_{i,j} * \left(\sum_t \left(\frac{I_{i,j,t} + I_{i,j,t-1}}{2}\right)\right)$. Note that number of inventory used is the average inventory which is calculated from the beginning inventory plus the ending inventory divided by two. Setup costs or costs of changeover when different products are subsequently produced and require different tools or methods can be written as $\sum_{i,j} SUC_{i,j} * SUT_{i,j} * \left(\sum_t p_{i,j,t}\right)$. Transfer costs are costs of transferring products between production centers and from production center to distribution center as well as from distribution center to retailers. Transfer costs can be written as $\sum_{i,j} k_{i,j} * TR_{i,j} * \left(\sum_t p_{i,j,t}\right)$. The total costs can be rewritten as

Total Costs= Inventory costs
+ Setup Costs
+ Transfer Costs

$$= \sum_{i,j} Inv_{i,j} * \left(\sum_t \left(\frac{I_{i,j,t} + I_{i,j,t-1}}{2}\right)\right)$$
$$+ \sum_{i,j} SUC_{i,j} * SUT_{i,j} * \left(\sum_t p_{i,j,t}\right)$$
$$+ \sum_{i,j} k_{i,j} * TR_{i,j} * \left(\sum_t p_{i,j,t}\right) \quad (1)$$

3.2. *Waiting Time*

Since different production or transfer batch sizes can affect the time waiting to fill up the pallet further transferred to next production center or distribution center or retailer, the waiting time is of importance and unavoidably must be considered. The waiting time can be written as $\sum_{i,j} TB_{i,j} * PT_{i,j} * k_{i,j} * \left(\sum_t p_{i,j,t}\right)$.

3.3. *Objective Function*

As mentioned earlier, the objective function is to simultaneously minimize the costs and time. These two measurements are different in units; therefore, the conversion factor, α, is necessary to equate the costs and time. With the conversion factor, the complete objective function can be written as follows.

$$\text{Min } Z = \alpha \begin{pmatrix} \sum_{i,j} Inv_{i,j} * \left(\sum_t \left(\frac{I_{i,j,t} + I_{i,j,t-1}}{2}\right)\right) \\ + \sum_{i,j} SUC_{i,j} * SUT_{i,j} * \left(\sum_t p_{i,j,t}\right) \\ + \sum_{i,j} k_{i,j} * TR_{i,j} * \left(\sum_t p_{i,j,t}\right) \end{pmatrix} + (1-\alpha)\left(\sum_{i,j} TB_{i,j} * PT_{i,j} * k_{i,j} * \left(\sum_t p_{i,j,t}\right)\right) \quad (2)$$

3.4. *Constraints*

To assure the possibility of problem, several constraints must be constructed. The first set of constraints is to ensure that the total time used in production including setup time does not exceed the time available considering period by period. The capacity constraints can be written as

$$\sum_i p_{i,j,t} * \left(PT_{i,j} * PB_{i,j} + SUT_{i,j}\right) \le C_{j,t} \qquad \forall t, j \in J. \quad (3)$$

Second set of constraints is to count inventory at each stage period by period. Inventory in any period equals the inventory at the beginning of that period minus units transferred from this stage to the next stage during that period plus units transferred from the previous stage to this stage during that period. The inventory at production centers or distribution center can be written as

$$I_{i,j,t} = I_{i,j,t-1} - p_{i,j,t} * k_{i,j} * TB_{i,j} + p_{i,j-1,t} * k_{i,j-1} * TB_{i,j-1} \qquad \forall i, t, j \notin R. \quad (4)$$

The retailer's inventory constraints can be written as

$$I_{i,j,t} = I_{i,j,t-1} - D_{i,t} + p_{i,j-1,t} * k_{i,j-1} * TB_{i,j} \qquad \forall i, t, j \in R. \quad (5)$$

The last set of constraints force the size of process batch to be multiple of the size of transfer batch which can be written as

$$PB_{i,j} = k_{i,j} TB_{i,j} \qquad \forall i, j \in J. \quad (6)$$

The complete nonlinear integer optimization model can be written as follows.

$$\text{Min } Z = \alpha \begin{pmatrix} \sum_{i,j} Inv_{i,j} * \left(\sum_t \left(\frac{I_{i,j,t} + I_{i,j,t-1}}{2}\right)\right) \\ + \sum_{i,j} SUC_{i,j} * SUT_{i,j} * \left(\sum_t p_{i,j,t}\right) \\ + \sum_{i,j} k_{i,j} * TR_{i,j} * \left(\sum_t p_{i,j,t}\right) \end{pmatrix} + (1-\alpha)\left(\sum_{i,j} TB_{i,j} * PT_{i,j} * k_{i,j} * \left(\sum_t p_{i,j,t}\right)\right) \quad (7)$$

Subject to

$$\sum_i p_{i,j,t} * \left(PT_{i,j} * PB_{i,j} + SUT_{i,j}\right) \le C_{j,t} \qquad \forall t, j \in J$$

$$I_{i,j,t} = I_{i,j,t-1} - p_{i,j,t} * k_{i,j} * TB_{i,j} + p_{i,j-1,t} * k_{i,j-1} * TB_{i,j-1} \qquad \forall i, t, j \notin R$$

$$I_{i,j,t} = I_{i,j,t-1} - D_{i,t} + p_{i,j-1,t} * k_{i,j-1} * TB_{i,j} \qquad \forall i, t, j \in R$$

$$PB_{i,j} = k_{i,j} TB_{i,j} \qquad \forall i, j \in J$$

$$0 \le \alpha \le 1$$

$I_{i,j,t}$, $p_{i,j,t}$, $PB_{i,j}$, $TB_{i,j}$, $k_{i,j}$ are nonnegative integers

4. Genetic Algorithm

In view of the fact that the mathematical model constructed is a nonlinear integer type and moreover NP-hard, it is impossible to obtain the optimal value within a reasonable time. In the real practice, good-enough solution is satisfied. To obtain an acceptable solution, a GA approach will be used. GA was first introduced in 1970s by Holland and has been widely used to solve a variety of problems. It is a randomized algorithm motivated from the study of cellular automata. The advantage of GA is that several solutions can be considered simultaneously with few problems with local optima. GA is superior to other meta-heuristics in that it keeps a set of solutions rather than a unique solution [1]. Currently, GA has been widely used in many optimization problems such as scheduling problems. Many successful applications of GA in industry can be found in [17].

GA uses a chromosome representing a solution which is probabilistically obtained based on randomization. Initial feasible solutions are randomly generated and their objective functions are calculated. Initializing with a good population and reasonable population size can increase the efficiency of genetic algorithm [18]. GA requires two genetic operators called crossover and mutation to combine and alter current solutions to generate new solutions. Hence, to perform crossover and mutation respectively, a pair of feasible solution is selected based on their objective function values. The better objective function value, the more chance to be selected. New solutions are then calculated. Good solutions will be stored and used as initial feasible solutions while poor solutions will be discarded. Crossover and mutation then take place and algorithm continues until either time is up or all iterations are completed. The outline of genetic algorithm can be summarized as follow.

- Initialization: A set of feasible solutions is generated.
- Evaluation: the objective function is calculated for each solution in the set of feasible solution.
- Selection: Given Z is the number of solutions that will be considered simultaneously, Z pairs of (parent) solutions are randomly selected from the set of feasible solution. Each pair will be used to generate a child solution subsequently. Note that better (parent) solution has more chance to be selected.
- Crossover: A randomly selected crossover point is assigned for each pair of parent solution. A crossover point is a point where two parent solutions are crossed to generate new (child) solution.
- Mutation: Each string in a child solution is randomly mutated according to mutation probability.
- Termination testing: the algorithm is terminated if stopping condition is satisfied; otherwise, go back to Initialization.

The parameters required for the genetic algorithm are assigned according to [18]-[20].

- Population size (Z) equals 100.
- Crossover probability is 1.0.
- Mutation probability for each string is 1.0.
- Number of iteration is 100.

5. Numerical Illustration

Given that a planning horizon time covers twelve periods and there are two products called products A and B which must be processed at production center called production center X according to the demand from retailer. The demand is assumed to be known and shown in Table 2. Table 3 includes values of the rest of parameters needed to solve the problem.

Table 2. Demand for Products A and B

Period	Demand for Product A	Demand for Product B
1	200	1000
2	250	1000
3	300	1000
4	500	1000
5	450	1000
6	350	1000
7	300	2000
8	350	2000
9	400	2000
10	500	2000
11	450	2000
12	300	2000

Table 3. Values for the rest of parameters

$Inv_{1,1}$	0.10	\$/unit
$Inv_{1,2}$	0.15	\$/unit
$Inv_{1,3}$	0.20	\$/unit
$Inv_{2,1}$	0.05	\$/unit
$Inv_{2,2}$	0.10	\$/unit
$Inv_{2,3}$	0.15	\$/unit
$SUC_{1,1}$	0.5	\$/minute
$SUC_{1,2}$	-	\$/minute
$SUC_{1,3}$	-	\$/minute
$SUC_{2,1}$	0.3	\$/minute
$SUC_{2,2}$	-	\$/minute
$SUC_{2,3}$	-	\$/minute
$SUT_{1,1}$	20	Minutes
$SUT_{1,2}$	-	Minutes
$SUT_{1,3}$	-	Minutes
$SUT_{2,1}$	15	Minutes
$SUT_{2,2}$	-	Minutes
$SUT_{2,3}$	-	Minutes
$PT_{1,1}$	8	Minutes
$PT_{1,2}$	-	Minutes
$PT_{1,3}$	-	Minutes
$PT_{2,1}$	5	Minutes
$PT_{2,2}$	-	Minutes
$PT_{2,3}$	-	Minutes
$C_{1,t}$	11,000	Minutes
$TR_{1,1}$	20	\$/batch
$TR_{1,2}$	40	\$/batch
$TR_{1,3}$	-	\$/batch
$TR_{2,1}$	10	\$/batch
$TR_{2,2}$	20	\$/batch
$TR_{2,3}$	-	\$/batch
α	0.5	

Table 4 shows the results of using a genetic algorithm approach to solve the problem. For Product A, production batch size, transfer batch size from production center X to distribution center, and transfer batch size from distribution center to retailer are 26, 13, and 20 respectively. For Product B, production batch size, transfer batch size from production center X to distribution center, and transfer batch size from distribution center to retailer are 32, 16, and 25 respectively.

Table 4. Results for numerical iIllustration

Decision Variables	Value
$PB_{1,1}$	26
$PB_{2,1}$	32
$TB_{1,1}$	13
$TB_{2,1}$	16
$TB_{1,2}$	20
$TB_{2,2}$	25

6. Conclusion

In this paper, the nonlinear integer optimization model is constructed to capture both costs and time when batch size is in consideration. This model can be used to determine (production) batch sizes to match up the flow of production at manufacturer with the demand at retailers and means of shipment (transfer batch size). At each stage of supply chain, the acceptable production and transfer batch sizes are obtained using the advantage of genetic algorithm. The results show that it is not necessary to use the same batch size at every stage when manufacturing and transferring.

References

1. P. Damodaran, P.K. Manjeshwar and K. Srihari, Minimizing makespan on a batch-processing machine with non-identical job sizes using genetic algorithms, *Int. J. Prod. Econ.* **103**, 882–891 (2006).
2. L. Dupont and C. Dhaenens-Flipo, Minimizing the makespan on a batch processing machine with non-identical job sizes: an exact procedure, *Comput. Oper. Res.* **29**, 807–819 (2002).
3. F.J. Ghazvini and L. Dupont, Minimizing mean flow times criteria on a single batch processing machine with nonidentical job sizes, *Int. J. Prod. Econ.* **55**, 273–280 (1998).
4. D.S. Hochbaum and D. Landy, Scheduling semiconductor burn-in operations to minimize total flow time, *Oper. Res.* **45**, 874–885 (1997).
5. Y. Ikura and M. Gimple, Scheduling algorithms for a single batch processing Machine, *Oper. Res. Lett.* **5**, 61–65 (1986).

6. C.L. Li and C.Y. Lee, Scheduling with agreeable release times and due dates on a batch processing machine, *Eur. J. Oper. Res.* **96**, 564–569 (1997).
7. S. Melouk, P. Damodaran and P. Y. Chang, Minimizing makespan for single machine batch processing with nonidentical job sizes using simulated annealing, *Int. J. Prod. Econ.* **87**, 141–147 (2004).
8. C.S. Sung and Y.I. Choung, Minimizing makespan on a single burn-in oven in semiconductor manufacturing, *Eur. J. Oper. Res.* **120**, 559–574 (2000).
9. C.S. Sung and Y.H. Kim, Minimizing makespan in a two machine flowshop with dynamic arrivals allowed, *Comput. Oper. Res.* **29**, 275–294 (2002).
10. C.S. Sung and S.H. Yoon, Minimizing maximum completion time in a two-batch-processing-machine flowshop with dynamic arrivals allowed, *Eng. Optimiz.* **28**, 231–243 (1997).
11. C.S. Sung, Y.H. Kim and S.H. Yoon, A problem reduction and decomposition approach for scheduling for a flowshop of batch processing machines, *Eur. J. Oper. Res.* **121**, 179–192 (2000).
12. C.S. Sung, Y.I. Choung, J.M. Hong and Y.H. Kim, Minimizing makespan on a single burn-in oven with job families and dynamic job arrivals, *Comput. Oper. Res.* **29**, 275–294 (2002).
13. R. Uzsoy, Scheduling a single batch processing machine with non-identical job sizes, *Int. J. Prod. Res.* **32**, 1615–1635 (1994).
14. C.Y. Lee, R. Uzsoy and L.A. Martin-Vega, Efficient algorithms for scheduling semiconductor burn-in operations, *Oper. Res.* **40**, 764–775 (1992).
15. Y. Pan, An improved branch and bound algorithm for single machine scheduling with deadlines to minimize total weighted completion time, *Oper. Res. Lett.* **31**, 492–496 (2003).
16. R. Uzsoy and Y.Y. Yang, Minimizing total weighted completion time on a single batch processing machine, *Prod. Oper. Manag.* **6**, 57–73 (1997).
17. C. Reeves, Genetic algorithms for the operations researcher, *Inform. Comput.* **9**, 231–250 (1997).
18. H. Ishibuchi and T. Murata, A multi-objective Genetic Local Search algorithm and its application to flowshop scheduling, *IEEE T. Syst. Man. Cy. C* **28(3)**, 392-403 (1998).
19. T. Murata, H. Ishibuchi and H. Tanaka, Genetic algorithms for flowshop scheduling problems, *Comput. Ind. Eng.* **30(4)**, 1061-1071 (1996).
20. T. Murata, H. Ishibuchi and H. Tanaka, Multi-objective genetic algorithm and its applications to flowshop scheduling, *Comput. Ind. Eng.* **30(4)**, 957-968 (1996).

AN APPROACH TO ANALYZING THE BIDIRECTIONAL VALUES

CHENYIN PAN
Glorious Sun School of Business and Management, Donghua University, 1882 Yan An Road West Shanghai, 200051, China

SUFEN WANG
Glorious Sun School of Business and Management, Donghua University, 1882 Yan An Road West Shanghai, 200051, China

Customer relationship describes a sort of interactions between enterprises and their customers, and customer relationship management always emphasizes on the research of customer value: from enterprise to customer and from customer to enterprise. In this paper, cognition process is introduced to demonstrate the two types of values are bidirectional and to analyze the bidirectional values, and the interaction mechanism of bidirectional values is explained in terms of the associated processes. Moreover, the factors in bidirectional values are identified via analyzing the Customer Satisfaction Index Model, and concretize the interactive relationships of bidirectional values. Meanwhile, the mathematic model is set up to demonstrate the effect of interactive relationships. Thereby a sound and stable relationship between enterprises and their customers can be realized via combination of bidirectional values based on cognition process.

1. Introduction

In an environment of fierce market competition, customers become a kind of particular important resources. The relationships between an enterprise and its customers are considered as a property of the enterprise. As we all know, not every customer has the same value. Consequently, enterprises are very interested in establishing sound and stable customer relationships with their customers. Hence, how to establish such customer relationship turns out to be a hot issue in customer relationship management (CRM) research.

Generally speaking, study of customer value is from two perspectives: the value that a customer carries to an enterprise from the perspective of the enterprise and the value that an enterprise delivers to customers from the perspective of the customers.

When addressing the first type of value, researchers focus on the so-called customer lifetime value (CLV). For instance, Hoekstra and Huizingh (1999) consider that the total value of direct contributions and indirect contributions to overhead and profit of an individual customer during the entire customer life cycle [2]. However, some scholars have different opinions, say Qi and Shu (2005) suggest that net values of the customer's margins during every transaction period of the entire life cycle [6]. These researches study from various aspects of economic benefits customers carry to the enterprise during the entire customer life cycle.

For second type of value, the customers' perception of satisfaction draws attentions from researchers. When discussing customer classification, Zhao et al (2005) refer to the major contents of customer value including customer value, customer perceived value (CPV) and customer delivered value (CDV) [11]. Dong and Jin (2004) have a direct discussion about value that an enterprise delivers to its customers and also demonstrates that the customer value is the most important factor for any enterprise to possess competitive advantage [10].

Customer relationship describes a sort of interactions between enterprises and their customers. It characterizes a series of processes of dynamic cognition, thus forming a closed loop. Neglecting this feature, researchers would intend to apply open-loop idea to model the customer relationship, so that their formulation would not be very appropriate. As pointed out by Malthouse and Blattberg (2005), it would lead to misclassification of customers [1] and improper allocation of limited human and financial resources. Enterprises and their customers continuously cognize and understand each other in all stages of customer life cycle [13]. Such continuous cognitions and understanding make the customer relationship more friendly (or estranged). Thus, the change of customer relationship will have impact on the change of customer values of two types ("the value the enterprise delivers to the customers" and "the value the customer carries to the enterprise"). For convenience in discussion, let the product value and customer value be the shortened form of the value that the enterprise delivers to its customers and the value that the customer carries to the enterprise respectively.

A survey shows that if enterprise' CSI (Customer Satisfaction Index) increases 1% annually, the return rate of assets after 5 years will increase 11.33% [7]. Therefore the customer relationship reflected via customer satisfaction index is of great significance for enterprises and customers, but the establishment of customer relationship is firstly based on interactive cognition.

This paper deals with customer relationship via combination of product value and customer value based on cognition process for the purpose of establishing a sound and stable relationship between enterprises and their customers. In this paper, it is considered that the two types of values are bidirectional and vary with the cognition processes of enterprises as well as customers. Then, the factors of causing the change of bidirectional values (the product value and customer value) are identified via Customer Satisfaction Index Model. This paper emphasizes analysis of the interactive relationships of bidirectional values in modeling.

2. The Relationship between Cognition Process and the Change of Bidirectional Values

There exists the certain relationship between the enterprise and the customers from the perspective of psychological cognition. Both parties can be either cognizing agent or cognized object (See Figure 1).

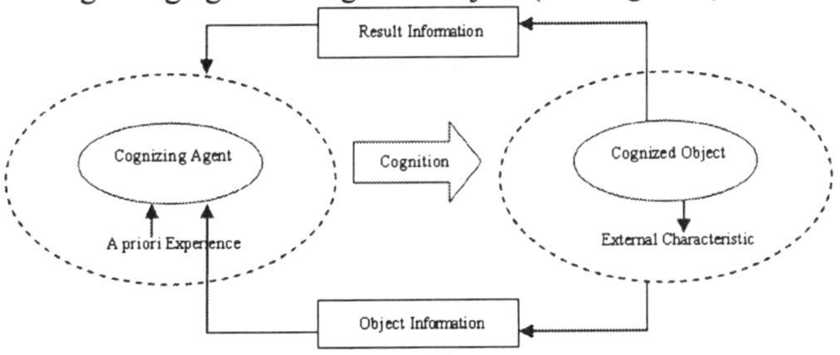

Figure 1. A Cognition Process Model

The enterprise is the cognizing agent and customers are the cognized objects. The enterprise identifies the object information from the external characteristics of the customers (e.g. age, gender, income, previous purchase records, *etc*) by means of combining them with the a priori experiences (e.g. the customers purchase information, the segmentation information of the customer, *etc*) to make the new judgment, and infer whether or not the customers are able to create the expected profit, before the enterprise takes the next action (e.g. retains, develops, or drives the customer). Then, the responses of the customers with respect to the enterprise's new actions (e.g. increase or reduce the quantity of purchase, recommend products or service, *etc*) will become enterprise's source of new (or posterior) experience via enterprise's refining.

Conversely, the customers also play roles as the cognizing agent and consider their supplying enterprise as the cognized object. The customers process is similar to the enterprise, identify the object information from the external characteristics of their enterprise (e.g. the products or services provided by the enterprise, the intangible properties such as brand and goodwill, *etc*) by means of combining them with a priori experiences (e.g. expectation, previous similar shopping experiences and feelings, *etc*) to make the new perception, and infer whether or not their enterprise are able to satisfy their requirements, before the customers takes the next action (e.g. repurchases or change their supplying enterprises). Then, the responses of the enterprise with respect to the customer's new actions (e.g. provides better products or services, cross-sales, *etc*) will turn out to be customer's new experience via customer's reconsidering.

In this way, the interactions between the customers and the enterprise are interactive cognition processes. In the bidirectional processes, the relevant input information is processed into the information on changes in the two types of values by the cognition agent, which becomes the base of the next round of cognition. The change in the bidirectional values has impact on action-taking of cognizing agent. As a result, cognition process causes the change of bidirectional values, and the change in bidirectional values will influence the cognition in next round. Thus, it possesses the functions of significance for balancing the bidirectional values and analysis of the relation of bidirectional values from cognition process.

3. The Relationships of Bidirectional Values

In 1989, Doctor Fornell in Quality Research Center of Business School of Michigan University suggest a set of factors (e.g. customer expectation, perception after purchase, and purchase price) to set up the logic model of econometrics [7]. Later, many countries have established their nationwide customer satisfaction index (CSI) systems, which carry out evaluation of CSI [9]. The America Customer Satisfaction Index (ACSI) is one example of them. We identify the factors of bidirectional values from ACSI model, and concretize the interactive relationships of bidirectional values.

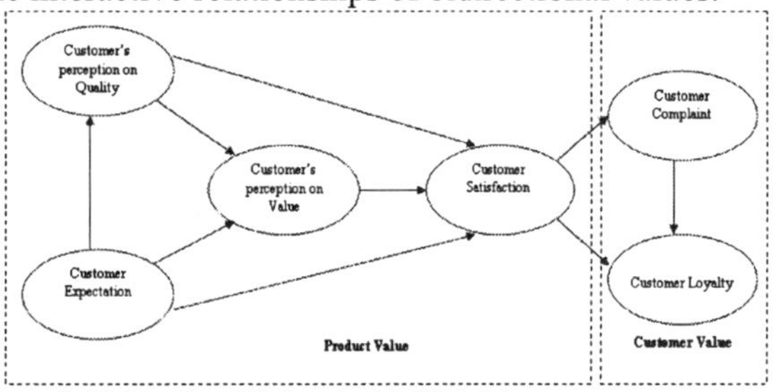

Figure 2. Bidirectional Values in ASCI Model

The left part of Figure 2 depicts the product value. First, the customers set up their expectation as a criterion for judging the value. Their expectation synthesizes their requirements, previous purchase experiences and their value orientation, and will form a criterion in the customers' mind, which finally poses the certain impact on the evaluation of the value. Second, the customers perceive the quality of the delivered products or services. The products or services quality has a direct effect on satisfaction of the customer's requirement. If they perceive the product quality is above their expectation and they are satisfied with the product quality, they will highly evaluate the product value and vice versa. Furthermore enterprise realizes the product or service quality in the customers' mind via the customers' perception on quality. Third, the customers' perception on value is similar to the perception on quality. The customers will compare the products or services with their demand and actual situations, apperceive the contribution the enterprise makes and the value the enterprise delivers. It not only affects the customers' satisfaction, but also has impact on the customers' evaluation of the product value.

Thus, with the efforts (e.g. publicity of overall image, establishment of brand image, improvement of product or service standard) that the enterprise makes for attracting more customers, enterprise can deliver product value to the customers, and raise the customer satisfaction to a higher level. Further, the product value can be obtained by means of the evaluation of the CSI, and then identified by the enterprise. So, product value can be derived through the process shown in the left part of Figure 2.

The right part of Figure 2 depicts the customer value. The customers react to the actions taken by the enterprise (e.g. the purchase of enterprise's products or services, forming purchase intentions, the customer loyalty, the complaint of the products or services, the positive or negative word-of-mouth, *etc*), resulting in the customer value either profitable or profitless. First, the customer loyalty is of particular importance in the customer value. Loyal customers mean financial and spiritually inputs to establishments [5], since their repurchases, their cross-sales, their willingness to express the positive word-of-mouth, and so forth, all of which demonstrates the benefits that the customers may bring to the enterprise. Furthermore, such benefits will be continuously improved in the long-term interaction of the enterprise with the customers, so the customer loyalty can be seen as a profitable aspect of the customer value. Second, the customer complaint may or may not be beneficial to the enterprise. Customers have direct or indirect complaints. If an enterprise deals with its customers' direct complaints in a right way, the customers will enhance their cognition of the enterprise and generate the intention of purchase behavior. So they would like to do more business with the enterprise such that the enterprise gains more customer value. However, if the enterprise deals with their direct complaints in a wrong way, the customers would be reluctant to keep business with the enterprise so that the enterprise loses the customer value. The indirect complaint is more difficult to be dealt with. A study shows that among all the unsatisfactory customers, about 13 percent will spread their complaints to other 20 persons in average while the rest 87 percent will do so to other 9 persons in average [7]. Customer behavior that negatively affects the enterprise's profit is complaints in the presence of other (potential) customers [2]. The negative effect of word-of-mouth will result in the loss of a large number of potential customers.

Thus, the customer loyalty and the customer complaint in the CSI Model reflect the customer's purchase behavior and affection representation. Whether or not the enterprise gains more customer value depends on the customer loyalty and the customer complaint. So, customer value can be derived through the process shown in the right part of Figure 2.

The product value and the customer value interact with each other. Figure 3 shows the process of bidirectional values, forming a closed loop. After purchasing products or service, the customers will normally compare them with their own psychological expectation to judge whether the ex ante demands can be satisfied and which extent the satisfaction can achieve, thus reducing the risk and uncertainty of the second purchase and laying the basis for repurchase. While earning the benefits, the enterprise can also obtain the orientation of customer demands in the interaction of each other, assesses the possibility of such demand, utilizes customer value (the earned benefits) and combines the rational customer demands to improve the product quality and service standard and provides the more appropriate products or service to the customer, satisfy the new round of customer demands, help the customers achieve the certain extent of satisfaction and perceive product value. Thus, the cycle comes into being, where bidirectional values become value-added in the interactive process and shows the basic nature of the relationship between the customers and the enterprise.

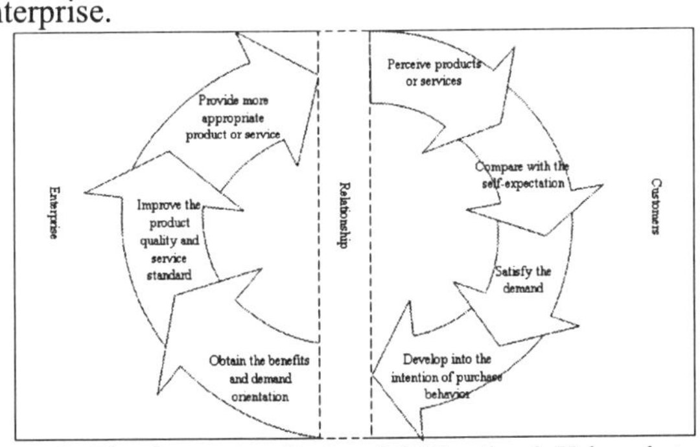

Figure 3. The Interactive Cycle of Bidirectional Values between Enterprise and Customers

4. A Quantitative Analysis Model

The above discussion is in a qualitative way, now we are going to make effect to quantitatively modeling the relation between bidirectional values. As the two key stages of the customer relationship management, the value between the customers and the enterprise are continuously added value. In the point of view of the enterprise, the customers randomly purchases the products or services provided by the enterprise and the customers can not necessarily make an overall comment on the social value, economic value and psychological value of the products or the service. The evaluation of the bidirectional values with the CSI only can stay at the qualitative level, so we will choose the corresponding contents of the bidirectional values from the CSI model and analyze the inner relationship of bidirectional values in combination with the customer's purchase information and quantitative measures at the standpoint of the enterprise.

Let CV_{1t} denote the customer value over the tth period while takes value randomly in a real space, and $\mu = E(CV_{1t})$. Let ϕ and Φ be the density and distribution functions of CV_{1t} respectively. Let CV_{2t} denote the product value over the tth period.

A customer can perceive the product value through the routine channels, but the customer's perception is subjective to the certain extent [8] and the perception varies from customer to customer. Assume that the product value cannot be fully perceived by the customers, that is, $CV_{2t} = CPV_{1t} + \zeta_t$, of which CPV_{1t} is the customer's perceived value over the tth period and ζ_t denote the loss the customer suffers while perceiving the value the enterprise delivers.

In addition, according to Oliver's disconfirmation-of-expectation paradigm, the customer satisfaction is a function of a cognitive comparison of expectations prior to consumption and actual experience [4]. If the product performed better than expected (perceived actual performance > expected performance), positive disconfirmation is expected to occur. This leads to customer satisfaction, strengthens customers' attitudes towards the service, and results in positive word-of-mouth. If however, in the customers' evaluation, the product performs worse than expected (perceived actual performance < expected performance), negative disconfirmation occurs. This may weaken future dispositions towards purchasing the product, and the customer may search for other products [3]. So we can assume the relationship between the customer's perceived value and the customer's expected value on products or services as $CPV_{1t} - CEV_{1t} = \delta_t$, where CEV_{1t} and δ_t denote the customer's expected value over the tth period and extent of the customer satisfaction, respectively.

As a result, there exists the following relationship between the product value (CV_{2t}) and the customer's expected value (CEV_{1t}):

$$CV_{2t} = CEV_{1t} + \zeta_t + \delta_t \tag{1}$$

Let $\hat{R}_t(CEV_{1t} - CV_{1t})$ be unit loss the enterprise suffers in the value delivery over the tth period. Then, we have

$$\hat{R}_t(x) = \frac{[x]^+}{N} + \frac{(M-P)[x]^-}{P^2} \qquad (2)$$

where N is the product quantities the customer purchases when he/she perceives acquired benefits, M is the product quantity and service quantity the customer is expected to purchase, P is the product quantities the customer purchases when he/she perceives lost benefits; assume $M \geq P$.

$\frac{[x]^+}{N}$: when the customer's expected value exceeds the value actually paid for the product or service rendered over the tth period, he/she is willing to pay for the product or service less than the original expectation, where the customer benefits from difference, but the enterprise loses the original opportunity to make profits and such loss is converted to unit loss; $\frac{(M-P)[x]^-}{P^2}$: when the customer's expected value is less than the value actually paid for the product or service rendered over the tth period, customer lost from difference and thus reduces the original expectative purchase quantities, and the enterprise loses the profits the customer would had originally created and such loss is converted to unit loss.

Let $R_t(CV_{2t})$ be the expected unit loss the enterprise suffers from the product value over the tth period, then

$$R_t(y) = E[\hat{R}_t(y - CV_{1t})] \qquad (3)$$

After plugging Expressions (1) and (2) in Equation (3), we obtain:

$$R_t(y) = E\left[\frac{[y - CV_{1t}]^+}{N} + \frac{(M-P)[y - CV_{1t}]^-}{P^2}\right]$$

$$= \frac{1}{N}\int_0^y (y-x)\phi(x)dx + \frac{(M-P)}{P^2}\int_y^\infty (x-y)\phi(x)dx$$

Since $R_t(CV_{2t}^*) = \min R_t(y)$,

$$\left.\frac{d}{dy}R_t(y)\right|_{CV_{2t}^*} = \left.\frac{d}{dy}\left(\frac{1}{N}\int_0^y (y-x)\phi(x)dx + \frac{(M-P)}{P^2}\int_y^\infty (x-y)\phi(x)dx\right)\right|_{CV_{2t}^*}$$

$$= \left[\left(\frac{1}{N} + \frac{M-P}{P^2}\right)\Phi(y) - \frac{(M-P)}{P^2}\right]_{CV_{2t}^*} = 0$$

Thus $$\Phi(CV_{2t}^*) = \frac{N(M-P)}{P^2 + N(M-P)}, \qquad (4)$$

$$CV_{2t}^* = \Phi^{-1}\left(\frac{N(M-P)}{P^2 + N(M-P)}\right), \qquad (5)$$

$$\frac{d^2}{dy^2}R_t(y) = \left(\frac{1}{N} + \frac{M-P}{P^2}\right)\Phi'(y) > 0, \qquad (6)$$

As a result, there exists the minimum value in the expected unit loss the enterprise suffers from the product value, that is, $R_t\left[\Phi^{-1}\left(\frac{N(M-P)}{P^2 + N(M-P)}\right)\right]$.

$CV_{2t}^* = \Phi^{-1}\left(\frac{N(M-P)}{P^2 + N(M-P)}\right)$ is the optimal allocation value of the product value, and excess (shortage) of the product value over the optimal allocation value will increase the expected unit loss of the enterprise to certain extent.

In a word, according to the different product or service quantities (N, M, P) the customer purchases under the different psychological states and the distribution function of the customer value (Φ) over the tth period, the analysis of how to attain the extreme value of unit loss in the product value can understand whether and how the value the enterprise brings to the customer can be optimally distributed and further reflect the relationships of bidirectional values.

5. Conclusion

The research of bidirectional values (the research of the value the enterprise delivers to the customers from the perspective of the customers and the research of the value the customer carries to the enterprise from the perspective of the enterprise) is the focus of the enterprise. Customer relationship characterizes a series of processes of dynamic cognition. The interaction mechanism of bidirectional values is clearly explained in terms of the associated processes. We draw the following conclusions through the analysis and discussions in each part:

- Analyze cognition process between enterprise and customer from the perspective of psychological cognition, and demonstrate the importance of the researches of the combination of bidirectional values.
- The factors in bidirectional values are identified via the customer satisfaction index model: the product value is reflected in the form of customer expectation, customer's perception on quality,

customer's perception on value and customer satisfaction from the left part of CSI model, while the customer value is reflected in the form of purchase behavior and affection representation arising from the customer loyalty and customer complaint from the right part of CSI model, both of which interacts with each other and develops into the cycle of bidirectional values demonstrating the basic nature of the value-added customer relationship.

- Set up the mathematic model of mutual relationships of bidirectional values and further demonstrate that there exists the certain relationships between product value and customer value. The product value can be rationally distributed according to the customer value, which can control and optimize the expected unit loss in the product value according to actual situations.

We develop into the new perspective of studying the customer relationship according to the combination of bidirectional values and provide the theoretical basis for the enterprise to make use of bidirectional values to manage the customer relationship. We identify it is very important for the enterprise to emphasize bidirectional values from the cognition process in developing the customer relationship management. Such research possesses the functions of theoretical significance and practical instruction to the certain extent. According to the factors in bidirectional values and the combination of certain historic data of customer purchase, the enterprise can rationally configure bidirectional values, and establish sound and stable customer relationship. Thereby, the enterprise can properly allocate the limited human and financial resources to the maximum extent to generate more considerable and efficient customer benefits, and stably develop and improve itself in the competitive market.

In future research, we will examine effectiveness of above conclusions via field study, and investigate the detailed rules for implementation in real situation.

Acknowledgments

Special thanks go to Professor Jingxian Chen, for his valuable advice.

References

1. Edward C. Malthouse and Robert C. Blattberg, Can we predict customer lifetime value? *Journal of Interactive Marketing* **19**, 2-16 (2005).
2. Janny C Hoekstra and Eelko K R E Huizingh, The Lifetime Value Concept in Customer-Based Marketing, *Journal of Market Focused Management* **3**, 257-274 (1999).
3. Sunil Erevelles, Shuba Srinivasan, and Steven Rangel, Consumer Satisfaction for Internet Service Providers：An Analysis of Underlying Processes, *Information Technology and Management* **4**, 69-89 (2003).
4. Tor Wallin Andreassen and Bodil Lindestad, Customer loyalty and complex services, International *Journal of Service Industry Management* **9**, 7-23 (1998).
5. A. Akin Aksu, Gap Analysis in Customer Loyalty: A Research in 5-Star Hotels in the Antalya Region of Turkey, *Quality & Quantity* **40**, 187-205 (2006).
6. Jiayin Qi and Huaying Shu, Evaluation, Modeling and Decision-Making of Customer Value, *Beijing University of Posts and Telecommunications Press*, 6-16 (2005).
7. Shanghai Academy of Quality Management., Evaluation of Customer Satisfaction, Shanghai Science & Technology Press, Shanghai, (2001).
8. Shouxiang Xie and Zhengshun Shen, Development of Corporate Core Competitive Capability Based on Customer Value, *Journal of Hunan Administration Institute* **5**, 21-22 (2004).
9. Xinyan Liu, Yanni Liu, Zhi Yang and Houfen Wan, The Construction of a New Customer Satisfaction Index Model Based on the Anaiysis of SCSB, ACSI and ECSI, *Nankai Business Review* **6**, 52-56 (2003).
10. Dahai Dong and Yufang Jin, Customer Value as the Key Premise of Competitive Advantage: A Case Study, *Journal of Management Sciences in China* **7**, 85-89 (2004).
11. Linjie Zhao, Shukun Tang and Daowu Zhang, Study on Customer Classification Model Based on CPV and CLV, *Value Engineering* **1**, 32-37 (2005).
12. Xiangyang Liu, Analysis of Dual Factors and Tolerance Zone of Customer Satisfaction-Margin Chain, *Journal of Zhongnan University of Economics and Law* **4**, 112-115 (2003).
13. Mingliang Chen, Customer Loyalty and Customer Relationship Life Cycle, *Journal of Industrial Engineering/Engineering Management* **2**, 90-93 (2003).

AN ONLINE FREQUENCY RATE BASED ALGORITHM FOR MINING FREQUENT SEQUENCES IN EVOLVING DATA STREAMS

M. BAROUNI-EBRAHIMI
Faculty of Computer Science, University of New Brunswick
Fredericton, NB, Canada

ALI A. GHORBANI
Faculty of Computer Science, University of New Brunswick
Fredericton, NB, Canada

Mining sequential patterns for discovering frequent sequences has been widely studied as a data mining problem. A challenging research is to extend its use to data streams. A data steam is an unbounded, continuously generated sequence of data transactions. In this paper, we propose an online single-pass algorithm called OFSD (Online Frequent Sequence Discovery), to mine the set of all frequent sequences in a data stream whose frequency rates satisfy a minimum user defined frequency rate (f_u). The algorithm significantly reduces the number of elements in the candidate set (a set of candidate sequences that should be kept for further exploration) that efficiently increases its performance in comparison with other general solutions. The simulation results show the effects of f_u variation and the application defined threshold (C_M) on the frequent phrase detection process.

1. Introduction

Frequent phrase miner algorithms [1, 6, 7] are provided with a static dataset containing a sequence of transactions, a user defined minimum support value and a list of transaction items. They find the maximal frequent sequences of items that satisfy the minimum support value. Incremental maintenance of frequent sequences in the presence of dataset updates is another approach in this area [8]. The algorithms attempt to reduce the number of scans performed on the unchanged section of the dataset.

Li et al. [5] have pointed out the differences between mining data streams and mining static datasets. From their perspective, firstly, each transaction within a data stream should be examined at most once. Secondly, a mechanism is needed to bind the number of candidate elements due to the continuous generation of new data elements. Finally, the mining result should be available whenever it is requested regardless of the stage of the process. The data stream minor algorithms [2, 4, 5] find the frequent itemsets in a data stream which satisfy a user defined minimum support value.

Charikar et al. [3] have proposed a one-pass algorithm for estimating the most frequent items in a data stream. The algorithm addresses the problem that comes up in the context of search engines, where there is a query stream sent to the search engine and the goal is to find the most frequent queries handled in some period of time. A query is an item in this algorithm, while in this paper, we are interested in finding the common phrases used in the user queries (a query is composed of a number of phrases). Each phrase is a word (generally an item) or a sequence of words. Our approach finds the frequent phrases used in a data stream of user queries.

Legacy frequent sequence mining algorithms define a threshold for the occurrence number of a phrase called min-support. A phrase whose occurrence number satisfies the min-support is a frequent phrase. However, min-support is not a suitable threshold in data stream mining due to the fact that there is unlimited number of transactions in a data stream. A phrase may be frequently present in a part of a data stream and satisfy the min-support. The phrase would be a frequent phrase in that period of time, but if it does not present in the data stream after that, its status should change to none frequent.

In this paper, we propose an algorithm for discovering frequent phrases in a data stream containing a sequence of transactions. A phrase is a subsequence of a transaction and a frequent phrase is a phrase (P) where its frequency rate (f_P) is greater than a minimum user defined frequency rate (f_u). A phrase is a frequent phrase as long as its frequency rate satisfies f_u. The proposed method is an online, one-pass algorithm, which means that each transaction in the data stream is examined only once. Consider a data stream of user queries submitted to a search engine as an input of our algorithm. Assume a phrase "New York city" is frequently used within queries such as "map New York city pdf", "New York city subway" and so on in a period of time. The algorithm initially considers three items "New", "York" and "city". Since the phrase is frequently used, the algorithm gradually combines the items and creates the phrase "New York city". The phrase is recognized as a frequent phrase while it is frequently used. When the frequency rate of the phrase becomes less than f_u, the phrase will die. It will be created again whenever its frequency rate goes to higher than f_u.

2. Problem Definition

The frequent sequence mining problem is defined in this section. The notations that we use in this paper are as follows:

- $\psi = \{I_1, I_2, \ldots, I_m\}$ is a set of literals, called items.
- A transaction $T=I_i \ldots I_j$ consists of a sequence of items.
- $DS = (\ldots, T_i, T_{i+1}, \ldots)$ is a data stream, which is an infinite sequence of transactions.
- $TL=[T_i, \ldots, T_j]$ is a transaction list containing a finite sequence of transactions from DS.
- A phrase $P=I_i \ldots I_j$ is a subsequence of T.
- $P \in T$ implies phrase P exists in the transaction T.
- $T:P_i \rightarrow P_j$ implies P_j immediately follows P_i in T.
- t_c is the current transaction number of the active transaction in DS.
- Phrase Birth Number (t_P) for a phrase P in TL is defined as: $t_P=i \Leftrightarrow (\forall T_i, T_j \in TL, P \in T_i \wedge P \in T_j \Rightarrow i<j)$
- n_P is the occurrence number of P in $TL=[T_{tp}, \ldots, T_{tc}]$.
- Phrase Frequency Rate (f_P) in $TL=[T_{tp}, \ldots, T_{tc}]$ is defined as:

$$f_P = \frac{n_P}{t_c - t_P + 1} \quad (1)$$

- $l(i,j)$ is a link from P_i to P_j.
- Link Birth Number ($t_{l(i,j)}$) for a link $l(i,j)$ in TL is defined as: $t_{l(i,j)}=k \Leftrightarrow (\forall T_k \in TL, \forall T_m \in TL, T_k:P_i \rightarrow P_j \wedge T_m:P_i \rightarrow P_j \Rightarrow k<m)$
- $n_{l(i,j)}$ is the occurrence number of $l(i,j)$ in $TL=[T_{tl(i,j)}, \ldots, T_{tc}]$.
- Link Frequency Rate ($f_{l(i,j)}$) in $TL=[T_{tp}, \ldots, T_{tc}]$ is defined as:

$$f_{l(i,j)} = \frac{n_{l(i,j)}}{t_c - t_{l(i,j)} + 1} \quad (2)$$

Given a data stream DS, the goal of mining frequent sequences is to find the phrases such as P in DS, where f_P is greater than a user specified minimum frequency rate (f_u). Here, f_u is a real number between 0 and 1. A frequency rate of zero for a phrase means that the respective phrase has not been observed in any of the transactions in DS, while a frequency rate of one implies that the phrase is present in all of the transactions in DS.

To clarify the notations used in this paper, consider the data stream DS_I in which transactions $T_1=A_1A_2A_4A_5$, $T_2=A_2A_4$, $T_3=A_1A_2A_3A_5$ and $T_4=A_2A_3$ are repeated periodically. The values of the notations introduced earlier in this section based on DS_I are as follows:

- $\psi = \{A_1, A_2, A_3, A_4, A_5\}$
- $T_1 = A_1A_2A_4A_5$, $T_2 = A_2A_4, \ldots$
- $P = A_2A_4 \Rightarrow P \in T_1$
- $P_i = A_2A_4 \wedge P_j = A_5 \Rightarrow T_1: P_i \rightarrow P_j$
- $P = A_3$ and $t_c=7 \Rightarrow f_P=0.6$.

Table 1. Frequent Phrases of DS_I

f_u	Frequent phrases
0.2	$A_1, A_2, A_3, A_4, A_5, A_1A_2, A_2A_3, A_2A_4, A_3A_5, A_4A_5, A_1A_2A_3, A_1A_2A_4, A_2A_4A_5, A_2A_3A_5, A_1A_2A_4A_5, A_1A_2A_3A_5$
0.4	$A_1, A_2, A_3, A_4, A_5, A_1A_2, A_2A_3, A_2A_4$
0.6	A_2

Based on the above definitions, the frequent phrases resulting from different f_u values are shown in Table 1. Phrases A_2 is present in every transaction ($f_{A2} = 1$), therefore it has been selected for all f_u values. All of the phrases in DS_I have a frequency rate higher than 0.25, thus they are all selected in the case where f_u is 0.2.

3. The OFSD Algorithm

The simplest solution for the problem defined in Section 2 is to create all the possible phrases based on the items in ψ and then count their occurrences in the data stream. The solution is not efficient due to its high time and space complexity. This is caused as a result of too many comparisons performed on the set of created phrases. The other deficiency of this simplistic approach is that ψ may not be known in advance and hence the creation of the phrases is not possible.

To overcome the high complexity of the previous approach, one can restrict the algorithm to only count the phrases extracted from the performed transactions. The algorithm extracts all possible phrases such as P_i for each transaction and increases P_i occurrence in a Candidate Set (CS) by 1. The total number of possible phrases for transaction $T=I_1I_2 \ldots I_k$ with k items (NP_T) is calculated as follows:

$$NP_T = \sum_{i=1}^{k} i = \frac{k(k+1)}{2} \quad (3)$$

In the worst case, the number of phrases that can be added to the candidate set is of order $O(k^2)$. Although it is known to an omniscient that the majority of transaction phrases are not frequent in real world cases, but the algorithm needs to add them to the candidate set to reach such conclusion in its subsequent phases. The bottleneck of this algorithm and generally most of the other proposed algorithms is that they need to search CS for each of the possible transaction phrases. This results in high time complexity for a large CS.

The proposed OFSD algorithm significantly reduces the number of phrases in CS. It consists of four major steps:

- **Step 1**: all transaction items are added to CS. Each added item is a single-element phrase.
- **Step 2**: if transaction phrase P_i is currently a member of CS, its occurrence number will be incremented by 1.
- **Step 3**: $\forall P_i \in T$, $\forall P_j \in T$, $P_i, P_j \in CS \wedge T{:}P_i \rightarrow P_j \Rightarrow$ link $l(i,j)$ is created and $n_{l(i,j)}=1$ for the first visit or $n_{l(i,j)}$ is incremented by 1 if it already exists.
- **Step 4**: $\forall$ $l(i,j)$ in Step 3, $f_{l(i,j)} > f_u \Rightarrow l(i,j)$ is deleted and phrase P_iP_j is added to CS.

The number of items added to CS in Step 1, and the number of links added between two single-element phrases in Step 3 are both of order $O(k)$ in the worst case for each transaction. The algorithm does not insert a phrase P_iP_j into CS unless it realizes that the frequency rates of P_i, P_j and $l(i,j)$ satisfy f_u. This procedure significantly reduces the size of CS.

Each transaction T is processed in the *parseTransaction* procedure shown in Figure 1. In line 1 of this procedure, each item in T is added to the *candidateSet* as a phrase, if the phrase does not already exist in the *candidateSet*.

In line 2 of Figure 1, the algorithm iterates through the number of items available in T denoted by *index*. For each *index*, the *headPhraseList* is a set of the phrases from T. Each phrase ends with the item in position *index* and is present in the *candidateSet*. The formation of the *TailPhraseList* is very much similar to the *headPhraseList* except that the item in position *index+1* is at the beginning of the created phrases.

To create candidate multi-element phrases that can serve as possible frequent sequences, the algorithm creates appropriate links between the phrases in *headPhraseList* (P_i) and *TailPhraseList* (P_j) through the

```
parseTransaction()
1: add T.Items to candidateSet with tP=tc;
2: for index=1 to T.size
3:    headPhraseList=findHeadPhrases(T, index);
4:    foreach phrase Pi in headPhraseList do
5:       increment Pi occurrence number by 1;
6:    end for
7:    tailPhraseList=findTailPhrases(T, index);
8:    foreach phrase Pi in headPhraseList do
9:       foreach phrase Pj in tailPhraseList do
10:         if (PiPj does not exist in candidateSet) then
11:           l(i,j)=updateLink(Pi, Pj);
12:           if (weight(l(i,j)) > CM) then
13:              delete l(i,j);
14:              add PiPj to candidateSet with tP=tc;
15:           end if
16:         end if
17:      end for
18:   end for
19: end for
```

Figure 1. The *parseTransaction* procedure.

updateLink function (line 11 of Figure 1). The *updateLink* function creates a link from P_i to P_j and keeps track of its occurrence number. The *weight* of $l(i,j)$ is compared with C_M (a threshold indicating the satisfactory frequency value) to see if the two ends of $l(i,j)$ should be merged to form a new phrase in the *candidateSet* (line 12 in Figure 1).

All of the frequent phrases can be retrieved from the *candidateSet* at any point of time through the *frequentPhraseExtraction* function. This function checks all the phrases in the *candidateSet* and selects the phrases with a *weight* more than the constant C_M.

3.1. *Weight Analysis*

The first visit of the phrase P_j immediately after P_i ($P_i, P_j \in T \wedge P_i, P_j \in CS$) will result in the creation of the link $l(i,j)$ (from P_i to P_j). $W_{l(i,j)}$ is the weight of $l(i,j)$ which is calculated in a specific transaction number (t_c) as follows:

$$W_{l(i,j)} = n_{l(i,j)} - (t_c - t_{l(i,j)} + 1) \times f_u \quad (4)$$

Theorem 1: Instead of $f_{l(i,j)} > f_u$, the condition $W_{l(i,j)} > C_M$ is a sufficient condition to create a new phrase P_iP_j.

$$W_{l(i,j)} > C_M \Rightarrow f_{l(i,j)} > f_u + f(t_c)$$

$$f(t_c) = \frac{C_M}{t_c - t_{l(i,j)} + 1} \quad (5)$$

$$\lim_{t_c \to \infty} f(t_c) = \lim_{t_c \to \infty} \frac{C_M}{t_c - t_{l(i,j)} + 1} = 0 \quad (6)$$

Proof: $W_{l(i,j)}>C_M$ is used as a precondition for merging two phrases P_i and P_j. Equation 5 has been derived from Equations 2 and 4. C_M is a constant and $t_{l(i,j)}$ is the birth number of the link that does not change while t_c increases, therefore $f(t_c)$ tends towards 0 (see Equation 6). This means that if $(f_{l(i,j)}>f_u)$ is true, then $(f_{l(i,j)}>f_u+f(t_c))$ will also be true after a specific t_c.

The algorithm uses Theorem 1 to create frequent phrases. Consider a phrase $P=P_iP_j$ in which $f_P>f_u$. The algorithm first creates P_i and P_j (they can also be a combination of other phrases) and a link $l(i,j)$ from P_i to P_j. $f_{l(i,j)}$ is greater than f_u because $f_P>f_u$. Therefore, the phrase P will be created after a specific t_c (line 12 Figure 1). W_P is the weight of phrase P in a give t_c which is calculated as follows:

$$W_p = n_p - (t_c - t_p + 1) \times f_u \quad (7)$$

Theorem 2: Instead of $f_P>f_u$, the condition $W_P>C_M$ is a sufficient condition for choosing P as a frequent phrase.

Proof: Similar reasoning as above is employed based on Equations 8 and 9.

$$W_p > C_M \Rightarrow f_p > f_u + f(t_c)$$

$$f(t_c) = \frac{C_M}{t_c - t_p + 1} \quad (8)$$

$$\lim_{t_c \to \infty} f(t_c) = \lim_{t_c \to \infty} \frac{C_M}{t_c - t_p + 1} = 0 \quad (9)$$

Theorem 3 (Correctness of the Algorithm): Let DS be a data stream and *FrequentSet* be the set of frequent phrases in DS returned from the *frequentPhraseExtraction* function in the OFSD algorithm. *FrequentSet* consists of all phrases in DS such as P_i where $f_{Pi}>f_u$.

Proof: We first show that the frequency rates of all elements in *FrequentSet* are greater than f_u. *frequentPhraseExtraction* function adds phrase P_i to the set only if weight(P_i)>C_M. Theorem 2 shows that the condition weight(P_i)>C_M satisfies $f_{Pi}>f_u$, therefore the frequency rates of all the phrases in *FrequentSet* are greater than f_u.

Secondly, we prove that all phrases in DS such as P_i where $f_{Pi}>f_u$ are added to *FrequentSet*. The proof is based on Strong Mathematical Induction.

- Basis step: The algorithm adds all the transaction items as single-element phrases to CS and keeps track of their frequency rates as time goes by, therefore, it can select the frequent single-element phrases by *frequentPhraseExtraction* function.
- Inductive step: Let $P=P_iP_j$ be an arbitrary multi-element phrase in DS where $f_P>f_u$. Since P_i and P_j have already been added to CS (induction supposition), *updateLink* function creates the link $l(i,j)$ from P_i to P_j. $f_P>f_u$, therefore, $f_{l(i,j)}>f_u$. Based on Theorem 1, the *parseTransaction* function creates $P=P_iP_j$ and adds it to CS. Since the algorithm keeps track of the frequency rates of all the elements in CS, phrase P will be selected by the *frequentPhraseExtraction* function.

Theorem 3 shows the correctness of the algorithm. In real world cases, however the algorithm needs to read sufficient number of transactions to create a multi-element phrase P from DS and calculate its frequency rate. The sufficient number of transaction is affected by the application constant C_M. The higher the value of C_M is, the longer it would take for the condition *weight*>C_M to satisfy, therefore setting C_M is an important issue in real world cases. The merge function will be very slow for large C_M values. Moreover, large TL is needed to find long frequent phrases. On the other hand, the merge will happen very quickly for small C_M values. The algorithm creates new multi-element phrases after a few subsequent occurrences. It adds the phrases to CS although the phrases have not been frequent in the long term. This causes CS to contain a large number of phrases which have been repeated in a small TL, but they are not frequent phrases in DS.

3.2. *Pruning*

When a new transaction (T) is read, the algorithm inserts the single-element phrases of T into CS. Some of these phrases do not satisfy the condition $f_P>f_u$ and need to be removed from CS after a while to keep CS as small as possible. Moreover, the algorithm creates new multi-element phrases such as P where $f_P>f_u$ based on Equation 5 and inserts them into CS. There are phrases that satisfy the condition $f_P>f_u$ in a small TL from DS, but not in the DS as a whole. These phrases should also be deleted from CS.

In the *prune* procedure, a phrase or link is deleted if its weight is less than 0. Conditions weight(P)≤0 and weight($l(i,j)$)≤0 result in Equation 10 which are the appropriate conditions for phrase or link removal based on previous definitions.

$$W_P \le 0 \Rightarrow f_P \le f_u$$
$$W_{l(i,j)} \le 0 \Rightarrow f_{l(i,j)} \le f_u \qquad (10)$$

The *prune* procedure needs to scan each phrase in CS and all its links, therefore the procedure is of order O(n) in an average case (O(n^2) in the worst case) where n is the number of phrases in CS. Since the *parsingTransaction* procedure (see Figure 1) is of order O(log n), it is not rational to call the *prune* procedure after each transaction parsing. The condition in Equation 11 is used for calling the *prune* procedure. In Equation 11, t_{lp} is the transaction number of the last prune and n_{cls} is the number of phrases in CS after the execution of the last prune. The condition reduces the order of the OFSD algorithm to O(log n) in average cases.

$$(t_C - t_{lp}) > \left(\frac{n_{csl}}{\log(n_{csl})}\right) \Rightarrow call\ pruneCandidateSet \quad (11)$$

4. Simulation Results

The algorithm was applied to a part of an Alta Vista 2002 query log containing 100,000 query transactions. The goal is to find the phrases (P) with f_P greater than a user defined f_u in the dataset. The factor f_u and the application constant C_M are examined in the experiments.

In the first experiment, C_M is set to 5 and the algorithm is executed for different f_u values. Figure 2 shows the number of frequent phrases for four different f_u values where the maximum number of transactions is 100,000. Figure 2(a) shows that the number of frequent phrases increases when f_u decreases. This is due to the fact that the less frequent phrases are selected for lower f_u values. The number of frequent phrases extracted from the dataset reaches a stable value after approximately 40,000 transactions. Figure 2(b) shows the number of multi-element frequent phrases in the experiment. Although the overall number of multi-element frequent phrases (Figure 2(b)) is less than the half of all frequent phrases (Figure 2(a)) but the variances observed in both diagrams follow a similar pattern which confirms the efficiency of the algorithm to create the multi-element phrases and follows their frequency rates. Figure 2(c) shows the number of frequent phrases that are older (t_c-t_p) than 10,000. The diagram follows Figure 2(a) with a shift of 10,000 transactions to the right. The comparison between Figures 2(a) and 2(c) illustrates that the set of frequent phrases in CS is a mixture of the phrases, which are frequent in a small TL called short-time frequent phrases and those, which are frequent in a large TL called long-time frequent phrases. Since the algorithm stores phrase birth numbers, it can classify the frequent phrases based on their persistency in DS.

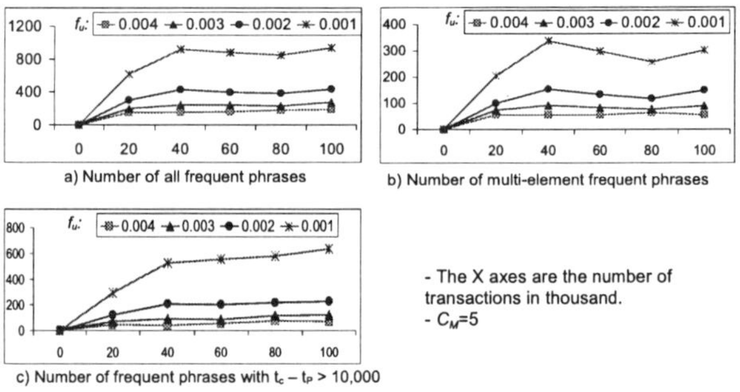

Figure 2. Number of Frequent Phrases for 100,000 transactions.

In the second experiment, f_u is set to 0.002 and the algorithm is executed with different C_M values. Figure 3 shows the number of frequent phrases for four different C_M values where the maximum number of transactions is 100,000. Figure 3(a) shows that the number of frequent phrases increases when C_M decreases because the short-time frequent phrases are also counted by the algorithm. As it is apparent from Figure 3(c), the number of long-time frequent phrases is approximately the same for different C_M values. The experiment confirms the importance of setting C_M for real world cases. On the one hand, C_M should be big enough to ignore the short-time frequent phrases while on the other hand; C_M should not be too big to make the algorithm very slow in finding the long-time frequent phrases.

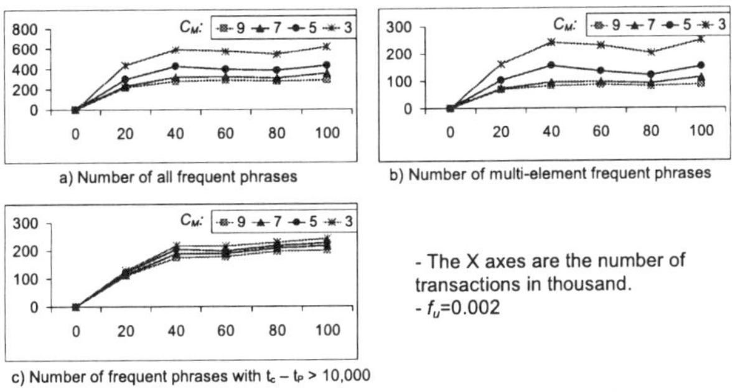

Figure 3. Number of Frequent Phrases for 100,000 transactions.

5. Discussion

The algorithm can be applied in different real world cases. A practical example of the application of this algorithm is to extract the frequent phrases from user queries in web search engines. By applying the algorithm, the frequent phrases of the queries are collected continuously in a dataset. We intend to discover the most frequent phrases used by previous web surfers for recommending appropriate phrases to new users. In this context, a user query is a transaction, each word in the query is a transaction item and blank is the separator of the items.

An important issue in this example is that the frequency rates of the phrases may change as time goes by. This is due to the fact that users' interests are not persistent in the long term. On the other hand, there are certain events (e.g. soccer world cup) which make short-time frequent phrases in the users' queries. As we said, the algorithm is able to extract a short-time frequent phrase in its related TL and then to forget it whenever it is not frequent anymore. This is because each phrase has a birth number in DS. The appropriate TL for a phrase starts from the transaction of its birth number and the algorithm keeps track of its frequency rate from that time. Therefore, a phrase has a chance to be born in different transaction lists, be selected as a frequent phrase and die after a while.

Another real world case that well suits the proposed algorithm is to find the frequent phrases in online news. The information is usable to analyze news (e.g. news directions). Each sentence is a transaction which ends with a dot, each word of the sentence is an item and blank is the separator of the items.

The maximum number of transaction items is a constant in the described examples. The algorithm searches each possible phrase of a transaction in the candidate set, therefore the number of search function calls is of order $O(k^2)$ for each transaction (see Equation 3) where k is the number of items in the transaction. If the maximum number of transaction items is not constant, the time complexity of the algorithm will be of order $O(k^2 \log n)$ where n is the number of elements in the candidate set.

6. Conclusions

This paper addresses mining sequential pattern problem in a data stream. The data stream is a sequence of transactions. Each phrase is a subsequence of transaction and is considered as frequent in the data stream if its frequency rate satisfies a minimum user defined frequency rate. The algorithm inserts the candidate phrases into a candidate set. It keeps track of the frequency rates of the candidate elements and removes the infrequent phrases from candidate set. The algorithm is of order $O(\log n)$, where n is the number of elements in the candidate set. Two efficient techniques are given to reduce the number of elements in the candidate set. First, the phrase $P=P_iP_j$ is inserted to candidate set only if P_i, P_j and the link $l(i,j)$ between them are frequent. Second the *prune* function continuously removes the infrequent phrases from candidate set. Further research in this direction may include a mathematic analysis to have a good judgment of appropriate C_M setting in different real world cases. We also intend to apply this algorithm to a web search engine query log to test it under real world conditions.

Acknowledgments

The authors graciously acknowledge the funding from the Atlantic Canada Opportunity Agency (ACOA) through the Atlantic Innovation Fund (AIF) and through grant RGPN 227441 from the National Science and Engineering Research Council of Canada (NSERC) to Dr. Ghorbani.

The authors would also like to sincerely thank the generous help of Jim Jansen for providing them with the AltaVista 2002 search engine query log.

References

1. R. Agrawal and R. Srikant, Mining sequential patterns, *11th International Conference on Data Engineering (ICDE'95)*, 3–14 (1995).

2. J. H. Chang and W. S. Lee, Finding recent frequent itemsets adaptively over online data streams, *Proceedings of the ninth ACM SIGKDD international conference on Knowledge discovery and data mining (KDD'03)*, 487–492 (2003).
3. M. Charikar, K. Chen and M. Farach-Colton, Finding frequent items in data streams, *Proceedings of the 29th International Colloquium on Automata, Languages and Programming (ICALP '02)*, 693–703 (2002).
4. C. Giannella, J. Han, J. Pei, X. Yan and P. Yu, Mining frequent patterns in data streams at multiple time granularities, *Proceedings of the NSF Workshop on Next Generation Data Mining*, 191-211 (2002).
5. H.-F. Li, S.-Y. Lee and M.-K. Shan, Online mining (recently) maximal frequent itemsets over data streams, *15th International Workshop on Research Issues in Data Engineering: Stream Data Mining and Applications (RIDE-SDMA'05)*, 11–18 (2005).
6. W. Xing and A. A. Ghorbani, Information domain modeling for adaptive web systems, *IEEE/WIC/ACM International Conference on Web Intelligence (WI'05)*, 684–687 (2005).
7. M. Zhang, B. Kao, C. Yip and D. Cheung, A gsp-based efficient algorithm for mining frequent sequences, *Proceedings of International Conference on Applied Informatics (IC-AI '001)*, 14-18 (2001).
8. M. Zhang, B. Kao, D. Cheung and C.-L. Y. ER. Efficient Algorithms for Incremental Update of Frequent Sequences, *Pacific-Asia Conference on Knowledge Discovery and Data Mining*, 186-197 (2002).

FORMAL NEGOTIATION MODEL FOR AUTOMATED AGENTS IN E-COMMERCE SYSTEMS

T. KIJTHAWEESINPOON

Faculty of Information Technology, Monash University
900 Dandenong Rd. Caulfield East, Victoria, 3145, Australia

P.L. ZHOU

Faculty of Information Technology, Monash University
900 Dandenong Rd. Caulfield East, Victoria, 3145, Australia

The impact of information technologies on negotiations is not limited to the use of electronic communication such as email, fax, telephone, etc. Information technology has changed the way a negotiation problem can be represented and a negotiation process structured. For example, e-commerce systems have created many more activities undertaken in negotiations, including, efficient matching of potential negotiators; exchange, comparison and categorization of information, and the use of tools for information gathering, problem structuring and analysis, and interpretation of offers. These new possibilities have led to the emergence of formal negotiation procedures and protocols, which are necessary for the use of rich and expressive information technologies in various stages of negotiation processes rather than solely for the exchange of messages. In this paper, we proposed a formal negotiation model for automated agents.

1. Introduction

In e-commerce systems, the computerization of negotiation processes increasingly affects the way organizations and individuals interact with each other. These include the involvement of two or more decision making agents. Each agent has specific needs and requirements. The agents may also differ in their perception of the problem and have different understandings of its solution. They negotiate because they are interdependent and no one can implement a chosen solution without the acquiescence of the other parties to the process. Automated negotiations promise higher levels of process efficiency and effectiveness, and most importantly, a higher quality and faster emergence of agreements [1, 2, 3]. The potential economic impact leads to an increased demand for appropriate automated negotiations for specific negotiation situations. Thus, both the design of suitable automated negotiation protocols and the implementation of relevant automated negotiation media largely lack systematic, traceable and reproducible approaches [1, 4]. Furthermore, the advancing of technologies led to the design of models and systems that often use little from the behavioral and economic body knowledge. In effect systems were developed that are appealing, easy to use and allowing users to delegate many complex decision and negotiation tasks but with not sufficient concern of the users' needs and expectations in particular of qualitative nature, and their cognitive capabilities and limitations [5]. More importantly, people biases, misconceptions and misunderstanding that have been shown to occur very often are not considered and countered with a sound decision and negotiation methodology embed in the system. The design and implementation of electronic negotiation media requires the consideration of insights from multiple relevant research areas in order to fulfill its promises and represent the richness and complexity of real negotiation scenarios in e-commerce.

In the following section we discuss the related work in the area of automated negotiation. In section 3, we present a formal automated negotiation model which describes characteristics and interaction among engaging parties including important properties that must satisfied by the system. Section 4 presents a shopping scenario between a buyer and a seller agent. From the shopping scenario we can see where negotiation processes arise and that these negotiations may comply with a negotiation model. We also provide an abstract theory of the states involved in the shopping scenario and derive the paths leading to a particular shopping state. We then give several negotiation protocols that can be followed by agents engaged in a negotiation process. Section 5 describes how an agent evaluates a proposal in order to reach a goal state. Section 6 concludes the paper.

2. Related Work

Sierra *et al* present a formal model of negotiation between autonomous agents [6]. The model defines a range of strategies and tactics that agents can employ to generate initial offers, to evaluate proposals, and to generate counter proposals. The intelligence of a negotiation agent is manifested by the use of an evaluation function for each negotiation attribute and a simple hand-coded monotonic concession negotiation strategy. The formal model proposed by Kraus *et al* consists of a set of agents, not necessarily cooperative, with the ability to exchange messages [3]. Their mental states are characterized by using the notions of beliefs, goals, desires, intentions, and local preferences. Each agent has a set of desires. The agent's activities are motivated by the will to fulfill these desires. At any given time, an agent selects a consistent subset of its desires. This serves as its set of current goals. An agent ascribes different degrees of importance to different goals. It prefers to fulfill goals of higher importance. The set of goals motivate the agent's planning process.

On the other hand, Sandholm *et al*, Kijthaweesinpoon and Zhou, and Indrawan *et al* developed a coalition formation model for bounded rational agents and present a general classification of coalition games [5, 7, 9]. They concentrate on the problem of computing the value of a coalition and in their model this value depends on the computation time available to the agents. The coalition formation of self-interested agents provides more benefits to the agents. In the case of a coalition of buyers, it is possible to get a cheaper price from the supplier because of greater market power possessed by the coalition compared to an individual buyer [5, 8].

3. The Proposed Formal Model for Automated Negotiation

In this section, we present a formal negotiation model based on the unified negotiation framework [9]. A formal model describes characteristics and interactions among engaging parties including properties that must be satisfied by the system. In the unified framework, negotiation can take the form of one-to-one, one-to-many, or many-to-many negotiation. In the case of one-to-many and many-to-many negotiation, an administrative agent is assigned to coordinate the activities of the many agents. Hence the administrative can be a Buyer Administrator (B_{Ad}) or a Seller Administrator (S_{Ad}).

We can formally describe an automated negotiation system as the following:

Definition 3.1 (Negotiation System) **A** negotiation system **N** is defined as unions of the following sets:

$N = \{A, M, NP, P_i, NS\}$

- ***A***, where $A \neq 0$, stand for the set of engaging parties in ***N***.
- ***M*** stands for messages. In order for engaging parties to do negotiations, a set of well-defined messages need to be defined and exchanged between them. In the unified negotiation framework, eight primitive operations have been introduced. They are Call-for-Proposal, Propose Proposal, Accept Proposal, Reject Proposal, Modify Proposal, Withdraw Proposal, and Terminate.
- ***NP*** stands for negotiation protocol. To conduct an automated negotiation, engaging parties must follow a proposed negotiation protocol, which specifies what alternative actions can be taken at different states of a negotiation process.
- P_i stands for a proposal which represents action regarding.
- ***NS*** stands for a Negotiation Strategy. In order to reach an agreement, engaging parties use their own negotiation strategies to evaluate the proposals.

Definition 3.2 (Engaging parties) *A negotiation system **N** consists of a set of engaging parties **A**, where **A** =* $\{BA, SA, B_{Ad}, S_{Ad}\}$.

- ***BA***, where $BA \neq 0$, stands for a buyer agent who wants to negotiation to buy a product or a service on the Internet.
- ***SA***, where $SA \neq 0$, stands for a seller agent who supplies a product or a service through the Internet.
- B_{Ad} stands for a buyer administrator agent who coordinating the negotiation among the participants of the coalition and negotiating with the other party on the behalf of the buyer coalition.
- S_{Ad} stands for a seller administrator agent who coordinating the negotiation among the prospectus participants of the coalition and negotiating with the other party on the behalf of the seller coalition.

Definition 3.3 (Message) *A negotiation N consists of a message **M**. **M** has the following messages:*

M={Call-for-Proposal, Propose Proposal, Accept Proposal, Reject Proposal, Modify Proposal, Withdraw Proposal, Terminate Negotiation}

Definition 3.4 (Negotiation Protocol) *A negotiation N consists of a Negotiation Protocol **NP**. **NP** has the following protocol:*

***BP**: Bilateral Negotiation Protocol*

***MP**: Multilateral Protocol*

***CP**: Coalition Protocol*

Definition 3.5 (Negotiation Proposal) *A negotiation N consists of a proposal P_i. P_i has the following properties:*

***Proposal** (P_i) = {Agent, P_{Id}, Content}*
***Agent:** Agent Identification*
***P_{Id}:** Proposal identification*
***Content** = {I_i, X_i}* for $i = 1, \ldots, n$]
I_i: *An item, which is a product or service*
X_i: *List of attributes for the item i, each element of the list has the following structure*
$X_i = \{A_j, Vmin_j, Vmax_j, W_j\}$ where j in $[1, \ldots, M]$
Where A_j: Attribute of an item
$Vmin_j$: Attribute minimum value
$Vmax_j$: Attribute maximum value
W_j: Utility function of attribute

Definition 3.6 (Negotiation Strategy) *A negotiation N consists of Negotiation Strategy **NS**. The negotiator used his/her strategy to make a decision in order to reach an agreement.*

Definition 3.7 (Importance of Attribute) Given decision information system $\mathbf{S} = (U, A, \{d\})$, if $\forall a \in A$, where relation matrix is $\mathbf{M}(I_a)$, then the **decision equivalence importance measurement** β of decision attribute d subject to condition attribute a is defined as

$\beta(a) = \Sigma$ (Number of "1"s in decision same matrix block) / Σ (number of matrix items in decision same blocks);

The **decision difference importance measurement** γ of decision attribute d subject to condition attribute a is defined as

$\gamma(a) = \Sigma$ (Number of "1"s in Decision difference matrix block) / Σ (number of matrix items in decision difference blocks); the **importance measurement** α of decision attribute d subject to condition attribute a is defined as

$\alpha(a) = \beta(a) / \gamma(a)$, where $\gamma(a)$ is not equal to 0.

4. The Negotiation Protocols

The proposed formal negotiation model can support all types of negotiation. Firstly, we view a bilateral and multilateral negotiation process as a set of software agents which interact in order to reach an agreement. Agents participating in a negotiation can interact directly without involving by an administrative agent. In other situations, the role of a party during the negotiation process is almost entirely carried out by the administrative agent. This is the case for instance in coalition formation, where the administrative agent acts on behalf of the coalition to negotiation with other party.

4.1. *Bilateral Negotiation Protocol*

In the proposed protocol, the bilateral negotiation involves only one Buyer Agent (*BA*) and one Seller Agent (*SA*). After each negotiation cycle (one proposal and counter proposal), *BA* evaluates the situation and takes the decision according to the current information.

In bilateral negotiation protocol, a negotiation transaction is started by *BA*, which issues Propose Proposal (P_i) on behalf of a buyer. Decisions need to be made with respect to the contents of the Propose Proposal. Alternative decision-action rules can be used to create the contents. For example, if the negotiation attributes (price, warrantee, quantity, and delivery date) form part of the data contents of a Propose Proposal, the initial values provided for these attributes can either be very close to what the issuer desires (i.e., the bottom lines) or exceed what the issuer desires with the expectation that the counterpart may bargain them down. Other rules can be applied to determine the proper initial values that are appropriate for achieving a negotiation goal defined in terms of profitability, time-to-agreement, and desire-for-relationship discussed before.

We represent the messages, which exchange during the negotiation process as follow:

***Proposal** (P_i)*: An agent *BA* who wants to buy a product or a service to announce a proposal message (P_i) to *Seller Agents (SA_1, SA_2, SA_3, ...)*

***Proposal** (P_i^*)*: A proposal message and a counter proposal message exchange between *BA* and other agents during a negotiation.

***Accept** (P_i^*)*: An agent wants to accept proposal P_i^*. Assume *BA* receives a proposal from the *SA* response to the buyer's proposal. After the analysis of its contents, some decision-action making needs to be applied to guide the acceptance decision. Some examples are given:

- All attributes of the proposal are within the difference of the desired values (between V_{min} and V_{max}).
- Global preference score derived from all the attribute values exceeds a certain threshold.

Reject (P_i^*): An agent wants to refuse proposal P_i^*. *BA* may decide to reject the current proposal. A rejection is different from a termination in that the negotiation process would continue. It simply informs *SA* that the received proposal is not acceptable, and requests the sender to modify and resubmit a proposal. Some decision-action rules for guiding the rejection decision are given below:

- The data conditions specified in the proposal are below the acceptable bottom-line values.
- Insufficient information is provided in the proposal.
- The data conditions specified in the proposal are acceptable but the receiver of the proposal wants its counterpart to do further concession

Modify (P_i^*): A user wants to modify proposal P_i^* into a new proposal that suits him/her. During the negotiation process, if the previous proposal has been rejected or received no response from its counterpart within time limit, *BA* or *SA* may trigger the modification in the previous proposal.

Withdraw (P_i^*): Similar to a proposal modification, a user may initiate the withdrawal of a proposal. Or rules can be defined to guide a negotiation server in making the withdrawal decision automatically. For example, if the financial condition of the issuer has changed, if the customer has changed his/her order, if the inventory has dropped to a certain level, or if the counterpart has not responded to the previous proposal after X time units, the proposal should be withdrawn.

Abort: An agent quits negotiating. The proposed negotiation protocol provides a set of well-defined "rules of engagement" for both parties to exchange proposals and counterproposals. The acceptance and termination states of the protocol are the states to which a negotiation process should converge. However, the protocol itself does not guarantee that these states will be reached since the negotiation parties may engage in an endless exchange of proposals. To ensure a negotiation transaction's convergence to one of the terminal states, decision rules which explicitly specify the conditions for termination, must be specified and applied. These conditions may depend on the data conditions presented in the previous proposals received. For example, the negotiation server can use the previous exchange of proposals to determine if the negotiation is converging or diverging, and if the counterpart is acting reasonably or not. If not, the negotiation process should be terminated. Some example termination rules are given below:

- The global preference scores derived for the received proposals indicate that the negotiation is moving away from the desired direction.
- The negotiation time exceeds time limit.
- The number of proposal exchanges limited times.
- Some combinations of the above.

Report the agreement: The buyer administrator agent (*BA*) has detected an agreement on current proposal.

Report Termination: An agent has detected the negotiation broke down. The termination is trigger by time constrain and also if either agent decides to quit the negotiation before the time deadline.

4.2. *Multilateral Negotiation Protocol*

The negotiation protocol found in these automated agents is based on traditional auctions such as English or Dutch auctions. These negotiation agents are efficient and simple to implement in current e-commerce application, fundamentally due to their simplicity. They follow a bidding style, which considers competitive offers between bidders flowing in one direction. However there is a significant limitation of auction-based negotiation. They do not allow for exchanging offers and counter offers, and exploiting the flow of information in both directions. Moreover, exercising different negotiation strategies with different parties cannot be implemented in auctions [7].

The proposed protocol solves some of these limitations. In our protocol, multilateral negotiation has more than two agents participating during the negotiation process. The interaction between Buyer Agent (*BA*) and the Seller Agents (SA_1, SA_2, SA_3,..) are performed simultaneously as one-to-one interaction.

With our approach, the agent B_1 can use different negotiation strategies to negotiate with different seller agents. In this protocol, we assume that B_1 gives the knowledge of the weight of each attribute of the item to the administrator agent (B_{Ad}) through the propose message. B_{Ad} performs negotiation process, and filters the offers from seller agents on behalf of B_1. B_{Ad} negotiate with seller agents through S_{Ad} by creating a number of one-to-one negotiations between B_{Ad} and each of seller agents.

4.3. *Coalition Negotiation Protocol*

The proposed coalition negotiation protocol is based on the unified framework for e-commerce negotiation [9] and relation matrix algorithm [8]. In the unified framework, an administrative agent is assigned to coordinate the activities of the many agents. Hence, the administrative agent can be a Buyer Administrator (B_{Ad}) or a Seller Administrator (S_{Ad}).

There are two rounds of negotiation involved during the buying and selling products or services using coalition. The first round of negotiation aims to find a common accepted proposal. In this round of negotiation the participants consist of the Agent administration and other agents who are interested in forming a coalition. The second round of negotiation aims to find the best offer form the opposing parties.

We use an example on the buyer side. B_{Ad} represents a group of buyer agent, $\{B_1, B_2, B_3, \ldots, B_n\}$, who want to form a coalition. Each of buyer agents will send the proposal based on their preferences to B_{Ad}. B_{Ad} will use the relation matrix algorithm to form a near optimal coalition based on the attribute importance measurement from every proposals sent by every buyer agents.

The following actions are performed by the agent on P_i^* during the negotiation:

Accept (P_i^*): An agent wants to accept proposal P_i^*.

Reject (P_i^*): An agent wants to refuse proposal P_i^*.

Modify (P_i^*): An agent wants to modify proposal P_i^* into a new proposal that suits it.

Other activities supported by the protocol are:

Abort: An agent quits negotiating.

Report Coalition Formed: The buyer administrator agent (B_{Ad}) has detected an agreement on current proposal and a coalition agent has been formed.

Report Termination: A buyer administrator agent (B_{Ad}) has detected that the negotiation broken down.

For solving the optimization problem of each coalition, we proposed an algorithm to solve a near optimal coalition based on the attribute importance measurement from a given information system, in this case it could be a primitive data table. Below we propose an attribute importance measurement method of relation matrix totally based on condition attributes.

From definition 3.7, we want the objects with same decision value to be tolerant/similar, that is the "1" of the decision same matrix block expected. If all matrix items of one decision same matrix block are "1", then it means the objects of the corresponding decision class subject to the decision same matrix block are tolerant, it is the best situation. At the same time, we want the number of "1" in the decision difference matrix block become minimal. The less of "1" in the decision difference matrix block, it means the consistency in the decision table is better. We can use the α to measure the relative size of β and γ. note, if γ=0, then the situation is more complex, because at that time the attribute importance measurement is also related to the related value of β. Normally, in real world problems, the γ might not be 0 subject to the relation matrices of the primitive attributes.

In the information system (data table), if two objects can be discerned using fewer attributes, then when increasing the number of attributes, those two objects are still discernible. This is represented by the matrix item with "0" of the relation matrix subject to the relation matrix, when increased new attributes, that matrix item will not become '1". So Optimal Coalition can be defined as the number of "0"s in the matrix items of decision difference matrix block in the relation matrix $\mathbf{M}(I_A)$ of the equivalence relation I_A between objects do not decrease. So to tell a attribute subset B whether is a Coalition or contains a Coalition, we only have to tell whether the "0" of the decision difference matrix block in the relation matrices between objects of the attribute set is corresponding to the "0" of the decision difference matrix block of the relation matrix $\mathbf{M}(I_A)$ of attributes set A.

Algorithm 4.1 To solve a near optimal Coalition based on relation matrix

Input: information system $\mathbf{S} = (U, A, \{d\}, \tau)$, where $A=\{a_1,a_2,a_{card(A)}\}$;

Output: one near optimal Coalition R of attribute set A;

Begin

Calculate the relation matrix $M(I_{ai})$ of every condition attribute a_i and the relation matrix $M(I_A)$ between objects;

Based on the relation matrix of attribute a_i, calculate attribute $\alpha(a_i)=\beta(a_i)/\gamma(a_i)$ of attribute a_i.

$\alpha_k=MAX(\alpha(a_1),\alpha(a_2),\ldots,\alpha(a_{card(A)}))$;

$R:=\{a_k\}$; /* current partial Coalition */

$B:=A-R$; /* current non-visited condition attribute set */

While the "0"s of decision difference matrix blocks of $M(I_R)$ and $M(I_A)$ do not correspond to each other

DO

Begin
To attribute set B calculate
$\alpha_k = MAX(\alpha(a_1), \alpha(a_2), \ldots, \alpha(a_{card(A)}))$;
IF $R \cup (a_k)$relation matrix reduces the "0"s inside the decision difference matrix block
THEN
$R := R \cup / \{a_k\}$;
Generate the relation matrix $M(I_R)$ of attribute set R; $B = B - \{a_k\}$
End;
End;
Output Coalition set R;
End.

5. Discussion

To evaluate the results of negotiation protocols is not an easy task. Because the agents are self-interested, when saying, for example, a "negotiation was successful" the question "successful for whom?" must be asked, since each agent is concerned only about its own benefits or losses from the resolution of the negotiation. However, there are certain parameters that can be used to evaluate different protocols: negotiation time, efficiency, simplicity, stability, and money transfer. These parameters are used for evaluate our negotiation protocols. The proposed protocols have shortened the negotiation time particularly in coalition negotiation formation. In term of efficiency, our protocols are very effective. We use multi-attribute utility theory and relation matrix to solve the pareto optimal agreement. We also introduce a negotiation process which is simple and easy to follow. Administration agents are created to manage the complexity of various negotiation processes.

6. Conclusion

In this paper, we proposed a formal negotiation model for automated agent in e-commerce. We provide a framework of terms and concepts which, in addition to formal approaches, facilitates an incorporation of results of multiple disciplines and especially of behavioral studies into an engineering approach. The proposed model provides effective and practical approach for enabling negotiation to interact with each other in a different ways. For example, in human negotiation, one of the strategies to increase the chance of maximizing the profit in negotiation is by forming a coalition. In the case of a coalition of buyers, it is possible to get a cheaper price from the supplier because of greater market power possessed by the coalition compared to an individual buyer. However, performing coalition between agents is not straightforward task in e-commerce due to the assumption that each agent works to maximize profit for its individual user. Hence, a model to allow negotiation to take place in order to form a coalition is needed. The coalition agent is formed to reduce the operating and transaction cost by sharing the cost among the participant agents. In the real business world, coalition negotiation should involve sharing of information among the participants. The outcome of the negotiation should be perceived to bring benefits to all the participants. The benefits sometimes are not only lowest price and reducing operating cost but also other attributes for example delivery time, warrantee, etc. In our model, we identified the role of administrator agents is to coordinate between agents who are interested in joining a coalition.

References

1. N.R. Jennings, P. Faratin, R. Lomuscio, S. Parsons, C. Sierra and M. Wooldridge, Automated negotiation: prospects, methods and challenges, *Int.J. of Group Decision and Negotiation* **10(2)**, 199-215 (2001).
2. M.P. Papazoglou, Agent-oriented technology in support of e-business, *Communications of the ACM* **44(4)**, 71-74 (2001).
3. S. Kraus, K. Sycara and A. Evenchik, Reaching agreements through argumentation: a logical model and implementation, *Artificial Intelligence*, 1–69 (1998).
4. I. Rahwan, R. Kowalczyk and H.H. Pham, Intelligent Agents for Automated One-to-Many e-Commerce Negotiation, *Proceedings of The Twenty-Fifth Australian Computer Science Conference (ACSC2002)*, 197-203 (2002).
5. M. Indrawan, T. Kijthaweesinpoon, B. Srinivasan, and A.S.M. Sajeev, Coalition Formation Protocol for E-commerce, *Proceedings of. The International Conference on Intelligent Sensing and Information Processing*, 403-408 (2004).
6. C. Sierra, P. Faratin and N. Jennings, A Service-Oriented Negotiation Model between Autonomous Agents, *Proceedings of 8th European Workshop on Modeling Autonomous Agents in a Multi-Agent World (MAAMAW-97)*, 17-35 (1997).
7. T. Sandholm and V. Lesser, Coalitions among Computationally Bounded Agents, *Artificial*

Intelligence, Special issue on Economic Principles of Multiagent Systems **94(1)**, 99-137 (1997).

8. T. Kijthaweesinpoon and P.L. Zhou, A New Relation Matrix Algorithm for Autonomous Agents Coalition Formation, *Proceedings of The 2005 International Conference on E-Business, Enterprise Information Systems, E-Government, and Outsourcing*, 219-225 (2005).
9. T. Kijthaweesinpoon, M. Indrawan and B. Srinivasan, A Unified Framework for E-commerce Negotiation Agents, *Proceedings of The Fifth International Conference in Information Integration and Web-based Application and Services*, 179-184 (2003).

STUDY ON THE THEORY OF USING SDN TO SOLVE A SUPPLY CHAIN BOTTLENECK PROBLEM

JING HE

College of Economics and Management, Shanghai Fisheries University
Shanghai, 200090, China

FU-YUAN XU

College of Management, University of Shanghai for Science and Technology
Shanghai, 200093, China

Constraint factors exist in any system will influence the whole value of the system. Bottleneck dilatation and bypass methods can only control Supply Chain (SC) bottlenecks. Therefore these two methods cannot solve the problem radically. As transformation to the traditional structure of SC, Supply and Demand Network with multi-functional and opening characteristics for enterprise (SDN) is a perfect method which can reduce the rate of SC bottleneck question from origin.

This paper aims to integrate the theories, methods and tools of Bottleneck Analysis (BNA) to analyze the bottleneck problems existing in Supply Chain (SC) through the means of both quantitative and qualitative. Any system can be imagined to consist of a chain of interlocked rings, and the firmness of the entire system is determined by the weakest ring, not the strongest one[1][2]. Likewise, for the supply chain system, every enterprise node is a ring of this value chain, and they may all be bottleneck nodes in the SC. To optimize output, efforts must be put on the weakest ring, that is, the bottleneck ring, in order to make obvious improvement.

1. Analysis on The SC Bottleneck Problem

At present, SC was defined as a chain structure mode which connects suppliers, manufacturers, distributors, retailers and final users as a whole. It surrounds core enterprises and begins from purchasing raw materials to manufacturing medium and final products, and finally delivers the products to consumers through a sales network[3]. Every node and process in the supply chain can then be divided into different levels of sub-nodes and sub-processes, and thereby forming interlocked rings in the SC with each sub-process creating value. On the other hand, Supply Chain Management (SCM) is to plan, coordinate and control material flow, information flow and capital flow reasonably, and to deliver the right products to the right users in correct number at the right time and place[4]. Although SCM tries to optimize SC at various stages of design and implementation, SC's structural characteristics cause the bottleneck problem to emerge unavoidably once SC is under the influence of complicated and uncertain elements both inside and outside, and in the extreme situation may cause the supply chain to break and SC's disintegration, bringing enormous loss to the whole supply chain alliance. As a result, searching for the bottleneck and its causes as well as breaking the bottleneck are of great significance.

1.1. *Analysis of the Causes of Bottleneck*

The causes of bottleneck can be summarized as follows:

1.1.1. Lagging response to the market.

Changes in outside market environment, sudden increase or decrease in customers' demand and sudden changes in demand propensity may all cause a certain ring of the supply chain fail to response in a short time, resulting in the emergence of a bottleneck, and may influence the long-term development of the enterprise if not dealt with timely[5]. For example, if the R&D department fails to satisfy customers' demand quickly or keep carrying out technological innovations, it may become the weak ring in the whole supply chain and influence the core competitiveness of the enterprise.

1.1.2. Unreasonable partnership choice and resource allocation.

The dominant core enterprise, when choosing outside SC strategic partners, may perform errors and result in surplus or shortage of some core advantages; moreover, unreasonable resource allocations may occur among various parts of member enterprises' inner SC. All these may lead to the bottleneck problem.

1.1.3 Conflicting organizational objectives among member enterprises.

Conflicting organizational objectives always occur in SC because various organizations are independent of each other, and SC's overall objective is hard to realize especially when a certain ring in the supply chain focuses on its own inner objectives myopically; meanwhile, non-cooperative games always exist among SC's enterprise nodes, and immoral behaviors happen from time to time, which is also an important reason in producing the bottleneck problem [6][7].

1.1.4 Information asymmetry among different members in the SC.

Because information asymmetry will cause enterprise nodes to forecast supply and demand of upstream and downstream mistakenly, even if there exist information feedback circuits in the SC, "time lag" will disturb them, causing the results of relevant actions to happen in a gradual way, and also derives the bottleneck problem. The beer game in Peter Senge's "The Fifth Discilpline" describes vividly the difficult situation in which suppliers, manufacturers and retailers fail to interchange information effectively with the presence of "time lag", and can be regarded as a typical inter-linked bottleneck case[8][9].

1.1.5. Unexpected sudden events.

When various man-made or non-man-made sudden events cause huge damage to a certain node, it will consequently become a bottleneck node in the SC.

1.1.6. There is not enough ability to solve the bottleneck problem.

Some member enterprises themselves are rather limited in resources like material, talents, management, technology, ideas as well as capital and lack enough support from league members, causing them to become potential bottlenecks in the SC; meanwhile, the competitive relationship with other SC makes it impossible to seek help from outside, leading to inability in solving the bottleneck problem and long-term existence of that problem.

1.2. *Analysis on the Influence of Bottleneck*

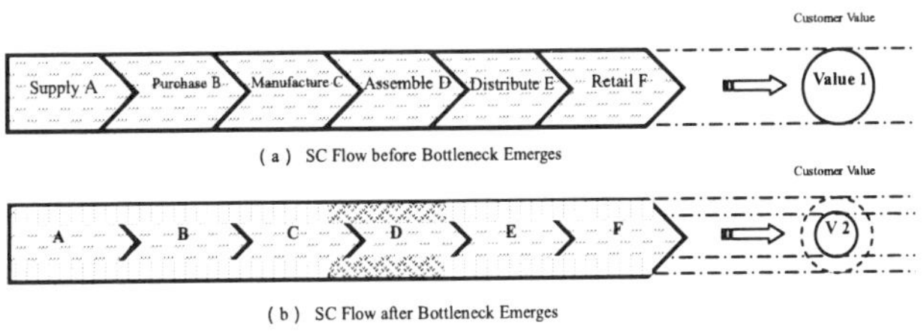

Fig.1 Bottleneck Effect and its Influence on the SC

Figure 1 (a) is the ideal situation of SC. In this situation, material flow, information flow and capital flow move smoothly through stages of supply, purchase, manufacture, assemble, distribute and retail in the SC, and the customer value created is the circle "Value 1" tangent to "the maximum value tube". Whereas in Figure (b), a bottleneck emerges at a certain node D, causing various "flows" to be blocked at that node with effects spreading to the entire supply chain and leaving resources of other nodes unused, thus greatly shrinking the ultimate output into circle V2 (Value 2). Figure 1 is merely the special case of a single bottleneck; in reality, however, bottlenecks may emerge simultaneously at different nodes, which means huge influence on the overall benefit of SC and may cause the entire SC to paralyze in extreme situations.

2. Discussion about the Methods to Solve the Bottleneck Problem in SC

Since SC can be treated as a system, it is quite objective for its inner bottleneck problem to exist. On the basis of detailed analysis on the system, we can take measures to eliminate system losses caused by the bottleneck problem, or at least reduce the probability of a bottleneck emergence by changing the system's structure.

Here we proposes three methods to eliminate bottleneck problems in the SC, they are: expanding the bottleneck, creating alternative routes and the SDN method. The former two keep the original SC theory and overall systematic structure intact and only make partial adjustments to eliminate bottlenecks and increase system benefit. The SDN method, however, makes revolutionary changes on the SC and is an ideal and more effective way in realizing system value output compared with the former two.

2.1. *Expanding the Bottleneck*

Although each stage in the SC plays an important role in realizing the final value output, the emergence of bottlenecks and relevant value output are decided by the weakest stage, which means we cannot equalize the development of each stage indistinguishably or else it will leave more resources unused in other stages. Therefore it is useless to equalize development among each stage of the SC. On the contrary, efforts must be made to eliminate constraints of bottlenecks, that is, to expand the originally narrow bottlenecks and bring about overall benefit[10].

In Figure 2, suppose that the normal output ratio of three stages A, B and C in the SC system is m_A : m_B : m_C ($m_A + m_B + m_C = 1$) and the total created value is Q, then in normal situations the three stages' output will be $m_A Q$、$m_B Q$ and $m_C Q$ respectively. The bottleneck causes the total output to change from Q to Q′ (Q′<<Q), and through careful recognition and comprehensive evaluation it can be diagnosed that stage B is weak. From Figure 2 it can be seen that the block of stage B cuts area of value S_{cdij} from S_{cdop}, if we suppose that $\gamma_B = \frac{S_{cdij}}{S_{cdop}}$, the value stage B fails to create will be $m_B \gamma_B Q$. Effected by the bottleneck and unused resources, stage A and C will fail to create value of $m_A \gamma_A Q$ and $m_C \gamma_C Q$ respectively, in which $\gamma_A = \xi_A \gamma_B$, $\gamma_C = \xi_C \gamma_B$ (ξ_A and ξ_C are factors of correlation). As a result, because of the unused resources, the whole SC fails to create value of:

$$S_{abgh} + S_{efkl} = m_A \gamma_A Q + m_C \gamma_C Q$$

$$= m_A \xi_A \gamma_B Q + m_C \xi_C \gamma_B Q = (m_A \xi_A + m_C \xi_C) \gamma_B Q$$

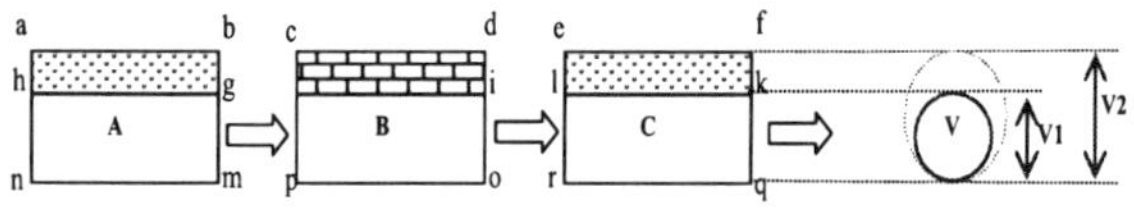

Fig.2 Expanding the Bottleneck

From the above analysis it can be seen that once a bottleneck emerges, the economic meaning of "expanding" that bottleneck can be expressed by the following coefficient:

$$\text{Bottleneck Expanding Value added Coefficient} = \frac{(m_A \xi_A + m_C \xi_C)\gamma_B Q}{m_B \gamma_B Q}$$

$$= \frac{\text{Losses caused by unused capital}}{\text{Losses caused by the bottleneck}}$$

$$= \frac{m_A \xi_A + m_C \xi_C}{m_B} \qquad (1)$$

Formula (1) defines losses of unused resources caused by unit bottleneck losses. In other words, it implies the effects that can be brought about once unit bottleneck is eliminated. This method is easy to use, and as long as the key bottleneck stage is found, it will only be necessary to increase resource input in that stage so as to expand the bottleneck. However, there are still many complicated decisions left such as who should be responsible for the input and how to carry it out.

2.2. *Creating Alternative Routes*

This is to add some parallel connections to the original SC bottleneck in order to create alternative routes, as shown in Figure 3. By adding additional route B′ to stage B and consequently allowing more flow to pass through stage B, the originally unused resources in other stages can be fully and reasonably utilized, which enhances the overall benefit of the SC. For example, if it is the supplier stage that constrains normal operation of the SC, more suppliers can be added in time to solve the problem; and if the bottleneck emerges at the manufacturer stage, cooperative exploitation, parallel project and outsourcing, etc. can be adopted accordingly. Creating alternative routes can be used not only in eliminating bottlenecks due to SC's inner resource shortage but also bottlenecks of other causes.

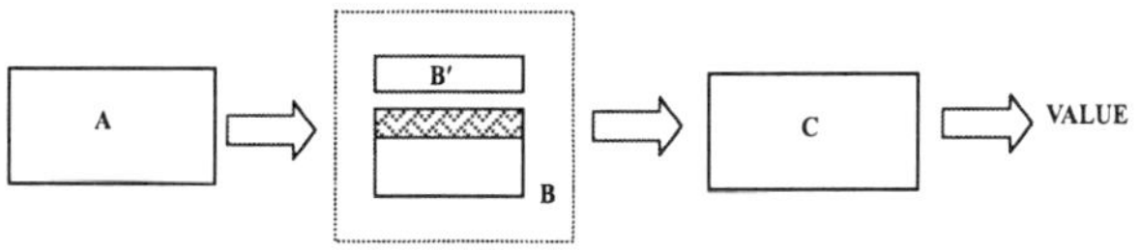

Fig.3 Creating Alternative Route by Adding B′

The common characteristics of the above two methods are that they both adopt the method of control after the bottleneck come into being. However, when practicing, these methods always lead to the contradictory of benefit-off. Let's look at the bottleneck of supplier again: it is indeed beneficial to increase extra number of suppliers, but it seems rather hasty to do so and consequently challenges its chance of success. Meanwhile, there is another difficult part in these two methods: the quantity of input and number of new partners. As a result, expanding the bottleneck and creating alternative routes have rather limited effects in solving SC's bottleneck problem.

2.3. *The Ideal Solution for SC's Bottleneck Problem---SDN*

The SDN method revolutionizes the existing SC's structure, changing it from chain mode to three-dimensional network. Because of its breakthrough in function and degree of opening compared with SC, SDN has become a better solution in solving the bottleneck problem.

2.3.1. The Concept of SDN

The Supply and Demand Network with multifunctional and open characteristics for enterprise (SDN) is a multifunctional and open supply and demand network in a global scope, formed among relevant enterprises by their interactive "Supply and Demand Flow", with the aim of access to global resource, manufacturing and marketing[11]. The SDN model is shown in Figure 4:

In the model of Figure 4, the "Supply and Demand Flow" is the media of supply and demand which flows among nodes in SDN. Compared with the "flow" in SC, the "Supply and Demand Flow" has a broader meaning, which includes dominant and recessive supply-and-demand such as materials, products, knowledge, talented persons, management ideas, funds and even "enterprise culture", etc.. The "Supply and Demand Flow" reveals dynamic changes all the time, with its scope expanding to the global market. Besides, the SDN network nodes are rich in variety, which include customers, distributors, manufacturers, suppliers and SC alliances, etc. and are not connected in series like those in the SC; any network nodes in SDN may have supply and demand relationship between each other, which reveals a great variety of association.

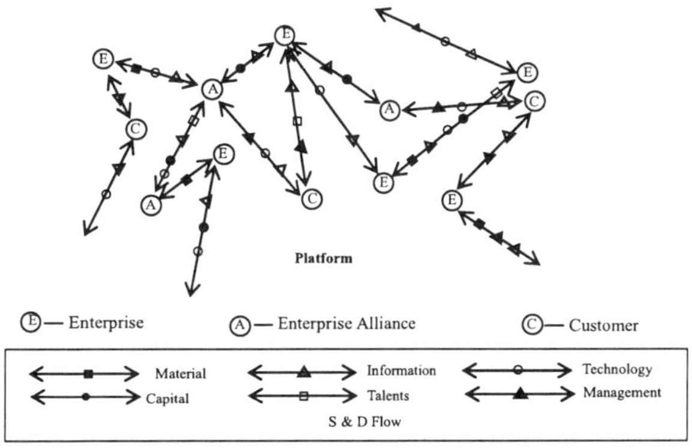

Fig. 4 The SDN Model

2.3.2. Eliminating Bottlenecks using SDN

Compared with the gradual improvement of "expanding the bottleneck" and "creating alternative routes", SDN requires thorough change in SC's concept and structure. Its characteristics of network, multifunction, opening and dynamic stability will fundamentally reduce the probability of a bottleneck emergence, or respond quickly and agilely as soon as a bottleneck comes into being so as to reduce losses to the minimum and increase overall system output. SDN can eliminate the bottleneck phenomenon from the following aspects:

a. Enhance enterprises' agility in adapting to market change. The network characteristics of SDN enable member enterprises to interchange needed "Supply and Demand Flow" directly, and effectively avoid slow response to market change due to gradual transmission of "flows" through various stages in traditional SC. In the unpredictable dynamic market environment, member nodes spreading across the world can satisfy customer's demand more rapidly by access to global resource, global manufacturing and marketing. Meanwhile, with the aid of information technology such as Internet/Intranet and EDI etc., every enterprise node in SDN can share each other's supply and demand information timely and completely on the uniform information platform, which greatly enhance enterprises' agility and ability in adapting to market change.

b. Reduce losses due to partner choice and misallocation of resources. In SDN, enterprises hold the idea of "all those who come are guests" in handling the competitive and cooperative relationship among each other, and replace possible "unilateral relationship" found in chain structure with "multilateral relationship" to reduce over-reliance on partners in chain structure. SDN with open characteristics can also make worldwide expansion of resource share, and form different levels and types of partnership according to cooperation range and depth, such as multiple flow strategic model, single flow strategic model, multiple flow affair model and single flow affair model as well as opportunity model, all of which compensate for the losses caused by single partner choice and misallocation of resources, and can realize higher levels of optimal resource allocation and worldwide value augmentation[12].

c. Restrain the opportunism tendency and promote cooperation among member enterprises. Multifunction emphasizes that besides realizing basic logistic functions, SDN also possesses other "Supply and Demand Flow" such as technology, capital, managerial ideas, information and talents, etc., even if one of these supply-demand relationship terminates, other relationships will still remain. As a result, enterprises in SDN will be able to maintain longer cooperation compared with those in SC, and the games among them will also change from limited, single-content and repeated ones to limitless, multi-level, multi-content and repeated ones. Considering the probability of being punished in the future (which means loss of long-term benefit), the optimal strategy for an enterprise will be to cooperate with others further so as to realize ideal Nash Equilibrium[13].

d. Enhance system's ability to cope with sudden events. In the short run, since SDN has a dynamic and stable network structure, transmission channels carrying Supply and Demand Flow through nodes are further widened, making common sudden event less striking on the entire network and consequently reduces the probability of a bottleneck emergence. When faced with a violent and sudden event, even if one of the sub-system connection breaks, the multi-relationship existing in the network will lead cooperation to other nodes immediately to avoid destructive strike on the entire SDN system. Besides, there are no risks that can be caused by hasty actions. In the long run, multifunctional SDN promotes various Supply and Demand Flow interchanges in material, technology, capital, managerial ideas and talents, etc. among member enterprises, and enhances each other's core ability in the process as well as the ability to cope with sudden events.

e. Reduce information asymmetry. The integrated information platform with three-dimensional network structure and seamless connection provides any enterprise node in the SDN with windows to share information and channels for communication, and allows network nodes to interact with each other directly independent of a third party, which effectively avoids distortion in transmitting SC information and the emergence of enlarged demand information effect. All these can greatly reduce information asymmetry and the probability of creating a bottleneck.

f. Alleviate the conflict of creating a bottleneck due to inadequate supply and demand. The opening of SDN is an advantage over SC alliances, which makes the frontier of cooperation more flexible and ambiguous. Meanwhile, the operational mode of international resource share, manufacturing and marketing is gradually harmonizing differences in value and culture among enterprises, and the hostile relationships among enterprises and SC's are changing into cooperative ones, which greatly alleviate the conflicts of inadequate supply and demand among enterprises in material, talents, information, managerial ideas, technology and capital, etc. and consequently enhance enterprises' ability to cope with bottlenecks.

From the above analysis it can be concluded that as an ideal solution, SDN has made breakthroughs over traditional SC both in structure and functions. In fact, it adopts preventions in advance to reduce the probability of a bottleneck emergence from the very beginning. At present, many famous international enterprises such as Microsoft, Dell and Apple have already make breakthroughs on the traditional SC concept, and have gained enormous profit by bringing themselves into the bigger system of SDN in their own ways[14].

3. Conclusion

The paper put forward solutions to SC bottleneck problem and made a detailed discussion. Expanding the Bottleneck and Creating Alternative Routes are taken after the bottleneck has emerged, while SDN adopts preventions in advance to solve the bottleneck problem. The former two methods may lead to conflicting benefits when carried out and are difficult in handling the degree to which they can be applied. According to the principle of "function decided by structure" in system science, the characteristics of inner network, multifunction, opening and dynamic stability in SDN make it more effective, intelligent and flexible. As a result, SDN is the ideal solution to bottleneck problem in SC system.

Acknowledgments

Jing He's and Fuyuan XU's work was partially supported by Chinese National Natural Science Fund (Grant No. 70472075) and Shang Hai Primary Subject Program (Grant No. T1103).

References

1. E M Goldratt and J. Cox, The Goal: a Process of Ongoing Improvement, The North River Press, (1992).
2. Xing-yuan WANG, Bottleneck analysis (BNA) of Enterprise and Its Application, *Industrial Engineering and Management* **5**, 41-45 (2000).
3. David Simchi-Levi, Philip Kaminsky and Edith Simchi-Levi, Designing and Management the Supply Chain- Concepts, Strategies and Case Studies, YuanDong Press, (2001).
4. Marshall L. Fisher, What Is The Supply Chain for Your Product? *Harvard Business Review* **75(2)**, 105-106 (1997).
5. R Anupindi and R. Akella, Diversification under supply uncertainty, *Management Science* **39(8)**, 944-963 (1993).
6. G N Evans, D R Towill and M M Naim, Business process re-engineering the supply chain, *Production Planning & Control* **6(3)**, 227-237 (1995).
7. David Boddy, Douglas Macbeth and Beverly Wagner, Implementing collaboration between organizations: an empirical study of supply chain partnering, *Journal of Management Studies* **37(7)**, 1003-1017 (2000).
8. Peter Senge, The Fifth Discipline, Shanghai: Shanghai SDX Joint Publishing Company, (2001).
9. Lee Hau et al., Information distortion in a supply chain: the bullwhip effect, *Management Science* **43(4)**, 546-558 (1997).
10. Hui-lin RAO, Urban Economics, Dongbei University of Finance & Economics Press, (1999).
11. Fu-yuan XU and Jing HE, Study on Enterprise Management Pattern under the Environment of Globalization, Science of Science and Management of S. & T., (2002).
12. Lu HAN, First Study on Supply and Demand Network with Multi-functional and Opening Characteristics for Enterprise, University of Shanghai for Science and Technology, (2002).
13. Wei-ying ZHANG, Game Theory and Information Economics, Shanghai SDX Joint Publishing Company, (2001).
14. David Bovet, Joseph Martha and R.Kirk Kramer, Value Network- Breaking the Supply Chain to Unlock Hidden Profits, People Post Press.

A HERMENEUTIC APPROACH TO 'INFORMATION ANALYSIS' FOR INFORMATION REQUIREMENTS

SUFEN WANG
Glorious Sun School of Business & Management, Donghua University
Shanghai ,200051, China

JUNNKANG FENG
University of Paisley, High Street
Paisley PA1 2BE, UK

Requirement analysis is an important stages in information systems development (ISD) but is characterized by informality and uncertainty. In this paper, we will look at how well-known information systems methodologies handle it, and identify main problems and their causes. Then we argue that an explicit information analysis stage would be required in order to alleviate these problems, the information that an agent in a domain requires is identified and formulated in this stage. Such a stage would need a mechanism. We describe how hermeneutics might enable us to construct the mechanism whereby information is created and information flow takes place.

1. Introduction

A formal information system uses structured data to represent information. To identify and formulate information required by an actor for a human purposeful activity and identify the data that will be able to represent required information is at the center of information systems design.

We have conducted an investigation in this area. In this paper, we will present a literature review and then in section 2 suggest that an 'information analysis' stage be included in ISD. . In section 3 we outline a hermeneutics foundation for a mechanism that can be used for such a stage. We conclude this paper with a summary.

2. The need for a mechanism for identifying and formulating required information

We argue our case for such a mechanism by looking at how well-known ISD methods approach the identifying and formulating of required information, and their problems.

2.1. *The content of IS requirements by the user*

The first issue we will look at is the content of IS requirements. It appears that there are a number of different approaches to this. STRADIS[1], YSM[2], and OOA ([3],[4]) do not seem to consider how to define problems that need to be tackled.

IE[5], SSADM[6], ISAC[7], and ETHICS[8]have an explicit phase of requirements analysis, which covers a variety of elements. In addition, UML BPR CRC (Classes, Responsibilities and Collaborators) uses a variety of elements to formulate requirements for the system to be designed[9].

SSM[10] based methodologies use a notional system and its activity model to capture users' views and interpretations of a problem situation, and their requirements are embedded in the notional system([11], [12], [13], [14], [15]).

It would seem that the main problem in the aspect of 'the content of IS requirements by the user' is that the requirements are modeled by a variety of conceptual models (normally a semantic data model and a process model of some kind, for instance in DFD), and the information required by the agent or user is not captured by means of some workable definition, concrete format and systematic procedure. This may be caused by the lack of a prominent appearance of the agent who the information requirements are for.

2.2. *How required information is identified*

There appear to be a number of approaches to this. The first and dominant approach to this is that information, in a variety of terms such as 'information category' [11], 'information flow' [15], 'information need' (in IE [5]), 'information base' [16], and 'information set' (in ISAC[7]), is identified as the necessary condition for an activity([11], [14], [13],[15]).

The second approach is to identify required information by looking at the input/output of an activity([7], [12]).

The third approach seems to identify required information without an explicitly stated basis.

The main problem with these approaches is that even all of them put together might still not be sufficient for an activity. Moreover these information related things are not necessarily the information that the agent really requires.

The main cause seems the lack of the realization of the need for an 'information analysis' stage, and its associated mechanism for connecting to the earlier problem appreciation stage and the later conventional conceptual modeling stage by using a data model or DFD, and the lack of the realization that the basic theoretical underpinnings for this stage might have been available for a while now. Consequently the requirements analysis of IS is often organized around the requirements of the new system by means of a data schema and a process model.

2.3. *Whether and how data are derived from required information*

The identification of data entities is seen as the beginning of the design stage of an information system[17]. STRADIS[1], YSM[2], IE[5], SSADM[6], OOA ([3],[4]), UML ([3],[9]), ETHICS[8], Multiview [12], Prior[13], Sawyer[14], Flynn do not seem to have such a concept of deriving a data structure from identified required information[16]. Instead either data structures are constructed from unstructured user requirements, or are constructed to represent the 'structure component' (i.e., an entity model) of a specification created through requirements analysis [16] or are constructed under the influence of a SSM conceptual model Multiview[12].

The second approach is that an 'information category' is seen as an aggregation or generalization of data[11]. The 'data content' of an information category is elaborated by using the hierarchical data model.

The third approach, which is taken by ISAC[7], is that information sets are in fact treated as attributes, and a data schema is constructed by using the concept of 'functional dependency' and principles of physical database design.

Finally the fourth approach exemplified by Miles' approach[15] is that some heuristic rules are given, such as 'to ask what are the entity types that will support the information flows and how they are related', and yet no concrete guidelines for how this is done are given.

It would seem that the main problems with these approaches are, first of all, a data schema is not derived from required information captured in a concrete format. As information and data are seen essentially the same thing despite different terms being used, to construct a data structure is a matter of data modeling through data consolidation, specialization, aggregation or step-wise refinement. That is to say, a data structure is not derived from required information. Secondly as a consequence of the first one, these approaches do not address the issue of how data in a machine bear information that can be derived by a user from them. There is no clearly defined concept of and mechanism for looking at how data are structured to bear required information. Batini et al.[18] raises the question of the 'information content' of a data schema, but does not seem to have provided an adequate solution. This question is not well acknowledged in the literature. This problem seems relevant to the problem of the 'gap' (or 'link') between SSM conceptual model and conventional data and function models.

The cause seems to be the lack of widely accepted theories that address the relationship between information and data, and systematic techniques for this, including the issue of the quality of a data schema.

Constructing data structures without considering information is problematic philosophically. As we mentioned earlier, according to Mingers[19] humans are always in a 'meaning system' and they cannot engage information in an unmediated way, let alone data, which should be seen as a collection of signs that carry information. Multiview's approach[12] namely constructing a data structure under the influence of the SSM conceptual model that is constructed beforehand, is also not convincing. Mingers[17] says that with Multiview[12] the move from the stage of analyzing a human activity to the subsequent stage of analyzing information (deciding the functions and entities for the new system) is 'singularly weak', and 'the soft analysis carried out... is really left up in the air,' and 'quite how this new system was decided upon and how the functions and entities relate to the conceptual model is left unclear.'

So it would seem that a solution for the problems having been identified will have to be based upon the following essential elements:

- The agent should be put at the center of the requirements analysis and modeling;
- Required information should be identified systematically and then formalized with a format that will provide concreteness and precision;
- Data schema construction will have to be systematically carried out from required information, and the notion of and some measure for 'information bearing capacity of a data schema' must be established.

To achieve these, an 'information analysis' stage would seem highly desirable, which should be inserted between problem appreciation and conventional data modeling and process (or function) modeling. This stage would require a mechanism, which should address the following problems:

- Where the information that an agent acquires, records and sends comes from, and the quantity of it;
- The quantity of and what (i.e., the content of) information an agent acquires, records and sends, and how to organize this information;
- How an 'acquiring, recording and sending' process takes place.

It would seem that such a mechanism has to be based upon a formal, useful and systematic treatment of the concept information. We suggest adopting Hermeneutics as such a perspective. We describe how Hermeneutics might enable us to look at the mechanism whereby information is created and information flow takes place in the context of information systems in the sections that follow.

3. A Hermeneutic approach to the problem of information in IS

3.1. *A new perspective on the essence of information*

How to understand and deal with the essence of information is obviously one of the key problems in IS field([19],[20]).

We suggest using results of advances in the research of 'information philosophy' in recent years[20] thereby to formulate a new perspective for obtaining a better understanding of the discipline of information systems and for investigating the essence of information.

We believe that information is carried by non-empty, well-formed and meaningful data [20], and an information system is a social system making use of IT. Thus the relationship among information, data and meaning can only be explored through communication and negotiations between humans. It is conducted within the never-ending cycle of 'information is carried/embodied/projected by data; meaning is created from information through interpretation of data; then further information may be created due to the intention of a human agent, which is again carried by data' Through communication and negotiations between them, people obtain understanding of the world around them and of themselves. So, 'why information is called information in the first place' must be considered form the viewpoint of human's existence.

The process above is that of information (impact) realization, and the associated mechanism is that of information realization. On the one hand this process captures the relationship between information, data and meaning. On the other hand, this process is accomplished through the interaction between the three. We believe that information is independent of informees (the receivers of information), borrowing Floridi's term[20]. But we also believe that the impact of information, which is concerned with the reason why a piece of information can be seen as such, namely due to its capability of informing, can only be materialized through the interaction between the three, i.e., information, data and meaning. This entails the involvement of human agents within the process, or the interpretation/creation of meaning. Information realization is concerned with how people use information, and how information supports people who need information. Therefore the process of information realization becomes a process of meaning interpretation and realization.

The informing process through accessing information is that of interpreting the meaning of information for the informee in the sense that what the information means to him/her. It would seem that this has not been adequately addressed. Furthermore, exploring meaning would seem a basic problem for hermeneutics. In the sections that follow, we will put forward a proposal on how a mechanism for exploring meaning might look like by drawing on hermeneutics.

3.2. *The general process of 'information realizing' mechanism*

Hermeneutics is the study of interpretation. Hermeneutics emerged as a concern with interpreting ancient religious texts and has evolved to address the general problem of how we give meaning to what is unfamiliar and alien([21], [22], [23]).

In the context of IS, data, information and meaning are in a state of co-existence. Information is borne by data, and meaning is created due to reception of information through looking at data or interpreting data. Thus these data are in the position of the target, i.e., 'text' in Hermeneutics.

We consider information systems as social systems that are technically and technologically implemented, so, we adopt Ricoeur's Hermeneutics as the theoretical foundation for our investigation into the mechanism that enables the realization of information and information flow within the context of information systems[23].

Ricoeur combines ontological Hermeneutics with methodological and epistemological Hermeneutics through linking Hermeneutics with the text theory.

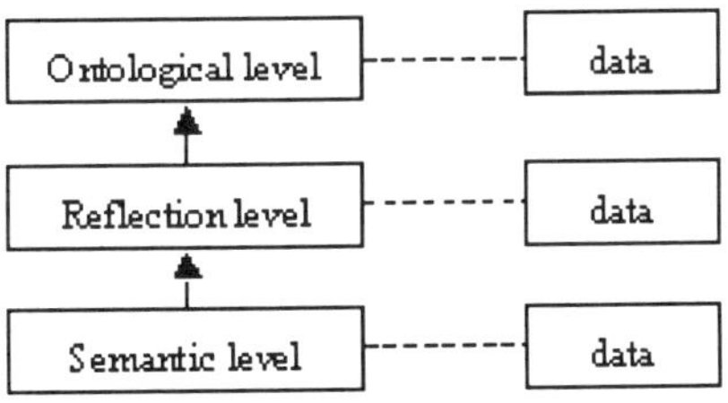

Figure 1. The general process of information realization

The general process of information and information flow realization (see Figure 1.) may be seen as having three stages, namely the Semantics Layer, Reflection Layer, and Ontological Layer. Each of the layers is connected with the 'text' (i.e., data) of the information system. The transformations between the three layers embody those between objective meaning (in the sense of being independent of the receiver of information), inter-subjective meaning and subjective meaning.

3.3. *The analysis of various elements in the 'information forming' process*

3.3.1. The data analysis

With Hermeneutics, data in information systems are read and interpreted as texts. We give data here slightly different characteristics from those that appear in more 'general' research of information systems([21],[22], [23]).

We think that data links information and meaning, which enables the communication between people. Through communication, people acquire self-understanding. Thus data should have the following characteristics:

- Data are fixed life expressions by being written. They have multiple meanings and multiple layers of meaning. There are literal meaning, sender's meaning, hidden and latent meaning produced by various factors.
- There is a dialectic relation between the sender's meaning and the meaning that may be seen as inherent to the data. They are inter-dependent, which shows the relation between data and information.
- The meaning created through the information that is carried by data and the importance of data are derivate from the dialectic relation between data and its receiver. The dialectic relation embodies the relation between information and meaning, and the relation is realized by jointing data and meaning. The meaning and the importance are achieved through the increase of the receiver's understanding of the world under the influence of the information carried by data, which is characterized by the reduction in the uncertainty of the receiver's understanding of the world.
- Data is not limited by their direct references; data enable people to enter a possible world from a given world, i.e., the data world.

3.3.2. Semantic analysis------ the analysis of information content

The analysis of the information content of data, through interpreting the data, we can obtain objective information content carried by the data. The objective information content is taken as the meaning that the sender of the data wishes the data to carry. So 'objective' here means being independent of the receiver of the data. Data may have various meanings, such as the literal meaning, which may in turn refer to a particular event.

Literal meaning is the direct and basic meaning, and the others are indirect, second or metaphoric meaning. These indirect meanings are nested within the direct meaning. This is similar in a way to information nesting[24].

We begin to interpret data that have multi-stipulations. But every kind of interpretation is based on its own frame of reference in order to seek agreement with the rich and multi-vocal meanings of data. The interpretation process of data is illustrated in Figures 2 and 3.

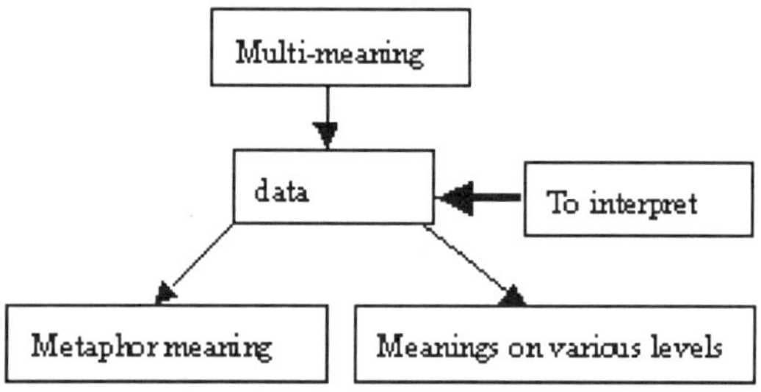

Figure 2. Various factors involved in semantic analysis

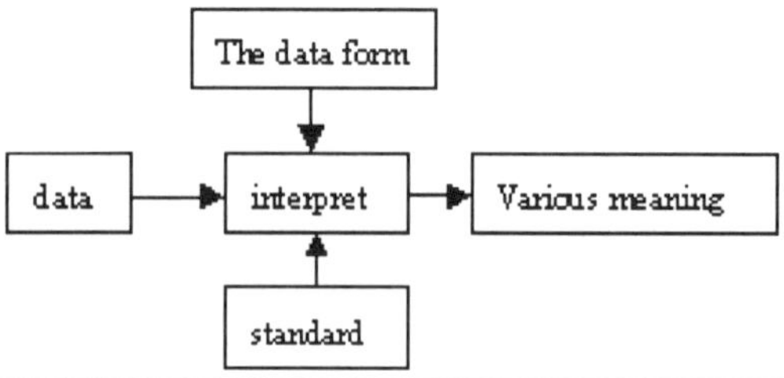

Figure 3. Interpretation procedure

3.3.3. *Reflection layer*

The information forming process embodies the communication between people by means of the inter-relationship of data, information and meaning. Its goal is for people to achieve understanding of themselves by communicating one another.

Thus our interpretation of data is not just the understanding of the information content that is carried by the data, but also the meaning of the sender of the data. The purpose of this is, through understanding the sender's meaning, to ascertain what world we ourselves are in, and make sure of what 'I' am, and what I should do. This is self-understanding, to achieve which there has to be a process of reflection.

Reflection is of course self-reflection, and not a concrete reflection on a particular event. Reflection is a process of transforming the 'otherness' of the data into an 'utterance event' for me. The receiver's 'utterance event' is a new event, that is, it is not the repetition of the ''utterance event' that created the data in the first place, but is new creation according to the requirement of 'speaking'. This way, the interpretation of reflection is completed. Thus, self-understanding is realized through reflection.

Reading links two incidents of speaking: data as utterance, and reading as new utterance (See Figure 4). Ricoeur makes use of Gardmer's 'fusion of horizons' to refer to the widening of the understanding of the subject after she/he has entered the world of data.

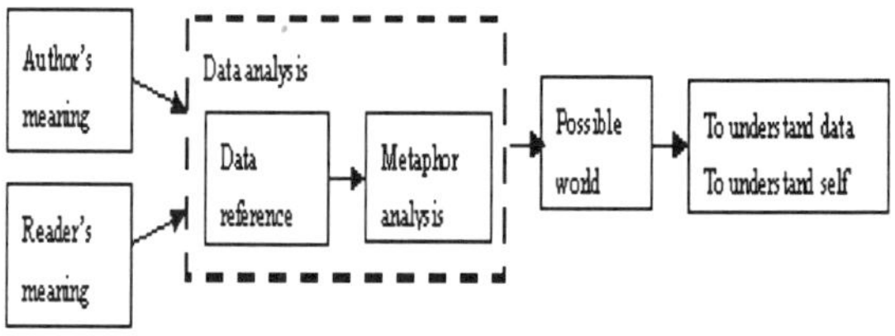

Figure 4. Reflection process

We place data at the position of a production medium. Through the interpretation cycle, more meaning is obtained; and through 'fusion of horizons', self-understanding is achieved.

Reflection process is completed through reading data and conversing with data, and reading through 'fusion of horizons' and game-playing.

3.3.4. *Ontological Layer*

After reflection, self-understanding comes into being according to the form in which it can exist, and it creates new data. This is not an end, but the beginning of a new cycle. This process of information and information flow formation constitute a basis of exchange between human being.

3.4. ***Concluding remarks***

Through semantic interpretation of the semantic layer, the receiver obtains the information content of the data sent by the sender. Much of the information content exists in the form of being implied and implicit, through obtaining which the receiver obtains her/his understanding of the sender. Through assimilation via reflection, the receiver strives to find the way to further understanding her/himself, namely to make something 'alien' to be of his/her own. Then on the ontological layer, the receiver expresses his/her own utterance with new data. Through such a never-ending cycle, human exchange is achieved, through which we increasingly under ourselves.

We identified the three problems in the previous sections concerning requirements of IS, namely,

- *The content of IS requirements by the user*,

- *How required information is identified*, and
- *How data that an IS will actually process are identified.*

These can now be looked at within such a never-ending Hermeneutic cycle. The content of information requirement from the point of the view of the user would now be what is needed for her/him to understand her/himself in the context of using an IS to approach and complete her/his tasks and the meanings that are subsequently produced. The required information should be identified through the stages of semantic understanding, reflection and ontological realization. Finally, the data that an IS processes should be among the original set of data and the new data. These can be seen in Figure 5. To work out the details of how a mechanism for analyzing information and information flow within the context of IS would require much more work and it is therefore beyond the scope of this paper.

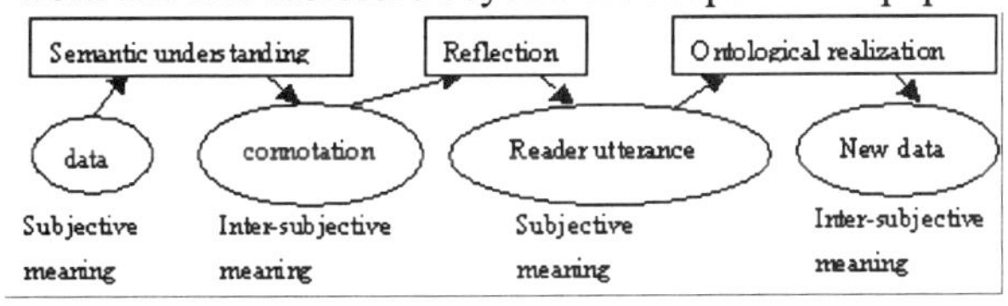

Figure 5. How to identify the required information through the stages of semantic understanding, reflection and ontological realization.

4. Summary

In this paper we have presented a literature review to support our observation that an 'information analysis' stage for information systems development would seem to be needed, in which the information that an agent in a domain requires is identified and formulated. Such a stage would need a mechanism. To develop such a mechanism, we suggested using Hermeneutic as the foundations and we outlined a Hermeneutic approach to information in information systems.

References

1. C.P. Gane and T. Sarson, Structured Systems Analysis: Tools and Techniques, Englewood Cliffs, New Jersey, Prentice Hall, (1979).
2. Yourdon Inc. Yourdon Systems Methods: Model-Driven Systems Development. Englewood Cliffs, New Jersey.Yourdon Press, (1993).
3. G. Booch, J. Rumbaugh and I. Jacobson, The Unified Modeling Language User Guide, Reading, Massachusetts, Addison Wesley, (1999).
4. P. Coad and E. Yourdon, Object Oriented Analysis, 2nd ed. Englewood Cliffs, New Jersey, Prentice Hall, (1991).
5. J., Martin, Information Engineering, Englewood Cliffs, New Jersey, Prentice Hall, (1989).
6. P.L. Weaver, Practical SSADM Version 4: A Complete Tutorial Guide, London, Pitman, (1993).
7. M. Lundeberg, G. Goldkuhl and A. Nilsson, Information Systems Development - A Systematic Approach. Englewood Cliffs, New Jersey, Prentice Hall, (1982).
8. E. Mumford, Effective Requirements Analysis and Systems Design: The ETHICS Method, Basingstoke, Macmillan, (1995).
9. P. Harmon and M. Watson, Understanding UML - The Developer's Guide with a Web-based Application in Java, San Francisco, California, Morgan Kaufmann Publishers, Inc., (1998).
10. P. Checkland and J. Scholes, Soft Systems Methodology in Action, Chichester, John Wiley & Sons, (1990).
11. B. Wilson, Systems: Concepts, Methodologies and Applications 2nd ed. Chichester, Wiley, (1990).
12. D.E. Avison and A.T. Wood-Harper, Multiview - an exploration in information systems development, *Australian Computer Journal* **18(4)**, 1986.
13. R. Prior, Deriving data flow diagrams from a 'Soft Systems' conceptual Model, *Systemist* **12(2)**, 65-75 (1990).
14. K. Sawyer, Linking SSM to DFD's: the two epistemological differences, *Systemist* **13(2)**, 76-80 (1991).
15. R. Miles, Combining "hard" and "soft" systems practice: grafting and embedding revisited, *Systemist* **14(2)**, 62-66 (1992).
16. D. Flynn, Information Systems Requirements: Determination & Analysis 2nd ed, London, McGraw-Hill, (1998).
17. J. Mingers, SSM and information systems: an overview, *Systemist* **14(3)**, 82-88(1992).
18. C. Batini, S. Ceri and S.B. Navathe, Conceptual Database Design: An Eentity-relationship Approach Redwood City in Calif, Benjamin/Cummings, (1992).
19. J. Mingers, Information and meaning: foundations for an intersubjective account, *Info Systems* **5**, 285-306 (1995).
20. L. Floridi, Is Information Meaningful Data? *Philosophy and Phenomenological Research* **70(2)**, 351-370 (2005).
21. R. Hirschheim, H.K. Klein and K. Lyytinen, Information systems development and data modeling, Cambridge University Press, (1995).
22. H. Gadamer, Philosophical Hermeneutics, University of California Press, Berkeley, (1976).

23. Ru-Lun Zhang, The inquire of meaning: contemporary western hermeneutics, Liaoning Publishing, (1985).
24. F. I. Dretske, Knowledge and the Flow of Information, Oxford, Basil Blackwell, (1981).

MAKING FOLKSONOMY MACHINE-UNDERSTANDABLE

PRABODH SHRESTHA
Information Systems, University of Maryland, Baltimore County, 1000 Hilltop Circle
Baltimore, MD 21250, USA

LINA ZHOU
Information Systems, University of Maryland, Baltimore County, 1000 Hilltop Circle
Baltimore, MD 21250, USA

A recent surge of interest in social tagging, also known as folksonomy, challenges the formal and structured knowledge representation in the Semantic Web. Social tagging is attractive in its low barrier to entry and personal and community aspects. However, the benefits of social tagging come at the cost of reduced machine-understandable and reduce effectiveness in information retrieval and organization. To address the above limitations, we propose a framework, UNITAG, to enhance existing social tagging systems with semantic information. It is shown that the framework facilitates information sharing in folksonomy while retaining the usability of folksonomy.

1. Introduction

Web 2.0 technologies enable the active involvement of great mass in content creation. For example, social tagging and tag sharing, also known as folksonomy [1], has transformed the cardinality of author-reader relationship from traditional one-to-many into many-to-many, where individuals play the role of both authors and readers. Driven by the popularity of web sites adopting folksonomy such as Flickr, Delicious, and YouTube, the Web grows significantly in both the volume of data and the size of user base. However, the lack of formal inclusion criteria for tags and relationships between terms hinders the effective use of tag information in folksonomy [2].

In folksonomy, users are not only sharing users' resources with others through self-selected tags, but also expressing their perspective on the resources, explaining their interest [3]. In view of individual differences in perspectives and preferences for tags, tagging and resources sharing is not a simple task.

Several recent studies have attempted to address the problem of folksonomy in support of effective information search and organization [4-6]. Existing technical solutions to the above problem can be grouped into three categories: directing users to converge to a smaller set of tags [7], asking users to specify the semantics of their tags [8], and resolving the ambiguities in user tags automatically [9]. All of them can benefit from the Semantic Web technologies.

The semantic web is built on a decentralized infrastructure that can facilitate data interoperability by means of standardized taxonomies and ontologies. Information in the Semantic Web can be easily processed and understood by machine, making it easier to share the data between different Web pages [10]. Therefore, the Semantic Web technologies have great potential in providing a robust and extensible basis for emerging Web. 2.0 applications [11]. On the other hand, Web 2.0 applications provide a platform for the Semantic Web technologies to reach the critical mass of user community.

In this research, we propose UNITAG, a method to improve the effectiveness in organizing user tags and associated information by enhancing Web 2.0 applications with Semantic Web technologies. The application of UNITAG is illustrated with several case studies, which demonstrate that the method can improve the effectiveness of information search and organization in folksonomy.

In the rest of this paper, we first review some background and related research on tagging. Then, we introduce our proposed framework, and evaluate the framework using popular social network tag sharing systems such as Delicious and Flickr. Finally, we end the paper with conclusions.

2. Background and Related Research

In a digital world, a tag simply is a keyword that is attached to resources such as files, pictures, articles, audio/videos and web URLs, which describes the property of a particular resource in a single word or sometime combination of words. A main purpose of tagging information is to make content searching easier. Tagging is not a new concept. There are many disciplines that have studied and proposed frameworks of tagging resources systematically to facilitate future retrieval.

2.1. *Meta-tag*

Meta tag is used for promoting websites by providing a "structured metadata about a web page." Meta tag is a tag that resides in html code, which does not have any direct *visible* effect. The initial goal of using meta-tags is to help search engines rank resources. Nonetheless, meta-tags have been abused to artificially boost website search rankings by including tags that contain the keywords or descriptions that do not match the content of the websites. For example, an online shoe business may include meta-tag such as apples, oranges, cars, restaurants, computers or any tags they desire—just to pull traffic to their sites [12]. Meta-tags are created and maintained by Web site authors, and other users had no control over the type of tags that they want to use or share. Further, a traditional web—which was designed for manual browsing and searching textual content—is becoming less adequate as more and more resources are generated in the web environment.

2.2. *The Semantic Web and Ontology*

The Semantic Web is an idea of connecting existing data on the Internet in a logical way so that Software agent can read and process [23]. The concept is similar as in relational database where data are logically connected to each other making it a powerful information resource.

Semantic Web does not require the recreation of the entire data on the Internet. Based on ontology, a formally defined controlled vocabulary that describes objects and the relations between them [23], the Semantic Web encourages the Web community to share existing data in a semantically-enriched and machine-friendly format. Librarians, scientists and ontologists have successfully standardized and categorized items through tagging systems, such as ISBN for books and Periodic Table for chemicals. Those systems have been proven to be unambiguous and precise. However, the Semantic Web, by design, does not allow individuals to express their perspectives using tags without restrictions but enforce semantic models on users. Users have to follow predefined concepts, relations, or axioms to annotate resources in the Semantic Web.

2.3. *Folksonomy and its Limitations*

The concept of Web 2.0 highlights a paradigm of information sharing among web users by tagging their content freely. Such a freely tagging culture has evolved into a very powerful social networking community. Delicious, Flickr, Google, Amazon, EBay and YouTube have successfully carried out an open-ended tagging system. These systems labelled as folksonnomy allow users to freely tag and share their content with other users.

Folksonomy is a web community where users tag their resources freely and shares them socially. It is a user generated social tagging system to describe information "to make a body of information increasingly easy to search, discover, and navigate over time [1]." These tags are very open-ended and unstructured. Folksonomy is usually created for tagging online items such as images, multimedia content and other specific site links. These tags are generated by users freely without any formal rules.

The community oriented tagging points to not only the object of interest, but also tells something about the tag creator herself. The benefit of using these folksonomy tags gives a sense of how one's personal views and concepts of contents represented by the tags are interrelated to others. "Harvesting individuals' knowledge through folksonomies therefore can benefit the whole society [13]."

However, the limitations of folksonomy become more evident as the tag size increases. First, user-created tags can be ambiguous due to a lack of systematic rules to guide the tag creating process. For example, when the same tag may mean different things and is used to annotate different contents, such an ambiguity is known as *polysemy*. When different tags are used for the same content, they are likely to be *synonymy*, as shown in Figure 1. These social annotations won't be of much use for Web agents and applications on the Semantic Web. Second, the tags created heavily reflect individuals' personal experiences, preferences, and skill level [14]. In addition, different individuals could link real-world objects with textual representations of these concepts in different ways. Third, even the same users may not be able to recall correctly how they tagged the information sometime earlier[5]. Fourth, folksonomy includes typographical errors and spelling variations [1]. In addition, plural and singular forms, conjugated words and compound words may be used, as well as specialized tags and "nonsense" tags designed as unique markers that are shared between a group of friends or co-workers [8]. For example, many folksonomy systems such as del.i.ci.ous allow for only single-word tags. Many users managed to create tags by combining more than one word with special characters such as underscore, hyphen, star, and slashes to describe resources.

The limitations of folksonomy have motivated some researchers to look for solutions in recent years.

2.4. *Enhancing Social Tagging with Semantics*

Enhancing the semantics of social tagging is a well recognized approach to addressing the limitations of folksonomy [11]. Understanding the semantic concepts of tags helps identify other tags or resources that are of interest to users [9].

'SynTag' is proposed to allow users to input tags and upload images with tags and their semantics and to allow searchers to explore more relevant images from Flickr using synonyms and polysemy of their tags based on WordNet [8].

A prearranged knowledge structure is a core component of an approach to bridging semantic and community tagging [15]. Users can organize their annotations in their own space by masking collection of users shared annotation into predefined shared knowledge structure. Specifically, they used Association for Computing Machinery (ACM) as a knowledge structure in a three-step iterative process: 1) selecting specific resources built in the ACM portal; 2) structuring individual interests in the resources by grouping them into desired metadata structure; and 3) making all collected individual metadata available to the entire community for knowledge evolution [15]. Although this approach creates some structure in user-generated tags, it also introduces the burden of tagging and classifying tags to users. For example, users have "to decide the best position… where to put the concept corresponding to the selected term classification [15]". Furthermore, it does not address how to process millions of existing tags into machine-understandable information.

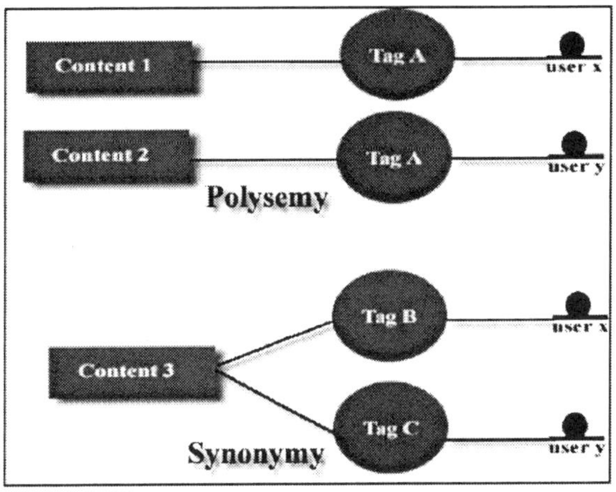

Figure 1. Polysemy & Synonymy

Several efforts have been put in leveraging the strengths of the Semantic Web infrastructure to facilitate mashup-like information sharing [11] such as semantics-enhanced RSS feeds, blogs, or wikis[16]. They expose wikipedia's fine-grained edited information in a standardized and machine-readable way by using the W3C standards on RDF, RDFS, and OWL. Machine tag, a triple tagging concept that allows RDF namespaces within tags, was recently adopted by Flickr, a photo sharing social networking site. A three-part geo-tag was previously introduced for photo blogging by overlaying photo on the map using geographical representation such as latitude and longitude. Although their fundamental ideas are similar to the method proposed in this study, they did not develop a formal methodology to bridge the gap between the semantic and social tagging worlds.

The manual and semi-automatic methods usually requires the user be familiar with the concept of ontologies and taxonomies. A framework has been outlined for utilization of machine common sense such as WordNet [17] and Cyc [18] for addressing the problem of search in folksonomy [5]. Driven by traditional research in text mining, some studies organized huge number of annotations in a semantic hierarchy to help users browse efficiently [9].

We propose a method that can enhance social tagging with semantics in this study.

3. An Integrated Tagging Framework

Although folksonomy offers unprecedented low barrier to entry and individual and community perspectives, retrieving information from clouds of tags becomes almost impossible as the cloud of tags starts to grow rapidly. There is a desperate need for making sense of and managing these rapidly growing tags. On the other hand, a machine-understandable well-structured system in the Semantic Web offers accuracy and consistency at the cost of being very restrictive and thus unattractive to users. The two types of systems could complement each other [11]. Therefore, we propose a framework that integrates Semantic Web into folksonomy. The goal of the framework is to minimize the ambiguity in user tags while keeping users' freedom in choosing their tags.

3.1. *A Motivating Example*

Figure 2 shows an image extracted from Flickr. The image, Rolling Cherry, is annotated with thirteen tags: *cherry, red, fruit, summer, spring, roll, dof, bokeh, macro, close, Nikon, D200, lela.*

Figure 2. Cherry:Flickr Photo

Just by looking at this picture, we can see that it is a red cherry and it is a fruit. From the tags, we can sense some additional meanings that the author of this image was trying to convey. For example, it is a fruit, which is rolling on the metal bar. It seems that the photo was taken during summer or spring and the photographer used Nikon D200 to capture the close-up shot. There are also a few tags such as dof and bokeh that may have some personal meanings to the author.

We made the following observations from the tags of the image. First, a tag can have multiple meanings. For example, cherry could refer to a tree, a color, or a fruit. Second, there is underlying semantic relationships between different tags used to annotate the image. For example, cherry is a type of fruit and is of red colour. Third, some tags such as dof and lela may be created for personal resource organization, which are not intended for information sharing with the public. This phenomenon is also noted elsewhere [8, 14]. Fourth, some tags are more indicative of the image than others. For example, cherry is more essential to describing the image than summer. As a result, new users are mostly likely to reinforce cherry in their tags and the tags for the images may converge to power law distribution over time [19]. Fifth, popular tags such as cherry and fruit are useful for grouping images into general categories, but are not sufficient to indicate the specific purpose of the image such as photography effect. It has been found that tags in Technorati are less effective in indicating the particular content of an article than suggesting broad categories [20]. To address the above issues, we propose a framework called UNITAG.

3.2. *UNITAG Framework*

The basic idea of UNITAG is to selectively map user-generated tags to an ontology repository. The framework aims to achieve two goals: 1) enrich the semantics of user-generated informative tags by mapping them to ontology classes; and 2) disambiguate the interpretations of user tags by associating co-occurrent tags with ontology properties. Thus, the framework is expected to create a path from ontology to folksonomy by making folksonomy tags machine-understandable and by associating ontologies with a wealth of user-generated tags.

There are there major components in UNITAG: tag filtering and normalization, ontology mapping, and resource networking (Figure 3). *Tag filtering and normalization* aim to select and transform user-generated tags into a normal form. *Ontology mapping* helps map normalized tags to classes in an ontology; and *Resource networking* builds the connection between candidate tags and other related tags. The tasks of each component are described in detail in the following.

During tag filtering and normalization, the top-N candidate tags are chosen from folksonomy tag clouds of a resource based on their popularity and importance. The choice of N depends on users' tolerance of noise. Next, a stemming and a synonym routine are applied to normalize all tags by removing duplicated tags and grouping synonymous tags. A segmentation routine is applied to process "compound words".

During ontology mapping, the ontology class is first identified for the most informative tag, and then for the next popular tag, if the first one fails, so on and so forth. To facilitate mapping tags consisting of polysemous words, we assess the similarities between co-occurred tags and ontology properties and definitions. In case that no match of an ontology classes can be found for any of the tags, the top tag can become a new ontology class with other related tags becoming candidate properties of the tag. In addition, ontology

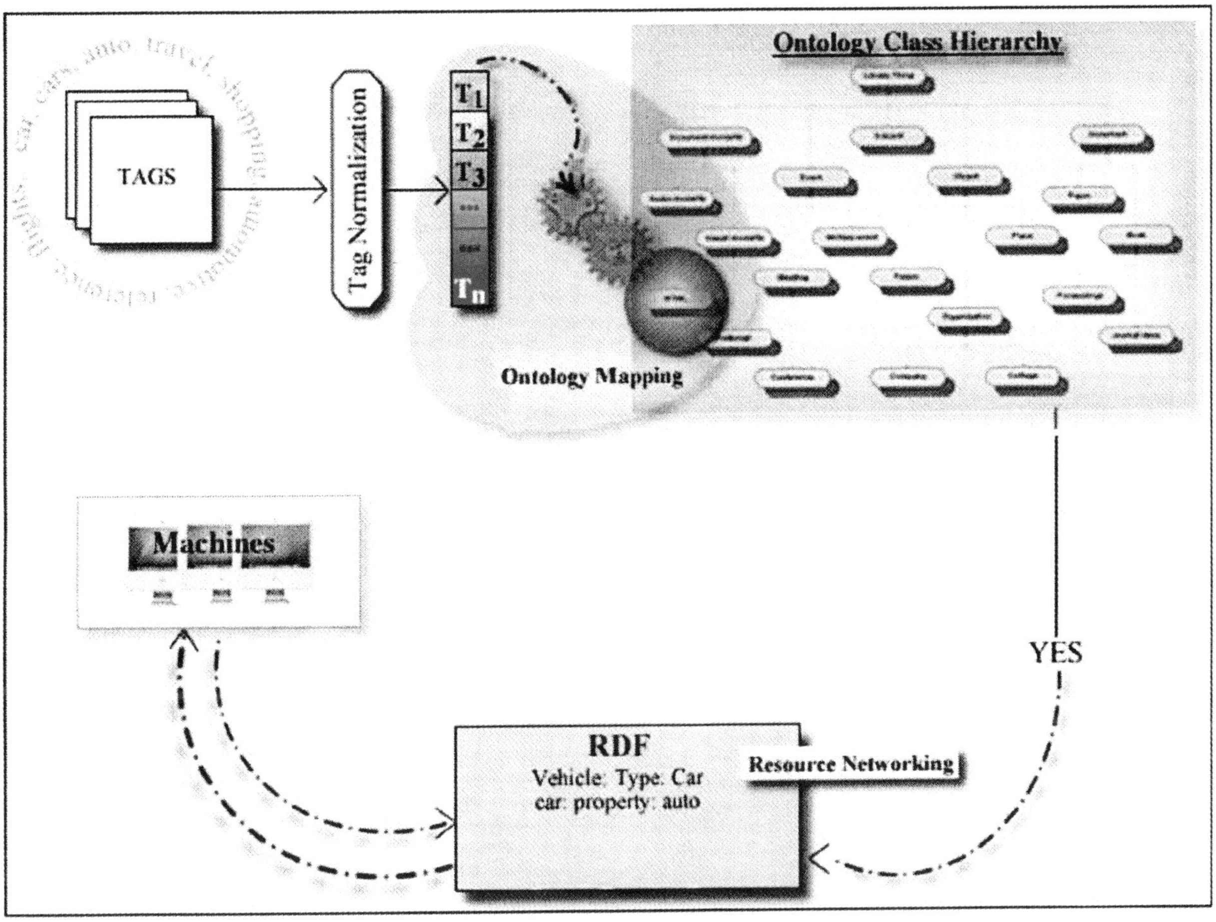

Figure 3. UNITAG Framework

mapping focuses on the lowest level of classes in an ontology hierarchy. For example, according to the ontology hierarchy shown in Figure 4, grape is mapped to fruit rather than food class.

During resource networking, the relationships between tags and ontology classes are constructed to link different resources using W3C's RDF and RDF schema. Other top-N tags that are associated with the identified ontology classes are treated as the property of the selected tag. The RDF based model helps generate specific statements about resources in a triple format: **subject :: predicate :: object.** For example, for the statement "The cherry is red", its RDF representation consists of "The cherry" as the subject; "is" as the predicate, and "red" as the object. RDF schema further enhances RDF with some standardized vocabulary.

3.3. *UNITAG Algorithm*

UNITAG identifies the ontology class and related tags for the candidate tag that is on focus. Once the candidate tag is associated with an ontology super class, we derived the relationship structure using RDF framework and its triple concept such as subject: has: object. Then, we linked remaining related tags as additional properties of the candidate tags. The following is a high-level

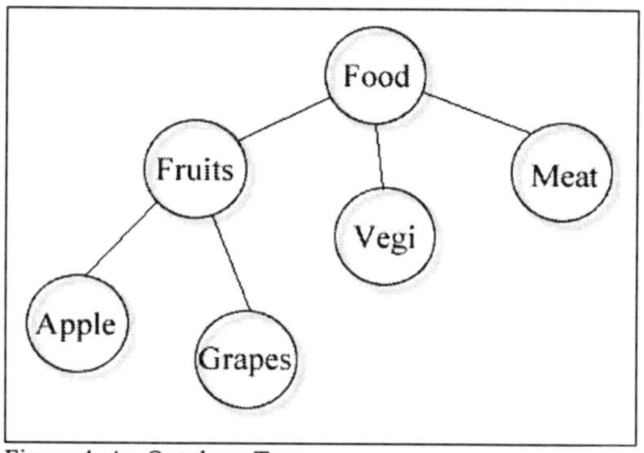

Figure 4. An Ontology Tree

UNITAG algorithm as described above:

```
/* Choose a candidate tag that points to a
specific resource */
    Get_candidate_Tag(){
Candidate_Tag = Input a tag;}

/* Find related tags, apply synonym filter to
the list of tags to combine similar, synonym
words into one common word */
    Quarry_related_tags(){
Related_Tags = Find Relate_Ttags for a given
(Candidate_Tag);
Synonym_Filter();
RelatedTtags_Count;}

/* build a relation structure using RDF
framework to create a formal relations
between the tags and its class */
    Ontology_Mapping(){
    //Ontology Mapping System
    If (Mach_Found==true){
RDF_Construct_Relation(){
associate candidate_tag with Ontology class
Connect_Related_tags as property of the
Candidate_Tag;}
    /* error handler */
else { return error ;} }
```

Interlinking tags make it possible to relate entire tag set with one another through the candidate tag. If a query is made from the Semantic Web, this system will help find a targeted resource through the path defined by RDF.

4. Case Studies and Discussion

We illustrate the application of UNITAG with two popular social networking Web sites and then discuss the implications of UNITAG in this section.

4.1. *Case Studies*

Delicious (http://del.icio.us) is a social bookmarking website which allows users tag and share their tags with others. We chose tag "car" from the website in this

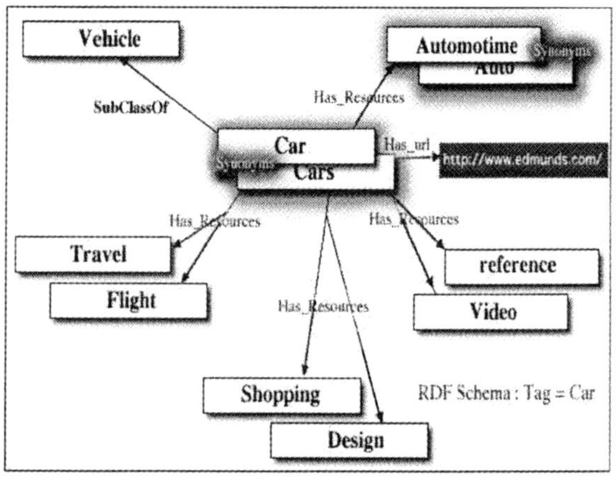

Figure 5. A case from del.icio.us

study. We searched tag "car" using the search feature from the main page of delicious, and the system returned 137,096 results and ten unique tags, including *car, cars, auto, travel, shopping, automotive, reference, flights, design,* and *video*.

Once all related tags are identified, we will apply a synonym filter to reduce duplicated tags and synonym tags. Words such as car and cars are combined into a single tag. Similarly, tags "auto" and "automobile" can be combined into a single tag (*Figure 5*). Then a candidate tag is mapped to an ontology repository containing the predefined class using Ontology Mapping System (OMS) [21, 22]. In this case, car is mapped to vehicle, which is represented as *Vehicle: Type: car*; and then the relationships between car and other tags such as travel are created such as ***car:*** *has_property: travel.*

Flickr is an online photo management and sharing application. Using Flickr's search feature, we retrieved the following tags for a photograph of a cherry: *cherry, food, red, macro, fruit, top20macro, 500v20f, nikonstunninggallery, kitlens, 28-80mmf/3.3-5.6G, nikkor,* and *wild*dreams*

First, noise such as nikkor and personal tags such as top20macro are filtered. During tag normalization, we segmented the compound words such as nikonstunninggallery, kitlens, and wild*dreams into their component words. Then, we mapped the tags to ontological classes using OMS. For example, given the ambiguity in word cherry, we infer from other related tags such as food that cherry should be mapped to class fruit rather than class tree, which was represented as *Fruit: Type: cherry*. Finally, the relationships between tags are created such as ***cherry**: has_property:red.*

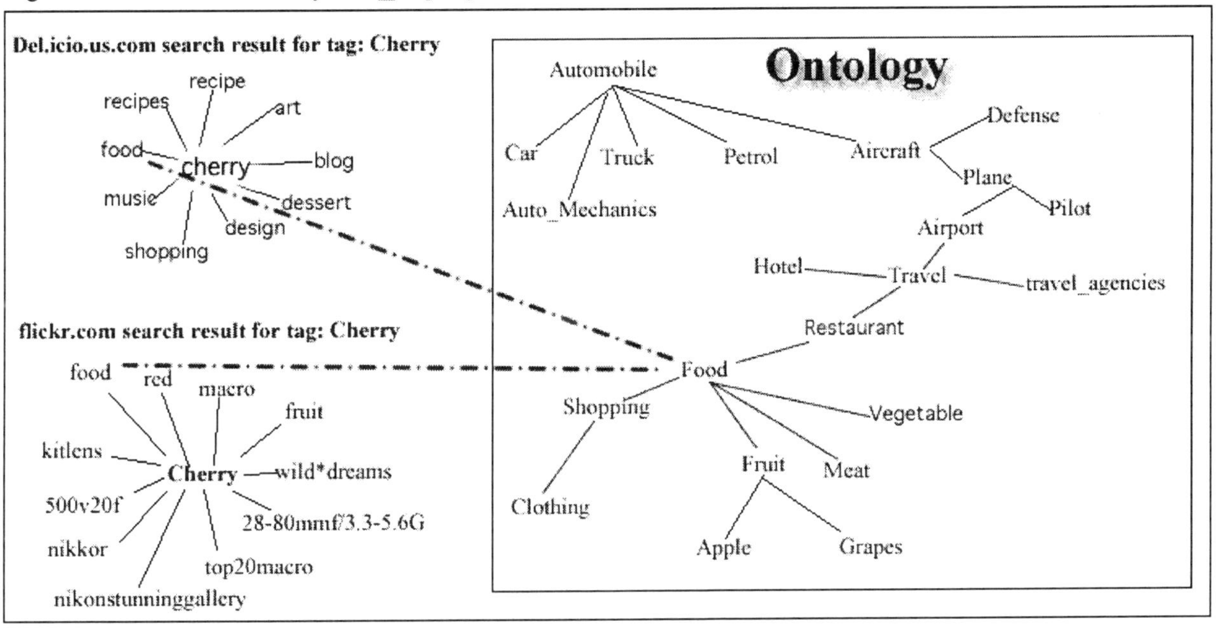

Figure 6. UNITAG Mapping

4.2. *Discussion*

It is demonstrated from the above two case studies that UNITAG has the potential to improve the search and organization of tags and related resources in a folksonomy Web site. Folksonomy users can directly benefit from UNITAG by getting access to semantically enriched information. In addition, UNITAG can support mashing up information from different Web sites. As shown in Figure 6, based on the search results for tag cherry from del.icio.us and those from Flickr.com, a system built on UNITAG can not only retrieve information about recipes including cherry from delicious but also display a professional photo shot of cherry from flickr. UNITAG essentially creates a pathway between folksonomy and the Semantic Web and between different folksonomy systems via machine-understandable semantic tagging. Further, UNITAG extends ontology mapping to a set of user-generated tags and allowed for ontology extension.

UNITAG lays the foundation for unifying social tagging with semantic tagging. It allows for access to other resources that are semantically related, and does not impose extra burden on users. Nonetheless, there are a number of issues that need to be addressed to build a real-world UNITAG system. First, automatic ontology mapping and extending an ontology with new concepts and instances are themselves challenging research issues. Second, a UNITAG system should retain the usability of folksonomy. Third, the system should personalize tags and resources to users' preferences and interests.

The state of the art Semantic Web technologies significantly improve machine-understandability of information on the Web. However, they impose a lot of constraints and structures on users, consequently many novice users tend to shy away from it. The Semantic Web technologies are yet to be widely adopted in folksonomy largely because social tags are ambiguous in nature. The UNITAG framework enables the Semantic Web to tap into enormous resources—beyond its current capacity—from the folksonomy world.

5. Conclusions

Folksonomy web sites contain an enormous amount of user-generated social tags, which is growing exponentially. However, those tags are not machine-understandable mainly due to their ambiguities and lack of formal inclusion criteria and structure. To address the fundamental limitations exposed by freely generated tags, we proposed a framework UNITAG to enhance folksonomy with semantic information in this paper. It is shown from the two case studies that UNITAG facilitates information retrieval and organization in folksonomy.

References

1. M. Guy and E. Tonkin, Folksonomies: Tidying up Tags? *DLib Magazine* **12(1)**, (2006).
2. H.L. Kim, S.H. Hwang and H.G. Kim, FCA-based approach for mining contextualized folksonomy, *Proceedings of the ACM symposium on Applied computing*, 1340-1345 (2007).
3. K.F. Lawrence and M.C. Schraefel, Freedom and Restraint Tags, Vocabularies and Ontologies, *Proceedings of International Conference on Information and Communication Technologies*, 1745-1750 (2006).
4. S. Bao, G. Xue, X. Wu, Y. Yu, B. Fei, and Z. Su, Optimizing web search using social annotations, *Proceedings of the 16th international conference on World Wide Web*, 501-510 (2007).
5. M. Nauman, and F. Hussain, Common Sense and Folksonomy: Engineering an Intelligent Search System, *Proceedings of International Conference on Information and Emerging Technologies*, 1-6 (2007).
6. Lux, M., Granitzer M. and R. Kern, Aspects of Broad Folksonomies, *18th International Conference on Database and Expert Systems Applications*, 283-287 (2007).
7. Del.icio.us tag cloud view, http://del.icio.us/tag/.
8. S.-S. Lee and H.-S. Yong, Component Based Approach to Handle Synonym and Polysemy in Folksonomy, *Proceedings of the 7th IEEE International Conference on Computer and Information Technology*, 200-205 (2007).
9. R. Li, S. Bao, Y. Yu, B. Fei, and Z. Su, Towards effective browsing of large scale social annotations, *Proceedings of the 16th international conference on World Wide Web*, 943-952 (2007).
10. T. Berners_Lee, J. Hendler and O. Lassila, The Semantic Web, *Scientific American* **284(5)**, 34-43 (2001).
11. A. Ankolekar, M. Krötzsch, T. Tran and D. Vrandecic, The two cultures: mashing up web 2.0 and the semantic web, *Proceedings of the 16th international conference on World Wide Web*, 825-834 (2007).
12. B.D. Davison, Topical locality in the Web, *The 23rd Annual international ACM SIGIR Conference on Research and Development in information Retrieval. Athens*, (2000).
13. H. Wu, M. Zubair and K. Maly, Harvesting social knowledge from folksonomies, *Proceedings of the seventeenth conference on Hypertext and hypermedia*, 111-114 (2006).
14. S. Golder and B. Huberman, The Structure of Collaborative Tagging Systems, Information Dynamics Lab: HP Labs, (2006).
15. D. Gendarmi, F. Abbattista and F. Lanubile, Fostering knowledge evolution through community-based participation, *Proceedings of WWW Workshop on Social and Collaborative Construction of Structured Knowledge*, (2007).
16. M. Völkel, M. Krötzsch, D. Vrandecic, H. Haller, and R. Studer, Semantic Wikipedia, *Proceedings of the 15th international conference on World Wide Web*, 585-594 (2006).
17. C. Fellbaum, Wordnet: an electronic lexical database, MIT Press (1998).
18. D. Lenat, CYC: A large-scale investment in knowledge infrastructure, *Communications of the ACM* **38**, 33-38 (1995).
19. H. Halpin, V. Robu, and H. Shepherd, The complex dynamics of collaborative tagging, *Proceedings of the 16th international conference on World Wide Web*, 211-220 (2007).
20. C.H. Brooks and N. Montanez, Improved annotation of the blogosphere via autotagging and hierarchical clustering, *15th international conference on World Wide Web*, (2006).
21. R. Viegas and V. Soares, Querying a Geographic Database using an Ontology-Based Methodology, http://www.geoinfo.info/geoinfo2006/papers/p51.pdf (2006).
22. N. Choi, I. Song and H. Han, A survey on ontology mapping, *SIGMOD Rec.* **35(3)**, 34-41 (2006).
23. X. Wu, L. Zhang and Y. Yu, Exploring social annotations for the semantic web, *Proceedings of the 15th international Conference on World Wide Web*, 417-426 (2006).

PART B

Electronic & Management

STUDY KM SYSTEMS FROM CAS PERSPECTIVE

MEIQI FANG
Economic Science Lab Renmin University of China Haidian District,
Beijing, 100872, China

YING LIU
Economic Science Lab Renmin University of China Haidian District,
Beijing, 100872, China

SHUGUANG SUO
Economic Science Lab Renmin University of China Haidian District,
Beijing, 100872, China

The most important productivity in information age may be the knowledge and human resource. A growing number of people and enterprises pay attention to the knowledge management in organizations. We believe the IT assistant Knowledge management (KM) system serves as both an extension and an integration of traditional e-business, and thus, it is necessary for a firm's innovation and the maintenance of competitive power. However, many problems present in the way of the design and implementation of KM systems. By treating the KM system as a complex system, we find a new way to solve these problems. We design the architecture of KM system with the methodology of complex adaptive system, and resolve many practical difficulties to some extent. Furthermore, the problem in technology is merely one aspect of the whole thing, more works in management and organization, such as corresponding regulations on evaluation and promotion, are needed to make sure a smooth implement of a KM system.

1. Introduction

Along with the development of technology, we depend on more and more electronic methods in the whole business processing. Information technology can not only be view as assistant method or tools, but it also brings forth the deep transform in work flow and management. As a result we face a fast-moving businesses characterized by short product life-cycles and rapid development. The only way to survive and succeed should be to keep the pace of the environment and find the compete advantage to surpass other competitors. We should aware that the most important productivity in modern society is knowledge and human resource. So we believe the IT assistant KM system is both an extension and an integration of traditional e-business, and it is necessary for firms' innovation and maintenance of competitive power nowadays.

2. Requirement for KM in the New Age

As many businesses are executed in electronic way, they can easily record and store a lot of data and information. There comes the ubiquitous requirement for the knowledge management system, which can effectively mine the knowledge from information and manage it. Though the concept and the range of knowledge keep changing with the environment, here we consider the most distinct property of knowledge is the capability of instruction for activities. In this section, we will emphasize the requirement of knowledge management in the e-business widespread circumstance.

From having been applied firstly to tools, processes, and products, knowledge is now being applied to workplace. [1] It is reaching a point where the structure of entire industries as well as competition itself will fundamentally change. The knowledge/capital-goods ratio today is almost reversed from what it was at the turn of the century. [2] It is therefore necessary to realize the increasing value of knowledge. Similar changes also take place in the labor structure. When Taylor set out to change the world by applying knowledge to work through management, nine out of every ten working people did manual labor and in the 1950s a majority of workers were still "working". By 1990 the figure was one-fifth and it will continue to shrink. With a workforce of less than one-tenth, as is predicted by 2010, it is obvious that something other than workforce efficiency will be the primus motor. [1]The productivity of non-manual workers sometimes is called intellectual capital.

In this new age, the new logic is most compelling in information businesses where the physical distribution costs are high. [3]The physical value chain becomes more streamlined for the sake of delivering information. As a result, there seems lavish information available in the whole business systems, which in turn becomes a cause for more changes, for instance, information accessibility facilitates the increasing of buyers' bargaining power and easier switching of suppliers; barriers to entry become smaller. These changes lead to big challenges to every firm. They have to face a more dynamic business environment, and manage to deal with the abundant information effectively and efficiently.

The only method to succeed should be knowledge management, in the sense of supplying knowledge to find out good ways of using existing knowledge and to define what kind of new knowledge is needed. So the conclusion here is that in a fast-moving business characterized by short product life-cycles and rapid development, knowledge management is the most important strategic resource of enterprises. [4] Since knowledge can be considered the most valuable strategic resource, the ability to acquire, integrate, store, share, and apply it becomes the most important way of sustaining competitive advantage.

3. Barriers in Traditional Perspective

We can find that a lot of firms begin to pay attention to the management of internal and external valuable knowledge in business, especially in the knowledge businesses like biotechnology, consulting and software design. [5] I have participated in a group to design and develop a knowledge management system in a software company. We had good plans and conceptions, but encountered many difficulties when we try to realize them. We believe that will be general in many firms. We will declare some typical problems in our work and will try to analyze and solve them in the following parts.

As an IT producer and service supplier, the firm is good at utilizing the electronic method for business and management. There are already some different information systems in the organization, such as Financial, HR, OA and CRM. So the enterprise's internal systems store vast of information, although they belong to different departments. And there is probably a lot of information resource valuable to the firm in external internet. It seems good thing to an organization, but unfortunate it makes many difficulties in the application. The overwhelming information seems great trouble to get access to the usable knowledge efficiently. Sometimes one can figure that a solution to the problem in the intranet or somebody who is expert in the field of the company, but they just can't find it or it will take too much time. So a big problem is how to extract the action-oriented knowledge from the dispersed and redundant information and make it easily available. We constitute the main objectives of the system: integrated knowledge management and storage, efficiently knowledge accessibility and application, and a knowledge cooperating platform and community.

To complete the objectives, we try to design and build an integrated system based on the ongoing systems. The system is supposed to assist the whole lifecycle of knowledge. (see Figure 1)

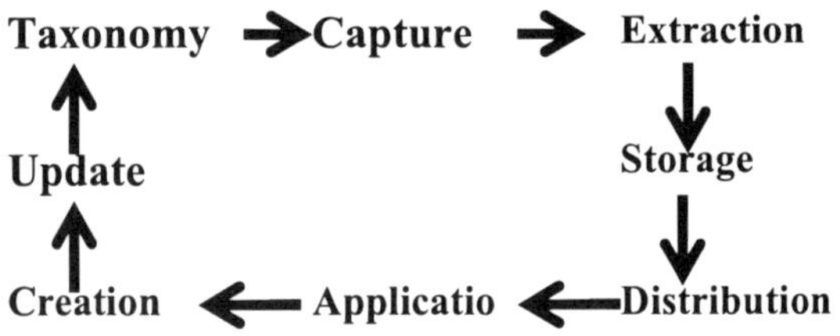

Figure 1 the lifecycle of knowledge

We try to create a hierarchical model or architecture for knowledge, similar to the encyclopedia, which would govern the collection and categorization of knowledge. We have thought the top-down collection and classification would be a laborsaving and feasible method. Soon we find our basic expectation that knowledge should be explicit, structured, organized in taxonomies, and semantically unambiguous seemed too idealized. When we try to use traditional "tree" describing the hierarchy of knowledge, we find it difficult to navigate through a tree, and new terms tended to be added at inappropriate levels of the tree. We also find a lot of important knowledge is hard to be expressed or recorded formally. This kind of tacit knowledge is based much on the experience and context, meanwhile is both more expensive and has greater potential rewards than the explicit knowledge like data and information. [6]

It is just the first step, when we want to build integrated knowledge storage as our resources. To improve the accessibility, we also should solve the problems in taxonomy. We find it's hard to give a uniform and standard classification. Even if we can give one, to let every one in the organization accept and follow it seems unimaginable

Another basic problem in the knowledge management should also be replied. How can the system tell who knows who or who knows what, and then provide the proper knowledge resource to proper person who request it. We may ask every one in the organization answer these questions when we build the system, but we can't guarantee their accuracy or timely, therefore it seems not so useful.

4. A New Concept Knowledge Management

To overcome the barriers we encountered in the design process, we have to understand the system more thoroughly and in a way more close to the reality. Here we propose a way to study and analyze the knowledge management system in a complex system view. In this section we will analyze the characteristics of knowledge management combined with the complexity theories. Meanwhile we will try to contrast it to the traditional perspectives that somewhat Utopian.

The collective theories of complexity and chaos, emerging from the scientific domains of quantum physics, theoretical biology, chemistry, and ecology, offer new perspectives to explore complex systems and fields. [7][8][9][10]Complexity science is an interdisciplinary field of study that embraces a wide range of approaches, yielding, at present, no single unified and coherent theory.[11] Non-linear dynamic systems theory, nonequilibrium thermodynamics, dissipative structures, the theory of self-organization, catastrophe theory, the theory of self-organized critically, antichaos, and chaos theory collectively refer to be complexity sciences.[12] Systems theories have exerted a profound influence on the study of understanding today's unpredictable, complex, and fast-paced organizational situation.

The first important thing we couldn't neglect is the relationship of parts and whole. Ludwig von Bertalanffy's General Systems Theory, introduced in the 1950s, explain relationships of parts to the whole as a dynamic interchange of energy, force and information. A system can be fully understood only by analyzing its parts in the context of the whole, when attention is shifted from objects to the networks of relationships among objects. [13]But the traditional knowledge analysis usually focus on the separated points and components and fail to put them in the reality related networks, so it seemed dispersed and hard to grasp.

Another thing should be noted are the concepts of linearity and nonlinearity, which is inherent in the evolving models of systems theories. In linear systems, interaction is based on one-way causality; outcomes are predictable and equilibrium conditions remain steady. In nonlinear systems, interaction is multidirectional, outcomes are unpredictable, and far-from-equilibrium conditions can undergo structural transformation. Dynamical systems are nonlinear systems that change, but from which changes in outcomes appear to bear no relationship to the changes in system input. [14][15] The knowledge business is characterized by very high unpredictability in both inputs and outputs. So we can tell in an organization, linear relations may be important for the stability, nonlinear relations should be emphasized to encourage innovation. We should aware that the nonlinear relationship in the system is not only inevitable but also the origin of creativity. If we emphasize the up-down control in the system there is a dangerous to lose the innovative capability.

5. Solve the Problems by CAS Theory

It sometimes seems as a dilemma, we want to utilize the knowledge effectively through control and management on one hand; and find it can't be controlled at all on the other hand, as neither the creative process itself, nor the new knowledge as outcome, can be planned or predicted follow a blueprint. After the analysis, we try to find a solution from a complex system perspective. We try to give some suggestions on system design and proposal a framework from a complex adaptive system view.

5.1. *Detecting Existing Knowledge Property*

To solve the problem about the codification and integration of the organization's knowledge especially tacit knowledge, we try to build an agent-orient, human and technology combined architecture. It means we respect that every person in the firm should be an adaptive agent in our system. They are the owners of existing knowledge and the creators of new knowledge.

This idea is especially useful in tacit knowledge related activities. We can store and maintain experts' information as the tacit knowledge deposit. Nowadays this procedure will be more effective and efficient, as some useful quantitative measure can be analyzed by SNA approach. SNA represents for Social Network Analysis. In other words now we acknowledge and respect experts' special importance to tacit knowledge, so instead of providing static, standard explicit knowledge, we focus on construct a distributed knowledge network. And SNA provides us effective approach to depict the status and understand it through deep quantitative analysis.

In this way, knowledge in the system is the outcome of individuals attempting to manage the inevitable tension between normative expectations (rules), individual dispositions, and local contexts. [16] So our effort to make a structured and hierarchical database for collecting and categorization changed to map the knowledge based on the users' phrase. The map breaks the boundary of departments and may be seems illogical, but is still more helpful to a user than a hypothetical knowledge model that is best understood by its creators, a rarely fully implemented. [17]

5.2. *Integrate Users' Intelligence*

Information technology can facilitate knowledge processing greatly in some way, but it can not resolve all of the problems as we have analyzed above. So we try to find a method to combine the intelligence of both technology system and human users. As users are integrated in the whole system, their operation behavior like posting, searching, updating of knowledge will be considered to improve the system's performance. We'll find users' intelligence can be effective in several aspects.

5.2.1 Knowledge Classification

Category methods are very important to knowledge management system, as it is the foundation to knowledge organization and retrieval. Some problems in system mentioned above are caused by the traditional category approaches. For example, information usually belongs to certain fixed category and the whole organization is typically tree-like.

From user-centered perspective, we propose this function be based on social tags. Tag is not a brand new concept in computer area, but recently many applications of information system show combining this technique in system will bring flexibility, convenience and even more unexpected effect. In fact there is a new term --- folksonomy[18] --- to express this approach. Capability of tagging information is provided to authors or users. Tags are the basic for information classification. Tags can be aggregated flexibly, so the category problems of ambiguous information are avoided. The category can be updated along with the massive usage. This mechanism guarantees that the current classification is most widely accepted and is not out of date.

5.2.2. Knowledge Recommendation

Classification and search engine can help users find information they need. Functions like recommendation make the system works more intelligent, in that it can provide probable useful information to users before they search. Of course, the recommendation and forecast are based on certain clues. There are lots of algorithms on this topic. Recommendations are usually made through analysis on similarity of relative users and information items. Systems can find out potential indirect connection among user and information items, so they can give useful suggestions. We can think this process as intelligence of systems. In fact, a totally perfect algorithm doesn't exist because of the complexity in human thoughts and decision. It may be not so reliable that completely relying on systems' intelligence. So we notice that effective system should combine both the intelligence of systems and that of human users. That means systems support user's collaboration. As systems are based on network, users' interactive is encouraged and reinforced. Users may maintain their friend list or interest league. So they can also get direct illumination from their friends. These two kinds of recommendation work synchronously and they can also facilitate each other. When a user build or supplement their list, he will consult to system's suggestion. When they make some choice and select in the recommendation, this kind of behavior can be recorded. It will be good feedback and useful implication to system algorism. So users' behavior does not only influence their current knowledge storage, it will also improve the system's performance.

5.2.3 .More Important Aspects Such as Diversity, Innovation...

The knowledge in the system is dynamic and near to the creator and context, so it also keeps the diversity of knowledge system. As Weick and Karl E noticed "Overload is not the problem but rather the limited variety of inputs". We welcome the diversity and also many people prefer to call the system "knowledge ecosystem". To survive and thrive in that ecosystem, companies are increasingly relying on their network of long term co-evolutionary relationships, which will be boosted by the knowledge value that their extranet adds to those relationships.

In this way our system also encourages innovation. The users are no longer passive recipients of finished ideas. The recursive and reflexive interaction between discourses and local contexts is important to understand the development of management knowledge in general; instead of "being applied" new ideas seem to trigger locally situated change processes which in turn inspire new ideas at a higher level. "In this new 'mode' of production knowledge is increasingly generated by users in the context of its application." [19]

Based on that system from the top view, we can let the market work, from the top we try to make knowledge as attractive and accessible as possible, and then observe what knowledge gets requested using what specific terms. So we can get a preferred usage and several possible synonyms for each certain knowledge request. Knowledge will bottom-up emerging. When the dispersed "knowledge center" proliferate, the high level system aims to pull together the data, organize and index them and make them easily achievable.

At last we can also start by understanding information holders and their relationships to information by watching what they publish and how they use information. It will help us to find the knowledge supplier and demander so help the system build a connection between them and realize our objective to provide proper knowledge to proper persons. Obviously this connection will be dynamic and updated in good time. We can so realize the distribution of knowledge in the system effectively and efficiently.

6. Conclusion and Future Work

In the paper we first analyze the necessary of knowledge management in the e-business widespread age. Then give some example of difficulties in practice when we try to design and construct a KM system. Through a system analysis we find organizations obsessed with extracting and measuring knowledge will not have much to measure unless they shift the focus of their knowledge initiatives to develop an open culture of communication and collaboration that is supportive to the sharing of innovative work and business practices. At last we try to design the system as a complex adaptive system (CAS) of people in communities co-located in the same space, physical and/or virtual, in which they cultivate relationships, tools, and practices for creating, integrating, sharing, and using knowledge. There are some principles to design bottom-up knowledge architecture in the last section, and that solve many difficulties.

Of course there are still many related works left for further study and research. The knowledge management focuses have evolved in the past years. The early technology-centric form focused on information sharing, information repositories, and intellectual capital accounting. The second generation brought in the concepts of tacit knowledge, social learning, situated and embedded knowledge, and communities of practice. There are still some areas need more studies in the early generations, for example intellectual capital accounting that can help us compare the invest and output for the system, and information search technology that is helpful to the accessibility of knowledge. Nowadays more demands appear in the research like the link between knowing and action, the organization structure and social network analysis, which are useful for a more practical knowledge management. The new generation knowledge management will require capability to manage change, social conflict and revolution. It will also require new institutional foundations that make productive conflict resolution possible. It will therefore also require that we understand better the cultural basis of knowing and social activity, as well as the ways in which social and organizational learning lead to new social practices. [20]

References

1. Peter F Drucker, From Capitalism to Knowledge Society, Post-Capitalist Society in The Knowledge Economy, ed. Dele Neef, (1993).
2. Grant Miles, Raymond E. Perrone Miles and Leif Vincenzo Edvinsson, Some Conceptual and

Research Barriers to the Utilization of Knowledge, *California Management Review* **40(3)**, (1998).
3. Philip B. Evans and Thomas S Wurster, Strategy and the new Economics of Information, *Harvard Business Review*, (1997).
4. Sarah Cliffe, Knowledge management: The well-connected business, *Harvard Business Review* **76(4)**, 20-21, (1998).
5. R E. Snow Miles, C C. Mathews, J A. Miles, G. Coleman and HJ Jr, Organizing in the knowledge age: Anticipating the cellular form, *The Academy of Management Executive* **11(4)**, 7-20 (1997).
6. Michael J Earl, Knowledge as Strategy: Reflections on Skandia international and Shorko Films, Strategic Information Systems: A European Perspective, Knowledge in Organizations ed. Laurence Prusak (1994).
7. S. A. Kauffman, At home in the universe: The search for laws of self-organization and complexity, Viking, (1995).
8. B. Mandelbrot, Towards a second stage of indeterminism in science, *Interdisciplinary Science Reviews* **12**, 117-127 (1987).
9. I. Prigogine, The end of certainty, New York: The Free Press, (1996).
10. H. R. Maturana and F. J. Varela, The tree of knowledge: The biological roots of human understanding, 263 (1987).
11. M. Cohen, Commentary on the organization science special issue on complexity, *Organization Science* **10(3)**, 373-376 (1999).
12. K M. Mathews, M C. White and R G Long, Why Study the Complexity Sciences in the Social Sciences? *Human Relations* **52(4)**, 439 – 462 (1999).
13. M. J. Hatch, Organization theory: Modern, symbolic, and postmodern perspectives, Oxford University Press, (1997).
14. R. Lewin, Complexity: Life at the edge of chaos. , Macmillan Pub. Co. ; Maxwell Macmillan Canada ; Maxwell Macmillan International, (x, 208), New York Toronto New York, (1992).
15. Mary A. Ferdig, Complexity Theories: Perspectives for the Social Construction of Organizational Transformation.
16. Tsoukas Haidimos, The Firm as a Distributed Knowledge System: A Constructionist Approach, *Strategic Management Journal* **17**, 11 – 25 (1996).
17. Thomas H. Davenport, Some Principles of Knowledge Management, Posted April 10, (1996).
18. Adam Mathes. Folksonomies - Cooperative Classification and Communication Through Shared Metadata [EB/OL].
19. http://www.adammathes.com/academic/computer-mediated- communication /folksonomies.html (2004).
20. Harry Scarbrough, and Jacky Swan, Knowledge Management and the Management Fashion Perspective, Refereed Paper submitted to *the British Academy of Management Conference*, "Managing Diversity", (1999).
21. Ilkka Tuomi, The Future of Knowledge Management, *Lifelong Learning in Europe (LLinE)*, **7(2)**, 69-79 (2002).

FINANCIAL PERFORMANCE AND ENTERPRISE RESOURCE PLANNING IMPLEMENTATION: A STUDY OF MANUFACTURERS IN TAIWAN

CHIEN-WEN SHEN

Department of Logistics Management, National Kaohsiung First University of Science and Technology No. 2, Jhuoyue Rd., Kaohsiung City, 811, Taiwan

Even though Enterprise Resource Planning (ERP) systems are increasingly implemented in today's business environment, results of ERP investments remain debatable. This study would like to investigate the financial impacts of ERP systems for the manufacturing sector in Taiwan. Findings demonstrate that most of performance indexes show no significant differences after ERP installation. Only two indexes such as "Inventory Turnover" and "Average Number Days Inventory in Stock" show significant improvement after 2 or 3 year ERP implementation. Other indexes such as "Return on Equity" and "Return on Assets" even have worse performance than before. This outcome implies that ERP systems have not shown significant benefits with respect to financial performance under our short-term observations. It may take longer period to see real financial advantages like the ERP vendors claimed.

1. Introduction

Over the last decade, enterprise resource planning (ERP) has emerged as an important information technology solution for many organizations that seek to streamline and integrate operation processes and information flows. According to AMR Research annual report in 2005, the global market for ERP software became a $23.6 billion business in 2004. The five biggest ERP vendors - SAP, Oracle (which bought PeopleSoft and J.D. Edwards), Sage Group, Microsoft's Business Solutions Group, and SSA Global account for almost 73 percent of total market revenues. AMR also predicted that the ERP sector will see a 6 to 7 percent compound annual growth rate from 2006 through 2009. These commercially ERP software packages promise seamless integration of all information flows: financial and accounting, human resource, operations, supply chain, and customer information, providing a unified view of the business, encompassing all functions and departments by establishing a single processed, monitored, and reported [16]. Therefore, ERP has become an important software product line since the mid-1990s.

In Taiwan, the ERP implementation rate and ERP outsourcing rate was 60.9% and 67.8% respectively. Meanwhile, Data Systems Consulting (DSC), SAP, and Oracle accounted for 52 percent of the ERP market in Taiwan [11]. Even though SAP dominates the worldwide ERP market, 476 of the top 1000 manufacturers in Taiwan adopt DSC products [1]. Another study conducted by Industrial Development Bureau in 2005 [7] indicates that there were 37.6% of the electronic information companies have implemented ERP systems. However, the ERP penetration rates for other traditional manufacturing sectors such as metal machinery and material chemical industry were only 10% around. This implies that many traditional manufacturing companies still hesitate about their ERP investments.

Cost is probably the most important concern for companies seeking ERP system to synergize their corporate resources. Based on the ERP survey from Meta Group in 2002, the average costs of ERP ownership were $15 millions. The average cost per user per year could be as high as $20,000. Another survey by Forrester Research reveals that 54% of responding organizations took more than 2 years to implement ERP [19]. Despite the expense and time-consuming, the returns of ERP implementations are not always positive. FoxMeyer Drug went bankrupt in 1996 and files a US$ 500 million lawsuit against SAP, an ERP software provider, blaming SAP for its woes [13]. Dow Chemical wrote off close to half a billion dollars when it switched from a mainframe-based ERP to a client/server architecture ERP system [12]. Some of the biggest ERP system implementation failures occur because the new software's capabilities and needs are mismatched with the organization's existing business processes and procedures [15]. Although the success of ERP implementation is not guaranteed, we also see many fruitful cases. For examples, the Daimler-Benz and

Chrysler merger was able to shave close to ten years in its integration effort by using SAP [17]. Owens Corning saved $50 million in logistics, materials management, and sourcing through its ERP [16]. Since the return of ERP investment is highly uncertain, it's worth discussing the real effect of ERP installation from different perspectives.

The aim of this paper is to analyze the impact of ERP implementation on financial performance for the manufacturers in Taiwan. Section 2 starts with literature review of ERP impacts. We then describe the financial performance indexes and methodology used in our study under section 3. Analysis results are discussed in section 4. Finally, we conclude our findings in section 5.

2. Literature Review of ERP Impact

ERP has been successful in many corporations and yet many others have struggled with their investments. Hitt et al. [5] found that firms that invest in ERP tend to show higher performance across a wide variety of financial metrics. Even though there is a slowdown in business performance and productivity shortly after the implementation, financial markets consistently reward the adopters with higher market valuation. Meanwhile, Mabert, Soni, and Venkataramanan [8] noted that companies of different sizes approach ERP implementations differently across a range of issues. Also, the benefits differ by company size. Larger companies report improvements in financial measures whereas smaller companies report better performance in manufacturing and logistics. Hunton et al. [6] examined the longitudinal impact of ERP adoption on firm performance by 63 firms with peer firms that had not adopted ERP systems. Results indicate that return on assets, return on investment, and asset turnover were significantly better over a 3-year period for adopters, as compared to non-adopters. Besides, Chand et al. [2] provided a balanced-scorecard based framework for valuing the strategic contributions of an ERP system. Using a successful SAP implementation by a major international aircraft engine manufacturing and service organization as a case study, this paper illustrates that an ERP system does indeed impacts the business objectives of the firm and derives a new innovative ERP framework for valuing the strategic impacts of ERP systems.

Most recent studies from Hendricks et al. [4] documented the effect of investments in ERP, supply chain management, and customer relationship management systems on a firm's long-term stock price performance and profitability measures. In the case of ERP systems, they found some evidence of improvements in profitability but not in stock returns. The results for improvements in profitability were stronger in the case of early adopters of ERP systems. Mabert et al. [10] compared and evaluated the use of regression analysis, logistic (logit) models, discriminate analysis and data envelopment analysis (DEA), for empirical data from a survey of ERP implementations in the US manufacturing sector. Their analysis illustrated that regression based tools are more valuable in developing predictive models, while logit and discriminate models are powerful in classifying the outcomes. Wieder et al. [18] conducted a survey on several aspects of organizational performance in companies that adopted ERPS and/or SCMS and the respective control groups. Their results contradict the claims of ERPS vendors insofar as no significant performance differences were found between ERPS adopters and non-adopters, either at the business process level, or at the overall firm level.

Relative research for the ERP impact in Taiwan also continues to thrive. Tsai [14] analyzed 28 companies who used ERP system in Taiwan. They found ERP systems improve employee productivity and raise the sales significantly. Wu and Wang [20] investigated different ERP implementation patterns and outcomes on a survey of two representative samples of "large size enterprise vs. medium size enterprise" and "electronics & science industry vs. traditional industry". Chiu et al. [3] presented an empirical research aiming to measure how business efficiencies in terms of scale efficiency and technical efficiency are influenced by the implementation of the ERP system. Six cases of large-scale companies in Taiwan were investigated. Data envelopment analysis and analytic hierarchy process are the two main analytic methods used in this measurement. From the above literature review, we see different studies having various measurements and outcomes. The success of ERP implementation also depends on many factors such as company size, region, and measurement approach. Comparing to previous studies, our research tempts to focus on the analysis of performance difference between the financial indexes before and after ERP system implementation.

3. Methodology

We started our study by collecting the data of ERP on-line year for those ERP-implemented manufacturers in Taiwan by contacting the big-3 ERP vendors (DSC, SAP, and Oracle). Here we define the on-line year as the year that the first module of ERP system is on line for daily operations. Due to business confidential, the big-3 vendors only released part of their customer lists for our academic research. From these lists, we skipped those manufacturers that were not publicly traded and then randomly selected a sample of 25 companies for further investigation. Since we want to analyze the financial performance differences before and after the ERP on-line year, we selected 10 financial performance indexes that are commonly used for enterprise financial evaluation in Financial Supervisory Commission in Taiwan. These indexes are: "Receivables Turnover" (RECT), "Average Number Days Receivables Outstanding" (RECD), "Inventory Turnover" (INVT), "Average Number Days Inventory in Stock" (INVD), "Fixed Assets Turnover" (FIXT), "Total Assets Turnover" (TOTT), "Revenue Growth Rate" (RGR), "Net Profit Rate" (NPR), "Return on Equity" (ROE), and "Return on Assets" (ROA). Financial statements of manufacturer samples during the period of 3 years before and after the ERP on-line year were collected for performance differences tests.

In order to evaluate the ERP impact on financial performance, our study used paired t test to check whether there exists a difference between i-year before and i-year after the ERP on-line year within each manufacturer for corresponding financial indexes (denoted as $\mu_{D,i}^{Index}$), where year i = 1, 2, and 3, *Index* = RECT, RECD, …, ROA. Let l denote the variable of the ERP on-line year for each manufacturer. Here in our approach, the data of i-year before (after) the ERP on-line year also include data of previous years. That is, the data of i-year before the ERP on-line year l include data of year $l - i$, …, $l - 1$, and the data of the i-year after "on-line" year l include data of year $l + 1$, …, $l + i$. Because all the manufacturers in our sample are publicly listed companies, our financial performance indexes can be retrieved from their financial statements. We first conducted hypothesis tests to see whether the difference existed in each financial index for i = 1, 2, and 3. When the difference of performance index is significantly positive, it implies that the financial performance before ERP on-line year is better than the one after ERP installation if larger index indicates better performance. Because paired t test is under the assumption that the sample of differences is normally distributed, we also conducted Anderson-Darling approach for normality testing. If the underlying sample did not follow a normal distribution, we would not perform the corresponding paired t tests for further analysis.

4. Data Analysis

In Section 4.1, we first present the descriptive statistics of the financial performance indexes i-year before and i-year after the ERP on-line year for all observations. Next, the results of hypothesis tests are discussed in Section 4.2. These results can infer whether the ERP system has positive impact on financial performances.

4.1. *Descriptive Statistics of Financial Indexes*

Table 1 shows the descriptive statistics of financial indexes based on the financial statements of $(l - 1)$-year and $(l + 1)$-year from our sample manufacturers, where l denote the ERP on-line year for each manufacturer. As we can see that most financial indexes show better average performance before ERP implementation except RECD, INVD, FIXT, and RGR. This may suggest that initial setup and maintenance costs deteriorate the financial health at the very beginning year of ERP implementation. As we know that the average cost of ERP ownership is $15 millions and the average cost per user per year could be as high as $20,000 according to the ERP survey by Meta Group in 2002, it's really a financial burden for most companies.

Table 1. Descriptive statistics of financial indexes between 1-year before and 1-year after ERP on-line year.

Financial Index	1-year before on-line year		1-year after on-line year	
	Mean	Standard Deviation	Mean	Standard Deviation
RECT	5.31	1.99	5.07	1.61
RECD	77.69	36.03	77.04	30.30
INVT	7.69	5.36	7.22	3.64
INVD	68.40	50.90	64.73	39.87
FIXT	4.02	3.83	4.45	4.67
TOTT	0.85	0.56	0.82	0.63
RGR	20.00	33.79	29.83	30.08
NPR	21.82	18.46	12.14	15.46
ROE	12.37	12.80	8.66	12.06
ROA	14.43	12.00	8.43	9.40

Table 2 summarizes the means of performance indexes i-year before and i-year after the ERP on-line year (i = 2, 3). Even though INVT and INVD show better average performance after ERP implementation, we still need to conduct hypothesis tests to confirm our inference. The improvement of INVT and INVD may be resulted from the basic capabilities of ERP systems such as integrating activities across functionality and executing best practices for corresponding business processes. However, most of other financial indexes show better average performance before the ERP implementation. In addition to the cause of heavy initial investments, worse performance after implementation may be resulted from our definition of on-line year, which is the year that first module goes live for daily operations. According to a survey by Forrester Research revealed that 54% of responding organizations took more than 2 years to implement ERP, 3-year observations after the on-line year may not have enough time length to demonstrate significant advantages. In section 4.2, we will perform necessary hypothesis tests to understand the impact of ERP implementation on financial performance.

Table 2. Comparisons of financial indexes.

Financial Index	2-year before and after on-line year		3-year before and after on-line year	
	Mean (before)	Mean (After)	Mean (before)	Mean (After)
RECT	4.61	4.72	5.12	5.05
RECD	79.11	78.70	69.63	72.41
INVT	6.01	6.68	5.72	6.49
INVD	71.28	64.09	59.34	54.74
FIXT	3.39	3.68	1.31	1.17
TOTT	0.80	0.68	0.69	0.59
RGR	30.72	26.84	30.40	25.46
NPR	18.93	13.12	20.18	9.30
ROE	23.13	12.01	21.94	6.99
ROA	17.66	9.15	16.53	6.45

4.2. *Hypothesis Tests*

Our discussions are going to separate into three subsections. In each subsection, we first perform Anderson-Darling (A-D) normality tests to check whether the underlying samples satisfy normal distribution. If the answer is yes, we then conduct the paired t tests to understand whether there is a significant difference between i-year before and i-year after the ERP on-line year for each financial index (H_0: $\mu_{D,i}^{Index} = 0$), where i = 1, 2, 3. If the difference exists, we further check the difference is positive or negative. Findings would help us understand the impact of ERP implementation on financial performances.

4.2.1. 1-year before and 1-year after ERP on-line year

The data we used for analysis is the difference of each financial index between 1-year before and 1-year after ERP implementation. We found all the samples of differences follow normal distributions according to Anderson-Darling tests. Paired t tests show no significant difference between 1-year before and 1-year after the ERP on-line year for most financial indexes except ROE and ROA (see Table 3). We further analyze the t statistic of null hypothesis $\mu_{D,i}^{Index} > 0$ when index = ROE and ROA. Significantly positive values of t statistic (3.00 and 3.03 for ROE and ROA respectively) imply that the financial performance of ROE and ROA are significantly better before ERP implementation.

Table 3. Results of normality test and paired t test (1-year before and 1-year after ERP on-line year).

Financial Index	p-value of A-D test	p-value of paired t test
RECT	0.250	0.327
RECD	0.313	0.872
INVT	0.181	0.488
INVD	0.978	0.423
FIXT	0.373	0.277
TOTT	0.748	0.559
RGR	0.518	0.342
NPR	0.354	0.101
ROE	0.625	0.006*
ROA	0.886	0.006*

*Significant at $\alpha = 0.05$

4.2.2. 2-year Before and 2-year After ERP On-line Year

Similarly, Table 4 summarizes the results of A-D tests and pair t tests for each financial index between 2-year before and 2-year after ERP on-line year. We found the sample of differences for index FIXT does not follow normal distribution and therefore we do not conduct further t test for this index. Additionally, the results of paired t tests show that indexes INVT, INVD, TOTT, NPR, ROE, and ROA have significant difference between 2-year before and 2-year after the ERP on-line year. Hence we want to investigate whether the difference is positive or negative for these indexes. Table 5 summarizes the test results of null hypothesis

$\mu_{D,i}^{Index} > 0$ for indexes INVT, INVD, TOTT, NPR, ROE, and ROA. It shows that only INVT and INVD perform better after ERP implementation (because lower INVD is better). On the other hand, indexes TOTT, NPR, ROE, and ROA show better results before ERP implementation.

Table 4. Results of normality test and paired t test (2-year before and 2-year after ERP on-line year).

Financial Index	p-value of A-D test	p-value of paired t test
RECT	0.189	0.606
RECD	0.858	0.909
INVT	0.668	0.049*
INVD	0.800	0.037*
FIXT	0.027*	-
TOTT	0.567	0.002*
RGR	0.926	0.655
NPR	0.354	0.001*
ROE	0.122	0.000*
ROA	0.202	0.000*

Table 5. Results of hypothesis test (H$_0$: $\mu_{D,i}^{Index}>0$).

Financial Index	t statistic	p-value
INVT	-2.04*	0.024*
INVD	2.15	0.981
TOTT	3.40	0.999
NPR	3.87	1.000
ROE	5.23	1.000
ROA	5.65	1.000

4.2.3. 3-year Before and 3-year After ERP On-line year

Finally, we analyze whether there is a difference between 3-year before and 3-year after ERP implementation for each financial index. We found samples of differences for indexes TOTT and NPR do not follow normal distributions. No further tests will be conducted for these two indexes. Next, we perform paired t tests for the remaining indexes (see Table 6). Our investigation shows that there exists no significant difference between 3-year before and 3-year after the ERP on-line year for most financial indexes except INVT, ROE and ROA. Further investigation was conducted to check whether the difference is positive or negative for these indexes. Table 7 summarizes the test results of null hypothesis $\mu_{D,i}^{Index} > 0$ for indexes INVT, ROE, and ROA. It shows that only INVT perform better after ERP implementation. On the other hand, index ROE and ROA show better results before ERP implementation, which are consistent with the results from subsection 4.2.1 and 4.2.2. Heavy initial ERP investments could be one of the important reasons for this phenomenon.

Table 6. Results of normality test and paired t test (3-year before and 3-year after ERP on-line year).

Financial Index	p-value of A-D test	p-value of paired t test
RECT	0.179	0.796
RECD	0.922	0.477
INVT	0.114	0.041*
INVD	0.888	0.146
FIXT	0.690	0.263
TOTT	0.063**	-
RGR	0.985	0.543
NPR	0.032*	-
ROE	0.768	0.000*
ROA	0.392	0.000*

*Significant at $\alpha = 0.05$, **Significant at $\alpha = 0.1$

Table 7. Results of hypothesis test (H$_0$: $\mu_{D,i}^{Index}>0$).

Financial Index	t statistic	p-value
INVT	-2.14	0.02*
ROE	5.68	1.00
ROA	6.23	1.00

4.3. *Analysis Summary*

The above hypothesis test results are summarized in Table 8. It shows that index ROE and ROA have better performance before ERP implementation. Most financial indexes show no difference between 1-year before and 1-year after ERP implementation. But it's interesting to see that more indexes have better results 2 years before ERP installation. As our previous literature review shows that average ERP implementation took 23 months to complete [16], it may imply that ERP could cause negative impacts on financial performance for the first 2 years. Finally, the only improvements from ERP implementation are inventory related indicators. This suggests ERP systems could lead to inventory reductions because staff can access up-to-date and accurate data for better inventory management, although the improvement may have to wait till 2 to 3 years of ERP implementation.

Table 8. Summary of indexes that differ significantly after ERP implementation

Financial Index	1-year before	1-year after
ROE	Better	-
ROA	Better	-
Financial Index	2-year before	2-year after
INVT	-	Better
INVD	-	Better
TOTT	Better	-
NPR	Better	-
ROE	Better	-
ROA	Better	-
Financial Index	3-year before	3-year
INVT	-	Better
ROE	Better	-
ROA	Better	-

5. Conclusion

Our study provides evidence that the benefits of ERP systems may not be seen quickly in the early years. It takes time and people to work together for matching the organization's existing business processes. Because our investigation only compares 3 years before and after the year that the first ERP module is installed for daily operations, it's interesting for future research to conduct similar investigation for longer period. Even though our study does not find positive impact on most financial indexes from ERP implementation, we found benefits existing on inventory related indexes. This observation may encourage manufacturers to seriously evaluate the possibility of ERP systems if inventory reduction is critical for them. But decline of financial performance seems unavoidable according to our analysis. As the growth rate of ERP sales starts to slow down, ERP vendors need to clear the doubts and concerns more proactively in order to keep their market growing.

References

1. Next generation ERP killer applications, *iThome*, 216 (2005).
2. D. Chand, G. Hachey, J. Hunton, V. Owhoso and S. Vasudevan, A balanced scorecard based framework for assessing the strategic impacts of ERP systems, *Computers in Industry* **56(6)**, 558-572 (2005).
3. R. K. Chiu, S. C. L. Koh and A. Gunasekaran, An empirical analysis of business efficiency from the implementation of enterprise information system, *International Journal of Business Information Systems* **1(4)**, 387-407 (2006).
4. K. B. Hendricks, V. R. Singhal and J. K. Stratman, The impact of enterprise systems on corporate performance: A study of ERP, SCM, and CRM system implementations, *Journal of Operations Management* **25(1)**, 65-82 (2007).
5. L. M. Hitt, D. J. Wu and X. Zhou, Investment in enterprise resource planning: Business impact and productivity measures, *Journal of Management Information Systems* **19(1)**, 71-98 (2002).
6. J. E.Hunton, B. Lippincott and J. L. Reck, Enterprise resource planning systems: Comparing firm performance of adopters and nonadopters, *International Journal of Accounting Information Systems* **4(3)**, 165-184 (2003).
7. Industrial Development Bureau, *Development project of the information service industry in Taiwan*, (2005).
8. V. A. Mabert, A. Soni and M. A. Venkataramanan, The impact of organization size on enterprise resource planning (ERP) implementations in the US manufacturing sector, *Omega* **31(3)**, 235-246 (2003).
9. V. A. Mabert, A. Soni and M. V. Venkataramanan, Enterprise resource planning: Managing the implementation process, *European Journal of Operational Research* **146**, 302-314 (2003).
10. V. A. Mabert, A. Soni and M. V. Venkataramanan, Model based interpretation of survey data: A case study of enterprise resource planning implementations, *Mathematical and Computer Modelling* **44(1-2)**, 16-29 (2006).
11. S. Shi, *TSIA company report*, Taiwan Securities (2005).
12. T. Stein, SAP Installation Scuttle - Unisource Cites Internal Problems for $168m Write-off, *Information Week*, 34 (January 26, 1998).
13. S. Tiazkun, SAP Sued for $500 Million, *Computer Reseller News*, 42–44 (August 26, 1998).
14. W. C. Tsai, *Performance Measurement of Enterprise Resource Planning*, Master thesis, National Taiwan University (2001).
15. E. Turban, J. E. Aronson and T. P. Liang, *Decision Support Systems and Intelligent Systems*, Upper Saddle River, Pearson Education (2005).
16. E. J. Umble and M. M. Umble, Avoiding ERP implementation failure, *Industrial Management* **44(1)**, 25-33 (2002).
17. B. Wallace, Now it's Cost-Cutting Time, *Computerworld* **32(47)**, 1 and 82 (1998).
18. B. Wieder, P. Booth, Z. P. Matolcsy and M. L. Ossimitz, The impact of ERP systems on firm and business process performance, *Journal of*

Enterprise Information Management **19(1)**, 13-29 (2006).
19. B. Worthen, Nestle's ERP Odyssey, *CIO*, (May 15, 2002).
20. J. H. Wu and Y. M. Wang, Enterprise Resource Planning Experience in Taiwan: An Empirical Study and Comparative Analysis, *Proceedings of the 36th Hawaii International Conference on System Sciences*, (2002).

USER AWARENESS AND ATTITUDE TO HOME WLAN SECURITY

FRODE EIKA SANDNES
Fac. Eng., Oslo University College, P.O. Box St. Olavs plas
N-0130 Oslo, Norway

UGO SANTUCCI
Fac. Eng., Oslo University College, P.O. Box St. Olavs plas
N-0130 Oslo, Norway

YO-PING HUANG
Comp. Sci. & Eng., Tatung University, 40 ChungShan N. Rd., Sec. 3
Taipei, Taiwan

Recent advances in technology have led to the wide availability of low cost wireless networking equipment. An increasing number of households are acquiring wireless networks. The low cost and convenience of not having wires around the house is appealing to users who want a tidy and clutter-free home environment. Simultaneously, there has been a growing attention towards security in wireless networks – both home networks and public networks. This study sets out to fill this gap through a quantitative and qualitative investigation. The results suggests that wireless equipment manufacturers can contribute to overall wireless security by providing simple security oriented user interfaces where options that violate best practices are hidden from the users.

1. WLAN and Convenience

An increasing number of households around the world have access to the Internet and many of these have some form of broadband access [1, 2]. Recently, WLAN (wireless local area network) equipment has become very affordable, fast and reliable.

The WLANs are attractive for a number of reasons. The absence of physical wires is both aesthetically pleasing and convenient. The average home has limited space and its residents usually want an environment not cluttered by wires. The lack of wires means that equipment can be placed nearly everywhere and the range of current wireless routers is sufficiently large to cover an entire apartment, including all its rooms.

Most of the wireless routers that can be bought today will work straight out of the box. This is convenient for most users who expect immediate deployment of their newly acquired equipment. If one walks around a residential neighborhoods with a WLAN enabled device, such as a PDA, it is common to see WLAN access points with the SSID "default". Such SSIDs indicate that the router is simply connected to the nearest Internet socket provided by the ISP (Internet Service Provider) and all default wireless router settings are used. The default is to impose no security (with the exception of the SSID itself which indicates to the client where access point is connected to). The consequences of this lack of security can be severe.

1.1. *WLAN threats and hacking tools*

Recently, there has been a focus on wireless security, and much have been written about WLAN security [1, 3]. The main issues include unconsolidated eavesdropping, denial of service attacks and man in the middle attacks [1]. With unencrypted traffic anyone within range of the WLAN network is able to eavesdrop on the communication and record all the contents. This is obviously not desirable when communicating sensitive information, such as credit card numbers. Furthermore, with an open network anyone within range can potentially access all the computing resources on the network, such as inspecting contents of files and e-mails. Finally, perhaps the most severe threat is identity theft whereupon someone in range can pretend to be the user and do various illegal transactions such as downloading child pornography. The owner of the network will be accountable as it is the owner's Internet line that has been used to commit the crime.

To overcome these problems most routers are equipped with a set of security mechanisms. Encryption is used to prevent eavesdropping and authentication is used to limit access to the network. First generation WLAN equipment was equipped with WEP (Wireless Equivalent Protocol) which is considered unsafe. Second generation equipment is equipped with WPA (Wi-Fi Protected Access) which is considered safer than WEP, but still has problems. New technology has emerged such as TKIP and AES [1].

Moreover, filters can be set up such that only machines with certain MAC-addresses are allowed to access the WLAN (each computer is associated with a unique MAC address). Another challenge is that shops do not always provide the necessary customer support.

When setting up a new access point experts recommend four basic steps [1]. First, broadcasting of the SSID should be turned off. Second, MAC based access control should be activated. Third, encryption should be enabled, and finally the power level of the access point should be lowered to prevent connections from outside the specified boundary. One way to achieve this is to set the maximum allowable communication rates to 5.5 Mbps.

There are several freely available security tools available that can be used for compromising the security of wireless networks. Some of these include AirCrack [4] which allows the wireless traffic to be monitored and WEP keys to be cracked. Another tool is WarLinux [5], a preconfigured linux installation that is designed for checking the strength of wireless networks.

1.2. *Users and technology*

Clearly, one needs certain technical insight to secure a wireless network. It is unrealistic to expect ordinary users to acquire sufficient insight. The responsibility of ensuring adequate security therefore falls onto the equipment manufacturers and software providers.

There are several interesting studies on how novice users relate to security. For instance, it has been demonstrated that novice users find it difficult to conduct an encryption task on a message [6] and hence find it difficult to protect e-mail messages. Another security feature that most users get in direct contact with is passwords and several studies have addressed how users compromise password security [7, 8]. Strategies for making more usable password systems include pass faces [9] and images [10]. Attitude to security has also been studied and it has been found that age is an important factor as younger users are more pragmatic about security than more senior users [11].

Studies from different areas of computer science repeatedly confirm that technology has different effects on different user groups. Especially, in the field of human computer interaction (HCI) it has been found that age has an impact on mobile phone usage [12]. Young users are more comfortable with the technology than older users, and young adults are again better than children. Gender has also been found to affect how users interact with technology [13]. Male users perform better at spatial tasks relying on spatial memory than females and that females are more emotionally driven. Finally, practice results in learning and consequently better performance [14].

The hypothesis of this study is that different user groups have different attitudes towards wireless technology. It is also relevant to study this diverse set of groups as an increasing portion of the general population is setting up wireless networks in their homes.

2. Quantitative Study

The quantitative study was conducted using a questionnaire. The purpose was to acquire general trends regarding user awareness and attitude towards wireless security.

2.1. *Method*

A total of 38 subjects completed the questionnaire. The subjects were hand-picked to widely represent gender and age. Subjects were mostly recruited from the international student population at Oslo University College.

The questionnaire comprised 20 multiple choice questions. The number of alternatives ranged from two to fourteen options. The questionnaires were printed on six sheets of one-sided paper and the text was written in English.

Subjects were contacted on a one-to-one basis and completed under the supervision of the second author. Some of the questionnaires were collected via e-mail and the others in person on hardcopies. It took about 10-15 minutes to complete the questionnaire.

2.2. *General trends*

Table 1 shows the general opinions about what a WLAN is. A total of 76.9 % of the subjects correctly identified a WLAN as a network that allows wireless communication. Interestingly, 7.7% of the subjects associate WLAN with laptops. This is understandable from the fact that laptop computers are the computer item most often connected to a wireless network. Surprisingly, 5.1% indicated that they did not know what a WLAN is. It is our guess that this is connected to unfamiliarity with the WLAN acronym WLAN and not necessarily the concept of wireless communication.

Table 2 shows the breakdown of responses to the trick question "Is wireless communication safer than communication through a wire?". Here, 43.6% of the subjects correctly reject this claim, while only 2.6% support it. Surprisingly, a massive 23.1% admit that they do not know, 12.8% claim that there is no difference and 17.9% think that a firewall will provide the necessary security.

Table 1. Responses to the question "What is a WLAN?".

What is a WLAN?	%
Net. that allows wireless communication	76.9
Accumulates on antennas	10.3
A way to get Internet access with a laptop	7.7
Don't know	5.1

Table 2. Responses relating to factors of security.

Wireless com. safer than through a wire?	%
Wireless is not safe	43.6
Don't know	23.1
Only unsafe without a firewall	17.9
There is no difference	12.8
Wireless is safer than cable	2.6

Based on these results we conclude that nearly 50% of the respondents have a correct fundamental understanding of wireless security while over half of the respondents have a distorted and inaccurate understanding of the problem.

Table 3 reveals the respondents' conception of the disadvantages of unencrypted traffic. Here 51.3% correctly perceive eavesdropping as a potential problem. Note that the term eavesdropping was replaced with an explanatory phrase on the questionnaire to make the option more clear to the less technical savvy respondents. An alarming 30.8% indicated that they do not know the disadvantages of unencrypted traffic. A total of 17.9% of the subjects indicated that unencrypted traffic makes the system more vulnerable to virus attacks. Although this is true in theory, it is less of a problem in practice. It is very surprising that none of the subject indicated computer hijacking as a potential danger of unencrypted traffic. Note that a more elaborate explanation of computer hijacking was used in the questionnaires.

Table 3. The role of a secure communication channel.

Disadvantages of unencrypted traffic?	%
Eavesdropping	51.3
Don't know	30.8
Virus easy access	17.9
Other	2.6
Computer hijacking	0.0

Table 4 enumerates elements that provide security according to the subjects. The results show that about a quarter of the subjects view WPA, WEP and VPN (Virtual Private Network) as technologies that provide security. The more recent WPA technology is also ranked before more dated WEP technology. A total of 17.9% of the subjects indicate that they do not know. Of the more ambiguous and misunderstood security practices included 20.6% of the subjects that username and password protection adds security, 17.9% believe that using a University WLAN is safe ("its provided by the university so it must be safe"), 5.1% believe using a Apple Machintosh computer is safe and 5.1% believe that installing the most recent Microsoft Windows XP service pack will do the same.

Table 4. Elements that provide security.

Elements that provide security?	%
WPA	28.2
WEP	25.6
VPN	23.1
Username and password protection	20.5
Use a university WLAN	17.9
Don't know	17.9
Other	5.1
Newest XP service pack	5.1
A Machintosh computer	5.1

2.3. *Effect of gender*

The largest cross-group difference was observed with respect to gender. Table 5 shows the breakdown of self-assessed Internet skills. There is a clear difference between males and females. Males express more confidence than females as 38% of the males view themselves as expert Internet users, while only 23% of the females viewed themselves as experts. Similarly, 50% of all males claimed to have "some" Internet skills, while only 23% of females did so. However, females were in majority (58%) in terms of having "little" Internet skills, while only 8% males thought the same.

Table 5. Self assessed Internet skills.

Level	male	female
expert	38.5	23.1
knows some	50.0	23.1
knows little	7.7	53.8
not an expert	3.8	0.0

Table 6. Awareness to threats.

Awareness	male	female
aware of threats	30.8	7.7
knows a little	34.6	30.8
do not know	30.8	53.8
don't know	3.8	7.7

Table 6 shows the subjects' self assessed awareness of wireless security threats. Again, males indicated a stronger awareness of wireless security threats than females as 31% males and only 8% females indicated awareness of wireless security threats. The males and females where approximately equally divided on knowing a little about security threats (35% males and 31% females) and females where in majority for the group that indicated no awareness (54% females and 31% males).

Table 7. Have installed WLAN?

Installed WLAN	male	female
Once	57.7	7.7
Many times	3.8	0.0
Tried but failed	7.7	15.4
Never	26.9	76.9
Not interested	3.8	0.0

Table 7 shows the gender breakdown with respect to practical experience with setting up a wireless network. Clearly, males express more familiarity with setting up a wireless network than females as a massive 58% males claim to have set up a wireless network once versus only 8% females. Next, 77% females reported never having installed a wireless network compared to 27% of the males. Only 4% males had set up a wireless network more than once. Next, 15% females and 8% males had attempted setting up a wireless network, but failed.

Table 8. How users handle difficulties.

Handling difficulties	male	female
pay technician	7.7	15.4
keep trying	46.2	0.0
ask a friend	34.6	76.9
Don't know	3.8	7.7
blame the manual	0.0	0.0
other	11.5	0.0

Table 8 shows how males and females would tackle difficulties while installing a wireless network. The general trend is that males report a willingness to try themselves until they are successful (46% males, 0% females), while females are more likely to seek help. Most subjects would ask a friend (77% females, 35% males). Others would be willing to pay a technician to complete the job (15% females, 8% males).

2.4. *Effect of age*

Results for the different age groups are similar to the ones obtained for the genders. However, there was not much effect of age between the young age groups, i.e. 21-25 and 26-30 years of age. There are generally more distinctive differences between subjects that are 21-30 and 31-50 years of age.

Table 9. Age breakdown of installing WLAN.

Installed WLAN	21-25	26-30	31-50
Once	50.0	53.8	0.0
Many times	5.6	0.0	0.0
Failed	0.0	7.7	37.5
Never	38.9	38.5	62.5
don't care	5.6	0.0	0.0

For example, Table 9 shows the differences between the different age groups with respect to experiences installing a wireless network. Generally, young adults have more experience with installing wireless networks than older subjects. There are not many differences between the two groups of young adults.

3. Qualitative Study

Subjects

Four subjects were recruited for the qualitative study. Computer users with no technical knowledge beyond office applications were chosen in order to acquire interesting qualitative data. The four subjects ranged in age from 20 to 50 and they were all female.

Materials

A DLink AirLink G DI-524 wireless router was used for the experiment, and a Dell Inspiron 1150 notebook computer with Microsoft Windows XP installed. The laptop had built in LAN and WLAN network cards and a CDROM drive. The wireless router was provided in the original packaging. The package contained the Wireless router, a power supply, a blue network cable, a quick installation CD with the router warranty and a multilingual instruction manual. The experiment was carried out on a desk next to wall with a university LAN socket. The university had also a WLAN with a unique SSID.

Procedure

The subjects were guided to the place of the experiment and told to set up a secure wireless network. The subjects were asked to unpack the contents of the WLAN router package and explore its contents.

Next the subjects where guided through the configuration. After successfully configuring the wireless router, and disconnecting the laptop from the Internet, the subjects were asked to test the wireless connection by logging into the configured network. The user had to open a webpage in browser to confirm the connection. The subjects were asked to "think aloud" and the sessions were recorded using a portable mp3 recorder. Each session lasted for approximately one hour.

3.1. *Results*

The subjects had no problems unpacking the contents of the wireless router package and identifying the various items. Two of the subjects looked at the installation manual but none of the subjects found the installation manual useful. The subjects complained that the manual did not contain sufficient background and explanation of terms and acronyms.

All the subjects quickly identified the quick-start installation CD with a yellow label giving the warning "insert into CD-ROM first" and successfully started the quick installation program. However, one subject discovered the CD with the yellow warning after having attempted to install the router from the instruction manual.

Subjects generally appeared uncertain about how things were to be connected. First, the laptop computer was to be connected to the wireless modem for configuration, and later connected to the LAN.

The setup CD was quite helpful in instructing the users how to connect things together. Illustrations were used allowing the subjects to make visual comparisons. One subject was confused by an illustration showing a tower computer case instead of a laptop computer but eventually deduced that the tower case was analogous to the laptop computer.

After guiding the subjects through the connections the router had to be configured. The user had to select a SSID, although no explicit explanation of this was provided. Next the subject had the choice to setup a security mechanism. The choices were no security (default), WEP, 64BIT and WPA-PSK, but no explanations of these were given. One subject initially ignored this setting and had to be corrected. All subjects had to ask which option to choose and WPA-PSK was recommended by the investigators with a simple explanation of why it is recommended. There was also a field for providing a password. Some subjects found the password field confusing when they were experimenting with the different encryption schemes as the allowable password characters are slightly different for each scheme.

Upon completing the installation, the subjects were asked to disconnect the laptop computer from the wireless router and test the wireless network. The subjects initially tried the connection by opening internet explorer, but with no effect. The users had to explicitly be told to establish a wireless connection by selecting the SSID they had set up and provide the password for the connection.

In summary, the installation procedure suffered from the following general problems: a) the subjects did not adhere to the specified order of the installation steps, b) the subjects had too little background information to understand the terminology and acronyms used, c) the printed manual provided no useful information and was only a disturbing element, d) the user was presented with too much choice and not enough insight to make a sensible decision, e) the setup CD did not help the users beyond installing the router as the subjects were totally on their own with regards to establishing a connection to the wireless network after completing the installation, f) the default option has no encryption and users are accustomed to accept the default settings when they are in doubt.

4. Conclusions

This paper addresses user awareness and attitude to wireless security. The results suggest that most users have insufficient knowledge about wireless network security to adequately install a secure WLAN, even with a quick start help program. Differences could also be attributed to gender and age. In particular, males are more confident about their wireless security knowledge than females, while females are more likely to seek professional help. There is clearly much to be desired from the wireless communication equipments manufacturers. The provision of quick-start help program is a good initiative, but these must be very simple, leaving no choice for the user in terms of security policy. Best practices should be followed to strengthen security. In addition it should also be possible to configure the router for advanced users. One cannot rely on users to follow recent advances in security. One solution would be to preset the wireless routers with a high security setting such as WPA as default, where the device is given a unique random SSID and a random password, also provided on a piece of paper in the packaging. Impatient novice users would then be able to immediately deploy relatively secure wireless networks in their homes.

References

1. W.C. Bhagyavati, Summers and A. DeJoie. Wireless Security Techniques: An Overview, *InfoSecCD Conference '04*, (2004).
2. T. Schmidt and A. Townsend, Why Wi-Fi Wan't to be Free, *Communications of the ACM* **46(5)**, 47-52 (2003).
3. Y. Zahur and A. Yang, Wireless LAN security and laboratory designs. *Journal of Computing Sciences in Colleges* **19(3)**, 44-60 (2003).
4. C. Devine, Aircrack. http://www.aircrack-ng.org
5. WarLinux. http://sourceforge.net/projects/warlinux/
6. A. Whitten and J.D. Tiger, Why Jhonny can't encrypt: a usability evaluation of PGP 5.0, *9th USENIX security symposium*, (2000).
7. A. Adams and M.A. Sasse, Users are not the enemy: why users compromise security mechanisms and how to take remedial measures, *Communications of the ACM* **42(12)**, 40-46 (1999).
8. A. Adams, M.A. Sasse, and P. Lutt, Making passwords secure and usable, *HCI'97 conference on people and computers XII*, (1997).
9. S. Brostoff and M.A. Sasse, Are passfaces more usable than passwords? A field trial investigation, *HCI 2000 conference on people and computers XIV - usability or else!* (2000).
10. R. Dhamja and A. Perrig. Deja vu: a user study using images for authentication, *9th USENIX security symposium*, (2000).
11. P. Dourish, et al., Security in the wild: user strategies for managing security as an everyday, practical problem, *Pers. Ubiquit. Comput.* **8**, 391-401 (2004).
12. M. Ziefle, S. Bay, and A. Schwade, On keys meanings and modes: The impact of navigation key solutions on children's efficiency using a mobile phone. *Behaviour and Information Technology* **25(5)**, 413-431 (2006).
13. C.A. Lawton, Gender differences in way-finding strategies: Relationship to spatial ability and spatial anxiety, *Sex Roles A Journal of Research* **30(11-12)**, 765-779 (1994).
14. A. Newell and P.S. Rosenbloom, Mechanisms of skill acquisition and the power law of learning, Cognitive Skills and Their Acquisition, J.R. Anderson, Editor. L. Erlbaum Associates, 1-55 (1981).

SAP BUSINESS ONE AND SIMERP: DIFFERENCES, SIMILARITIES, AND APPLICATIONS

MINGYANG YANG
School of Information, Renmin University of China
Beijing, 100872, China

MEIQI FANG
School of Information, Renmin University of China
Beijing, 100872, China

Two important classes of ERP systems, real ERP systems and ERP simulation systems can be used to support ERP teaching and learning. While both systems help learners to have an understanding and experience of ERP, the features and applications of real ERP systems and ERP simulation systems are different. In this paper, we present a comprehensive comparison between these two classes of systems. We discuss the differences and similarities of SAP Business One, which is a Business ERP system, and SIMERP, which is an ERP Simulation system designed and implemented by Economic Science Laboratory, Renmin University of China. Both systems have been used to support ERP teaching and learning in Renmin University of China since 2004. We describe how the two types of systems can be used differently in education.

1. Introduction

ERP system may well count as 'the most important development in technology in 1990s' [4]. It can either boost or doom a company, if implemented successfully or unsuccessfully. Most organizations realize the potential of ERP systems, but still struggle to materialize real benefits. 25 percent ERP projects is over budget and 20 percent are terminated before completion. There are many reasons that contribute to the low success rates, yet one common aspect that prevails is a misunderstanding of ERP [2].

Good teaching and training can help users to accept the new information systems and technology quickly [3]. But the pressures faced by practitioners as they innovate are not easily replicated by conventional teaching means. So simulation systems are introduced, which carry out the theory of "Learning By Doing" [5].The use of simulation and virtual worlds that compress time and space as microcosms of real settings can be tailored to give participants an experiential taste of how practitioners learn [6].

The purpose of this article is to discuss how to successfully develop an ERP simulation system. Real ERP system is very complex in both business process and software architecture, while simulation system has to be designed much simpler for the sake of teaching. Thus, how to extract the core theory of ERP becomes an important research area. In this paper, we give a comprehensive comparison of a real ERP system (SAP Business One 7.0) and an ERP simulation system (SIMERP 2.0), discussing their characteristics and how they can be used for teaching.

The paper is organized as follows. Section 2 presents an overview of SAP Business One and Section 3 SIMERP. Section 4 discusses the differences and similarities of the two systems and their applications in teaching. Section 5 offers our conclusion and future work.

2. An Overview of SAP Business One

SAP Business One is an ERP system for emerging and dynamic businesses ranging in size from ten to several hundred employees. It is developed by SAP and has been used by more than 10,000 enterprises all over the world [7]. Designed specifically for small and midsize businesses, the system is simple yet powerful. Business owners can use SAP Business One to automates their critical operations, including sales, finance, purchasing, inventory, and manufacturing. At the same time the system offers an accurate, up-to-the-minute picture of the business. SAP Business One 7.0 is subdivided into ten modules to cover each of these functions. Figure 1 depicts the modules in SAP Business One.

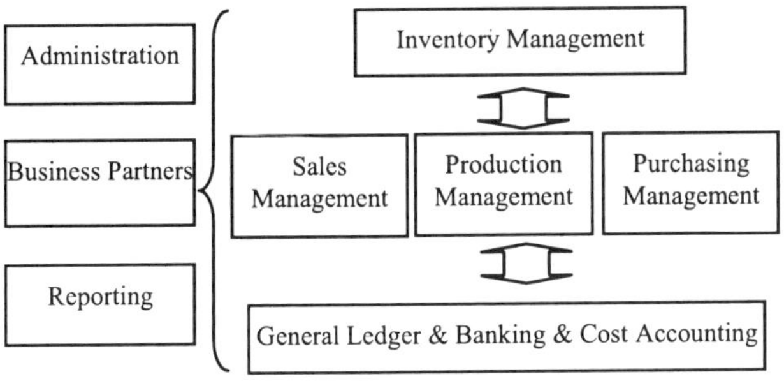

Figure 1. Modules in SAP Business One

1. Administration
This module contains the basic system settings, such as currency exchange rates, authorizations, online alerts, data import, and export functions.
2. Business Partners
In this module, users store the master data for all business partners, including all relevant information about customers, dealers and vendors.
3. Sales and Accounts Receivable
This module concentrates on sales processes, from calculating the price, entering customer orders, to issuing an invoice and accounts receivable.
4. Purchasing and Accounts Payable
In this module users manage all transactions with vendors. This module maps the entire buying process from purchase requisitions to vendor invoicing.
5. Inventory Management
In this module, users can manage all inventory including warehouse stocks, price lists, special pricing agreements, and warehouse transactions.
6. Production
The function in this module is to handle bills of materials (BOM) and work orders.
7. General Ledger
This is the module for managing financial accounting data, such as general ledger and budgets.
8. Banking
In this module, users can efficiently handle all of their monetary transactions, including cash receipts, check writing and bank reconciliation.
9. Cost Accounting
In this module, users define profit centers and organize auxiliary account assignments of postings.
10. Reporting
This module enables users to compile reports with corporate data and information.

3. An Overview of SIMERP

SIMERP is a web-based ERP simulation platform. We have designed and implemented this platform to help users learning and experiencing what "real" ERP is like.

SIMERP is based on the management of an international manufacturing enterprise. In this platform, users can play five kinds of roles in an enterprise's management, which are Sales Manager, Purchasing Manager, Production Manager, Inventory Manager and Finance Manager. Each enterprise in the simulation system should have these five roles played by five users, they work together to manage the enterprise.

In order to focus the users on the management of an enterprise, we introduce some auto roles, such as suppliers, customers and bank. Besides, SIMERP allow administrator to configure the system to fit different industry and the needs of the market can be changed by setting orders manually.

We use an example to illustrate the main process in SIMERP.

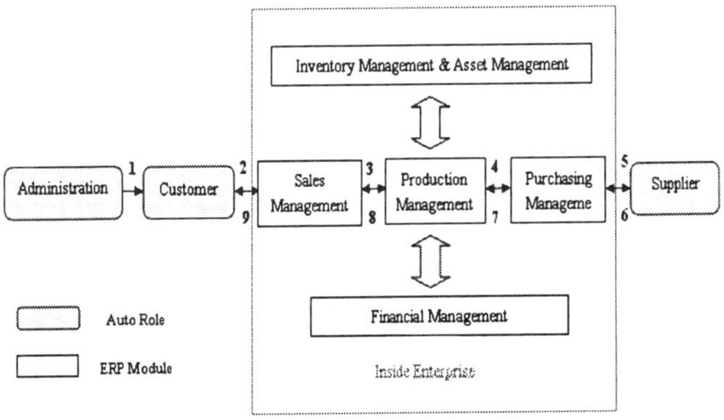

Figure 2. Modules in SIMERP

1. The process starts from Administration Module. In this module system administrator adds some orders for the market.
2. After that, Sales Manager competes for the orders offered by customers which are auto roles in the system.
3. The order information is integrated in SIMERP so that it can be shared by Production Manager.
4. When receiving the order, Production Manager breaks down the order and generates MPS (Master Production Schedule), MRP (Materials Requirement Plan) and Purchasing Plan.

5. According to the Purchasing Plan, Purchasing Manager buys materials from the suppliers which are also auto roles in the system.
6. When materials arrive at the time of delivery, Inventory Manager receives the materials and stores them in the warehouse.
7. When all materials are ready, Production can start according to the MPS.
8. When producing finishes, products are moved from product line to the warehouse.
9. At last, Sales Manager delivers goods to the customer at the time of delivery.

During the whole business process, Finance Manager has to deal with the Accounts Receivable and Accounts Payable.

We have depicted a representative process in SIMERP, basing production on sales prospects. The process is organized as follows: competing for orders, generating MPS and MRP, purchasing raw materials, executing production and delivering goods. Actually the process in real business world is more complex, so we offer relevant choices in SIMERP. Users can decide their own processes, for example purchasing raw material or executing production by forecast.

4. Comparison between SAP Business One and SIMERP

In this section we discuss the differences and similarities between SAP Business One and SIMERP. We focus on the major differences in system functions and what they can do for education.

We compare the systems along two main dimensions: general perspective and module perspective. First, general perspective shows the main differences of the two systems, and then module perspective depicts the differences and similarities of each module in detail.

4.1. *General Perspective*

4.1.1. System Design

The main differences of the two systems were summarized in Table 1.

Table 1. SAP Business One vs. SIMERP

Systems	SAP Business One	SIMERP
Objectives	For business	For education
Functions	Complex & Powerful	Simple & Simulated
	10 modules	7 modules
Supply Chain	Real	Simulated
Auto roles	None	Flexible auto roles

1. Objectives

SAP Business One is an ERP system designed specifically for small and midsize businesses. It has been used by more than 10,000 enterprises all over the world [7]. On the other hand, SIMERP is an ERP simulation system developed for education by Economic Science Laboratory, Renmin University of China. It has been used to support E-Commerce and ERP teaching since 2004.

2. Functions

As a real business system, SAP Business One has complex and powerful functions provided by ten modules, covering all aspects of enterprise management. Compared to SAP Business One, SIMERP is designed much simpler for the sake of simulation, including only seven modules. We will discuss the differences and similarities between the modules of these two systems in detail later.

3. Supply Chain

SAP Business One provides users with different roles and relevant authorizations. As a real business system, SAP Business One supports management inside the enterprise, at the same time business owners have to communicate with their partners on the supply chain to purchase material or sell goods.

On the other hand, SIMERP is a simulation system for education and no real partner exists in the system. In order to solve this problem, two kinds of auto roles are introduced as the "head" and "tail" in the supply chain: The head role provides supply chain with material and the tail role acts as customer. These auto suppliers and auto customers are played by background applications in the system.

4.1.2. Applications

Both SAP Business One and SIMERP can be used to support ERP teaching and training in both colleges and enterprises. But the two systems are appropriate for different kinds of users.

Both systems have been used in ERP teaching in Renmin University of China since 2004. From our teaching practice, we find that SAP Business One has complex and powerful modules which are fit for learning the details of each module in ERP system. In colleges, it can be used to give advanced courses to students who have already got some basic knowledge of ERP. In enterprises, it may help training employees from a certain department about the usage of the relevant module. But it is not suitable for the beginners. It is so complex that it's not easy for learners to understand ERP in a short time. That's why we develop SIMERP to help ERP teaching.

SIMERP is designed much simpler but it represents the kernel of ERP: Information Sharing, BOM (bills of materials), SCM (Supply Chain Management), etc. It helps learners to have a general understanding of ERP system in a short time. In colleges, it can be used to support ERP course for beginners. In enterprise, it can help training middle to top managers who don't bother to know the details of the ERP system but only need to have a general understanding. SIMERP simulate the whole process in supply chain by providing some auto roles. In this way, participants are able to experience the real business process and understand the importance of focusing on strategy and taking a long-term perspective to their decision making.

4.2. *Module Perspective*

In this chapter, we will compare some modules of the two systems in detail. Table 2 depicts the modules in SAP Business One and SIMERP.

Table 2. Modules in SAP Business One and SIMERP

SAP Business One	SIMERP
Sales and Accounts Receivable	Sales Management
Purchasing and Accounts Payable	Purchasing Management
Inventory Management	Inventory Management
	Asset Management
Production Management	Production Management
General Ledger	Financial Management
Bank Transactions	
Cost Accounting	

4.2.1. Sales Management

Sales and Accounts Receivable Module in SAP Business One provides comprehensive functions to help business owners complete the entire sales cycle. Two kinds of functions are provided, sales operation and sales opportunity management [7].

The representative process in Sales and Accounts Receivable Module is organized as follows: from quotation, order, delivery note to invoice. First, user issues a price quote to a customer. Second, customer order has to be entered, and a notification is sent to warehouse about the potential updating of stock balances. This can help maintain the safety stock. Third, delivery note is created and both stock balances and financial data are updated at the same time. At last, user creates the invoice, recording the stock and journal transactions.

SAP Business One offers sales opportunity management functions to record and analyze every sales opportunity, from the first phone call to the successful close of a transaction, logging various details of the whole selling process, providing easy-to-use tools such as win/loss opportunity table, open/closed opportunities, forecast reporting, and sales channel.

Sales Management Module in SIMERP is very different from that of SAP Business One. The entire sales cycle is very complex and our purpose of developing SIMERP is to provide a simulation system for education. Thus we extract the most important part of a sales process, competing for orders with other enterprises. And we neglect the details of quotation, customer order, delivery note and invoice.

Compared with SAP Business One, various new functions are introduced in SIMERP in order to fulfill the supply chain in the simulation system.

1. Orders in the market can be set by administrator in Administration Module. This function enables administrator to configure the system so students can have experiences of different industries.
2. In the beginning of the period, users have to decide how much they will spend on advertising. After that, users are ranked according to their spending. Each user can choose an order once a time according to their ranking order, which means the more a user pays on advertisement, the earlier and the better he can choose orders.
3. As we've mentioned before, users in the simulation system run international enterprises. In order to represent the characteristics of

international competition, we divide the market into three kinds: local market, national market and international market. These functions provide more decision making opportunities for users. The exploitation of different market swill cost enterprises certain amount of money. On the other hand, if an enterprise realizes global presence, it can sell to more than one market and spread the risk of doing business. So managers have to make decision whether to spend more to adopt differentiated strategy

4.2.2. Purchasing Management

Purchasing and Accounts Payable Module in SAP Business One can manage all transactions with vendors, mapping the entire buying process from purchase requisitions to purchase orders and delivery, right down to vendor invoicing [7].

SIMERP extracts the most important part in Purchasing Management, providing materials for production just in time. So the concepts of purchase delivery note and purchase invoice are ignored. Purchasing Manager just creates purchase order and then pays money on the date of payment. Supplier is an auto role in the system, which sells raw materials to enterprises. Several kinds of materials are provided and their prices, time of delivery and date of payment are different. This function gives users more choices, and at the same time keeps the simplicity of the system.

4.2.3. Inventory Management

Inventory Management Module in SAP Business One offers various tools and processes, including warehouse stocks, price lists, special pricing agreements, transfers between warehouses, and warehouse transactions [7].

Users can manage all item information, including name and code, measures, prices, and even the item's picture. Price Lists can be defined as many as needed and was associated with customer or vendor. Besides the common price lists, special prices can be set for unique customers or vendors. In addition, Inventory Management Module manages stock receipts or releases not connected directly to an AP (Accounts Payable) or AR (Accounts Receivable) document. Transfer between warehouses and stock transactions are also supported by the system.

Inventory Management Module in SIMERP provides much simpler functions compared with SAP Business One, since it is not the most important module in the system. Item information is also stored although not so complex. The concept of Price List is not introduced in the system, instead of that users can input certain price at the point of sale. However, the system will display the cost of the product to help users making decision. Asset Management Module is extracted to help users better understanding the differences between fixed assets and current assets.

4.2.4. Production Management

Production Management in SAP Business One is not very powerful compared with other modules. This module only handles bills of materials (BOM) and work orders. If an enterprise is a wholesaler or a retailer which means it doesn't produce anything, Production Module will not be used.

Production Management Module plays an important role in the process. It provides users the experience of BOM (Bills of Materials), MPS (Master Production Scheduling) and MRP (Materials Requirement Planning).

When receiving the order, Production Manager uses BOM to breaks down the customer order and generates MPS. Then MRP and Purchasing Plan are generated according to MPS and the current inventory.

4.2.5. Financial Management

SAP Business One divides Financial Management in to three modules, which are General Ledger, Bank Transactions and Cost Accounting [7]. In this chapter we will discuss the details of these modules.

1. General Ledger

In General Ledger Module, Finance Manager can manage all financial accounting data, defining all accounts and their hierarchical relationships, entering or finding manual journal entries, automatically allocating each transaction to a project or profit center and dealing with exchange rate differences.

General Ledger Module also provides powerful reporting functions, providing trial balance report, profit and loss statement, balance sheet, comparative report and budget report.

2. Bank Transactions

Bank Transactions Module helps Finance Manager to manage financial processing of the enterprise. This module can deposit cash, credit cards, or checks to the bank, issue checks for vendors, employees, or other creditors. It can also write and print a check and update the creditor balance accordingly.

3. Cost Accounting

Cost Accounting Module is much simpler compared with General Ledger Module and Bank Transaction Module. In this module Finance Manager defines profit centers and organizes auxiliary account assignments of postings. Some related reports are also provided by the system.

Financial Management Module in SIMERP integrates basic financial functions together. As we've discussed above, financial information in the real business world is extremely complex. However, the objective of the simulation system is not to make users master every aspect of financial management, but the kernel process of ERP. Therefore SIMERP ignores some complicated financial details and extracts the most important parts of financial management in an ERP system.

Accounts Receivable and Accounts Payable are deposited in Financial Management Module. Finance Manager pays suppliers at date of payment and receiving from customer are also managed. SIMERP automatically generates the most important reports for enterprise, which are Balance Sheet, Cash Flow Statement and Profit and Loss Statement.

SIMERP provides a virtual bank, which is an auto role played by the system. The most important function of the bank is to provide loans. When enterprise encounters financial problems or needs more cash flow, it can get loan from the bank. Both short term loans and long term loans are supported which provides more choices for enterprises.

5. Conclusions and future work

This paper summarizes the differences and similarities between SAP Business One and SIMERP. SAP Business One is a real ERP system designed for small and midsize businesses and SIMERP is an ERP simulation system designed for teaching. Both systems have been used to support teaching and learning in Renmin University of China, but they are appropriate for different kinds of users.

From our teaching and learning practice, we find that SAP Business One provides powerful and comprehensive functions. It is suitable for learners who already have some basic knowledge of ERP and want to learn farther more about details in certain modules. On the other hand, SIMERP is designed much simpler. It extracts the kernel of ERP system and introduces auto roles to simulate the whole process in supply chain. It is appropriate for the beginners and middle to top managers who only want to know the general process.

It must be noted that the simulation system SIMERP focuses only on daily management of the enterprise and does not take into account the Business intelligence (BI). BI applications are decision support tools that enable real-time, interactive access, analysis and manipulation of mission-critical corporate information [1]. Future research by the authors will focus on introducing BI in to SIMERP.

References

1. Cherry Tree & Co, Business Intelligence - the missing link, available at: http://www.ittoolbox.com/peer/bi.pdf, (2002).
2. ComputerWorld, Why ERP projects cause panic attacks, (2001).
3. A. Crowley, Training Treadmill-A Rigorous Plan of End-User Education is Critical to Whipping ERP Systems into Shape, *PC Week Online*, (1999).
4. T.H. Davenport, Putting the enterprise into the enterprise system, *Harvard Business Review* **76**, 121-131 (1998).
5. Hua Cheng, Meiqi Fang, Lin Guan and Zuqiang Hong, Design and implementation of an E-Commerce platform, *Journal of Electronic Commerce in Organizations* **2(2)**, 44-54, (2004).
6. P. McHardy and T. Allan, Closing the gap between what industry needs and what HE provides, *Education and Training* **42(9)**, 496-508 (2000).
7. SAP, http://www.sap.com, (2006)

JOINTLY MANAGED INVENTORY MODEL AND IMPLEMENT ANALYSIS*

GUOLING LAO

School of Information Management and Engineering, Shanghai University of Finance and Economics
Shanghai, 200433, P.R. China

LEI XING

School of Information Management and Engineering, Shanghai University of Finance and Economics
Shanghai, 200433, P.R. China

This paper briefly introduces the theory about supply chain, inventory management, and Jointly Managed Inventory (JMI). By a real-world case study, it discusses the status analysis, implement strategy and result evaluate of Jointly Managed Inventory (JMI) model about cigarette assistant material management in Shanghai Tobacco CORP.

1. Introduction

Supply Chain Management has been defined as a "set of approaches utilized to efficiently integrate suppliers, manufacturers, warehouses, and stores, so that merchandise is produced and distributed at the right quantities, to the right locations, and at the right time, in order to minimize system wide costs while satisfying service level requirements" [1]. Applying an advanced information technology, SCM leads to share much information, such as demand forecasting, inventory planning and production planning. However, it is hard to share information among the companies requires for SCM because the cooperation between the companies, which is the minimum composition unit of a supply chain, is inadequate. As the development of SCM, many problems need to be solved, especially the problem of inventory.

Inventory management in supply chain involves not only requirement forecasting and replenishment but optimization of customer service and profit. It covers evaluation of inventory strategies, lead time and changes of transportation with business modeling technology, considering effect from enterprises in supply chain while deciding economic variables, determining the right service level according to inventory status. There are four inventory management models that use different management agents: traditional model, Vendor Managed Inventory (VMI), Jointly Managed Inventory (JMI) and Collaborative Planning Forecasting & Replenishment (CPFR). In this paper, we discuss characters of the Jointly Managed Inventory and its implement base on case study of Shanghai Tobacco CORP.

2. Theory of JMI

Each point company in supply chain has its own inventory model that enlarges inventory demand (bullwhip effect), so the efficiency is low and the cost is high. Jointly Managed Inventory (JMI), a new inventory management model based on VMI, solves the problem by sharing information, responsibilities and risk among companies. JMI emphasizes the strategy and cooperation relationship between companies in supply chain. In the JMI system, all of the point companies make inventory plan together, considering the correspondences of supply and demand in the whole supply chain. So inventory is not more or less than its demand and inventory management is a process of cooperation [4].

The JMI strategy is different from the traditional model in which each company does things in its own way, and avoids limitations of VMI and bullwhip effect. It also controls risks efficiently in supply chain. JMI, developing with integrated supply chain concept corresponding with market requirements, is an integrated inventory management theory based on information sharing in supply chain.

Types of information that can be shared between supply chain partners in a JMI partnership include inventory levels and position, sales data and forecasts, order status, production and delivery schedules and

* This work is supported by 211 project foundation of Shanghai University of Finance & Economics.

capacity, and performance metrics. Sharing information yields many benefits to supply chain members, especially reducing the uncertainty and inventory fluctuation. JMI makes balance measures of risk, cost and benefit in supply chain, and companies share the inventory management risk, inventory and distribution cost, and get benefit according to their risk and cost. Suppliers and manufacturer share information through JMI Center, which strengthens the supply chain.

3. Comparison between JMI and other Inventory Models

The development of inventory management model in supply chain is related to the collaboration level between point companies, from simple business processing to collaborated planning and decision making, then inventory management in integrated supply chain. Inventory in the whole supply chain is controlled by collaborated inventory plan, not by a single company. The separation of inventory ownership and control makes sure the collaboration between inventory agents, decrease of inventory cost and risk and stability of supply chain. We can obtain connotation of jointly inventory management and a more efficient management model through comparing JMI and others.

Table 1 Comparison between JMI and other inventory model [2][3][4][5][6][7][8][9]

	Traditional model	**VMI model**	**JMI model**	**CPFR model**
Management agent	Point companies	Suppliers	Core company/ United agent	The workgroup for cooperated plan
Independency of point companies	Highest, managing its own inventory	High, helping supplier make inventory plan	Low, making, implementing and managing inventory plan together	Lower, managing business process and sharing information
Direction of information flow	Single-direction in supply chain	Double-direction between point firms and supplier	Double-direction between point firms and core firm	Double & complex direction among point firms
Reduction of demand uncertainty & risk level	Reducing risk resulted from demand uncertainty inefficiently, enlarging requirement	Supplier gets enough demand information but risk level is related to cooperation in supply chain.	Companies share inventory information and cooperate with others, avoid bullwhip effect.	Companies share completely information and get high level of demand forecast with an efficient supply chain.
Cost analysis	High inventory cost	Reducing inventory cost of suppliers and retailers	Lower inventory cost but high cooperation cost	Finding a right point between low inventory cost and high sharing information and cooperation cost
Request for point firms	Each firm has its own inventory and low collaboration level others, detesting risk.	Suppliers have enough market information and ability to direct-inventory. Backward companies can't manage inventory with information technology and infrastructure.	Point companies have good communication and faith with each other. A JMI center with high transportation level is needed	All companies have IT system and infrastructure. Keep identical business process and fixed cooperation relationship with others. The supply chain can forecast exact demand and respond to customer demand.
Technology support	MRP/MRP II, order-point method, double/multi-stack system	EDI/Internet, bar code technology, Continuous Replenishment system, MIS	ERP, SCM, CRM, communication system based on internet/intranet	Interactive system based on SCM/CRM/ERP, advanced planning and decision system, business intelligence
Implement strategy	Confirm self-inventory and make order strategy, safety inventory.	Set customer information system, sale network system, and cooperation frame agreement and organization innovation.	Build collaboration rules for demand and supply; enlarge resources planning function of manufacture and marketing. Build rapid-response system with third-part logistics.	Make agreement during supply chain partners, e.g. co-business plan, sale forecast and project collaboration plan.
Implement problems	High inventory level, great bullwhip effect and less communication during inventory management	Choice for suppliers; satisfaction for all partners; making collaboration agreement; evaluation system for VMI.	Build collaboration union and operation center with high level intendance.	Operating from demand forecast to order production, not considering customer demand, is not perfect.

Information economic benefit	Information stays inside enterprises uselessly.	Sharing inventory information with suppliers optimizes demand forecast and reduces inventory cost.	Inventory information flowing among point firms keeps their demand expectation clear and avoids demand enlarged effect. Information is full useful.	Sharing information completely in supply chain is good for business process management as well as inventory management.

4. Implement Analysis of JMI Model in Shanghai Tobacco CORP.

From the comparison in Table 1, we know JMI as a new inventory management strategy, emphasizes collaboration concept in supply chain. It advocates business cooperation and information sharing among all the companies. From its implement in Shanghai Tobacco CORP., we can know clearly about its advantages of reducing inventory cost and increasing efficiency.

4.1. *Background analysis*

4.1.1. Brief introduction

Shanghai Tobacco CORP was built in 1993 including many subsidiary companies, such as modernization tobacco Manufacture Company, tobacco logistics, printing, and machine and materials companies. It has business in industries of commerce, logistics, hotel and financial insurance, and is a great company of diversification, intensive and modernization. In 2004, it provided the tax of more than 19 billion, including benefit of 8 billion; its net capital is 33 billion. Shanghai Tobacco CORP is the number one in the tobacco industry in China [10].

Lack of the tobacco materials limits the development of Shanghai tobacco industry. In order to get enough resource, the company builds ten tobacco leaf bases and seven procurement bases in twelve provinces. After restructure, Shanghai Tobacco CORP consists of Shanghai Cigarette factory, Shanghai GaoYang International Tobacco Company, Beijing Cigarette factory and Tianjin Cigarette factory. The four companies have great demand of cigarette assistant materials, valued 2 billion RMB each year.

4.1.2. New stock problem after restructure

After restructuring, Shanghai Tobacco CORP faced many stock problems, such as the following:

1) According to the production, the whole company has a large stock and high cost, especially in Beijing and Tianjin.

2) In order to reduce its inventory, Shanghai Tobacco CORP improves inventory management and removes inventory press to material suppliers by asking them to prepare stocks of one month in their warehouse, which increases suppliers' cost.

3) The correspondence between plan and manufacture should be improved. The challenge of inventory management is to modulate the inventory level according to the manufacture in time.

4) There is not an efficient system of material management and sometimes four factories make measures it.

5) The demand is enlarged in supply chain and the cost is increased, which is called a "bullwhip".

The current status analysis of inventory management in three areas including four factories is show in table 2 to table 4.

Table 2. Status of cigarette assistant materials

Material \ Item	Percent in total procurement	Importance	Position of suppliers	Supply ability	Cooperation relationship
Brand paper	41%	5	5	5	5
Thread	13%	5	4	4	4
Wrapping paper	12%	3	3	3	3
Cigarette paper	7%	4	5	5	5
Essence	6%	4	5	5	5
Aluminum foil paper	5%	3	4	4	4
Box	4%	3	5	4	5
BOPP pellicle	3%	3	3	4	3
Yew paper	2%	3	3	4	4
Others	7%				

Table 3. Evaluation of recent inventory management condition

Item \ Area	Shanghai	Beijing	Tianjin
Hardware	A	B	D
Level of worker	B	B	C
Infomationization level	B	B	D
Service level	A	B	C
Stock turnover time	B	B	C
Inventory management ability	B	C	C

Table 4. Status of sale and stock condition

Item \ Area	Shanghai	Beijing	Tianjin
Income (billion)	30	1.6	1
Stock capital at the end of month (billion)	1.1	0.35	0.23
Stock turnover time	1.3	0.5	0.32
Warehouse area (M^2)	30000	15000	12000
Number of workers	80	20	30

In order to improve the inventory management and reduce the cost, Shanghai Tobacco CORP decides to build JMI model in cigarette material management.

4.2. *JMI strategy in cigarette material management*

4.2.1. Basic analysis

Base on investigate and analysis, we got the operation flow of cigarette material management, see figure 1. Then decided the basic structure of JMI model in cigarette material management, see figure 2.

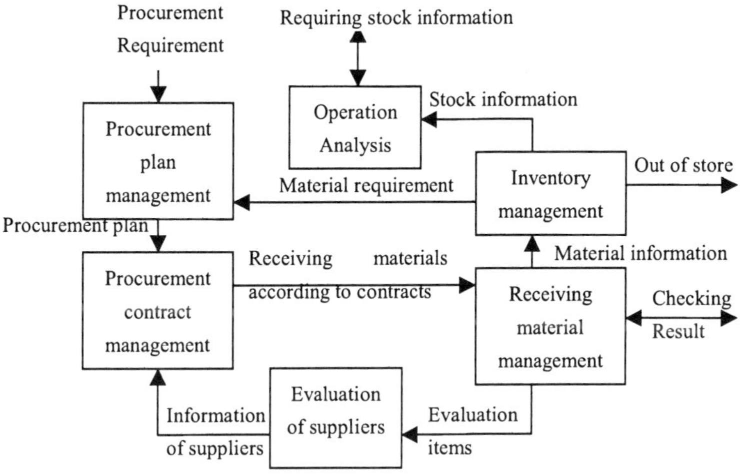

Figure 1. The operation flow of cigarette material management

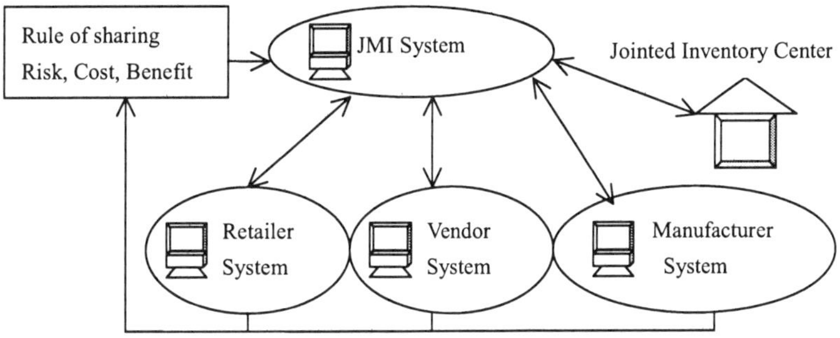

Figure 2. JMI framework of Shanghai tobacco Corp

4.2.2. Measures of JMI implement

For success of JMI, several measures to implement the jointly managed inventory of cigarette materials of Shanghai Tobacco CORP have been established.

1) Consummating the planning system and Implement inventory management by regarding planning as its core. Indetermination of planning is the main reason leading to increase of inventory. Daily Material demand plan in every month will be calculated automatically in the information system by comparing the BOM and the daily manufacturing plan provided by the manufacturing management department. Once the plan is changed, Material demand plan and manufacturing plan of providers can be changed too.

2) Construct information platform and Implement digital management of inventory. Material management system is a module of material management in the ERP system of Shanghai Tobacco CORP, which can be directly connected to manufacturing system, planning system, finance system, quality system etc. Through such a system, we can achieve information management of the inventory and achieve digital management of inventory by launching bar code management. Moreover, such a system has powerful statistical analysis function and querying function by automatically generating material demand plan. At the same time, website of inventory management is established, which can give orders to providers, perform financial settlement, release demand and delivery information. Material management system will be launched among main material providers.

3) Perfecting the management and communication of providers and Establish strategic cooperation. Conforming providers: wash out providers which cannot satisfy supply chain demand by evaluating quality, capital, price, management, logistics etc.

Assessing providers: assess the quality guarantee capability, supplying capability, development, respond capability etc.

4) Achieve JIT delivery and Guarantee manufacturing demand. According to material requirement plan, the information system creates order form and sends it to the right supplier through material website after optimized manually. The order should be sent 10 days before next month to make sure the suppliers have enough time to prepare the materials.

5) Quality, quantity inspection and Inventory management. There are two methods adopted, quality system assurance and ahead inspection, so that, quality of products can be guaranteed to satisfy the manufacturing demand and efficiency can be improved.

6) Application of third party logistics. In order to conform and improve transportation, delivery can be entrusted to third party logistics companies.

7) Delivery of logistics centers. Logistics centers will be set up in Shanghai and Beijing-Tianjin, which are responsible for receiving, storage and delivering materials which are unable to be transported from door to door, such as imported materials, small-batch materials etc. The whole East China can radiate from Shanghai center and North China can radiate from Beijing-Tianjin center in the future.

8) Establish safe inventory strategy. The way to set safe inventory is described as follows:

Safe inventory volume of single sort =(X1+X2+X3)* daily consumption in last year

X1=least manufacturing time after order is given (manufacturing volume is daily consumption in last year)

X2=average time of delivery from provider to tobacco factory

X3=average delivering time of materials of tobacco factory

When setting up the safe inventory, Beijing-Tianjin and Shanghai centers should be considered synthetically. It takes about 16 hours to transport goods between the 2 centers, so they should be complementary to each other.

9) Form a mechanism in with all parties is in harmony. Indetermination resulting from trust crisis, Information Island, profit conflict etc. in the supply chain should be eliminated. Such a phenomenon that an enterprise destroys the mutual profit of the supply chain in order to protect its own profit should be avoided. An effective communication mechanism should be formed between suppliers and customers, that is, these two parties exchange information face to face on problems and challenges in daily manufacturing by periodic or aperiodic meetings, in order to harmonize the partnership between two parties equally and friendly.

10) Form an index system of inventory management capability. Main index to be studied are: degree on JIT, respond capability, time of using safety stock, average monthly inventory value, weekly turnover etc.

11) Periodic evaluation and improvement on jointly managed inventory. Effect of the jointly managed inventory should be surveyed from the whole supply chain view. Problems and chance of improvement should be seek, so that, jointly managed inventory pattern can be perfected, inventory cost of the whole supply chain can be reduced and all enterprises in the chain can share the success.

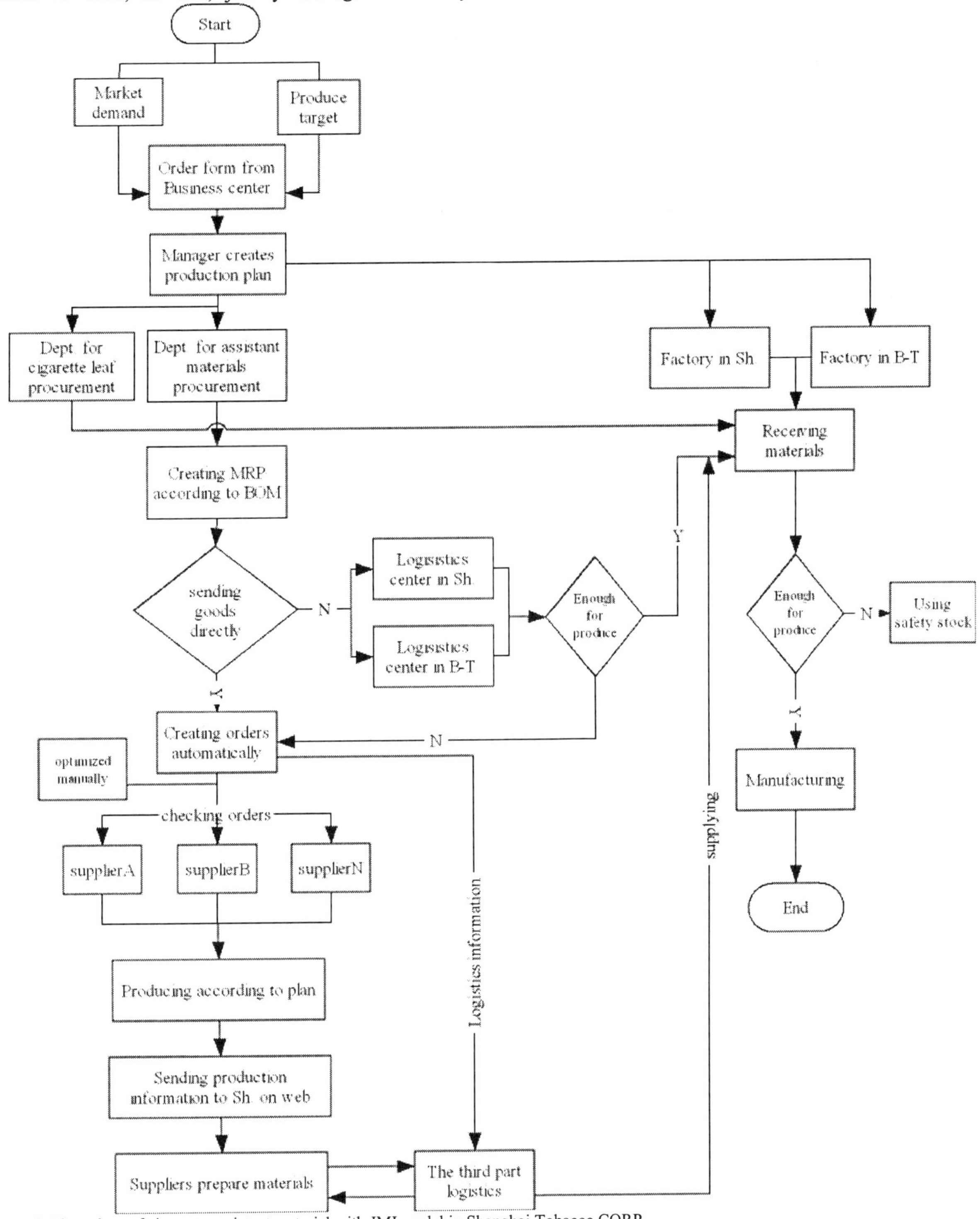

Figure 3. Flow chart of cigarette assistant material with JMI model in Shanghai Tobacco CORP

4.2.3. Detailed flow chart of JMI

Figure 3 shows the detailed flow chart of cigarette assistant material with JMI model.

4.3. *Implement effect analysis*

It brings effect on three aspects after launching the supplementary materials management of Shanghai Tobacco.

1) Logistics chain reduced and working-efficiency improved. After launching the jointly managed inventory and information management, the share of information and inventory resources between four plants located in three places and their suppliers are improved, the unnecessary chains in logistics are reduced, the coordination between corporations and suppliers are greatly enhanced, which leads to the improvement of manufacturing efficiency.

2) Supply chain construction strengthened by consistent correspond. After launching the jointly managed inventory, the link between supplies becomes closer. The construction of the information platform can greatly improve the contact between the suppliers, simplify the business process, reduce the chain and boost the working-efficiency.

3) Inventory cost of whole supply chain reduced. After launching the jointly managed inventory, inventory cost of whole supply chain will be reduced; estimate data is show in table 5.

Table 5 Comparison of before and after practicing JMI

Items	Before		After	
	Shanghai	Beijing &Tianjin	Shanghai	Beijing &Tianjin
Procurement (billion)	2.0	0.5	2.0	0.5
Stock capital at the end of month (billion)	1.30	0.58	0.90	0.37
Stock turnover time	15.38	8.62	22.22	14.29
Warehouse area (M^2)	30000	27000	15000	12000
Number of workers	80	50	80	50

5. Conclusions

Jointly Managed Inventory (JMI), a new inventory management model based on VMI, solves the problem by sharing information, responsibilities and risk among companies. JMI emphasizes the strategy and cooperation relationship between companies in supply chain. In JMI system, all of the point companies make inventory plan together, considering the correspondences of supply and demand in the whole supply chain. So inventory is not more or less than their demand and inventory management is a process of cooperation, not a single one. As the development of SCM and e-business, JMI technology will be widely used in companies to improving inventory management and valued companies and customers.

References

1. D. Simchi-Levi, P. Kaminsky and E. Simchi-Levi. Designing and managing the supply chain, McGraw-Hill Higher Education, (2000)
2. Dong Rui, SCM & 3PL, China Economy Press, (2003).
3. Min Hokey and Zhou Gengui, Supply chain modeling: past, present and future, *Computers and Industrial Engineering* **43(1-2)**, 231-249 (2002).
4. Feng Wang, Dali Jiang and Xilong Yang, Introduction to Logistics, China Communications Press, (1992).
5. Guohua Wang, Supply Chain Management, National Defense Industry Press, (2005).
6. Pengfei Liu and Ruhe Xie, The Comparalive Study on Modern Inventory Management Approaches Based on Supply China, *Commercial Research* **2**, 170-174 (2006).
7. W. W. C. Chung and S. W. F. Leung, Collaborative planning, forecasting and replenishment: a case study in copper clad laminate industry, *Production Planning & Control* **16(6)**, 563-574 (2005).
8. Funda Sahina and E. Powell Robinson, Information sharing and coordination in make-to-order supply chains, *Journal of Operations Management* **23(6)**, 579-598 (2005).
9. Arun Kanda and S.G. Deshmukh, A coordination-based perspective on the procurement process in the supply chain, *International Journal of Value Chain Management* **1(2)**, 117- 138 (2006).
10. http://www.sh-tobacco.com.cn/

THE ROLE OF THIRD PARTY TRUST MECHANISMS UNDER C2C ENVIRONMENT IN CHINA

TAO ZHOU
Management School, Hangzhou Dianzi University
Hangzhou, 310018, P.R.China

YAOBIN LU
School of Management, Huazhong University of Science and Technology
Wuhan, 430074, P.R.China

Third party trust mechanisms are of great importance in establishing a secure and credible C2C transaction platform. Under C2C environment, these trust mechanisms include feedback system, an escrow service, C2C intermediary and e-commerce laws and regulations. This paper used a questionnaire survey, collecting 115 samples and analyzing it with PLS Graph3.0. Results showed that escrow services, C2C intermediary and feedback systems played significant roles in establishing consumer's trust in sellers, which in turn reduced consumer risk perception and enhanced his transaction intention.

1. Introduction

C2C (customer to customer) online transactions are becoming increasingly common in China. The transaction volume of domestic C2C market attained 13.51 billion Yuan in 2005, an increase of 280 percent over 2004 [1], with Taobao and eBay China being the dominant players. Besides these two well-known websites, there are many other new C2C stores such as Paipai and Dangdangbao. However, C2C transactions depend on trust and, unlike in other e-commerce modes (B2B, B2C), the participants of C2C transaction are all individuals whose credibility is difficult to verify because China lacks an intact personal credit system. A certification method adopted by C2C websites is to verify sellers through Identification Card. By passing the verification, sellers can set up their stores in websites and begin to sell products. It is doubted that with only identification verification can the credit of sellers be guaranteed.

In order to enhance buyer's trust in sellers and promote C2C transactions, C2C websites generally take third party trust mechanisms to create a credible environment. Typical third party trust mechanisms include feedback systems, escrow services and C2C intermediaries. Furthermore, e-commerce laws and regulations will play some role. From the perspective of C2C websites, they anticipate to promote trust and C2C transactions by using these mechanisms. The ultimate goal is to make profit from managing the market However, whether consumers recognize and perceive the effectiveness of these trust mechanisms is the core of problems. Consumers need to build trust in sellers and conduct transactions in websites. Thus, this study will empirically analyze the roles of third party trust mechanisms and explore whether these mechanisms can significantly enhance consumers' trust, which in turn will influence their transaction intention.

2. Research Model and Hypotheses

Compared with B2C (business to customer) and B2B (business to business) e-commerce modes, risk involved in C2C mode is greater because China does not have an intact personal credit system, making it more difficult to verify the trustworthiness of individuals than of enterprises. Consumer trust depends on effective trust mechanisms. A central role of a C2C website is to establish a credible and secure transaction platform, thus reducing the consumer's perception of risk so as to facilitate transactions. This research describes a model wherein this is achieved by using four kinds of third party mechanism: feedback systems, escrow services, C2C intermediaries, and e-commerce laws and regulations,. It should be noticed that sellers in the model do not refer to any individual seller, but to the entire body of sellers in a market, the seller community. The model is shown in Figure 1.

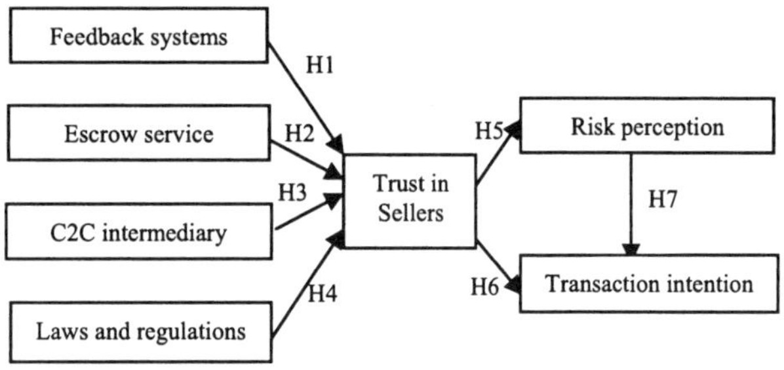

Figure 1. The roles of third party trust mechanisms

2.1. *Feedback systems*

A feedback system is also called as reputation system, which is one kind of third party trust mechanisms widely adopted by C2C marketplaces. After the completion of transactions, both buyer and seller rate and comment on the other. Ratings often include three kinds, that is, positive, neutral and negative, which separately represent score 1, 0, -1. The reputation score of a seller is the sum of his positive and negative ratings. This past information (include reputation score and comments) provides important reference to future participants. Consumers often judge the credibility of a seller by his reputation score.

Because of the importance of the reputation score, a few sellers often take advantage of loopholes of feedback systems to forge and quickly improve their reputation scores. For example, multiple sellers frequently transact among them and give each other positive rating. Also sellers can employ a few persons acting as consumers and let them give positive ratings. Although C2C websites have taken many technical measures to curb these behaviors, it is still possible to forge reputation scores. Furthermore, a few problems cannot be solved only by technical measures. For example, sellers can accumulate reputation scores by initially selling low value products. When his reputation score attains a level, he may utilize consumer's trust and cheat them in the last transaction involving high value products [2]. In sum, feedback system is an efficient but not intact mechanism. Consumers can perceive different level of effectiveness towards the same feedback system, which will influence their trust in sellers. More effective consumers feel feedback system, more trust they will give to sellers.

H1: Consumers' perception of the effectiveness of feedback systems will positively influence their trust in sellers.

2.2. *Escrow services*

Escrow services are third party payment services provided by a C2C website. The service solves the problem of "who acts first". That is, without escrow services, when a buyer and seller agree on a transaction, one side must first act. Either buyer first sends payment to seller or seller first sends products to buyer. The party who acts first will place itself in the vulnerable position and face potential risk. The emergence of escrow services solves the problem. The workflow of escrow services is as follows [3]. First, a buyer puts payments into escrow. Then the escrow service tells the seller to deliver the products to the buyer. When the buyer receives and is satisfied with the products, he goes to the escrow service and confirms products. Last, the escrow service sends the payments to the seller. The escrow service thus acts as the payment intermediary. Figure 2 shows the working process of the escrow service. Some C2C websites in China use escrow services. Both Taobao and eBay China have escrow services, separately named as "Zhi fu bao" and "An fu tong".

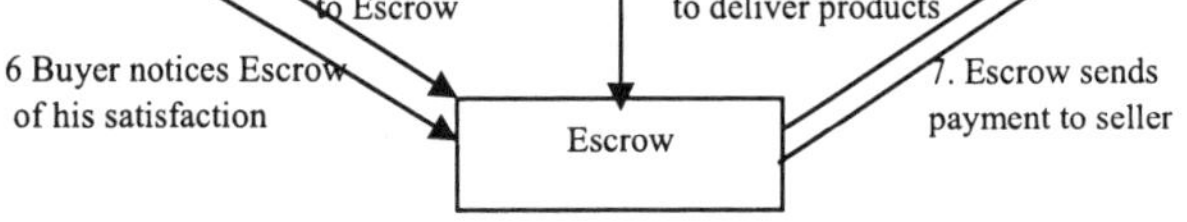

Figure 2. The workflow of escrow services

The essence of escrow services is that the C2C website acts as a reliable third party payment intermediary. Sellers who adopt escrow services will be more trusted by consumers. The shortcoming of escrow services is that consumers do not fully understand it. If consumers find escrow services are effective they will be more likely to engage with sellers.

H2: Consumers' perception of the effectiveness of escrow services will positively influence their trust in sellers.

2.3. *C2C intermediary*

C2C intermediary refers to C2C website itself. In addition to adopting feedback systems and escrow service, C2C websites take many other measures to safeguard transaction security. For example, Taobao has Web Policemen, who fully monitor online transactions and cooperate with public security departments to fight against web deception. EBay China also has this mechanism. Furthermore, eBay China provides 1000 Yuan transaction security fund to consumers who suffer from loss. With these measures, C2C websites try to establish a secure and reliable transaction platform, prevent sellers' opportunistic behaviors, enhance consumers' trust and promote transaction.

Consumer's trust in C2C intermediary may be influenced by many factors, such as reputation of C2C website, consumer's familiarity with website etc [4]. According to trust transfer principle [5], when consumers trust C2C websites more, they will give more trust to sellers in the websites.

H3: Consumers' trust in C2C intermediaries will positively influence their trust in sellers.

2.4. *E-commerce laws and regulations*

Although e-commerce laws and regulations in China are not intact, their roles in enhancing consumers' trust cannot be neglected. The effect of laws and regulations is to restrict online transaction behaviors and ensure transaction security. Thus, they can establish a macro environment for trust. In 2005, China government issued the first law on e-commerce, that is, electronic signature law. This law recognizes that electronic signature has the same effect with handwriting signature. With this law, electronic signature will be trusted and recognized by consumers, which will greatly promote the development of online transaction. Besides this law, there are many e-commerce related regulations in China. It is obvious that these laws and regulations will promote the shaping of an environment under which sellers are self-disciplined and credible. Consumers' perceived effectiveness of e-commerce laws and regulations will influence their trust in sellers. When consumers feel laws and regulations can effectively protect transaction security, they will trust sellers more.

H4: Consumers' perception of the effectiveness of e-commerce laws and regulations will positively influence their trust in sellers.

2.5. *Trust in sellers, risk perception and transaction intention*

The sellers in "trust in sellers" does not refer to any individual seller but to the whole sellers in a marketplace, or seller community. Only when consumers trust the whole seller community, they will be willing to transact with some individual seller in the marketplace. Due to the difficulty in measuring the actual behavior, this research tests transaction intention as the substitute of actual transaction. According to TRA (theory of reasoned action) and TPB (theory of planned behavior) [6], behavioral intention will lead to actual behavior. Thus, this substitute is feasible. Trust and risk perception are two opposite concepts. When consumers trust sellers more, they will perceive lower risk and be more willing to transact with sellers.

H5: Consumers' trust in sellers will negatively influence their risk perception.

H6: Consumers' trust in sellers will positively influence their transaction intention.

H7: Consumers' risk perception will negatively influence their transaction intention.

3. Research Method

This research adopted questionnaire survey methods. First, items measuring every factor were designated. Except that items of "laws and regulations" were designed by researchers, other indicators were adapted from existing literature. The purpose of adaptation was to be fit for Chinese reading customs and be easy for their understanding. The questionnaire includes 7 factors and 23 items. Each item is measured with 7-point Likert, which ranges from 1(strongly disagree) to 7 (strongly agree). After the questionnaire was completed, it was first sent to three e-commerce experts for their advice. They suggested that some items should be revised for more clean description. Then researchers revised the questionnaire and conducted a pilot test among 20 students with shopping experience in C2C websites. Results showed that the scale had a good reliability and validity.

The investigation was implemented among juniors majoring at e-commerce and MIS in a university. We felt that students were suitable samples for this research. As a new thing, C2C shopping was very popular among youngsters, especially young students, which were the main body of C2C shoppers. According to the 17th CNNIC report [7], one third of Internet users were students. Researchers first selected out those students who had C2C shopping experience. Then questionnaires were delivered among them. In sum, 123 questionnaires were returned. These questionnaires were examined by researchers and some unqualified papers (for example, the questionnaire with all items having same answers) were dropped. In the end, 115 papers were got as valid questionnaires.

Statistics of sample characteristics showed that 50.43 percent of students were male. All of them were in the age from 18 to 24. And 54.78 percent of students had used Internet for1~3 years, 33.04 percent for 4~6 years, 10.43 percent for more than 6 years. Among them, 78.26 percent had shopping experience on Taobao and 41.74 percent on eBay China.

4. Results

First, SPSS11.5 was used to conduct PCA (Principle Component Analysis) and examine scale's validity, including convergent and discriminant validity. Results showed that KMO value was 0.829 and the value of Bartlett test of sphericity was significant at 0.000. Thus, data were suitable for PCA [8]. Table 1 shows the component matrix with varimax rotation. In the table, some abbreviations are used. BEH represents for transaction intention, FED for feedback system, ESC for escrow service, TRU for consumer's trust in sellers, RISK for risk perception, LAW for e-commerce laws and regulations and IME for C2C intermediary. Totally, seven factors extracted 75.62% variance. The last row of table 1 lists the explaining variance of every factor. As shown in Table 1, each item loaded much higher (>0.7) on its related factor (shown as bold) and low on other factors, thus indicating a good convergent and discriminant validity.

Table 1. Component matrix after Varimax rotation

	BEH	FED	ESC	TRU	RISK	LAW	IME
FED1	.050	**.757**	.215	.192	.131	.076	.117
FED2	.224	**.791**	.204	.042	.059	.141	.128
FED3	.146	**.765**	.032	.183	-.173	.029	.262
FED4	.147	**.729**	.096	.201	.008	.094	.182
ESC1	.202	.164	**.746**	.244	-.085	.224	.071
ESC2	.229	.110	**.752**	.247	-.083	-.035	.195
ESC3	.002	.235	**.817**	.062	-.128	.171	.124
IME1	.164	.353	.348	.178	-.050	.008	**.716**
IME2	.213	.216	-.054	.234	.029	.126	**.772**
IME3	.065	.202	.234	.132	-.016	.121	**.785**
LAW1	-.026	.106	.085	.244	.076	**.836**	.021
LAW2	.043	.154	.216	.019	-.047	**.835**	-.004
LAW3	.085	.015	-.003	-.033	-.077	**.805**	.200
RISK1	-.184	.068	-.105	-.185	**.824**	.087	.118
RISK2	-.160	.039	-.015	-.072	**.824**	-.063	-.069
RISK3	.014	-.068	-.121	-.038	**.845**	-.061	-.057
TRU1	.202	.374	.184	**.718**	-.208	.053	.213
TRU2	.213	.206	.247	**.766**	-.165	.120	.298
TRU3	.201	.209	.215	**.814**	-.087	.116	.144
BEH1	**.807**	.113	.156	.146	-.056	.161	.204
BEH2	**.750**	.120	.017	.253	-.162	-.017	.068
BEH3	**.801**	.114	.215	.058	-.098	-.071	.079
BEH4	**.837**	.173	.028	.065	-.062	.074	.063
Var.%	13.12	12.88	10.26	10.00	9.96	9.88	9.52

Second, SEM analysis was conducted to examine the hypotheses of this research. We adopted PLS Graph3.0 as analysis tool. Due to small sample of data (115 students), it was not suitable to adopt LISREL for analysis. And PLS was appropriate under this condition because PLS had not strict demand for sample size and data distribution. According to PLS guides, sample attaining ten times the larger one of below two figures is enough: the factor which has the most paths leading to it or the factor having the most formative items [9]. In our model, all items were reflective. And the factor having most paths leading to it was TRU. Four paths pointed to it. Thus, 40 samples was threshold. This research had sample of 115 students, which was enough to conduct PLS analysis. Table 2 shows composite reliability (CR), average variance extracted (AVE) and correlation coefficients of every factor. As shown in the table, AVE of each factor was larger than its correlation coefficients with other factors. All AVEs were larger than 0.5 and all CRs exceeded 0.7. Thus, the scale had good reliability and validity [10].

Table 2. Factor correlation coefficients (sub diagonal) and AVE (diagonal and bold)

	FED	ESC	IME	LAW	TRU	RISK	BEH
FED	**0.682**						
ESC	0.446	**0.734**					
IME	0.572	0.467	**0.745**				
LAW	0.266	0.306	0.244	**0.714**			
TRU	0.557	0.556	0.569	0.278	**0.840**		
RISK	-0.04	-0.24	-0.08	-0.04	-0.31	**0.723**	
BEH	0.382	0.381	0.387	0.134	0.473	-0.269	**0.707**

Figure 3 shows path coefficient and significant value with bootstrap resampling. Explained variances of each dependent variable are also provided (shown as bold). It is worthy to notice that PLS Graph does not provide model fit index, such as GFI, CFI etc., which are presented by LISREL.

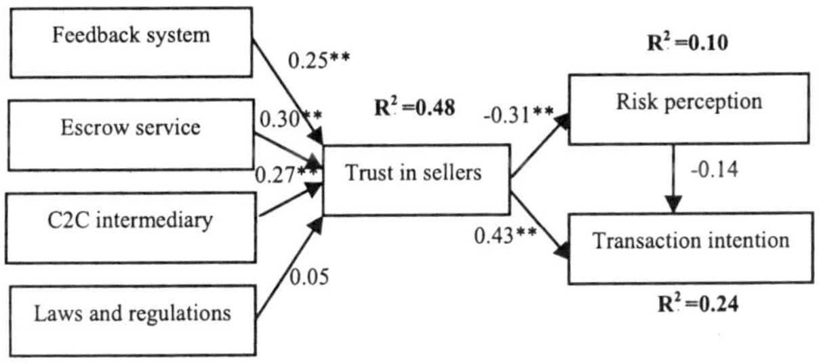

Figure 3. Result of PLS Graph analysis

(**, P<0.01; **R^2**: explained variance)

5. Discussion

As shown in figure 3, H1, H2, H3, H5 and H6 are supported, all path coefficients of which are significant at 0.01. H4 and H7 have no significant path coefficient and are not supported. The Explained variances of trust in sellers, risk perception and transaction intention were separately 48%, 10% and 24% respectively. Among factors influencing trust in sellers, escrow services has largest effect. Then C2C intermediary and feedback systems have smaller effect. Results show that e-commerce laws and regulations have no significant role in consumers' trust in sellers. Trust in sellers significantly influences risk perception and transaction intention. However, no significant relation is found between risk perception and transaction intention.

Among four trust mechanisms, escrow service has the largest effect on consumers' trust. This shows that consumers think highly of escrow services provided by C2C website. Escrow presents a secure payment tool to consumers and alleviates their anxiety of online shopping, thus promoting consumers' trust in sellers and ensure the success of transaction. This result also provides valuable suggestions for C2C website managers. At present, they should attach great importance to escrow services. In China, except a few well-known C2C websites such as Taobao and eBay China, other C2C websites have not establish their own escrow services. For these new and small C2C websites, one feasible way is to cooperate with existing escrow services to take use of their services. Otherwise, they can build their own escrow services. With the development of e-commerce in China, escrow services will be gradually adopted by more C2C websites.

C2C intermediary is another important factor influencing consumers' trust in sellers. The task of C2C website is to construct a secure, credible and efficient transaction platform for buyers and sellers. Although at present there are not many C2C websites in China, competition among them is much intense. Many C2C websites commit to provide free service for both sides of transactions to attract customers. However, free service may be a short-term plan. For C2C websites, they should pay great attention to improve itself, including providing high quality service and establishing a credible transaction environment to acquire consumers' trust. Only by this, websites not only attract more customers but also can make sizable profit. This may be a long-term plan.

Feedback systems also play a significant role in trust. However, compared with escrow services and C2C intermediary, feedback system has a smaller effect. This may indicate that shortcomings of feedback systems influence consumers' trust in them. With the development of e-commerce, feedback systems face many challenges. How to truly and efficiently reflect reputation of buyers and sellers should be paid more attention by C2C website in future. Nevertheless, feedback systems are still one of important trust mechanisms in C2C transaction at present and in future.

The research does not find the significant role of e-commerce laws and regulations on consumers' trust. This result can be explained by situations in China. Currently, although there are a few laws and regulations on e-commerce, it is still not enough for e-commerce development. Furthermore, many of them are not intact. Thus, they cannot produce a significant effect on consumer trust. In fact, in e-commerce transaction, consumers will not turn to laws for help in the last minute. Because of the virtual characteristics of online transaction, it is difficult to get proof. Moreover, the cost of enforcing laws is much higher and sometimes may exceed the price of consumer's purchased products. Therefore, laws and regulations may take a role of deterrence at most time, by which they reduce possibility of sellers' pursuing opportunistic behaviors and have no direct role in consumers' trust.

Consumers' trust significantly influences their risk perception and transaction intention, which has been verified in many empirical studies [11], showing the important role of trust in online transactions. However, this study does not find significant effect of risk perception on transaction intention. This may be biased by data sample. Subjects of this study are those who have C2C shopping experience. They are familiar with processes of online shopping. Thus, to them, risk may be not a significant and strong factor influencing their transaction intention. However, to those new comers, risk perception may be very high and a significant factor.

6. Conclusion

Third party trust mechanisms are vital to construct a credible and secure C2C transaction environment. This paper empirically studied the effect of four trust mechanisms on consumer's trust and transaction intention in China, which is the largest developing country and has the most attractive e-commerce market in the world. Results show that escrow service, together with C2C intermediary and feedback systems play significant roles in consumers' trust in sellers, which in turn reduces their risk perception and increases transaction intention. This suggests that e-commerce managers should pay attention to apply and improve third party trust mechanisms, thus enhancing consumers' trust and promoting transaction. Eventually, sustainable development of C2C market can be realized.

References

1. The Internet Research Center of China Academy of Social Sciences, Survey report on China e-commerce market in 2005, http://www.cass.net.cn (2005).
2. P. Resnick, R. Zeckhauser, E. Friedman and K. Kuwabara, Reputation systems, *Communications of the ACM* **43(12)**, 45-48 (2000).
3. X. Hu, Z. Lin, A.B. Whinston and H. Zhang, Hope or hype: on the viability of escrow services as trusted third parties in online auction environments, *Information Systems Research* **15(3)**, 236-249 (2004).
4. P.A. Pavlou and D. Gefen, Building effective online marketplaces with institution-based trust, *Information Systems Research* **15(1)**, 37–59 (2004).
5. K.J. Stewart, Trust transfer on the World Wide Web, *Organization Science* **14(1)**, 5-17 (2003).
6. I. Ajzen, The theory of planned behavior, *Organizational Behavior and Human Decision Processes* **50(2)**, 179-21 (1991).
7. CNNIC, 17Pth Statistical survey report on the Internet development in China, http://www.cnnic.net.cn, (2006).
8. Z.G. Guo, Social statistical analytical methods—SPSS software application, *China Renmin University Press* **12**, 92-93 (1999).
9. W.W. Chin, B.L. Marcolin and P.R. Newsted, A partial least squares latent variable modeling approach for measuring interaction effects: results from a Monte Carlo simulation study and an electronic-mail emotion/adoption study, *Information Systems Research* **14(2)**, 189-217 (2003).
10. D. Gefen, D.W. Straub and M.C. Boudreau, Structural equation modeling and regression: guidelines for research practice, *Communications of the AIS* **4(7)**, 1-79 (2000).
11. S. Grabner-Krauter and E.A. Kaluscha, Empirical research in online trust: a review and critical assessment, *International Journal of Human-Computer Studies* **58**, 783-812 (2003).

DYNAMIC COOPERATION DESIGN OF SUPPLY CHAIN BASED ON REPUTATION

GUIQING QI†

Business Administration, Northeastern University, No.11, Lance 3, Wenhua Road, Heping District Shenyang, Liaoning Province,110004,China

XIHUAI YANG

Business Administration, Northeastern University, No.11, Lance 3, Wenhua Road, Heping Disrict Shenyang, Liaoning Province,110004,China

Reputation can impel and restrict players' behavior, based on which, the paper regards reputation as the information reflecting the historic records and characteristics of players, and describe the dynamic mechanism to cooperate in the supply chain between the upstream and the downstream enterprises. Pursuant to the mechanism herein, agents' reputation are updated in accordance with Bayes' Law, therefore, the paper further establishes task distribution model and cooperation return rate model, through which, such problems as adverse selection and moral hazard can be effectively overcome before or after signing agreement.

1. Introduction

The research on contract management of supply chain mainly deals with the design of decision-making variable, and the determination of which will exert significant influence on the behavior and motive of supply chain members and the overall performance [1],[2],[3]. Therefore, the design of agreement decision-making variable has become an important part of supply chain operation. Essentially, the relation between enterprises on the upstream and downstream nodes of supply chain is principle-agency, in contrast to the common principle-agency relation. Cooperation between enterprises of the supply chain is long term, dynamic and multistage, and the reputation of enterprises should play a vital role in concluding and implementing supply chain agreement. So the conventional mechanism design based on combining restriction and encouragement is quite limited when being used for supply chain operation [4], [5], [6],[7].

Research on reputation transaction theory has pointed out that reputation is an important asset of an enterprise. The establishment, accumulation and publication of reputation and its underlying encouragement and restriction on players' behavior brought by gains and losses of benefits have made it become a solid guarantee for just and honest transaction [8],[9],[10]. The reputation information theory regards reputation as the information reflecting the historic records and characteristics of players, through exchanging and disseminating the reputation information among profit-related parties, the information flow, system and network are established, which manifests the reputation information and effectively restricts information distortion, enhances transaction transparency and reduces transaction cost [10],[11],[12].

As to the principle-agency relation and agreement design between enterprises of supply chain, the documents that regard reputation as a critically influential factor are few [1],[5],[13]. In practice, the cooperation and agreement conclusion between enterprises of supply chain are directly related with enterprises' reputation, for instance, Dongfeng-Citroen Automobile Co., Ltd. and the medicine sales agencies affiliated to Sinopharm Medicine Holding Co., Ltd. will always check the reputation of distributors so as to guarantee their returned capital, additionally, they will set up distributors' records before sales operation, register the reputation of each distributor, based on

† Work partially supported by grant70603005 of the Chinese National Science Foundation.

which, they will specify sales limitation, and offer different preferential policies to old, new, long-term and temporary distributors respectively for enhancing the trust between enterprises of the supply chain[1] The principle of reputation-based agreement can be traced from the bilateral and multilateral reputation mechanism based on repeated game and the social reputation mechanism based on associated game [14], [15].Therefore, in the course of designing agreement, it is theoretically and practically significant to take enterprises' reputation as an important factor to be considered.

This paper analyzes reputation-based cooperative mechanism against the adverse selection and moral hazard encountered in cooperation between enterprises in the upstream and downstream of supply chain, and establishes math models of some main factors that affect dynamic cooperative agreement by means of transmission and manifestation principle of reputation.

2. Assumed Condition and Related Explanation

2.1. *Definition and Measurement of Enterprises' Reputation*

The relatively more influential definition on enterprises' reputation was given by Gotsi Wilson in 2001, saying that enterprises' reputation is reflected in the overall appraisement of profit-related parties according to their experiences, behavior of related enterprises and the information of major competitors with the passage of time [9]. However, the enterprises' reputation discussed in this paper indicates the overall evaluation based on the fulfillment condition of one party in the course of communication and cooperation between enterprises on the upstream-and-downstream nodes of supply chain.

The main tools used for measuring enterprises' reputation include GAMC, the most globally popular company used by *Fortune* Magazine, "Comprehensive Reputation" put forward by *German Managers* Magazine, "Reputation Quotient Model" established by Fombrun and Harris as well as "Two-dimensional Evaluation Model" by Manfred [4],[20],[22],[23]. However, the indicating system and measuring model of enterprises' reputation in supply chain environment is quite different from the aforesaid tools. The standard for evaluating enterprises' reputation covers many factors like price, quality, service and delivery date, etc. For enhancing the research, the paper regards the probability of observing the historic information of agents (downstream enterprises) by the principle (upstream enterprises) as a measurement of agent's reputation. The principle updates his appraisement on agent's reputation by following Bayes' Law, judges the type of agent and modifies the agreement accordingly.

2.2. *Assumed Condition*

Supposing an infinite sequence $t = 0,1,\cdots$, in which, there are two players, one is the principle (upstream enterprise) who is a uninformed player and the other is the agent (downstream enterprise) who is an informed player, they are both risk-neutral. The task distributed by the principle to the agent is 1 unit, which can be partly or wholly distributed to the agent. The principle will fix the task quantity Q_t and return rate R_t in terms of his appraisal on agent's reputation and offers agreement $\{Q_t, R_t\}$. The undistributed task will be finished by the principle himself and the return rate is r. The principle adopts liquidation technique that will affect the earnings of delinquent agent based on their default behavior. Assuming an agent is too small to own special resources available for additional task, he can only depend on his reputation to obtain the distributed task; in case the task distributed by the principle cannot be finished, he will be incapable of paying off the returns of principle.

Agent can be classified into two kinds: good agents who will have the motives of choosing cooperation and opportunism behavior, and bad agents who will be always apt to opportunism behavior. Just supposing the reputation of the agents account for $c \in (0,1)$ before the cooperation, which can be asset by the principle in advance. The two kinds of agents are provided with the same fixed discount factor $\delta \in (0,1)$.

At the beginning of stage t, the agent type and his strategies to be selected belong to private information, while the agreement clauses and the agreement fulfillment history h_t of the agent before stage t are common information. Regarding $p_t(h_t)$ as the probability of historic information h_t that can be obtained by the principle, it is called as agent's reputation herein. Reputation is quite important for agents, because the principle is not inclined to cooperate with bad agents. The principle updates $p_t(h_t)$ in accordance with Bayes' Law so as to judge the type of agents and modify the agreement accordingly. In addition, the agent will select their optimal strategy guided this law.

Assumption 1: Agent who adopts cooperation strategy will obtain earnings of aQ_t, who takes opportunism action will get earnings of bQ_t with the probability of $\alpha \in (0,1)$ and obtain 0 with the probability of $1-\alpha$.

Of which $\alpha b < r < a < b$. (1)

The unit earnings b obtained by opportunism behavior is more than the unit earnings a by cooperation, the unit earnings a gained by the agent is more than the unit earnings r of principle by finishing the task himself and the anticipative earnings gained by adopting opportunism strategy is less than r.

To avoid the adverse selection problems and the moral hazard problems in the supply chain, the design of the cooperation mechanism must meet the follow constrains,

$$\text{(i)}\ c \geq \frac{r/a-\alpha}{1-\alpha} \tag{2}$$

$$\text{(ii)}\ \alpha < \frac{a-r}{(1-\delta)(b-a)+a-r} \tag{3}$$

Constraint (i) proposes the initial reputation of the agent when $t=0$, supposing the good agent has no default behavior, then the minimum return rate of cooperation obtained by the principle is $R_0 = r/c + \alpha(1-c)$, if $c \geq \frac{r/a-\alpha}{1-\alpha}$, $R_0 > a$, the good agent will not accept such agreement, and more possibly incline to adverse selection.

Constraint (ii) proposes the probability requirement of the agent to participate in the supply chain. Defining $V_\infty \equiv (a-r)/(1-\delta)$, if $\alpha < \frac{a-r}{(1-\delta)(b-a)+a-r}$ and $R_t > r$, the anticipative earnings brought by agent's opportunism behavior is always more than losses, then agent's motive of choosing moral hazard is stronger.

2.3. *Description of Equilibrium State*

Bad agents don't want to be recognized by the principle, so they will accept the same clauses and show the same signal for becoming a member of the supply chain and obtain tasks, which make it hard for principle to identify the agent type in one game stage. For achieving more earnings and preventing from adverse selection, the principle will design an agreement that can only be accepted by good agents. According to such agreement, when realizing the equilibrium state of game, good agents have no choice but to cooperate rather than take opportunistic action, or else, the unit anticipative earnings of the principle will be less than r. Therefore the equilibrium belongs to a separating equilibrium based on the behavior selected by the agent. In any stage, if the agent cannot fulfill the agreement, the principle will regard him as bad and delete him from the cooperation list. Since the good agent chooses cooperation strategy and the bad agent adopts opportunism strategy, under equilibrium condition, the cooperation return rate R_t of the principle must be more than or equal to r.

The principle pays more attention to the agreement that can maximize the earnings of good agent so as to avoid adverse selection. The reputation of any agent who doesn't accept the agreement will be down to 0, and deleted from the list of candidate agents. The equilibrium path meeting such condition is composed of a series of cooperation quantity $\{Q_t\}_t^\infty$ and cooperation return rate $\{R_t\}_t^\infty$ that can maximize the earnings of good agents. If the agent cannot fulfill the agreement in a certain stage, the principle will delete him from the cooperation list, so the good agent finds it beneficial to select cooperation strategy in each stage. The cooperation return rate R_t is more than or equals to r, the reputation p_t of the agent who has never broken the agreement will be updated in accordance with Bayes' Law. In equilibrium, only bad agent who adopts opportunism strategy and obtains 0 earnings will break the agreement, because the earnings of delinquent enterprise are destroyed by the liquidation technique [16].

3. Establishment of Models

Definition 1: If assumption (1), constrain (i) and (ii) are tenable, there is game equilibrium path. The principle will only cooperate with the agent who has never broken the agreement, and the good agent chooses cooperation. The reputation of the agent who has never default will be updated in accordance with the formula below:

$$p_{t+1} = \frac{p_t}{p_t + \alpha(1-p_t)}$$

$$p_0 = c\ (c \text{ is constant}) \tag{4}$$

In any stage, good agent will never break the agreement, while bad agent fulfill the agreement with the probability of α, once the agent breaks the agreement, his reputation will drop to 0, based on which, formula (4) is written.

The design of task distribution and cooperation return rate follows forward-looking viewpoints, i.e. standardizing the future behavior of agent ahead of schedule by considering his current and future earnings so as not to make good agent choose opportunism behavior.

The cooperation return rate required by the principle towards the agents who has never default follows the formula below:

$$R_t = R(p_t) = \frac{r}{p_t + \alpha(1-p_t)} \qquad (5)$$

Formula (5) considers the probabilities for good agent and bad agent to fulfill the agreement and given that the good agent never default, well then with the increase of his reputation, the anticipative cooperation return rate R_t payable will decrease gradually, when his reputation tends towards 1, R_t will be much closer to r.

The agreement $\{Q_t, R_t\}_{t=0}^{\infty}$ under equilibrium state is the result of maximizing the earnings $\sum_{t=0}^{\infty}\delta^t Q_t(a-R_t)$ of good agent by selecting cooperation strategy in each stage, which meets the following constraints:

(I) $R_t \le a, Q_t \le 1$, i.e. the good agent is capable of paying the promissory returns stipulated by the agreement to the principle when choosing cooperative behavior;

(II) $r \le R_t(p_t + \alpha(1-p_t))$, i.e. given that the bad agent breaks the agreement with the probability of $1-\alpha$, but the good agent will fulfill the agreement, it is beneficial for principle to distribute the task to the agent who has never default;

(III) $$\sum_{T=t}^{\infty}\delta^{T-t} Q_t(a-R_T) \ge \alpha(Q_t(b-R_t) + \sum_{T=t+1}^{\infty}\delta^{T-t}Q_t(a-R_T))$$

i.e. in a given period, threatened by the possibility of being deleted from the future cooperation list, the good agent would rather choose cooperation instead of opportunism behavior;

(IV) $p_t = p_t/(p_t + \alpha(1-p_t))$, $p_0 = c$, i.e. given that the bad agent breaks the agreement with the probability of $1-\alpha$, but the good agent will always fulfill the agreement, the reputation of the agent who never breaks the agreement will be updated in accordance with Bayes' Law.

When $(1-\alpha)\sum_{T=t}^{\infty}\delta^{T-t}(a-R_T) \ge \alpha(b-a)$, constrain (III) meets $Q_t = 1$, $T = t, t+1\cdots$, the task obtained by the agents can come to the maximum. When $Q_t \le 1$, $\sum_{t=0}^{\infty}\delta^t Q_t(a-R_t)$ can be maximized on this condition. When R_t is closer to r and $(1-\alpha)(a-r)/(1-\delta) > \alpha(b-a)$, there is stage τ, meeting the condition

$(1-\alpha)\sum_{T=t}^{\infty}\delta^{T-t}(a-R_T) \ge \alpha(b-a)$ since stage τ, well then $Q_T = 1$, $T = \tau, \tau+1\cdots$,

When $t < \tau$, it can be found out from (III):

$$Q_t = \frac{(1-\alpha)}{\alpha(b-a)-(1-\alpha)(a-R_t)} \times \sum_{T=t+1}^{\infty}\delta^{T-t}Q_t(a-R_t) \qquad (6)$$

Using (6) to calculate Q_{t+1} and incorporating it into Q_t, when $t < \tau - 1$, it can be found out that:

$$Q_t = \frac{\delta\alpha(b-a)\times Q_{t+1}}{\alpha(b-a)-(1-\alpha)(a-R_t)} \qquad (7)$$

According to (5) and Q_t=1, when $T = \tau$, $\tau+1\cdots$, $t = \tau - 1$, it can be found out:

$$Q_{\tau-1} = \frac{\delta(1-\alpha)\sum_{T=\tau}^{\infty}\delta^{T-\tau}(a-R_T)}{\alpha(b-a)-(1-\alpha)(a-R_{\tau-1})} \qquad (8)$$

According to (7) and (8), it can be found out that before stage τ

$$Q_t = Q(p_t) = \frac{(\delta\alpha(b-a))^{\tau-t-1}\times\delta(1-\alpha)\sum_{T=\tau}^{\infty}\delta^{T-\tau}(a-R_T)}{\prod_{T'=t}^{\tau-1}(\alpha(b-a)-(1-\alpha)(a-R_{T'}))} \qquad (9)$$

Defining $V_t = \sum_{T=t}^{\infty}(a-R_T)$ as the maximum earnings obtained by the good agent who chooses cooperation strategy since stage t, i.e.

$Q_t = 1, T = t, t+1\cdots$,

if choosing opportunism behavior, the agent will lose earnings of V_t with the probability of $(1-\alpha)$ and obtain earnings of $(b-R_t)-(a-R_t)$ with the probability of α . Because with the passage of time, the cooperation return rate will decrease, but $(1-\alpha)V_t$ increases. At stage τ , $(1-\alpha)V_t \ge \alpha(b-a)$, the task distributed to the agent will amount to the upper bound 1.

When $T=\tau-1$, formula (9) can be written below:

$$\alpha(b-a)Q_{\tau-1} = (1-\alpha)(a-R_{\tau-1})Q_{\tau-1} + (1-\alpha)\delta V_\tau \quad (10)$$

If Q_t reaches the upper bound 1 at stage τ or after the stage, then at $\tau-1$ stage, the anticipative earnings of the agent who chooses opportunism behavior will equal to the anticipative losses.

At stage $t<\tau-1$, formula (8) can be written below: $\alpha(b-a)Q_t = (1-\alpha)(a-R_t)Q_t + \delta\alpha(b-a)Q_{t+1}$ (11)

Formula (11) points out that the extreme point of task distributed to the agent will be reached when the anticipative earnings and losses are equivalent. Formula $\delta\alpha(b-a)Q_{t+1}$ indicates the discounted value of losses suffered by the agent who may be eliminated from the supply chain after stage $t+1$ for his opportunism behavior in stage $t+1$. According to the aforesaid description, it can be deduced that:

Deduction 1: If assumption (1),constrain (i) and (ii) are tenable, the cooperation return rate R_t will decrease with the passage of time and gradually be closer to r . When $t<\tau$, Q_t will increase gradually with the passage of time.

It is obvious that the agent newly joining the supply chain should spend much more time on establishing reputation so as to obtain lower cooperation return rate and more tasks.

Deduction 2: $Q_t \in \{0,1\}$, the cooperation can be realized when meeting $(1-\alpha)V_0 \ge \alpha(b-a)$; when $c \ge \dfrac{r/a-\alpha}{1-\alpha}$ or $(1-\alpha)(\dfrac{a-r}{1-\delta}) \ge \alpha(b-a)$, the cooperation cannot be realized because of agents' strong intention of adverse selection and moral hazard.

Deduction 3: If the agent newly joining the supply chain has enough patience, the agreement clauses concluded will be relatively less oppressive. With the increase of δ , and under the condition of keeping the potential earnings constant, the losses induced by agents' opportunism behavior will increase accordingly.

4. Numerical Example

In order to guarantee the returned capital, Dongfeng-Citroen Automobile Co., Ltd. records each distributor's reputation, based on the check of their reputation, the company will define sales limitation and grant different return rate to distributors of varied reputation. Supposing the total sales volume is 1 unit. For preventing from adverse selection and moral hazard encountered in cooperation, the principle A (Dongfeng-Citroen Automobile Co., Ltd.) determines to conclude a reputation-based dynamic agreement with agent B (distributor). The initial reputation assess of the agent $c=3/8$. The return rate of the task done by the principle is $r=0.1$. Agent who adopts cooperation strategy will obtain earnings of $0.2Q_t$, who takes opportunism action will get earnings of $0.4Q_t$ with the probability of $\alpha=0.2$ and obtain 0 with the probability of $1-\alpha=0.8$. And the two kinds of agents are provided with the same fixed discount factor $\delta=0.5$. We can get the result as in table 1. It can be found that the cooperation return rate R_t decrease with the passage of time and gradually be closer to $r=0.1$, Q_t increase gradually with the passage of time. The result meets the needs of the agreement design.

5. Conclusion

Through describing the reputation-based cooperation between enterprises in the upstream and downstream of supply chain, and the dynamic agreement based on updating agents' reputation model by Bayes' Law, the reputation and fulfillment probability of agents can be concluded before cooperation, which effectively inhibits the occurrence of adverse selection. By utilizing the accumulative effect of reputation, relate the distributed task and return rate with agents' reputation, try to realize that the more the reputation, the more the task, the less the interest paid to principle, in this way, the reputation can effectively hold back moral hazard. The result of numerical simulation is rightly coincident with design theory, and such agreement design can strengthen the encouragement effect and improve the efficiency of supply-chain cooperation.

Table 1. Reputation, the cooperation rate and the task assigned in different stage

Stage (t)	Reputation (p_t)	Cooperation rate (R_t)	Task assigned (Q_t)
0	0.3750	0.2000	0.0022
1	0.7500	0.1250	0.0089
2	0.9375	0.1053	0.0178
3	0.9868	0.1011	0.0638
4	0.9973	0.1002	0.5000
⋮	⋮	⋮	⋮

References

1. S. J XU and S. H. MA, On the trust mechanism between enterprises in supply chain, *Industrial Engineering and Management* **6**, 5-8 (2000) (in Chinese).
2. Besanko and D. S. Sibley, Compensation and transfer pricing in principal – agent model, *International Economic Review* **32(1)**, 55 – 681 (1991).
3. I. Giannoccaro and P. Pontrandolfo, Supply chain coordination by revenue sharing contracts, *International Journal of Production Economics,* **89(2)**, 131 – 139 (2004).
4. Cole, Harold, James and D. Default, Settlement, and signaling: lending resumption in a reputation model of sovereign debt, *International Economic Review* **36**, 365-385 (1995).
5. Douglas Diamond, Reputation acquisition in debt markets, *Political Economy* **4**, 828-86 (1989).
6. G. D. Eppon and A. V. Iyer, Backup agreements in fashion buying - the value of upstream flexibility, *Management Science* **43**, 1484-1489 (1997).
7. M. J. Maloni and W. C. Benton, Supply chain partnerships: opportunities for operation research. *European Journal of Operational Research* **101(3)**, 419 – 429 (1997).
8. Dunbar, L. M. Roger, Schwalbach and Joachim, Corporate Reputation and Performance in Germany, *Corporate Reputation Review* **3**, 115 – 123 (2001).
9. Fombrun and J. Charles, The reputation landscape, *Corporate Reputation Review* **1**, 5-14 (1998).
10. J. George, Mailath and S. Larry, Who wants a good reputation, *Review of Economic studies* **68**, 415-441 (2001).
11. M. Gotsi and A. M. Wilson, Corporate reputation: seeking a definition corporate communications, *An International Journal* **6(1)**, 24 – 30 (2001).
12. Edmund Gray, R. Ballmer and M. T. John, Managing corporate image and corporate reputation, *Long Range Planning* **31**, 695 – 702 (1998).
13. Y. Hoffner and S. Field, Contract driven creation and operation of virtual enterprises, *Computer Networks* **37(2)**, 111 – 136 (2001).
14. H. S JIA, B. WU, Reputation-based private mechanism, *Nankai Economic Studies* **6**, 16-51 (2004) (in Chinese).
15. L. Lode, Information sharing in a supply chain with horizontal competition, *Management Science* **48(9)**, 1196 – 1212 (2002).
16. J. F. Mahon, Corporate reputation: a research agenda using strategy and stakeholder literature, *Business and Society* **41(4)**, 415 – 447 (2002).
17. C. Martinelli, Small firms, Borrowing constrains, and reputation, *Journal of Economic Behavior & Organization* **33**, 91-105 (1997).
18. S. Manfred, Components and parameters of corporate reputation: an empirical study, *Schmalenbach Business Review* **56(1)**, 46 – 72 (2004).
19. J. R. Mason and D. Towill, Information enrichment: designing the supply chain for competitive advantage, *Supply Chain Management* **2(4)**, 137 – 148 (1997).
20. C. Schneeweiss, K. Zimmer and M. Zimmermann, The design of contracts to coordinate operational interdependencies within the supply chain, *International Journal of Production Economics* **92(1)**, 43 – 59 (2004).
21. Mahon, J. F. Steven and L. Wartick, Dealing with stakeholders: how reputation, credibility and framing influence the game, *Corporate Reputation Review* **6(1)**, 19 – 35 (2003).
22. S. Manfred, Components and parameters of corporate reputation: an empirical study, *Schmalenbach Business Review* **56(1)**, 46 – 72 (2004).
23. Prema. Nakra, Corporate reputation management : "CRM" with a strategic twist, *Public Relations Quarterly* **45(2)**, 35 – 42 (2000).
24. J. Sobel, Information control in the principal-agent problem, International Economic Review, **34(2)**, 259 –269 (1993).

SEMTOUR : HK – A TOURIST INFORMATION SYSTEM

TOBY H.W. LAM

Department of Computing, The Hong Kong Polytechnic University
Hung Hom, Kowloon, Hong Kong

JAMES N.K. LIU

Department of Computing, The Hong Kong Polytechnic University
Hung Hom, Kowloon, Hong Kong

Current Internet search engines do not always return results that users find useful, not least because the markup languages that are typically used only allow keyword searches. Semantic Web is a collection of web technologies that include a number of markup languages, such as RDF, OWL and RDFS, which can be used to model domain ontologies. Domain ontologies provide humans and computers (software agents) with a common understanding of a resource structure and help the creation of more effective web search systems. In this paper, we use Web Ontology Language (OWL) to model a travel domain ontology. Rather than inviting an expert to model the ontology, we create the travel ontology by collecting and analyzing the structural information from a number of travel related websites. The model is used to implement a tourist information portal, SemTour:HK, which is constructed using Semantic Web technologies.

1. Introduction

Internet search engines such as Google and Yahoo use keyword searching, which works by using techniques such as frequency- inverse document frequency (tf-idf) [1] to ascertain the importance of a word in a document. Such keyword searches locate web pages using input keywords without reference to semantics. The use of semantic information, perhaps in conjunction frequency-based search methods, could be expected to produce meaning-based searches that are more directly related to user's search queries.

Meaning-based or semantic searches cannot be conducted without semantically-oriented technologies. One such technology that could facilitate semantic searches is Semantic Web [2]. Semantic Web uses agent technology, ontology, and a number of standard markup languages such as RDF, OWL and RDFS to formally model information represented in web resources. The modeled information is accessible to humans and computers working co-operatively, perhaps with the assistance of intelligent network services such as search agents. This kind of knowledge interoperability is dependent on the ontology, which is a hierarchical relationship between terms of a domain. A domain-specific ontology is a tool for modeling resource structures and meanings and can allow software programs to do automated tasks for users, such as searching, customizing, and scheduling.

Given that two domains are sufficiently similar, one way to model a domain ontology is to reuse or extend an existing ontology. However, it is difficult to model a domain ontology completely from scratch. The most common way to model a fresh ontology is to invite an ontology expert to model the domain ontology. But there are few such experts. In this paper, instead of using experts for the ontology modeling, we model the ontology by using structural information. In this case, we gathered the structural information from web sites and analyzed this information in order to produce a travel-related ontology. This paper describes in detail how to construct such an ontology. For evaluation purposes, we used the ontology to develop a semantic tourist information portal, SemTour:HK.

The rest of this paper is organized as follows. In Section 2, we provide an overview of Semantic Web and some related work. In Section 3, we provide details of the travel ontology. Section 4 provides details of the system architecture of SemTour:HK. Section 5 presents the experimental results and Section 6 offers our conclusion and future work.

2. Background and Related Work

2.1. *Background*

The World Wide Web Consortium (W3C) has made two particular recommendations for the Semantic Web, Resource Description Framework (RDF) and the OWL Web Ontology Language (OWL) [3]. In this section, we describe RDF, OWL and related work.

2.1.1. Resource Description Framework (RDF)

The Resource Description Framework (RDF) is a language for representing information about resources in the World Wide Web [4]. RDF can also be used to represent information about resources that cannot be directly retrieved on the web. RDF is a framework for expressing and exchanging information between applications. The use of RDF allows applications designers to use RDF parsers and processing tools. In addition, the information in an application can be used by both users and applications, facilitating knowledge reuse and sharing. However, RDF is limited as it describes resources by using named properties and values only. A semantic extension of RDF, RDF Schema (RDFS), can describe the relationships between resources and groups of related resources such as classes, subclasses, domains and ranges.

2.1.2. Web Ontology Language (OWL)

Web Ontology Language (OWL) extends RDF(S) to make it easier to express meaning and semantics. Compared with XML, RDF and RDFS, OWL is better able to represent machine interpretable content on the Web [5]. There are three different sublanguages in OWL: OWL Lite, OWL DL and OWL Full. OWL Full is the superset of OWL Lite and OWL DL. OWL DL is based on description logic and its subset OWL Lite is based on the less expressive logic.

OWL Lite supports users' basic need for hierarchy classification and simple constraints. OWL DL maximizes expressiveness while retaining computational completeness. OWL Full maximizes expressiveness but with no computational guarantees.

2.2. *Related Work*

There are a number of research projects related to the travel domain. Most of them are guiding systems rather than tourist information portals. CRUMPET is a research project funded by the European Union. The main aim is to create user-friendly and personalized mobile services for Tourism [6]. CRUMPET adopted multi-agent technology and GPS technology to create a context-aware system. CRUMPET provides tourists with two different kinds of information: static and dynamic information. Static information is the information collected according to the user's profile and request. Dynamic information is the information gathered according to the user's location. CRUMPET also learns user preferences and interests to further filter irrelevant information. CRUMPET does not adopt reuse knowledge from other domains.

Cyberguide [7] is a personalized tourist guide for museum visitors. The tourist guiding system provides information to users based on data about the user's position and orientation. There are two different types of Cyberguide: indoor and outdoor. However, similar to CRUMPET, it provides only weak support for knowledge sharing and reasoning.

MyCampus [8] is a research project developed at Carnegie Mellon University. MyCampus is a semantic web environment for context-aware mobile services. The current implementation of MyCampus combines a number of technologies including OWL, reasoning, context-aware agent and OWL Rule Extension. The system can provide location-based movie recommendations and weather information. MyCampus is a user-friendly and intelligent application. It fully utilizes the latest Semantic Web technologies.

Johanna and Schubert [9] created a web-based virtual exhibition system (VES) based on an XML-based digital archive. They defined a rich layered set of metadata of image and text artifacts. These metadata make it easier to develop and maintain the content in the system. The idea of a virtual exhibition system is similar to our proposed portal. VES uses XML for processing, which provides syntax for structured documents but is not burdened by semantic constraints such as string literals. In this paper, we show how we integrated a tourist information portal with the latest Semantic Web Technology.

3. Travel Ontology

In this section, we describe how we collected the structural information and designed the ontology for the travel portal. In subsection 3.3 we describe the specific properties of our ontology and how they are made available for reuse. The travel ontology is related to areas such as accommodation, dining and sightseeing and this is a large domain so in this model we have defined only the upper-level ontology. This can provide a set of generic concepts which can be shared and reused by different users. To model this upper-level travel ontology, we collected and analyzed a number of travel guide related websites. The travel ontology was then used to develop a tourist information portal.

3.1. *Structural Data Collection*

We collected structural information from a number of travel related web sites. This included terms used in the site map and the website menu. Web developers often group related contents into categories. The use of such a site structure is a common way for people to define a domain (e.g. travel). Instead of inviting an ontology expert to model the ontology, we collected and recorded the structural information from a number of websites.

We collected a number of websites that related to Hong Kong Travel from Google Web Directory and Open Directory (domz.org). In Google Web Directory, there are 27 websites that are related to Hong Kong Travel (Regional > Asia > Hong Kong > Travel and Tourism > Travel Guides). In Open Directory, there are 31 websites that are related to Hong Kong Travel (Regional > Asia > Hong Kong > Travel and Tourism > Travel Guides). Since Google Web Directory integrates its search technology, PageRank [10], with Open Directory for searching, some websites in Open Directory are duplicated in the Google Directory. After removing duplicates, we were left with 32 websites (2 of them were unreachable). Table 1 provides the names and addresses of these websites.

We visited each website and recorded their structural information, including 153 different terms. After filtering and grouping processing, the most common term was "Shopping". Twelve websites contained this term. Table 2 shows the top ten most common used terms in Hong Kong Travel-related websites. We further filtered and grouped together terms with similar meanings (See Table 3). This information was then adopted to model the upper-level travel ontology.

Table 1. Names and addresses of websites related to Hong Kong Travel Guides.

No.	Name	Address
1	Lonely Planet - Hong Kong	http://www.lonelyplanet.com/dest/nea/hong.htm
2	Footprint Guides Hong Kong	http://www.footprintguides.com/Hong-Kong/
3	Regi Tour	http://www.regit.com/regitour/hongkong/regitour.htm
4	Dr Martin Williams	http://www.drmartinwilliams.com
5	Walk The Talk	http://www.walkthetalk.hk/
6	Arthur Frommer's Budget Travel Online	http://www.frommers.com/destinations/hongkong/
7	rec.travel Guide to Hong Kong	http://www.math.toronto.edu/~joel/hongkong.html
8	Hong Kong Tourist Guide +	http://www.yp.com.hk/yptourist_e03/en/html/tourist_index.aspx
9	PassPlanet.com - Hong Kong +	http://www.passplanet.com/HK/index.htm
10	Hong Kong Hotels Guide	http://www.hong-kong-hotels-guide.com/
11	12hk : The Unofficial Guide	http://www.12hk.com
12	Hong Kong FastFacts	http://www.hkfastfacts.com/
13	Hong Kong Travel	http://www.hong-kong-travel.org/
14	Writing, Photography and Nature Tourism in East Asia	http://martinwilliams.tripod.com/index.html
15	Travelocity's Destination Guide	http://dest.travelocity.com/DestGuides/geo_main/0,1743,TRAVELOCITY|2771,00.html
16	Stuie's Hong Kong Page	http://uk.geocities.com/expatbeamish/SB/HK/
17	Hong Kong Tong	http://www.hongkongtong.net/
18	Hong Kong Travel Guide	http://www.luketravels.com/hong-kong/
19	Hong Kong on Web	http://www.hongkongonweb.net/
20	Hong Kong Help	http://www.hongkonghelp.com/
21	Visiting Hong Kong	http://www.visitinghongkong.co.uk/
22	Hong Kong Travellers	http://home4u.hongkong.com/lifestyle/travel/hktravellers
23	Discover Sai Kung	http://www.discoversaikung.com/

24	Travallo: Hong Kong	http://www.travallo.de/laender/asia/china/hongkong.html
25	Worldsurface.com - Hong Kong Guide	http://www.worldsurface.com/browse/location-country.asp?locationid=112
26	BootsnAll	http://www.BootsnAll.com/asiatravelguides/hk/hk.shtml
27	CNN City Guides: Hong Kong	http://www.whatsontheplanet.com/wow/ptnr/cnn/page.jsp?fx=destination&loc_id=147486&xml_set=wow.city
28	Asia Friends Network - Hong Kong Tourism	http://www.countries.asiafriendsnetwork.com/HongKong/
29	Explore Sai Kung	http://www.exploresaikung.com/
30	Hong Kong Streets	http://www.hkstreet.com/
31	I Love Hong Kong	http://free.hostdepartment.com/i/iheart hk/
32	UnRealHongKong.com	http://www.unrealhongkong.com/

+ - dead link

Table 2. Ten most commonly used categories in Hong Kong travel guide websites

Rank	Category Term	Frequency
1	Shopping	12
2	Hotel	6
3	Getting Around	6
4	Link	6
5	Food	5
6	History	5
7	Attraction	5
8	Festival	5
9	Accommodation	5
10	Transportation	4

3.2. *Ontology Design*

An upper-level ontology is provides a set of basic concepts. If we modeled all of these basic concepts, the ontology would be too specific and would not be reusable. After collecting and analyzing the structural information, we modeled the upper-level travel ontology, which is reusable by different users in different regions. The travel ontology contains seven main classes, each with subclasses. Fig. 1 shows the details of the class relationships in the travel ontology.

Table 3. Ten most commonly used categories after filtering and grouping

Rank	Category Term	Frequency
1	See / Sightseeing / Sight / Spots / unique Sights / Interesting Places / Attractions / Landmarks / Places to visit / Getting Around / Go Arround	18
2	Food / Cruises / Restaurant / Dining / Eat / Bars and Restaurants / Eating and Drinking / food & Drink	16
3	Shopping / Shop / Shopping & Malls / Buy	15
4	General Information / General / Overview / General HK Info / City Facts & Info / Country Info / History	14
5	Accommodation / Places to stay / Sleep / Hotels	13
6	News & Events / News / Events / Festivals and Events / Festival / Festivals and Holidays / Public Holidays	11
7	Transportation / Transport / Getting There	10
8	Others / Misc / Link	6
9	Nightlife / Night	5
10	Weather / Local Weather	4

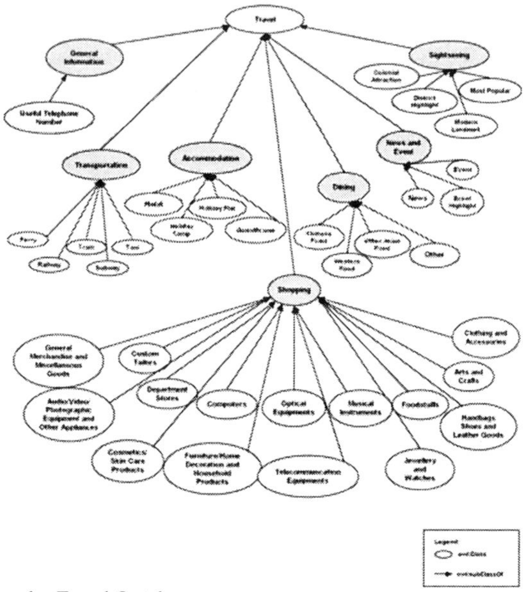

Figure 1. Travel Ontology

The travel ontology was modeled using Protégé [11]. Protégé is a free, open-source platform with a friendly user interface that provides a set of tools for constructing domain models and knowledge-based applications with ontologies. We modeled the travel ontology by using Web Ontology Language (OWL). Fig. 2 presents a partial OWL serialization of the travel ontology. We also created three other ontologies: Cuisine, Shop, and District. Fig. 3 shows the class relationships of the cuisine ontology.

```
<owl:Class rdf:ID="Custom_Tailor">
 <rdfs:subClassOf rdf:resource="#Shop_Type"/>
</owl:Class>
<owl:Class rdf:ID="Useful_Telephone_Number">
 <rdfs:subClassOf>
  <owl:Class rdf:ID="General_Information"/>
 </rdfs:subClassOf>
</owl:Class>
<owl:Class rdf:ID="Handbags_Shoes_and_Leather_Goods">
 <rdfs:subClassOf>
  <owl:Class rdf:ID="Shopping"/>
 </rdfs:subClassOf>
</owl:Class>
 <owl:Class rdf:ID="Hotel">
 <rdfs:subClassOf>
  <owl:Class rdf:ID="Accommodation"/>
 </rdfs:subClassOf>
</owl:Class>
<owl:ObjectProperty rdf:ID="hasCuisine">
 <rdfs:range rdf:resource="#Cuisine_Type"/>
 <rdfs:domain>
  <owl:Class>
```

Figure 2. The partial OWL serialization of the travel ontology.

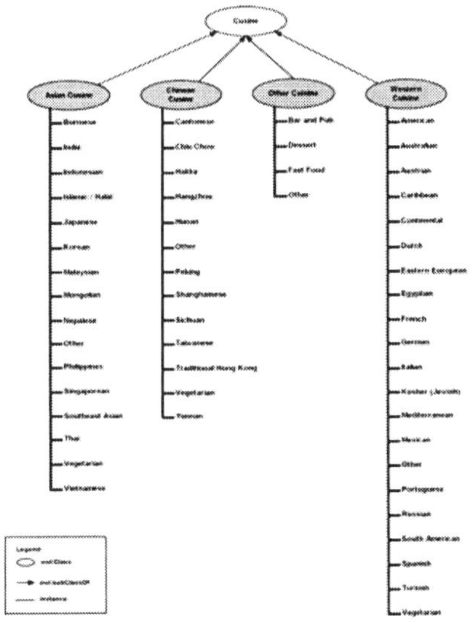

Figure 3. Cuisine Ontology

4. Travel Ontology

In this section, we describe the details of the system architecture of the semantic tourist information portal – SemTour:HK. In addition, we present a customized function called "My Travel Interest" and function "My Travel List", similar to a wish list in an e-commerce website. These functions can help users to collect information about places they are interested in. Users can also record this information in RDF format for use in personal devices.

4.1. *SemTour:HK*

SemTour:HK is a tourist information portal which lets tourists search for information about accommodation, sightseeing and dining in Hong Kong. The portal was developed using Semantic Web technology and implemented in Java on the Jena Semantic Framework. Fig. 4 depicts the system architecture of SemTour:HK. Users can access the information portal through the web browser. Fig. 5 shows the homepage of SemTour:HK. The tourist information server is a web server that handles user requests. In this prototype, we employed Apache Tomcat [12] as the tourist information server. After the information server receives the user request, the information server forwards the request to Jena Framework [13] to gather the related information. Jena is an open source Java framework for building Semantic Web applications. It offers a number of APIs for handling RDF, RDFS and OWL. Jena is chiefly used to parse and query the travel ontology. Jena searches the data from the travel ontology by using the SPARQL Protocol and RDF Query Language (SPARQL). SPARQL is a query language and protocol for accessing RDF which is designed by the W3C RDF Data Access Working Group. The SPARQL search result returns an RDF graph and is sent back to the tourist information server. Then, the server generates a result page and displays the result to the user. Fig. 6 shows a screenshot of a shopping page in SemTour:HK.

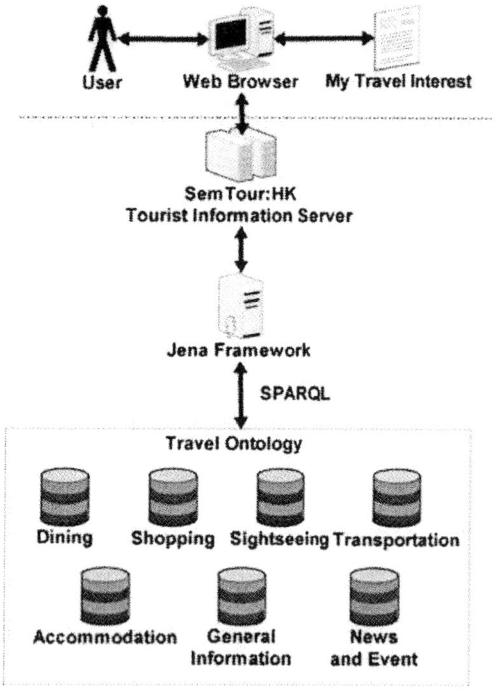

Figure 4. System architecture of SemTour:HK

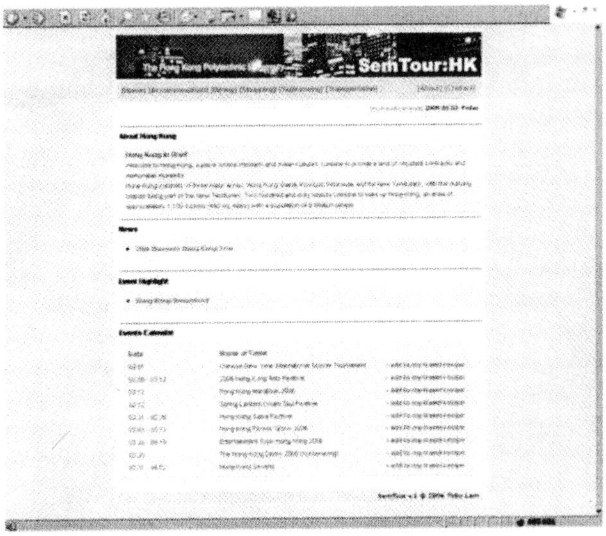

Figure 5. Screenshot of SemTour:HK Homepage

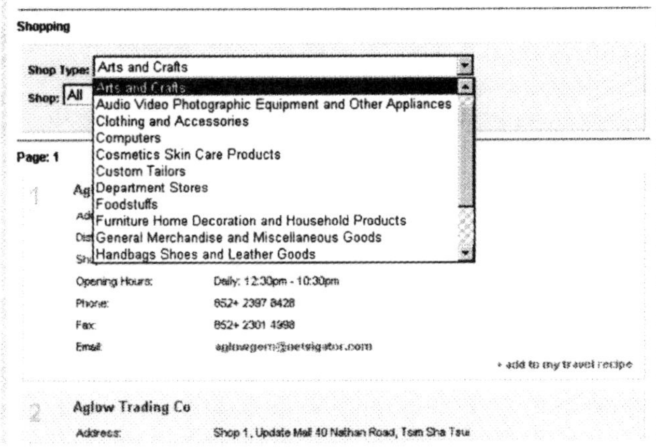

Figure 6. Screenshot of a shopping page in SemTour:HK.

4.2. *My Travel Interest*

SemTour:HK contains a function called My Travel Interest. This is similar to a wish list function in an e-commerce web site. If users are interested in a place, a shop or a hotel, they can click the hyperlink “add to my travel interest” and then the system will collect the information. Fig. 7 shows the “add to my travel interest” hyperlink in the shopping page. Unlike other wish list functions, users can save the interest to their own computer. The travel interests are maintained in a RDF file which contains the name and universal resource identifier (URI) of each item. Users can further save the interest information to a personal device such as a pocket PC or mobile phone. When users arrive in HK, they can use this information to find the place they are interested in.

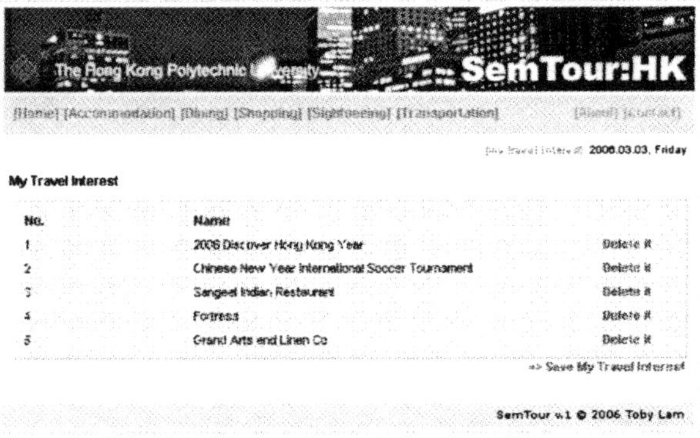

Figure 7. “My Travel Interest” page in SemTour:HK

5. Performance Evaluation

A prototype of a tourist information portal – SemTour:HK is developed by using Java Server Pages (JSP) based on a Jena framework. The tourist information server is installed in a P4 1.8GHz computer with 768MB memory. The main objective of the experiment is to evaluate the performance of the travel ontology.

5.1. *Processing Time*

SemTour:HK has six main pages: home, accommodation, dining, shopping, sightseeing, and transportation. We recorded the processing time required to generate the result page. Each page is requested ten times and the processing time is recorded. Fig. 8 shows the processing time for each page. The home page has the longest processing time at 3240.5ms. The transportation page has the shortest processing time at 829.6ms. The long processing time of the home page can be attributed to the fact that it provides four different classes of information. The SemTour:HK home page shows four different types of information: About Hong Kong, News, Event Highlight and Events Calendar. These mainly come from the News and Event and General Information classes in travel ontology. Since the home JSP page required four different SPARQL query to get the related information, the processing time is longer than that of the others. The transportation page has the shortest processing time as the SPARQL query is simple compared with other pages. Table 4 shows the average processing time for each page.

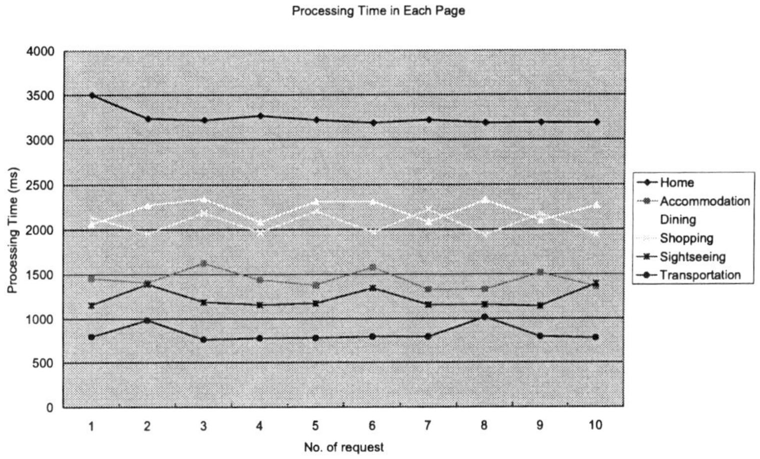

Figure 8. Processing time for each page

Table 4. Average processing time for each page

Name of the page	Average Processing Time (in ms)
Home	3240.5
Accommodation	1440.6
Dining	2214
Shopping	2068.7
Sightseeing	1224.9
Transportation	829.6

6. Conclusion and Future Work

This paper has described how we modeled the ontology by collecting and analyzing structural information from a number of websites. Using Google Directory and Open Directory, we collected 32 Hong Kong related travel guide websites. The terms used in the structural information were collected for analysis. After grouping and filtering terms with similar meanings, we defined seven main classes for use in the travel ontology. Each class had its own subclasses and properties. We input around 400 instances based on the travel ontology. To demonstrate how the ontology works, we used Java and Jena Semantic Framework to develop a semantic tourist information portal called SemTour:HK.

In summary, this work has offered a new approach to modeling a domain ontology. We have successfully developed a travel ontology and then used this ontology to develop a semantic web application. In the future, we would like to further develop a mobile, intelligent, interactive mobile tourist guide device that uses this ontology to assist tourists.

References

1. G. Salton and C. Buckley, Term-weighting approaches in automatic text retrieval, *Information Processing & Management* **24(5)**, 513–523 (1988).
2. T. B-Lee, J. Hendler and O. Lassila, The Semantic Web, *Scientific American*, 34-43 (2001).
3. W3C Semantic Web, http://www.w3.org/2001/sw/ (2007).
4. Resource Description Framework (RDF), http://www.w3.org/RDF (2007).
5. Web Ontology Language (OWL), http://www.w3.org/TR/owl-features (2007).
6. S. Poslad, H. Laamanen, R. Malaka, A. Nick, P. Buckle and A. Zipf, CRUMPET: creation of user-friendly mobile services personalized for tourism, *Proceedings of 3G 2001-Second International Conference on 3G Mobile Communication Technologies*, 62-74 (2001).
7. G. D. Abowd, C. G. Atkeson, J. Hong, S. Long, R. Kooper and M. Pinkerton, Cyberguide: A mobile context-aware tour guide, *ACM Wireless Networks*, 421-433 (1997).
8. N. Sadeh, E. Chan, Y. Shimazaki and L. Van, MyCampus: an agent-based environment for context-aware mobile services, *Proceedings of AAMAS02 Workshop on Ubiquitous Agents on Embedded, Wearable, and Mobile Devices* (2002).
9. J. C. Lim and S. Foo, Creating virtual exhibitions from an XML-based digital archive, *Journal of Information Science* **29(3)**, 143-157 (2003).
10. S. Brin and L. Page, The Anatomy of a Large-Scale Hypertextual Web Search Engine, *Proceedings of the 7th International World Wide Web Conference*, 107-117 (1998).
11. Protégé, http://protege.stanford.edu/ (2007).
12. Apache Tomcat, http://tomcat.apache.org/ (2007).
13. J. J. Carroll, I. Dickinson, C. Dollin, D. Reynolds, A. Seaborne and K. Wilkinson, 'Jena: Implementing the Semantic Web Recommendations, ' Proceedings of the 13th international World Wide Web conference (WWW 2004), 74-83 (2004).

PART C

IT Systems & Applications

AN INTEGRATED DISTRIBUTED SYSTEM FOR WEB NEWS RETRIEVAL

MAN-CHUNG CHAN
SPEED, Hong Kong Polytechnic University
Hong Kong, P.R. China

WEI-DONG LUO
Department of Computing, Hong Kong Polytechnic University
Hong Kong, P.R. China

JAMES N. K. LIU
Department of Computing, Hong Kong Polytechnic University
Hong Kong, P.R. China

This paper highlights the problems of information explosion and the incapability of currently available search engines in finding what we mostly want. In particularly, these search engines cannot offer users the facility of specifying the categories and time frames they receive and cannot provide the online news information with the required frequency. To address these problems, we present the design and implementation of- "Ai-Times", a distributed web news retrieval system which can accurately retrieve and organize the web news information. We describe the optimized crawler algorithm, the news extraction algorithm, and explain how MapReduce is used in "Ai-Times" and can be improved to get better performance.

1. Introduction

As the result of the online information explosion, currently available search engines [25] are often unable to find what we mostly want effectively. They cannot offer users the facility of specifying the categories and time frames they receive and cannot provide the online news information with the required frequency.

In order to accurately retrieve and organize the web news information better, we have designed and implemented Ai-Times, a web-based news retrieval system which is comprised of an optimized crawler, an inverted index engine, a retrieval module, and an automatic summarization module. The system provides the following functions:

- Fetch the web pages from pre-defined websites periodically.
- Extract the news from the fetched web pages.
- Index the extracted news.
- Abstract the extracted news.
- Provide a friendly user interface for user to retrieve news.

The remainder of this paper will be organized as follows: Section 2 gives a survey of the related work on news retrieval systems. Section 3 defines key terms and describes the operation of Ai-Times. Section 4 presents the distributed architecture and algorithm. Section 5 gives experiments results. The final section offers our conclusion and future work.

2. Related Work

2.1. *News Information Retrieval*

News information retrieval has been well studied [1, 2, 16, 18, 19, 20]. Many studies have been done on the architecture of news information retrieval. For example, Ariki and Sugiyama [2] present a system that automatically classifies TV news articles using keywords; Renals et al. [19] describe the THISL news retrieval system maintaining an archive of BBC radio and televisions news records; Aggarwal and Hung [1] introduce the WIRE-a WWW-based information retrieval and extraction system; Sanderson and van Rijsbergen [20] present the design of a news retrieval tools based on an existing database of some newspapers such as Times. Morrison and Jose [16] developed VideoSqueak, which records continuous news broadcasts and facilitates online querying and retrieval of the video archive created. Lim and Ng [13] developed DatAQs which analyzes, identifies, and categorizes languages used in HTML documents and extracts information from HTML documents of interest written in different languages. However, none of them describes the core modules such as the crawler module and the news extraction module in detail.

2.2. *Data-rich Part Extraction*

The datarich part extraction algorithm has been discussed in literature. For example, Mukherjee et al. [20] describe an algorithm for automatically partitioning the html document into tree-like semantic structures, which expose the implicit schema. However, it can't perform reasonably well on all types of html pages when used in news extraction. Lately, we presented a keen tag based extraction algorithm [14] which is resilient to most html pages.

2.3. *Web Crawler*

Boldi et al. [4] and Shkapenyuk and Suel [21] introduce means of how to implement a web crawler. Many studies have been done on implementing a domain-specific crawler. Hu and Wong [11] presented a simple probabilistic model for intelligent Web crawlers. Bergholz and Childlovskii [3] developed a crawler starting from the PIW (Publicly Indexable Web) to find entry points into the hidden Web. Lately, we presented an optimized web crawler [15] which is applicable to be used in news information retrieval system. Details are given in Section 3.

2.4. *Parallel Crawler*

Parallel crawler is a crawler whose fetching tasks are executed in parallel in different machines. Shkapenyuk and Suel [21] and Boldi et al. [4] describe the architecture of the parallel crawler. Cho and Garcia-Molina [6, 7] introduce means of implementing and evaluating a parallel crawler. Buzzi [5] proposed a scheme to permit a parallel crawler to acquire information about the global state of a Website before the crawling process takes place. However, this scheme requires Web server cooperation in order to collect and publish information content which is needed for enabling a crawler to tune its visit strategy. The parallel crawler's performance is relatively poor when it is directly applied in a news retrieval system.

2.5. *MapReduce*

MapReduce is firstly introduced by Dean and Ghemawat [9] in Dec 2004. MapReduce is a programming model and an associated implementation for processing and generating large data sets. Users are more interested in MapReduce since it has been successfully used in Google (e.g. [10, 24]). However, there are few academic literatures about MapReduce except the paper published by Google Inc in December 2004. The traditional MapReduce is not able to estimate the executing time of the individual tasks, which make it fail in some cases. The authors present an improved MapReduce to solve this problem in section 4.

3. The Architecture and Algorithm of Ai-Times

In this section we describe the basic framework of the Ai-Times. We also describe the optimized crawler module and news extraction module in detail.

3.1. *Architecture*

Figure 1 shows the architecture of Ai-Times system. It contains several classic web based information retrieval system modules such as a web crawler, an auto-categorization module, an index engine, a search module, and an auto-summarization module. We discuss the parallel crawler module and the news-extraction module in the following sections.

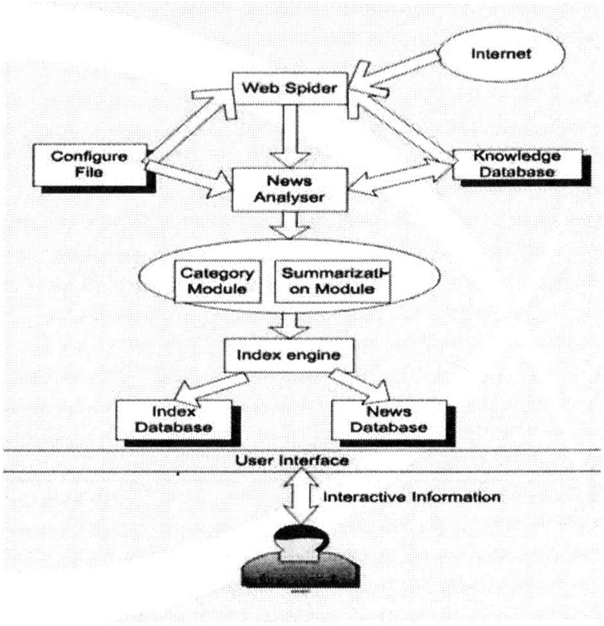

Figure 1. The architecture of the Ai-Times

3.2. *Optimized Web Crawler*

One of the fundamental and important components of news information retrieval system is the web crawler that can collect the web document automatically (e.g. [22]). Ai-Times focuses on the news collecting from some predefined news web sites, so an optimized web crawler algorithm is designed which is different from the classic crawler algorithm. In order to shorten the crawler executing time, we need to categorize the web news documents into 3 subcategories: valueless web document, news content web document and index/list web document. The definitions of valueless web document, news content web document, index/list web document are given below:

Valueless web document: The web documents that contribute nothing to the news retrieval, for example, the advertisement page.

News content web document: Web news documents that mainly contain the news text content or the news images or other multimedia sources.

Index/list web document: Web documents that mainly contain hyperlinks linking to the News content web document with relevant caption; often, the caption is the news title.

During the fetching period, the crawler can send request to the web server and analyze the return http header from the web server to get the last modified time of the web document. Thus, the crawler will determine whether to refresh the downloaded web document or not. However, even the crawler can get the last modified time through the HTTP header, it still wastes much request time and system resources. Many HTTP servers even do not provide the last modified time in the HTTP header. Therefore, one of the common refresh policies is to revisit all web documents to find the update information. However, this is very time-consuming. Another refresh policy is to select some important pages for revisit and this method often loses information.

Generally, more than 90% web documents of a news web site are news content web documents and these web documents are seldom or never modified or updated. By defining the three types of web documents, the Ai-Times web crawler needs not request all web documents during the update interval. This saves much time and makes the refresh interval shorter.

3.3. *News Extraction*

The news content strings spatially cluster (e.g. [23]) together in the html source and are accompanied with the Tag “<p>” and “</p>”. Universally, the tags such as “<p>”,” </p>”,”
”,” <font>”,” <img..>” can always be a web site’s keen tag. We define a list containing universal keen tags as below:

The list: <p>, </p>, <font*>, </font>, <b>, <a href*>, </a>, <img*>, <br>, <strong>, </strong>, <div>, </div>, <center>, </center>.

The string tokens of the html source of the web document are divided into 3 types:

1. The html tag that is a keen tag. 2. The html tag that is not a keen tag such as <!==* and <form> 3. The string tokens that are not html tag.

<u>*News extraction algorithm*</u>

1. Separate the html source code into many parts by the type 2 tags; therefore, each part contains the type1 and type3 strings. After that, the html source of the news document would look like this:

tag1-tag1-tag3-tag3 tag2 tag3-tag3-tag1 tag2 tag3-tag1 ......
part1 part2 part3 ......

2. Score each part, the scoring formulation is:

$$\text{Score (i)} = \sum_{k=1}^{ni} len(k) \qquad \text{----1}$$

where:

i: the sequence of the part. For i=1,2,...n (n is the total number of the parts).
ni: the total number of type3 tags in the current part.
k: the sequence of the type3 tags in the current part. For k=1,2,...ni.
len(k)—the length of the kth type3 tag in the current part.

3. Select the score winner part as the data-rich part.
4. Evaluate the selected part to see if it is a news content web document. The equation is as below:

$$\text{evaluate()}=\text{fin}(scorei)*\text{ tin(hrenum)} \qquad \text{----2}$$

scorei: the score obtained from equation 1.
hrefnum: the number of hyperlink html tags in that part.

$$fin(k)=1 \text{ while } k>N$$
$$fin(k)=0 \text{ while } k \leq N$$

N: the predefined low range of the news content’s length. Any news document whose content length is shorter than N will not be considered to be a useful news web document.

$$tin(k)=1 \text{ while } k<T$$
$$tin(k)=0 \text{ while } k \geq T$$

T: the predefined upper range of the total number of the link tags in a news content. Any news document that contains more than T link tags within the news content will not be considered a useful news web document.

5. If the evaluate() = 1, this web document can be regarded as a news content web document, and then the

selected data rich part will be extracted as the news text content. Let the caption we got before be the news' title. Let current time be the download time of this news. Besides the universal keen tags we have defined before, there are still some website-relevant keen tags that we can derive by training.

4. Parallel Strategy

As the size of the web grows; it is difficult for a single crawler/index node to finish downloading/indexing pages within a reasonable amount of time. In order to address this problem, we apply MapReduce to Ai-Times to achieve scalable parallel retrieval. In MapReduce, the computation takes a set of input key/value pairs, and produces a set of output key/value pairs. A whole round computation consists of two functions: Map and Reduce. Map applies a function to each element of a list to get a transformed version of the list which consists of a set of intermediate key/value pairs. The intermediate key/value pairs will then be passed to the Reduce. The Map function can be described as following formula:

Map (k, v) -> <k', v'>,

where <k, v> is the input pairs which we called it "raw data". <k', v'> is the intermediate pairs generated by Map function.

Reduce merges all intermediate values associated with the same intermediate key. It takes a function and runs it against items in the intermediate list, resulting in a single value for each invocation. The Reduce function can be described as following formula:

Reduce (k', v') -> <k', v''>,

where <k', v'> is the intermediate pairs generated by Map which is the input data for Reduce. <k', v''> is the result pairs generated by Reduce. Reduce merges all intermediated values associated with the same intermediate key and obtains the derived value v'' associated with key k'.

4.1. *MapReduce Architecture Design*

We completely rewrote the indexing system in Ai-Times. The Execution flow of the distributed indexing module using MapReduce is shown in Figure 2. The input data of the Map function will be partitioned into M splits associated with the number of the available nodes. These spits can be processed in parallel on distributed Map task nodes. Reduce tasks are also distributed by partitioning the intermediate key space into R pieces. At the end of the computation, all the reduce results will be collected as whole output.

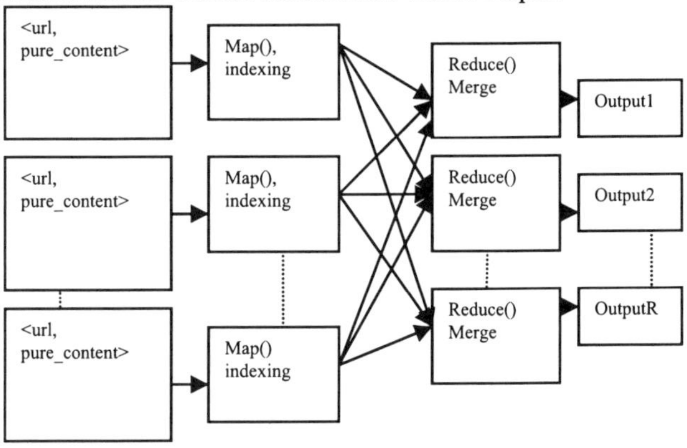

Figure 2. Execution flow of Indexing module using MapReduce

4.2. *Task Estimation Algorithm*

In a MapReduce system, when a job is partitioned into multiple tasks and the tasks are executed in parallel, the completion time of the job is determined by the last finished task. In a distributed indexing module using MapReduce, it is common that one of the map task nodes takes unusually longer time to finish its task. The whole system is waiting that node's result for Reduce use. A clever mechanism is to start a backup execution of the remaining tasks in-progress when the job is close to completion. The task will be marked as finished when the primary task or backup task gets finished.. This works in most scenarios.

However, in our experience of using MapReduce, the backup task mechanism doesn't always work. A recent problem we experienced is the parallel crawler using MapReduce, the input data is partitioned by the hash value of the url's hostname. Thus, a task node is responsible for fetching web pages from a set of websites (Assume 1 website here for simplicity). If a website is hard to connect due to the bandwidth or server problems, the task node which is responsible for fetching the pages of that website (Any page assigned to task nodes respectively is based on its host hash value, so pages from the same website will be assigned to the same task node) will take long time to complete the task and the backup tasks doesn't work.

In order to address this problem, the MapReduce system needs to take the task completion time into account when partitioning the input data. We used an algorithm to estimate the task executing time based on historical data, which we call Task Estimation algorithm.

Assume we have N1 data records to be partitioned. Each record has T attributes: attribute1....attributeT. From the past MapReduce processing, we get N2 data records' processed time. The data structure of the record looks like this:

Record{
attribute1
attribute2
......
attributeT
processedtime //null if the record has not been processed
estimatedtime
}

Records can be partitioned into Ct categories according to the tth attribute's value. In the same category, the tth attribute's values of the records are same or similar. In Ai-Times, the String attribute or the discrete attributes are partitioned by their hash value; the continuous attributes are partitioned by their range; Ct is configurable.

We calculate the average executing time of the records in each category:

$$AverageTime(tj) = \frac{\sum_{i=1}^{n_{tj}} record(i).processedtime}{n_{tj}} \quad (1)$$

where:

AverageTime(tj): average processedtime of the records which belong to the jth categories according to the tth attribute.

n_{tj}: total number of the records belonging to the jth categories according to the tth attribute.

$$\overline{AverageTime(t)} = \frac{\sum_{j=1}^{Ct} AverageTime(tj)}{Ct} \quad (2)$$

where:

Ct: the number of the categories according to the tth attribute.

Then we calculate the variable Determine of each attribute using following formula.

$$\text{Determine}(t) = \sqrt{\frac{\sum_{j=1}^{Ct} (AverageTime(tj) - \overline{AverageTime(t)})^2}{Ct}} \quad (3)$$

The attribute having the larger Determine value is considered to govern the task executing time more directly. Among the T attributes, we selected the top K attributes which are considered to eventually determine the task executing time. In Ai-Times, we make the k to be 1. Then we update the records' estimatedtime using the top K attributes' average time value, which we get from formula (1)

$$record.estimatedtime = \frac{\sum_{i=1}^{K} AverageTime(ij)}{K} \quad (4)$$

where:

K is the number of the top attributes we selected.

AverageTime(ij) is the average processedtime obtained from formula (1). The record belongs to j^{th} category according to the ith attribute.

After selecting the most important K attributes. We can then partition the data records to be processed using following three formulas:

Compute the record's hash value to partition the data records into K splits.

Hash (record[i]) mod K (5)

where:

record [i]: the ith record to be processed.

K: the number of the data splits we want to partition the data into.

Sum up all the records' estimated processing time in the same split to get the split's estimated executing time.

$$TotalTime(k) = \sum_{l=1}^{nk} record(l).estimatedtime \quad (6)$$

where:

TotalTime (k): the estimated executing time of the kth data split.

l: the sequence of the records in the kth data split.

nk: the total number of the records in the kth data split.

estimatedtime: the estimated processing time of the lth record.

The deviation between any two splits' estimated executing time should be less than a predefined threshold.

$$|TotalTime(i) - TotalTime(j)| < CONSTANTTIME \quad (7)$$

where:

TotalTime (i), TotalTime (j): the estimated executing time of the ith and jth data split respectively.

CONSTANTTIME: the predefined deviation threshold of the estimated time between any two data splits.

5. Experimental Results

Ai-Times is running on several pc servers. Server configuration is: CPU: p4 2.4 GHz; RAM: 512 MB; Bandwidth: 1MB.

5.1. *Ai-Times Single Optimized Crawler vs. Single Traditional Crawler*

Our crawler processed 3.53 million web documents in roughly six days. Assume that the traditional crawler has also processed the same number of web documents in a certain number of days; we then start a new round of web crawling. As stated earlier, our optimized crawler should only revisit the index or list web documents (in our experiment the number of the index or list web documents is 0.37 million) while the traditional crawler should revisit all web documents (in our experiment the number of all web documents is 3.53 millions). The consumed time and network traffic are both linear to the number of the web documents the crawler visits. Results gave an obvious improvement in terms of the fetch efficiency of our optimized crawler algorithm compared to the traditional algorithms. We consider the most important properties addressed by [6] including: Coverage, Overlap and Quality. Ai-Times parallel optimized crawler can achieve 100% coverage and 0 Overlap. For quality evaluation, we can approximate the recall and precision in next section..

5.2. *Ai-Times Parallel Crawler Based on MapReduce vs. Other Parallel Crawler*

In the scenario where the backup task algorithm doesn't work, we use the task estimation algorithm to estimate the task executing time, thus we can partition the input records more reasonably. Table 1 shows the result comparison in crawler module:

Table 1: Traditional MapReduce vs MapReduce Using Task Estimation Algorithm in crawler module

	Traditional MapReduce	**Using Task Estimation Algorithm**
Attributes selected as the Determine attribute		Hostname
Number of Input records	2.1 millions	2.1 millions
Size of the input records	3.38 GB	3.38 GB
Number of the tasks	250	250
Number of unusual tasks	21	3
Total completion time	12hrs 10mins	8hrs 01mins

In traditional MapReduce system's crawler module, we partition the pages based on their host value for task nodes to fetch. Thus the pages from the same website will be assigned to the same task node. Each node will be assigned same amount of pages. If a website is hard to connect due to the bandwidth or web server problems, the task node which is responsible for fetching the web pages of that website will take long time to complete the task. Actually the bandwidth or web server problems are very common, therefore the unusual tasks in traditional system are much more than the system which applied task estimation algorithm.

Table 2: Traditional MapReduce vs MapReduce Using Task Estimation Algorithm in indexing module.

	Traditional MapReduce	**Using Task Estimation Algorithm**
Attributes selected as the Determine attribute		Size of the page/document to be indexed
Number of Input records	1.5 millions	1.5 millions
Size of the input records	41 GB	41 GB
Number of the tasks	200	200
Number of unusual tasks	6	1
Total completion time	3hrs 3mins	2 hrs 45mins

Table 2 shows the result comparison in indexing module. In traditional MapReduce indexing module, we assign the pages/documents for task nodes to index based on their host hash value which is the same as crawler module. From the experiment we observed that the unusual tasks happened when a particular website has much more big files in PDF/DOC/PPT formats which are hard for parsing and indexing than other websites. The task nodes which are responsible for indexing this website then took unusual long time to complete. Using task estimation algorithm, we reduced the number of unusual tasks nearly to zero, and shorten the job's total completion time.

5.3. *News Extraction Performance*

Using the keen tag list defined earlier, our system has downloaded totally 1.46 million news documents. To measure the effectiveness of the news extraction (e.g. [12]) module, two ratios are used: precision and recall. Precision is the ratio of the number of correctly fetched web news documents to the total number of fetched web news documents that may contain some useless information. Recall is the ratio of the number of correctly fetched web news documents to the total number of web news documents in all predefined news websites. Because it is difficult for us to obtain the total number of web news documents or to verify each fetched web document to see whether it is correct or wrong, we approximate the recall and precision::

$$pre=num(r1)/num(N1)$$

where: pre is the precision. N1 is a set of documents randomly selected from fetched web news documents. r1 is the correctly fetched web news documents in N1. num(S) is the function to obtain the number of the units in the downloaded news collection S.

rec=num(r2)/num(N2)

where: rec is the recall. N2 is a set of documents randomly selected from total web news documents. r2 is the web news documents in N2 fetched by our system. num(S) is the function to obtain the number of the units in the downloaded news collection. We then select 1,000 web news documents from fetched web news documents and the number of correctly fetched documents in them is 915. We also select 1,000 web news documents from total web news documents and the number of fetched web news documents is 876. Therefore, we can obtain the approximation as below:

pre=915/1000=0.915 rec=876/1000=0.876

Note that we use the "keen tag" analyzing method to extract the news content so we need not implement different extractors for different news website, the effectiveness of our system is relatively acceptable.

6. Conclusion

In this paper we present the design and implementation of- "Ai-Times", a distributed web news retrieval system the goal of which is to accurately retrieve and organize the web news information. We describe the optimized crawler algorithm and the news extraction algorithm of "Ai-Times". Also we describe how MapReduce is used in "Ai-Times" and how we improved the traditional MapReduce model to get better performance.

In summary, we believe that our paper offers some useful guideline for the news information retrieval system designer, helping them for example, design and implement a parallel retrieval system using MapReduce, optimize their MapReduce and implement a more flexible news content extractor. Also, the incorporation of web ontology [e.g. 8, 17] shall be useful for information retrieval. This is the subject of next paper.

Acknowledgement

The author would like to acknowledge the partial support of the departmental grant 1-ZV41 of The Hong Kong Polytechnic University.

References

1. Sudhir Aggarwal and Fuyung Hung, WIRE - A WWW-based Information Retrieval and Extraction System, *Proceedings of the 9th International Workshop on Database and Expert Systems Applications*, 887-892 (1998).
2. Yasuo Ariki and Yoshiaki Sugiyama, A TV News Retrieval System with Interactive Query Function, *Proceedings of the 2nd IFCIS International Conference on Cooperative Information Systems*, 184-192 (1997).
3. A. Bergholz and B. Childlovskii, Crawling for domain-specific hidden Web resources, *Proceedings of the 4th International Conference on Web Information Systems Engineering*, 125–133 (2003).
4. Paolo Boldi, Bruno Codenotti, Massimo Santini, and Sebastiano Vigna, Ubicrawler: A scalable fully distributed web crawler, Proceedings of AusWeb02, *The 8thAustralian World Wide Web Conference*, (2002).
5. M. Buzzi, Cooperative crawling; Web Congress, *Proceedings of the 1st Latin American*, 209–21 (2003).
6. Junghoo Cho and Hector Garcia-Molina, Parallel crawler, *Proceedings of the 11th International World--Wide Web Conference*, (2002).
7. Junghoo Cho and Hector Garcia-Molina, Effective Page Refresh Policies for Web Crawlers, *ACM Trans. Database System* **28(4)**, 390-426 (2003).
8. C. Comparot, O. Haemmerle and N. Hernandez, Conceptual graphs and ontologies for Information retrieval, U. Priss, S. Polovina and R. Hill (Eds.): *ICCS 2007, LNAI 4604*, 480-483 (2007).
9. Jeffrey Dean and Sanjay Ghemawat, MapReduce: Simplified Data Processing on Large Clusters, *Proceedings of the OSDI'04*, 137-150 (2004).
10. Sanjay Ghemawat, Howard Gobioff and Shun Tak Leung, The Google File System *CSE497 WWW Search Engines*, (2004).
11. Ke Hu and Wing Shing Wong, A probabilistic model for intelligent Web crawlers, *Proceedings of the 27th Annual International Conference on Computer Software and Applications*, 278-282 (2003).
12. S. F. Liang, S. Devlin and J. Tait, Evaluating, Web search result summaries, *Proceedings of the 28th European Conference on Information Retrieval*, LNCS 3936, 96-106 (2006).
13. SeungJin Lim and Yiu-Kai Ng, Categorizing and Extracting Information from Multilingual HTML Documents Database Engineering and Application

Symposium, *IDEAS 2005. 9th International*, 415-422 (2005).
14. James N. K. Liu, Weidong Luo and Edmond M. C. Chan, Design and Implement a Web News Retrieval System, *Proceedings of KES05* **3**, 149-156 (2005).
15. J. N. K. Liu, W. D. Luo and M. C. Chan, Design and Implementation of a High Performance Distributed News Retrieval System, *Proceedings of ICITM2007*, 26-33 (2007).
16. S. Morrison and J. A. Jose, Comparative study of online news retrieval and presentation strategies, *Proceedings of IEEE 6th International Symposium*, 403-409 (2004).
17. Saikat Mukherjee, Guizhen Yang, Wenfang Tan and I. V. Ramakrishnan, Automatic Discovery of Semantic Structures in HTML Documents, *Proceedings of ICDAR'03*, 245-249 (2003).
18. G. Pant and P. Srinivasan, Link Contexts in Classifier-Guided Topical Crawlers, *IEEE Transactions on Knowledge and Data Engineering*, **18(1)**, 107-122 (2006).
19. Steve Renals, Dave Abberley, David Kirby and Tony Robinson, The THISL system for indexing and retrieval of broadcast news, *IEEE Signal Processing Society 1999 Workshop on Multimedia Signal Processing*, 77-82 (1999).
20. M. Sanderson and C.J. van Rijsbergen, NRT - News Retrieval Tool, *Electronic Publishing, EP-odd* **4**, 205-217 (1991).
21. V. Shkapenyuk and T. Suel, Design and implementation of a high-performance distributed Web crawler, *Proceedings of the 18th International Conference on Data Engineering*, 357-368 (2003).
22. A. Silva and E. Veloso, CoBWeb – A Crawler for the BrazilianWeb, *Proceedings of the String Processing and Information Retrieval Symposium & International Workshop on Groupware table of contents*, 184 (1999).
23. S. C. Smith and M. A. Rodriguez, Clustering-based searching and navigation in an online news source, *Proceedings of the 28th European Conference on Information Retrieval*, LNCS 3936, 143-154 (2006).
24. http://www.commerce.net/wiki/MapReduce_for_Decentralized_Computation.
25. Search engine watch. http://www.searchenginewatch.com.

FSAM: A FUZZY-BASED MIDDLEWARE FRAMEWORK FOR CONTEXT-AWARE ADAPTIVE SERVICES

RONNIE CHEUNG

Department of Computing,Hong Kong Polytechnic University
Yuk Choi Road, Hong Kong

We describe a middleware framework for context-aware applications. The key component in our framework is the Service Adaptation Model. The middleware infers the best service policy by making use of the fuzzification of different kinds of contextual information and by measuring and comparing the degree of fit between the current context and a predefined optimal context. Our system enables automatic service adaptation in changing contexts and provides best QoS services for pervasive applications.

1. Introduction

For mobile applications to operate efficiently in mobile environments, they have to be able to sense and reason about the current operating context and then adapt its service to the context so as to optimize system performance. One difficulty associated with this is that certain types of context information are highly variable. For example, the network bandwidth of a PDA can change dynamically while a person walks through a building or travels in a vehicle.

In this paper we describe a novel framework for fuzzy context-aware service adaptation using a Fuzzy-based Service Adaptation Model (FSAM) [1,4,5,6,7]. The middleware uses an inference engine to calculate and infer which middleware service is the most suitable one to be delivered according to the current context. It does this based on a fuzzification of different kinds of contextual information and by measuring and comparing the degree of fit between the current context and a predefined optimal context, The FSAM framework considers situations where multiple sources of context information may be available and defines different services for each application. Different policies can be provided for each service, depending on the quality of context attributes (e..g Network bandwidth). For example, a campus assistant application may provide a chat service. The middleware will provide adaptation decisions that suggest a suitable policy for the service, such as video chat, voice chat and text chat policies. When the campus assistant application contacts the middleware, the middleware suggest the most suitable policy for the application, depending on the network bandwidth. Our middleware is intended to offer adaptation with good performance, suggesting the best policy for context requirements by referring to a context repository, which stores a list of policies and their corresponding context requirements.

2. Related Work

Most context-aware middleware uses reflective architecture with mechanisms for the dynamic deployment and re-configuration of the underlying services [3]. The WebPADS project at the Hong Kong Polytechnic University [8] proposed actively deployable and dynamically reconfigurable service chaining for adapting to dramatically changing contexts in mobile environments. Much work [9] has been done to define context-aware computing and identify the requirements for building context-aware applications. Context Toolkits were developed to enable rapid prototyping of context-aware applications. These, however, did not provide a generic mechanism for organizing low level contexts and formulating high level abstract contexts

The CARISMA project [3] is a context-aware middleware system consisting of adaptable services. It uses context-aware application-specific semantic information in an "Application Profile" encoded in XML. The middleware checks the application profile document and compares with the current execution context to evaluate which behaviour or policy the service component should use. CARISMA proposed a microeconomic approach that relies on a particular type of sealed-bid auction to resolve service policy conflicts at execution time.

Systems have also been developed to directly address adaptation issues. The Chisel system [10] introduced a dynamic services adaptation framework which decomposes aspects of a service object into multiple possible behaviours. Whenever the context information changes, the service object is adapted to use different behaviours according to the adaptation policy. The Functionality Adaptation method [12] describes proxy-based context-aware adaptation of service code modules, by which the functionality of a service is adapted based on an estimate of the resource usage required for the execution. Policy-driven Mobile Agents [15] and Case-based Situation Assessment [14] are also proposed for adaptation in context-aware systems.

Our service adaptation model formulates and designs a policy selection mechanism, and we employ the fuzzy theory to solve the general problem of developing a generic service adaptation model. Existing works either work on a specific problem or focus on the software realization of services and policy rules.

Fuzzy-based methods have been used for control and adaptation. Indeed, fuzzy logic has been widely used since fuzzy set theory was first introduced by Zadeh [16]. Fuzzy logic controllers are very effective for complicated and imprecise processes, for which either no mathematical model exists or where the mathematical model is severely non-linear. The performance of fuzzy logic controllers is comparable with that of human experts in poorly defined environments.

A survey of techniques for using fuzzy theory to adapt quality of service (QoS) requirements in communication networks can be found in [11]. An example described in [13] uses fuzzy control theory for QoS adaptation in distributed multimedia applications. An application is associated with an observation task, an application task and a state of the application. The observation task monitors the state of the application task, and when the level of resources is low, the observation task will depress the requested rate of the application task, thereby decreasing requests for resources. In this work, fuzzy control theory is used to translate depressed requested rate values into tuning actions with enhanced parameter-tuning possibilities or re-configurations.

With the advances in context-aware computing, the sophisticated preferences in diversified applications domains impose strict requirements on quality of service requirements. The QoS-related approaches are usually developed for a specific domain (e.g., multimedia applications), and the related QoS parameters just constitute a subset of context information (e.g., bandwidth). Again, these approaches not targeted at a generic service adaptation model. They are targeted at specific types of applications, while our fuzzy-based model deals with application-independent service adaptation. The adaptive services are provided through a middleware implementation.

3. Middleware Architecture

Our mobile middleware infrastructure integrates context collection, fuzzy context composition, context delivery, adaptive middleware services, ToS and QoS. The advantage of introducing the adaptation mechanisms in the middleware layer is that the middleware has knowledge of the mobile application, the operating system, and the operating environment. This approach allocates resources fairly among mobile applications, at the same time fulfilling the requirements of individual application and achieving optimal overall system performance.

In our implementation of the mobile middleware infrastructure, there are four major system modules cooperating with each other to achieve a high level of context awareness: The first module is the *Context Space*, which contains *Context Detectors* and *Fuzzy Context Composers* that reason and compose low level contexts into higher level representations. Examples of context detectors include wrappers for OS events, which could also be directly communicating with the device drivers. At a higher level, context detectors could also be detecting an application's communication and computational activities. A fuzzy context composer gathers low level information, marshalling the dynamism and uncertainty of the mobile environment, and describes the current context in a more generic and coarser form. For example, a fuzzy context composer could be monitoring all the network related detectors to determine the quality of network connectivity – good, average, poor, or no connectivity. High level contextual information is also useful for adaptation with mobile applications.

The second module is the *Middleware Service Space*. This is the execution environment for both *Public Middleware Services* (one set of services that are shared among all mobile application) and Application Specific Middleware Services (each mobile application has its own set of services). These adaptive middleware services are categorized by their service nature into either public or application specific, e.g. a Web caching and prefetching middleware service is categorized as public since the cache pool benefits from economies of scale and the operations involved are generic among different mobile applications; a media transcoding service is categorized as application specific since, for the media transcoding service to work properly, different applications have different data semantics that require different settings.

The third module is the *Fuzzy Adaptation Engine*, which adjusts the middleware services according to the current context and the requirements of a mobile application's specific ToS and QoS requirements. In order to control the middleware services, the adaptation engine is aware of the programmable properties of the middleware service. To adjust quantitative controllable parameters for the middleware services, the adaptation engine calls the corresponding adjustment functions. The middleware services are responsible for exporting the required interface for adaptation control and adjusting the internal logic in line with specifications of the adaptation engine.

The fourth module is the *Middleware Manager Space*. The middleware manager space contains five system managers which coordinate all aspects of the operations within the mobile middleware.

The *Administration Control* component manages the admission of mobile applications that subscribe to the services of the middleware. Its duties include authentication, ToS and QoS negotiation, service subscription and un-subscription. For ToS and QoS negotiation, the strategy is based on a predictive rather than a reservation approach. A reservation approach reserves resources and guarantees all the time for each mobile application. This can often leave reserved resources idle and lead to new admissions being rejected for lack of resources. A predictive approach allows middleware to predict resource utilization according to the access pattern and to maintain the ToS and QoS requirements of all the connected applications.

The *Context Manager* controls the runtime environment for the context objects, including the low level context detectors and high level fuzzy context composers. The context manager coordinates the subscription of other entities to the middleware and the mobile application, answers queries, and reports changes in context to the subscribed entities.

The *Context Repository Manager* stores and manipulates the records regarding all contextual information. This allows queries on context history And the use of past records for predicting future trends in contexts.

The *Middleware Service Manager* controls both the public and application specific execution environments for the middleware services. The service manager coordinates with admission control. It also allocates and controls the resources for newly subscribed services.

The *ToS and QoS Enforcer* is used to monitor the ToS and QoS levels for each connected mobile application. If the ToS or QoS levels for a specific mobile application drop below the guaranteed margin, a warning is issued to the middleware service manager so that appropriate adaptive action can be carried out to restore the ToS and QoS level. Otherwise the admission control would have to carry out a re-negotiation of ToS and QoS with the affected mobile application. Instead, the ToS and QoS Enforcer module seamlessly and holistically integrates existing platforms.

4. Adaptation Operations

The core module of the FSAM framework is the Fuzzy Service Adaptation Engine. In the inference process where adaptations take place, we implemented the adaptation operations [1] as shown in Fig. 1. The inference process consists of three steps:

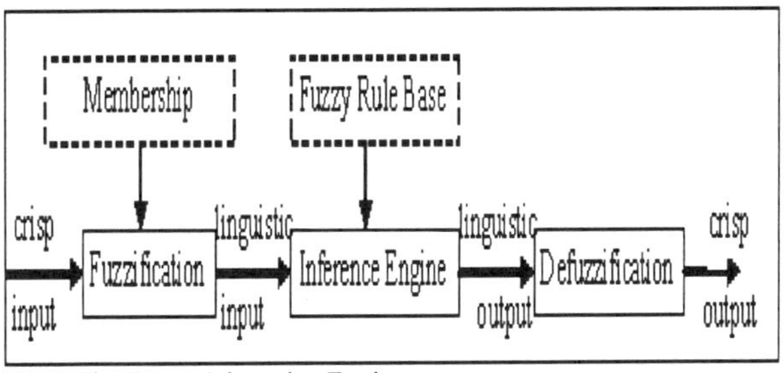

Fig.1. The Fuzzy Adaptation Engine

Step 1 Fuzzification: Each item of contextual information is represented by a linguistic variable. Each linguistic variable may be associated with several linguistic values (e.g. the linguistic variable *Network_maxRate* may be associated with two linguistic values, "*high*" and "*low*"). Each linguistic value is represented by a predefined application-related membership function (e.g. $\mu_{\text{Network\_maxRate high}}$ (x) and $\mu_{\text{Network\_maxRate low}}$ (x), where *x* is the crisp value of the corresponding linguistic variable). Using the membership functions, we translate the input context crisp value into a set of pairs, each consisting of a linguistic value and a membership degree for that value. This fuzzified context information is then combined into a fuzzified context situation.

Step 2 Calculation of degree of fit: In context-aware mobile middleware, a service can be delivered using several policies and each policy is associated with a particular context situation. We assume that a service can be delivered using only one policy at any time. During the inference process, each policy will be assigned a fit degree indicating to what degree the policy is suitable for being used in the current context situation. The degree of fit is assigned by using a fit function, which calculates the fuzzy distance between the policy's most suitable context situation and the current context situation. The degree of fit will increase as the fuzzy distance decreases. The most suitable context situation is the one having the maximum degree of fit.

Step 3 Adaptation: For a requested service, after each available policy has been assigned a degree of fit, the policy with the largest degree of fit will be selected as the best policy for delivering the service under the current context situation.

The inference engine refers to the predefined fuzzy rule base to derive the linguistic values for the intermediate and output linguistic variables.

In context-aware mobile middleware, a service can be delivered according to several policies and each policy is associated with a particular context situation. It is assumed that a service can be delivered using only one policy at any time. During the context reasoning process, each policy will be assigned a degree of fit indicating to what degree the policy is suitable for use in the current context. The degree of fit is assigned by using a fit function, which calculates the fuzzy distance between the policy's most suitable context and the current context. The degree of fit will decrease as the fuzzy distance increases.

Defuzzification takes place once the output linguistic values are available to produce the final crisp values. For any particular service, after the calculation of degree of fit for each policy, the policy with the largest degree of fit will be selected as the best policy for delivering the service in the current context.

5. Middleware Service

Our middleware platform provides facilities for implementing context-aware adaptation. In order for applications to co-operate with the middleware framework, we provide the following features:

- An API for tracking the context of resources and to provide facilities for notifying the application when certain threshold values are reached.
- Facilities for defining QoS parameters for adaptation decisions.

Table 1 lists the examples of contextual information that can be identified by the system. The device type include processor, network, storage, power, audio and display. For each device type, we list the possible contextual information that can be collected from the corresponding device. The abstracted contextual information is collected through the middleware.

Table 1. Examples of contextual information

Unit Type	Contextual Information
Processor	CPU type, clock rate, utilization
Storage	RAM size, free space, Secondary Storage size, free space
Network	Network type, capacity, data rate, delay, error rate
Power	Battery maximum lifetime, remaining lifetime
Display	Color type, depth, screen resolution
Audio	Type of sound supported
Operating System	OS name, version
Browser	Browser name, version

One of major features offered by the middleware is to sense external events, monitor and allocate resources. The adaptation process is achieved through a collaborative partnership between the OS and individual applications. This strategy characterizes the design space between two extremes. At one extreme, the system provides total transparency, particularly, the user can request policy changes from the middleware, e.g. switching from a color display to a black-and-white display window whenever the bandwidth is low. This policy is implemented in the public middleware services. In the other extreme, each mobile application copes with mobility on it own. This is achieved by defining the application-specific middleware services.

Another contribution of our approach ensures the best service to be delivered to meet the QoS requirements by calculating the fuzzy degree of fit, i.e. the distance between the current context and the best policy for specific application. The function FF below is used as the degree of fit function,

$$FF(SI(current),SR) = \frac{1}{\sum_{i=1}^{size\_of(SR(p_i^j))} \left|\mu(best\_value\_of(c_i)) - \mu(value\_of(c_i, current))\right|^{l_i}}$$

SI(current) is the current context, SR denotes the standard context that is most suitable for the specific service, C denotes the context and the factor l is an empirical value used to adjust the calculation of the fit distance. High-level service adaptation is achieved by allowing the Fuzzy Adaptation Engine to determine which currently available service is best adapted to the current context. The application can then switch to that service. For example, if a mobile device moving in a tunnel while accessing simultaneously offering image and voice services is faced with a dramatic drop in network bandwidth,, the image service may be dropped while the quality of the voice service is maintained.

In addition to system-wide service adaptation, we also provide a set of API for implementing finer-grain application-specific adaptation control. The middleware programming platform allows reconfiguration at the individual application level. The developers can extend the event system and the environment monitor. They can subscribe to a service that reacts to the context space and allow it to react to the event messages by adjusting its internal parameters to best adapt to the changes in the environment. An example of this would be an image transcoding service that offers different ratios of compression, using a different compression ratio based on the reported bandwidth from a bandwidth checking event source. Consequently, the image transcoding service can keep optimizing the transcoding performance for the varying bandwidth.

6. Conclusion

We have implemented a middleware service architecture for pervasive computing applications. The core module of the middleware framework is the Fuzzy Service Adaptation Engine. Given the abstract contexts from applications, the middleware provides services for each application. For each service provided by the middleware, the service adaptation engine provides the policy that matches the maximum quality of service. As part of our ongoing research, we are evaluating the effectiveness of the middleware infrastructure by implementing and testing with various pervasive computing applications.

Acknowledgments

This project is supported by RGC Grant Number PolyU5200/04E of the HKSAR.

References

1. J. Cao, N. Xing, A.T.S Chan, Y. Feng and B. Jin, Service Adaptation Using Fuzzy Theory in Context-aware Mobile Computing Middleware, *Proceedings of the 11th IEEE International Conference on Embedded and Real-Time Computing Systems and Applications*, 496–501 (2005).
2. L. Capra, Mobile Computing Middleware for Context-Aware Applications, *Proceedings of the 24th International Conference on Software Engineering*, 723 – 724 (2002).
3. L. Capra, W. Emmerich, and C. Mascolo, CARISMA: Context-aware Reflective Middleware System for Mobile Applications, *IEEE Transactions on Software Engineering* **29(10)**, 929 – 945 (2003).
4. Ronnie Cheung, An Adaptive Middleware Infrastructure for Mobile Computing, *Proceedings of 14th International World Wide Web Conference*, ACM Press, 996–997 (2005).
5. Ronnie Cheung, An Adaptive Middleware Infrastructure Incorporating Fuzzy Logic for Mobile Computing, *Proceedings of the International Conference on Next Generation Web Service and Practices*, (2006).
6. Ronnie Cheung, Jiannong Cao, Gang Yao and Alvin T.S. Chan, A Fuzzy-based Service Adaptation Middleware for Context-aware Computing, *Proc. 2nd IFIP International*

Conference on Embedded and Ubiquitous Computing, Seoul, Korea Lecture Notes in Computer Science, Springer-Verlag, (2006).

7. Ronnie Cheung, Gang Yao, Jiannong Cao and Alvin T.S. Chan, A Fuzzy Service Adaptation Engine for Context-aware Mobile Computing Middleware, *International Journal of Pervasive Computing and Communications*, (2007). (to appear)
8. S. N. Chuang, A. T. S. Chan, J. Cao, and R. Cheung, Dynamic Service Reconfiguration for Wireless Web Access, *Proceedings of the Twelve International World Wide Web Conference*, ACM Press, 58–67 (2003).
9. A. K. Dey, et al. A Conceptual Framework and a Toolkit for Supporting the Rapid Prototyping of Context-Aware Applications, Anchor article of a special issue on Context-Aware Computing, *Human-Computer Interaction (HCI) Journal*, 16 (2001).
10. J. Keeney and V. Cahill, Chisel: a Policy-driven, Context-aware, Dynamic Adaptation Framework, *Proceedings of IEEE 4th International Workshop on Policies for Distributed Systems and Networks*, 3 – 14 (2003).
11. C. Koliver, J. -M. Farines and K. O. Nahrstedt, QoS Adaptation Based on Fuzzy Theory, *Soft Computing for Communications*, L. Wang, Ed. Springer-Verlag, 245–267 (2004).
12. Vivien Wai-Man Kwan, Francis Chi-Moon Lau and Cho-Li Wang, Functionality Adaptation: a Context-aware Service Code Adaptation for Pervasive Computing Environments, *Proceedings of IEEE/WIC International Conference on Web Intelligence*, 358 – 364 (2003).
13. Baochun Li and K. Nahrstedt, A Control-based Middleware Framework for Quality-of-service Adaptations, *IEEE Journal on Selected Areas in Communications* **17(9)**, 1632 – 1650 (1999).
14. Anders Kofod Peterson and Angar Aamodt, Case-Based Situation Assessment in a Mobile Context-Aware System, *Proceedings of the Artificial Intelligence in Mobile System Workshop*, (2003).
15. Kun Yang, Alex Galis and Chris Todd, Policy-driven Mobile Agents for Context-aware Service in Next Generation Networks, *Proceedings of the 5th IFIP International Conference on Mobile Agents for Telecommunications*, 8-10 (2003).
16. L.A. Zadeh, Fuzzy Sets, *Information and Control* **8(3)**, 338–353 (1965).

CRM PROJECT MANAGEMENT IN THE SERVICE INDUSTRY IN HONG KONG

CHI WAH MAN

Department of Computing, Hong Kong Polytechnic University
Hong Kong, P.R. China

HARETON LEUNG

Department of Computing, Hong Kong Polytechnic University
Hong Kong, P.R. China

This paper proposes a project management model for customer relationship management projects for the service industry. It presents key findings from a survey of companies from the service industry and suggests that good communication management can increase the success rate of CRM projects. The other important project management areas are scope management, time management and project planning. The three key success factors are user involvement, executive commitment and process analysis. And the top three best practices for CRM project management are getting staff and management support and commitment, focusing on business not the technology, and managing stakeholder expectation. The findings confirm that people are critical to the success of CRM project management.

1. Introduction

The service sector includes trading, retailing, wholesaling, transportation, financial services, information technology, government and entertainment. The major challenge in service industries is said to be customer-focus, that is, managing customer demand and maximizing customer lifetime value to the service company. Managers encounter different challenges in different service categories [25]. To meet these challenges, service companies can use the latest technologies to strengthen their customer-oriented strategies to gain competitive advantage [13, 18]. The competitiveness of a service company depends on its abilities to apply technologies to meet customer's needs in terms of cost, quality, delivery requirements, level of service customization and service flexibility through its service operational and delivery systems, such as, transaction, sales force automation, order fulfillment, and customer information system [22].

Customer relationship management is the most important element in the success of a service company. A number of studies in different industries and companies have focused on the relationship between customer satisfaction, loyalty and business performance [23, 24]. Some have found that customer relationship management (CRM) software projects spread rapidly from the early adopter industries, such as telecommunications companies and banks to consumer goods and healthcare. Service companies try to develop integrated CRM systems consisting of operational CRM components, analytical CRM tools as well as collaborative devices so as to provide instant customer information for them to derive day-to-day marketing and sales activities [17]. Many retail banks in Hong Kong have recently started to develop different kinds of CRM systems such as sales force automation, marketing campaign system, internet banking and phone banking. However, implementing CRM systems is not easy. Research studies [4,8] indicate that 50% to 80% CRM implementations fail.

Our previous study focused on financial institutes and found that good communication is essential to the success of a project [20]. This paper presents our follow-up study which has been expanded to a much wider sample of service industries. Our project aims to explore an effective software/CRM project management model for the service industry in Hong Kong. In Section 2, we propose a software project management model for service industry. Section 3 focuses on the survey approach. Section 4 presents some key findings from the survey. It is expected that the research findings could help to understand the current Software/CRM project management practices, and difficulties as well as insights to improve the success rate of Software/CRM implementation in the service industry.

2. A CRM Project Management Model

In developing our model, we first review various CRM models [1, 2, 5, 7, 8, 21] and the popular software project management models [3, 6, 9, 10, 12]. The implication of each model on software project management in service industry is identified. In addition, after reviewing several case studies of CRM implementation [11], we identified some key success factors for software project management (SPM). We then developed a Software/CRM Project Management model for service industry, as shown in Figure 1. Our model consists of four major elements: environmental factors, project lifecycle management, project management area, and service value chain management.

Eight primary business environmental factors are identified. They are customers, market competition, technology, suppliers, industry, infrastructure, company culture and regulations. Among the environment factors, customer is of the most important, because the fundamental idea of any CRM software project is customer-centric [17].

Within the context of software project management environment, it is the layer of generic project management life cycle (project initiation, planning, execution, control, closing and evaluation). It provides a framework to define the basic project management components in the second layer. Among all, scope management, quality management, cost management and time management are the core areas to be focused on to increase the chance of success for the CRM project.

The third layer of the proposed CRM software project management model contains elements of the service value chain, which includes customer portfolio analysis, customer intimacy, network development, value proposition development and manage the customer life cycle. They are recognized as the critical areas for the design and implementation of the whole CRM system [17]. To what extent a CRM software project is successful depends on the integration of the service value chain propositions into the project management aspects. In fact, the integration is largely relied on people, as they are the key to bring the principle of service value chain, that is, 'customer-focus'. It was suggests that people is the most important critical success factor for the success of the CRM project implementation [17]. People have direct impact on customer satisfaction and customer retention. Yet, the ultimate goal is to achieve customer profitability which is the core of the model.

3. Methodology

The objective of our study is to validate the CRM software project management model proposed as well as to try to understand how to implement a successful CRM software project in the service industry in Hong Kong. To testify the proposed model and its assumptions, a research study was conducted with organizations in different service industries, including trading, retails, IT, financial and public utilities. In particular, the research focused on testing the hypotheses specified in Table 1. The hypotheses are derived with reference to the literature and research works of authors [20] and others [8, 9, 12, 15-19].

A survey questionnaire had been sent out to service companies. The questionnaire was designed with mostly closed-end questions, grouped into two sections. Section I was mainly for understanding the background of the interviewee's company. Section II focused on the project management aspects. In late March 2006, emails were sent out to targeted service companies and interviewees to ask support for doing the questionnaire. In total, 100 questionnaires were sent out to service organizations. Emails and telephones were used to follow up and motivate the feedback. By mid of April, 38 completed questionnaires were obtained through returned emails, giving a response rate of 38%.

4. Findings

4.1. *Profiles of Respondents*

In total, there were 38 respondents for the research study. 32% (12) had their CRM software project management experience in the financial service industry, 21% in IT and trading, 16% in retails and education, 3% in public utilities, and 16% in other industries.

Respondents included both business users (project managers, CRM managers, quality managers and directors) and technical staff (system analysts, IT managers and application system managers). They came from both local and multinational companies.

Most of the respondents (50%) worked in large companies with over 2,000 employees, 29% respondents worked in companies with less than 500 employees, and 10.5% respondents worked in companies with 500 to 1,000 employees. The remaining 10.5% respondents worked in companies with 1,001 to 2,000 employees.

4.2. *Project Implementation Area*

The most common type of CRM project found was internet/web project (37%), followed by data warehousing / database development (21%). Marketing management, service automation, analytical tools were the third CRM project implementation areas. Sales force automation was less common (5%).

Matching the CRM project implementation areas with the company size, it was found that large service companies with more than 2,000 employees focused more on service internet / web development (55%). Besides, large service companies had more CRM projects covering different areas than the others. They had projects in marketing management (15%), data warehouse / database development (15%) and analytical tools (15%).

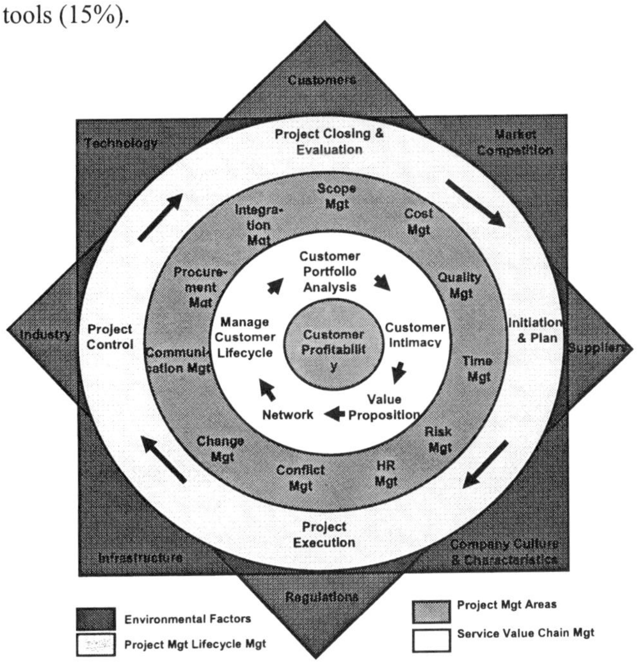

Figure 1. A CRM SPM Model for Service Industries

Whereas the small service companies with less than 500 employees focused on building their customer database (29%). The findings matched with hypothesis H1.

4.3. *Project Objectives*

The most common CRM project objectives found were improve customer services (21%), improve communication (18%), decrease cost (16%), and improve marketing effectiveness (10%). Our research results indicated that the company size is not a determinant factor for the CRM project objective. Since majority of small and large companies reported the same four project objectives, hypothesis 2 was not held.

4.4. *Implementation Approach*

Regarding the implementation approach of whether to employ external consultants or use in-house software project team, it was found that 37% respondents adopted the practice of hiring external consulting firm to work with internal project team for their CRM software management projects. It seemed to be an ideal approach to leverage on consultants' expertise to support the internal IT project team who knew the culture and the practice of the company. The second common type of implementation approach was recruiting experience staff to run the CRM project (24%) and total outsourcing.

Table 1. Hypotheses to be Tested

H1	The CRM software project implementation areas in the service industry are related to the size of the service company. Service companies with bigger size tend to emphases on internet / web project and data warehouse development because their operation is more diverse and complex than small service companies. There is huge cost saving impact for their operations by doing internet /web project and data warehouse management.
H2	Related to hypothesis 1, CRM project objective is related to the size of the service company. The large size companies are mostly with project objectives of overall cost reduction and customer service quality. Whereas the small size companies focus on either sales effectiveness or improve communication.
H3	The implementation approach of whether to employ external consultants or use in-house software project team is related to the size of the service company. Service companies with bigger size tend to employ external consultants or recruit experience personnel to work with their internal IT team because their IT team has a good knowledge of the company requirements and what they need from external consultants is the expertise on SPM and latest CRM technology. Small service companies are more cost conscious and they tend to adopt total outsourcing and standard software package.
H4	Business users are the key members in the project team. By including them in the project team, it helps getting a better understanding of needs of customers/ suppliers.
H5	Customers, technology, suppliers and competition are the four most important environmental factors that affect the CRM software project management.
H6	Scope, cost, quality and time management are the most important project management areas for the CRM software project in the service industry.
H7	People factor is the most important but also most difficult project management area.
H8	The three most critical successful factors for the CRM project management in the service industry are clear project scope, good project communication and customer driven system development.

Relating project implementation approach with company size, both large and small companies tended to adopt the approach of having external consulting firm to work with internal project team. The advantage of mixing external consultants and internal project team was to leverage on consultant's expertise and also trained up internal staff. Besides, large companies also took the approach of recruiting experienced staff to monitor the project. The findings suggested that hypothesis 3 was not held; the implementation approach of whether to employ external consultants or use in-house software project team was not related to the size of the company.

4.5. *Project Team Structure*

The key people involved in defining the CRM software project requirements were said to be the business users (68%) and internal IT staff (63%). This could be because they were the people who were dealing with the day-to-day customer services and hence they had a better understanding of the customer needs.

92% respondents replied that their major project team members were business users and IT professionals. 71% respondents reported that their project team had included senior management staff. 34% respondents answered that they had process specialists in their project team as it was believed that they could help in process redesign, ensuring that the system requirements met the business needs. It was worth to note that finance people (32%) were also involved in the project team. Normally, finance people played the cost control role in the project team. However, only 13% respondents replied that they involved quality assurance personnel in the project team.

The findings confirmed hypothesis 4 that the participation of business users in the project team was vital to the implementation of the CRM software project.

4.6. *Criteria for Measuring the Success of CRM Software Project*

82% respondents replied that the criteria for measuring the success of CRM software project was meeting project objectives. Meeting schedule was ranked the second most important, followed by the level of user acceptance. It was interesting to find that finishing on-time and meeting budget were less of concern.

4.7. *Environmental Factors Affecting the CRM SPM*

According to [18], there were ten major environmental factors affecting the CRM software project management at different degree, as shown in Figure 2. In this research, out of the ten environment factors seven of them were ranked above the average rate of 3 (out of maximum rate of 6). They were technology, customers/ suppliers, competition, infrastructure, industry, regulation, and parent company/ subsidiary.

The findings support hypothesis 5. However, technology was recognized as more important than customers / suppliers. It might imply that the CRM principle of customer-centric was limited by the technology applications.

4.8. *Importance of the Project Management Areas*

Regarding the importance of the project management areas, respondents were asked to rate the importance of project management areas from 1 to 6, where 1 indicates not important and 6 indicates the most important. All the thirteen project management areas were rated above the average of 3. Project planning was recognized as the most important project management area. The second important tier of project management areas included scope management, time management and communication management. They all got a score of 4.6 out of 6. The third important tier of project management areas included cost control and quality management. They got the same score of 4.4. Procurement management was of less concern as it got the lowest rating of 3.2.

The findings suggested that hypothesis 6 was not held. Scope, time, cost and quality were not the most important project management areas for the CRM software project management in the service industry. In this research, project planning was recognized as the most critical project management area. Same results were obtained in our earlier study with the financial industry [20]. The findings are in line with the view that project planning is the most important step in project management as it sets the foundations for the project implementation afterwards [15, 19]. Besides, communication management was rated more important than cost and quality management.

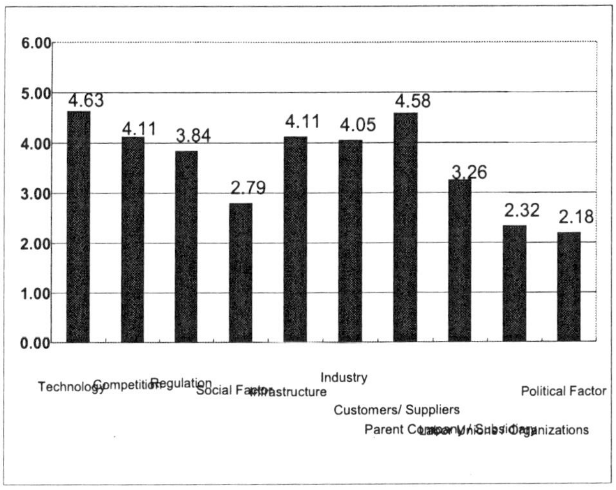

Figure 2. Environmental Factors Affecting the CRM SPM

4.9. *Difficulties encountered during project implementation*

The top three difficulties were:

1. Difficult to define system requirements (52.6%)
2. Employee's resistance to changes (44.7%)
3. Conflict among interest parties (44.7%)

Two of these were related to people management. It might imply that people issues were more difficult to handle than other issues. When mapping the project difficulty with project type, it was found that sales force automation experienced more difficulties than other project types. The difficulties were employee's resistance to change, difficult to define system requirements, poor data quality, poor planning, inadequate manpower, and conflict among members.

No	Project Management Areas	Avg Rating (max. 6)
1	Integration Management	4.2
2	Project Planning	4.9
3	Scope Management	4.6
4	Time Management	4.6
5	Cost Control	4.4
6	Quality Management	4.4
7	Human Resources management	3.9
8	Communication Management	4.6
9	Risk Management	4.1
10	Procurement Management	3.2
11	Change Management on People	4.0
12	Conflict Management	4.0
13	Measurements for Project Control	4.2

Figure 3. Importance of Project Management Areas

Different industries might experience different project management difficulties. In this research study, it was found that the trading and the retail industries were most likely to encounter employee's resistance to change and conflict among interest parties whereas the finance and the education industries were mostly found with difficulty in defining system requirements (83%). The IT industry, however, had its major difficulties in integrating highly diverse legacy systems (63%) and handling conflict among interest parties (63%). In general, the retail industry was reported to have more different types of difficulties than other industry. Typically, the difficulties in the retail industry were related to people issue, like employee's resistance to change (67%), conflict among interest parties (67%) and inadequate manpower resources.

4.10. *Comments on the last CRM implementation*

Among the 38 respondents, 84% claimed that their last CRM software projects were completed successfully. Only 16% reported that their last CRM software projects failed to achieve their project objectives.

To get a better understanding of the characteristics of a successful CRM software project management, all respondents were asked to give their comments on their last CRM software project implementation. A comparison of the comments between failure and successful cases were made.

For the successful cases, there were seven major project management characteristics identified:

1. The project plan was clearly communicated to all participants (90.6%)
2. System development was customer driven (87.5%)
3. The project scope was clearly defined (84.4%)
4. The project has well defined milestone for progress tracking and control (84.4%)
5. Compromise and collaboration were the most commonly used methods to handle conflicts (81.3%)
6. The project has a proper documented procedure for regular review of the status (81.3%)
7. The project cost was control properly (71.9%)

These seven characteristics covered areas of communication, customer focus (stakeholder management), scope management, progress tracking (time management), conflict management, quality management and cost management.

Table 3 compares the comment from the failure and successful cases. Large variances between the failure and successful cases were found in areas of:

1. Change management on people were handled

successfully (52.1%)

2. Software vendors were properly managed (49.0%)
3. Project risks were identified and monitored closely (42.7%)
4. Conflicts were properly managed (39.6%)

In a nutshell, the results supported hypothesis 8 that the three critical success factors were scope management, communication management, and customer driven system development. They were the pre-requisites for a successful CRM software project management.

Table 3. Comparison of Failure and Successful Cases

Comments on the Last CRM Software Project	Failure Cases	Successful Cases	Variance
The project plan was clearly communicated to all participants	66.7%	90.6%	24 %
Project scope was clearly defined	50.0%	84.4%	34%
The project has well defined milestone for progress tracking and control	66.7%	84.4%	18%
The project cost was control properly	33.3%	71.9%	45%
Has proper documented procedure for regular review of the status the projects	33.3%	81.3%	39%
Project team members worked well together	66.7%	43.8%	15%
Well established communication channels to collect feedbacks from users	50.0%	59.4%	6%
Project risks were identified and monitored closely	16.7%	65.6%	43%
Software vendors were proper managed	16.7%	68.8%	49%
Change management on people were handled successfully	16.7%	56.3%	52%
Conflicts were properly managed	16.7%	50.0%	40%
Compromise and collaboration were the most commonly used methods to handle conflicts	50.0%	81.3%	31%
Managing stakeholders was more important than technical aspects	50.0%	59.4%	9%
System development was customer driven	83.3%	87.5%	4%
Key performance indicators were developed to assess project success	66.7%	68.8%	2%

4.11. *Best practices for the CRM implementation*

Respondents were further asked to select the three major factors that contributed to the success of the CRM software project implementation. The results were very clear. User involvement was the top on the list (71.1%), executive commitment was the second (47.4%) and followed by process analysis (42.1%).

The top three best practices are:

1. Get employee and management to support and commit in the project (86.6%)
2. Focus on business not the technology (52.6%)
3. Manage stakeholder expectation (36.8%)

The results further indicated that people aspect was the most critical CRM software project management area and supported the findings of previous sections.

5. Conclusions

In summary, all hypotheses are supported, except hypotheses 2, 3, and 6. A limitation of our study is the lack of qualitative information for in-depth analysis as the questionnaire was designed mostly with closed-end questions. Subsequent research could aim to explore the integration of service value chain elements with project management areas. Comparing the CRM software project management practices with different service industries could be done in further detail so as to obtain more insights into the development of the CRM software project management model for service industries.

References

1. Neil Russell-Jones, Customer Relationship Management, Financial World Publishing, (2002).
2. N.L. Petouhoff and Jon Anton, Customer relationship management: The bottom line to optimizing your ROI, Prentice Hall, (2002).
3. Dwayne Phillips, The Software Project Manager's Handbook – Principles that work at work, IEEE Computer Society, (1998).
4. Gartner, CRM Benchmarking Study Key Findings, (2001).
5. Koos Koen, Technology and Customer Relationship Management, http://www.suntimes.co.za/2001/11/25/business/news/news13.asp, (2001).
6. Terrence L. Foran, A Structured Approach to Implement CRM, http://www.destinationcrm.com/articles/default.asp?ArticleID=1712 , (2001).
7. Stephen Redmond, http://workhelp.org/index2.php?option=content&task=view&id=65.
8. META Group. 2002/2003 trends – customer relationship management infusion, http://www.dmreview.com/article_sub.cfm?articleId=6347, (2002).
9. Thamhain and D. Wilemon, Criteria for controlling projects according to plan, *Project Management Journal* **17 (2)**, 75-81 (1986).
10. Bob Hughes and Mike Cotterell, Software Project Management, McGraw-Hill Publishing, (2005).

11. J.W. Ross, Travelers Insurance: Process Support through Distributed Technologies, Cambridge, Massachusetts: MIT Sloan School of Management Center for Information Systems Research, working paper 282, (1995).
12. PMBOK, A Guide to the project management body of knowledge, Project Management Institute, (2004).
13. M.E Porter, Strategy and the Internet, *Harvard Business Review* **79(3)**, 62-78 (2001).
14. James J. Jiang, Gary Klein and Joseph Balloun, Ranking of System Implementation Success Factors, *Project Management Journal*, (1996).
15. Harvey Maylor, Project Management, third edition, Prentice Hall, (2003).
16. Deloitte Consulting LLC, CRM. A Guide to Marketing, Sales and Service Transformation, Deloitte Consulting LLC, (1999).
17. Francis Buttle, CRM Concept & Tools, Elsevier Butterworth – Heinemann, (2004).
18. Bennet P. Lientz and Kathryn P. Rea, Project Management for the 21st Century 3rd ed. Academic Press, (2002).
19. Marsha D. Lewin, Better software project management: a primer for success, John Wiley & Sons, (2002).
20. Chi Wah Man, Wing Yee Winnie Kong, Wai Hung Eddie Yui, Pui Fan Jessie Tam and Hareton Leung, A Study of CRM Implementation in Financial Industry, International Conference on e-Learning, e-Business, Enterprise Information Systems, e-Government, and Outsourcing, (2006).
21. Adrian Payne, Customer Relationship Management, http://www.ittoolbox.com/peer/AP_website.htm.
22. Richard D. Metters, Kathryn H. King-Metters, Madeleine Pullman and Steve Walton, Successful Service Operations Management, South-Western of Thomson Corp., (2006).
23. C.D. Ittner and D.F. Larcker, Are non-financial indicators of financial performance? An analysis of customer satisfaction, *Journal of Accounting Research* **36**, 1-46 (1998).
24. N. G. Carr, Marketing: the economics of customer satisfaction, *Harvard Business Review* **77(2)**, 15-16 (1999).
25. Roger Schmenner, How can service businesses survive and prosper? MIT Sloan Management Review, (1986).

A CONCEPT FOR APPLYING MODEL-DRIVEN ENGINEERING TO APPLICATION INTEGRATION

CLEMENS DORDA
Institute of Parallel and Distributed Systems (IPVS), University of Stuttgart
Universitätsstr. 38, 70569 Stuttgart, Germany

UWE HEINKEL
Institute of Parallel and Distributed Systems (IPVS), University of Stuttgart
Universitätsstr. 38, 70569 Stuttgart, Germany

BERNHARD MITSCHANG
Institute of Parallel and Distributed Systems (IPVS), University of Stuttgart
Universitätsstr. 38, 70569 Stuttgart, Germany

Modern software for Enterprise Application Integration (EAI) provides tools for modeling integration scenarios. A drawback of these tools is the lack of functionality for exchanging or integrating models from different EAI products. Consequently, developers are only partially able to describe real heterogeneous IT environments. Our goal is to avoid the creation of these so-called 'integration islands'. For that purpose we present an approach which introduces an abstract view by technology-independent and multivendor-capable modeling for both development and maintenance. With this approach, we propose a toolset- and repository-based refinement of the abstract view to automate implementation with real products and deployment on real platforms.

1. Introduction

The history of integration projects in enterprises is almost as long as the usage of information systems itself. People often refer to the advantages and positive effects of application and system integration, e.g. faster and more automated business process execution, but they very often disregard the risks for the IT infrastructure. For example, integration projects endanger the agility of the IT infrastructure because they link together previously autonomous application systems, considerably reducing the overall system agility and making it difficult to adapt subsequent changes.

This agility decreases more with every new integration project. During an integration project, developers build large distributed systems which we will refer to as large distributed systems integration landscapes. In such integration landscapes, we have dependencies between existing stand-alone applications. The poorer the documentation, the greater the problem since knowledge of the integrated applications is usually distributed over many people or organizations inside an enterprise.

The result is a situation where central applications cannot be enhanced because the risk becomes too great that there might be an unintended negative impact on other critical systems. Therefore, with an increasing grade of integration, it becomes more and more difficult, complex, and expensive to adapt the system landscape to changing needs. The agility gets lost.

In this paper, we present methods to maintain agility over the whole lifecycle of an integration landscape. We introduce both an approach, which describes a process model for integration projects, and an appropriate generic tool support for development and documentation. The goal of this approach is to improve especially documentation aspects compared to the state-of-the-art of available integration solutions. However, our approach does not address semantic integration problems, for example semantic data heterogeneity. This topic is very complex on its own, and there are other researchers who address this problem [1][2].

This paper is structured as follows: in Section 2, we discuss main problems of integration projects and introduce typical integration scenarios. In Section 3 we give an overview of related work. Section 4 introduces our RADES (Reference Architecture for the

Development and Support of EAI Solutions) approach and describes its concepts as well as its tool support. In Section 5, we give a short conclusion and a view of future work.

2. Typical integration problems and scenarios

To motivate our RADES approach, we have a closer look at typical integration problems and scenarios. First, we identify three main problems of integration projects. These problems are difficult to handle with current tools. Second, we derive and discuss the most important scenarios of application and system integration. From our point of view, tool support for application and system integration should focus on these scenarios.

2.1. *The Main Problems of Integration Projects*

In general, integration projects suffer from three inherent problems: (1) divergence between system documentation and the current state of system runtime, (2) heterogeneity, and (3) distribution of systems and organizations.

The first problem we discuss is the *divergence between system documentation and system runtime*. During an information system's life cycle, there are for example changes to interfaces or message formats from time to time. Unfortunately, many people forget to update the related documentation. The consequence is inconsistent system documentation, and as a result of that an often unknown system state of the participating application systems.

A problem that comes along with inconsistent documentation is informal documentation, which often leads to varying interpretations by different readers. The consequence is an extensive reengineering of the system's runtime environment.

The second problem, *heterogeneity*, intensifies the first problem. Due to the fact that system landscapes become more and more heterogeneous, people have to deal with different integration products from different vendors. Consequently, they also have to deal with different philosophies of tool support and meta data management. This makes it more and more difficult to get a consistent view over the whole integration landscape. However, heterogeneity is not only limited to systems and applications – heterogeneity also applies to people. Integration projects are often done with different partners, who use different processes, documentation methods, or notations. Consequentially, heterogeneity is a problem for all integration project artifacts.

The *distribution of IT systems and organizations* is the third problem. Looking at distributed systems and applications, it is obvious that people have to put big effort to do consistent changes, because they have to be done on many places. These changes are error-prone, because developers mostly have to perform them manually. Looking at organizations, distribution of responsibilities over different people and departments leads to a troublesome retrieval of required information.

People usually try to solve these three problems by keeping them technologically and organizationally simple. On the one hand, many of these solutions are good and very important, and they are the precondition for our approach. On the other hand, it is necessary to introduce additional concepts, because these solutions are not sufficient to solve all of the problems mentioned above.

First of all, organizations need a central point for application and system documentation. The documentation stored in this central point should allow a consistent and homogeneous up-to-date view onto the runtime environment of integration solutions. We call this a central documentation system in the succeeding sections. Second, a defined process model has to guarantee the consistency between documentation and runtime, supported by appropriate tools. Finally, this process model must fit seamlessly into existing engineering processes.

2.2. *Four Scenarios for Application Integration*

To define an approach which addresses the requirements mentioned in the last section, it is necessary to look at some typical scenarios in integration projects. An appropriate process model must support these scenarios.

The first scenario is the *management of documentation*. This scenario is primary because it affects the others. We already mentioned the need for a central documentation system, but more difficult is the creation of good and sufficient documents. However, our focus here is not metrics for measuring documentation quality. For our needs, a good solution is to get as much documentation as possible from meta data. Together with human-made documentation, we need an automated way to collect this documentation and store it into the central documentation system.

The second scenario is a *new development of an integration solution*. Usually, developers start working from a preliminary design and refine it step by step towards a runtime environment. From our point of view it is important that developers store their in-between work into the central documentation system mentioned above. Another important requirement is the capability to check the results of a refinement step for consistency with the results from the step before. This requires a precise definition of the development approach as well as a precise definition of the result notation. After the last development step it should be possible to generate all required configuration data or code for the integration platform. For that purpose, developers should check out the meta data from the central documentation system.

The third scenario, *management of changes and maintenance*, is quite similar to the second scenario. This scenario requires the support of two different alternatives, changes on meta data or changes in code. The first one is similar to the new-development scenario and includes the documentation of changes into the repository, which leads to several refinement steps until generation of program code or configuration data. The second one is a scenario which is more difficult to handle. In this scenario, developers do their changes within the code or configuration data of the integration product, e.g. to fix a problem quickly. Here, mechanisms must be available, that detect these changes and propagate them to the central documentation system. After that, consistency checks must follow and must implicate well-defined steps to propagate these changes backwards to the higher development levels. Subsequently, the central documentation system should guarantee that all documentation is consistent again.

The fourth and final scenario is a very common one, the *migration of integration products*. From time to time, enhancements to integration technology require the migration of an integration product to another version, or to another product from another vendor. We mentioned in Section 0 the problem of different meta data, which results often in a complete reimplementation.

The existence of a consistent central documentation makes it possible to use the content as an interchange format between integration products. Together with applicable generators and adapters for the target product, which are required anyway for the scenarios before, this information shortens the implementation for the migration project.

3. Related Work

In this section, we discuss commercial approaches and scientific work which partially solve some of the problems we identified in Section 2.

3.1. *Commercial Approaches*

Software producers of commercial EAI products have integrated various mechanisms into their bundled development tools, which discard the common bottom-up approach for application integration. Instead, they provided tools which allow or force developers to use a top-down approach for development. This solves some of the problems mentioned in Section 2, but some requirements are not implemented yet.

One of these requirements is the lack of common standards, which makes it difficult to replace one EAI product by another product from a different vendor. This drawback reduces the agility especially of large enterprises, because different requirements for integration projects implicate the usage of different products, as well as the evolution of IT systems implicate heterogeneity. Finally, this means for development, documentation and maintenance of integration solutions, that the incompatibility among EAI products anticipates the implementation of common practices for integration development, based on the packaged tools. Consequently, existing technology cannot solve satisfactory the problems mentioned in Section 1.

3.2. *Scientific Work*

There are some research projects which try to address the problems under consideration here from different point of views.

The Model Integrated Computing (MIC) approach [3] describes a method how developers can model all relevant information about a system in development with domain specific modeling. Related to our needs, one drawback of this approach is both the lack of a well-defined domain model for EAI and a standardized modeling language.

Nevertheless, the idea behind this approach is one of the fundamentals of the Model Driven Architecture (MDA) standard [4] from the Object Management

Group (OMG). Methodically, MDA specifies a top-down process model with three abstraction layers, which provide platform independent models (PIM), platform specific models (PSM) and code. At present, many vendors support MDA with their tools, or plan to support MDA in the near future. Related OMG standards are for example UML [5] and the Query/View/Transformation (QVT) specification [6].

A more general approach than MDA is the Model Driven Engineering (MDE) approach, which was outlined by Stuart Kent, as stated in [7]. We can say that MDE is a superset of MDA, because MDE postulates in a more common manner multiple abstraction layers. Each abstraction layer is generally spoken a refinement of its predecessor, which is a layer with higher abstraction [8].

There are other approaches that focus on the topic of EAI and MDA. In [9] for example, the authors present a five model approach to realize a Model-Driven Architecture for EAI. Each model represents a different aspect of the EAI problem. Nonetheless, it lacks of a clear definition how the models relate to each other, as well as of a prototypical implementation.

4. The RADES Approach

RADES (Reference Architecture for the Development and Support of EAI Solutions) is a research project founded in cooperation with DaimlerChrysler Research & Technology. The project's goal is the development of a reference architecture to implement, document and maintain integration scenarios. The reference architecture includes concepts for both development methods and tools.

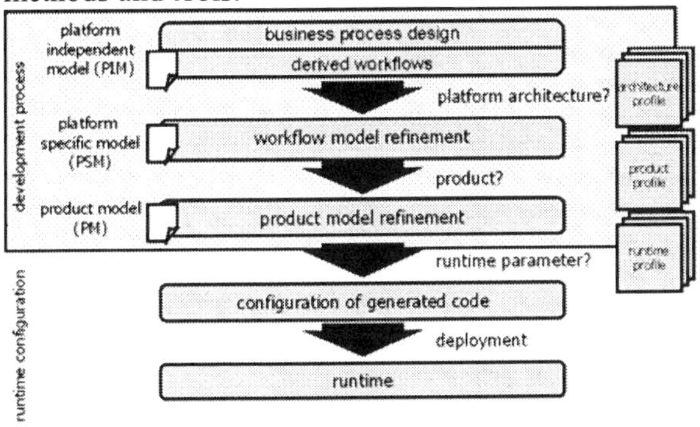

Figure 1. RADES Process Model

One part of this approach is the usage of a central repository, which contains all necessary information about applications and systems being part of an integration landscape. A well-defined development process is supposed to guarantee the consistency of all development data, including documentation, models, source code, and binaries (see Figure 1). Each stage in the whole lifecycle postulates on the one hand results in a specific syntax and semantic, but allows developers on the other hand a flexible organization of the tasks inside of each lifecycle stage.

4.1. *RADES Development Stages*

Compared with MDA, our RADES development process defines four abstraction layers by introducing the concept of a product model (PM). In the following sections, we discuss the reason for this decision.

4.1.1 Business Process and Workflow Modeling

One task, which is often disregarded, is the design of the business process that defines the underlying workflow of an integration scenario between applications and systems. This task is, from our point of view, one of the most important ones to finish an integration project successfully. After mapping the business processes to workflows, developers are enabled to make a decision about the integration strategy. They can decide whether to extend an existing interconnection between systems with the so far used EAI technology, or to replace such an existing integration technology with another one.

Therefore, the RADES approach defines the modeling of platform-independent workflows in the first development stage. Developers have to model applications, systems and resources, as well as their logical dependencies to each other. In this stage, it is sufficient to model only components whose functions and data are required for workflow execution from the application perspective.

The collection of these models is called the platform-independent model (PIM), and it reflects an overview over the integration landscape.

4.1.2 Detailing Workflows

In the next development stage, developers have to refine the platform-independent model to a platform-specific model. A platform-specific model is a description of the integrated systems within the targeted integration architecture without determining on a specific integration middleware technology or product. An example for a possible integration architecture is a "hub and spoke"-architecture, which is most commonly used, or a bus architecture. By choosing an integration architecture, developers limit on the one hand possible integration products to a certain product family, but does not commit to a specific product on the other hand.

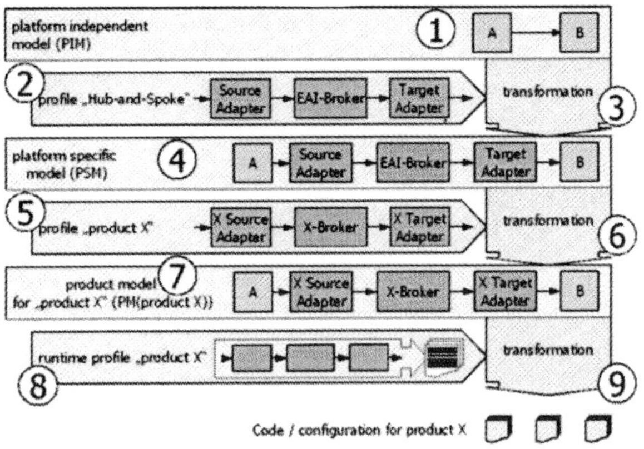

Figure 2. Schematic example illustrating model transformations with RADES

To get an initial platform-specific model, we use model transformations (Figure 2). The generator software ③, which is used for transformations, gets its input from the PIM ① and from a specific transformation profile ②. The transformation profile describes the integration architecture of the targeted integration middleware product. After the transformation, developers detail the models to get a complete product-independent description of the integration landscape ④. For example, to get a precise description of activities during workflow execution, developers have to detail the sequence and activity diagrams from the PIM.

4.1.3 Detailing the Product Model

The third development step starts similar to the second step. First of all, developers have to transform the PSM ④ to the product model (PM, ⑦). As before, the input for the transformation engine ⑥ are both the PSM models ④ and a transformation profile describing the targeted integration product ⑤, for example IBM WebSphere Business Integration Message Broker. Subsequently, developers have to refine the generated PM ⑦ so that the PM is well prepared for the code generation engine.

4.1.4 Configuration and Runtime

The last step in our development process is code generation for the targeted integration platform. For that purpose, developers need an appropriate code generation engine ⑧&⑨, which is enabled to compile the PM ⑦ to executable configuration data or runtime code for the targeted integration product. Due to the fact that the PM is a very detailed description of the integration product's metadata, the code generation is a simple mapping task in general. However, the reason for the necessity of the PM development stage before is simple. The PM describes all necessary interfaces, messages and flows of a specific integration product very detailed – but it does not describe a concrete configuration of this product. Therefore, this must be done by code configuration in this development stage.

4.1.5 Deployment

This development stage is not part of the RADES development approach. Usually, developers use tools for deployment which are bundled with the integration product. Nevertheless, it is possible that deployment fails. In this situation, it is necessary to go one or more development steps backwards to solve the problem on a higher abstraction layer. After that the succeeding development steps have to be done again.

4.2. *Modeling*

Modeling techniques are very important in the context of model-driven engineering. As a basic principle, the RADES approach does not commit to a certain modeling language or modeling tool. However, it is required that all models can be transformed into a unified model interchange language to process the models with different tools. For our research and prototype development, we use UML for modeling, and the XML Metadata Interchange (XMI) format [10] for model interchange.

We defined a modeling syntax and semantic subset for RADES based on the "UML for Enterprise Application Integration" profile from the OMG [11]. The advantage of this definition is the strong semantic explanatory power. This subset provides two typical modeling approaches for UML, collaboration modeling (class diagrams and collaboration or sequence diagrams) and activity modeling.

4.3. *Prototype Implementation*

Our current work focuses on the implementation of a prototype for model transformations (Figure 3), based on the Eclipse framework [12]. With this prototype, we want to provide a proof of concept for both our process model as well as our modeling approach. Our transformation plug-in modules, which will implement the transformation from PIM to PSM, PSM to PM, and PM to Code, build on top of the EMF framework [13] and the UML2 [14] libraries.

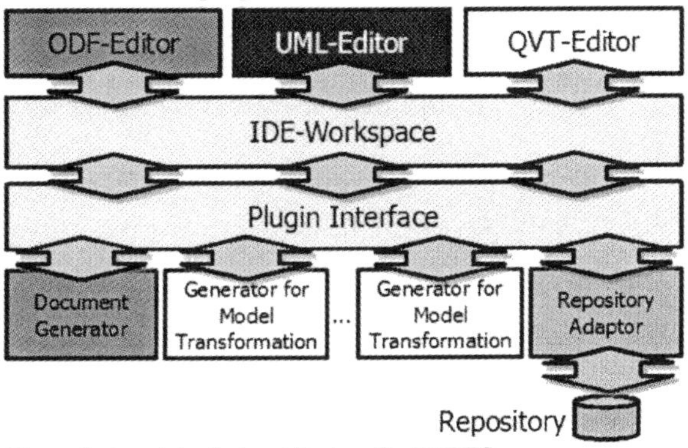

Figure 3. A prototypical architecture for RADES

Currently, we successfully implemented a plug-in module for the transformation of PIM to PSM models. The implementation of a transformation from PSM to PM models is ongoing. Our prototype will be the platform for the implementation of further research results, for example algorithms implementing reverse engineering approaches or concepts for the generation of human readable documentation.

4.4. *Evaluation*

We discuss in this section in which way the RADES approach supports the scenarios introduced in Section 2.2.

The first scenario we described was the management of documentation. RADES supports it in two ways. First, RADES uses a repository for the centralized storage of models and additional documentation. In some cases, such a repository already exists for some documents, so working with RADES will complement the existing documentation. In other cases, such a repository must be set up first. Second, the usage of a unified model interchange language enables a better tool-based metadata preparation for documentation without limiting the choice of usable modeling tools.

Our second scenario, the new development of an integration solution, is supported by the RADES process model. This process model defines a thread throughout the development process, and offers various views over the integration solution by providing different abstraction layers.

These abstraction layers provide starting points for the third and fourth scenario, depending on whether changes should be reflected to workflows, architecture, or the product model.

5. Conclusion

Agility and flexibility are important factors in enterprise application integration. This factor is underestimated and undervalued by many experts. The ongoing evolution of new IT concepts and technologies and their usage in enterprises leads to instable configurations of system landscapes. Developers can handle these instable configurations pretty good if they choose not to change the integration product. But if they choose to replace an integration product with a system from a different software producer, they can not just reuse the meta-information implemented in the existing systems.

The RADES approach offers a way to eliminate this drawback. We avoid an early commitment on specific integration products through high-level modeling in the beginning, and provide precise, reusable models of the integration landscape through several refinement steps. It is obvious that our approach does not make the initial implementation of an integration scenario less complex.

However, the return of investment comes with reuse, maintenance and request for standardized documentation, and we think that this benefit is worth to invest some more efforts in the first implementation.

Further work will focus especially on model transformation techniques and reverse engineering problems, because this is an essential feature for developers to adopt approaches like RADES.

References

1. AnHai Doan, Natalya F. Noy and Alon Y. Halevy, Introduction to the special issue on semantic integration, ACM SIGMOD RECORD **33(4)**, (2004).
2. Alon Y. Halevy, et al., Enterprise information integration: successes, challenges and controversies, ACM SIGMOD: Proceedings of the 2005 ACM SIGMOD international conference on Management of data, (2005).
3. Janos Sztipanovits, Gabor Karsai, Model Integrated Computing, *Computer, IEEE* **30(4)**, (1997).

4. Richard Soley, et al., Model Driven Architecture, (2000).
5. OMG, Unified Modeling Language, www.uml.org.
6. OMG, MOF QVT final adopted specification, (2005).
7. Marcus Alanen, Johan Lilius, Ivan Porres and Dragos Truscan, Model Driven Engineering: A Position Paper, *MOMPES*, (2004).
8. Frédéric Fondement and Raul Silaghi, Defining Model Driven Engineering Processes, WiSME, (2004).
9. Adra Al Mosawi, Liping Zhao and Linda Macaulay, A Model Driven Architecture for Enterprise Application Integration, *HICSS: Proceedings of the 39th Hawaii International Conference on System Sciences*, (2006).
10. OMG, MOF 2.0/XMI Mapping Specification, v2.1, (2005).
11. OMG, UML Profile and Interchange Models for Enterprise Application Integration (EAI) Specification, v1.0, (2004).
12. Eclipse Foundation, Eclipse Open-Source Community, http://www.eclipse.org/.
13. Eclipse Foundation, Eclipse Modeling Framework (EMF), http://www.eclipse.org/emf/.
14. Eclipse Foundation, EMF-based UML 2.0 Metamodel Implementation. http://www.eclipse.org/uml2/.

NEW DEVELOPMENTS IN E-LEARNING THROUGH MULTI-INSTITUTIONAL COLLABORATIONS – A CASE STUDY OF THE HKCYBERU

RONNIE CHEUNG

Department of Computing, Hong Kong Polytechnic University
Hong Kong, People's Republic of China

PAMELA LAM

International Graduate School of Business, University of South Australia
Adelaide, SA5001, Australia

Hong Kong CyberU (HKCyberU) is a company co-founded by the Hong Kong Polytechnic University (HKPolyU) and the Pacific Century CyberWorks (PCCW). As universities are investing in e-learning for Asynchronized Learning Networks (ALN), HKCyberU provides a business model for developing ALN in the Asia Pacific Rim. HKPolyU provides expertise and academic awards in professional education; PCCW provides investment, technical infrastructure, support, broadband capabilities, marketing and administration of courses. In addition to offering various HKPolyU awards, HKCyberU has developed strategic alliance with a number of universities in overseas and China to offer asynchronized/web supporting learning network. As higher education institutions are planning to finance e-Learning courses, HKCyberU model provides a good example of developing and offering courses online in Hong Kong and China.

1. Introduction

E-learning is becoming a popular mode of study. Working adults with full-time jobs are the largest audience for online education because it provides them not only the convenience but also the flexibility to advance their education and career [7]. Tertiary institutions in China are starting to adopt such new education approach to provide a high degree of flexibility in the learning and teaching process.

In order to provide better quality for e-learning in both course content and marketing management, collaboration is formed between industry and university. The traditional culture of academia and industry are very different. However, technological advances have brought them closer. It is realized that the co-operation can bring out the best of both parties' expertise. There are many successful examples of forming an industry/university partnership to provide e-learning in China and Hong Kong, similar to HKCyberU.

The next step forward will be the collaboration between e-learning institutions, by applying the concept of learning hubs to achieve the final goal of forming a global learning network. As a result, a well-developed, effective, diversified and national wide e-learning network can be seen in the near future.

2. Related Work

In this paper, we present the development of e-learning for higher education in China, including Hong Kong, based on the collaboration between industry and education institutions.

2.1. *E-learning in China*

E-learning refers to the wide range of technology applications, strategies, and tools that offer students the means to increase their knowledge and improve their skills [13]. Nevertheless, the availability of increasingly powerful communication and information technologies have opened the way for enhancing traditional teaching and learning in both distance and conventional education using synchronous and asynchronous tools [9]. Table 1 [10] shows the relationships between inventions and affect on distance learning.

According to the information announced by the China Ministry of Education, there are 67 universities in China supporting e-learning in its own institutions [4].

Table 1. Relationships between inventions and distance learning

Inventions	Effect on distance learning
TV, radio	1930's real-time, pre-schedule time
Video recorder	1960's time-independent. Inter-student, student-teacher communication limited

PC -> two-way video conferencing, Disk, CD-ROM, Internet	1980's email, BBS, computer aided teaching, computer simulation, remote communications

More than millions of students have applied e-learning in their courses. After three years of fast expansion at the development stage, the focus of e-learning is shifting to quality. It can be observed that some universities mainly open e-learning courses for full-time undergraduate level, and the entry requirement is not consistent with the regular full-time courses. This trend is unhealthy because e-learning courses are more suitable for part-time mode of study. Therefore, the China Ministry of Education (Document No.8 2002) released a list of suggestions in 2002. They recommended that e-learning should focus on part-time courses for working people. If e-learning institutions follow the government's instruction, a well-developed network-learning environment will be established in China for working people.

2.1.1. Analysis of E-learning in China

According to a research report released in May 2005 [8] about e-learning in China, the following results are obtained (as shown in Figures 1, 2 & 3).

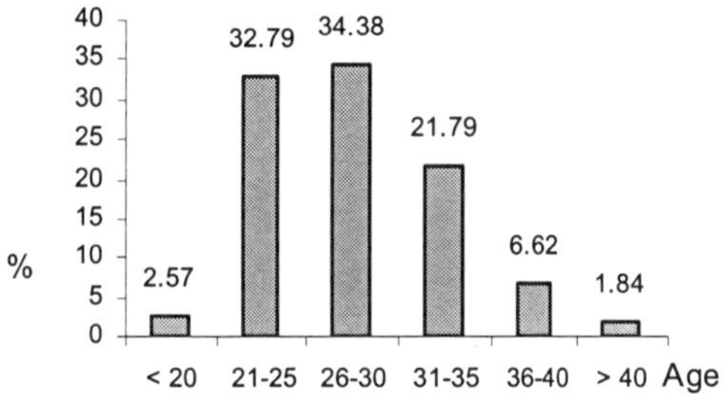

Figure 1. Age Distribution (%)

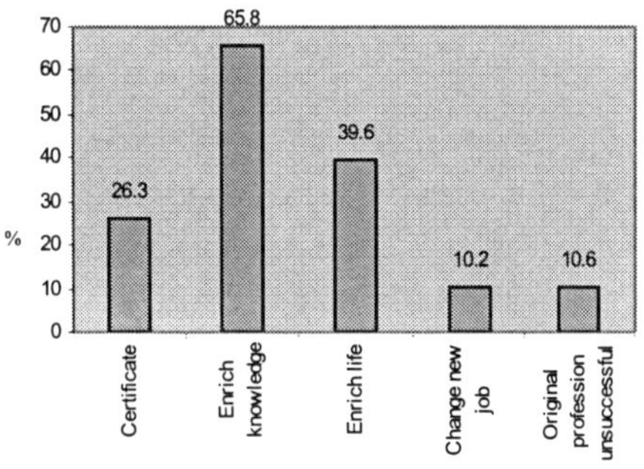

Figure 2. Motivation (%)

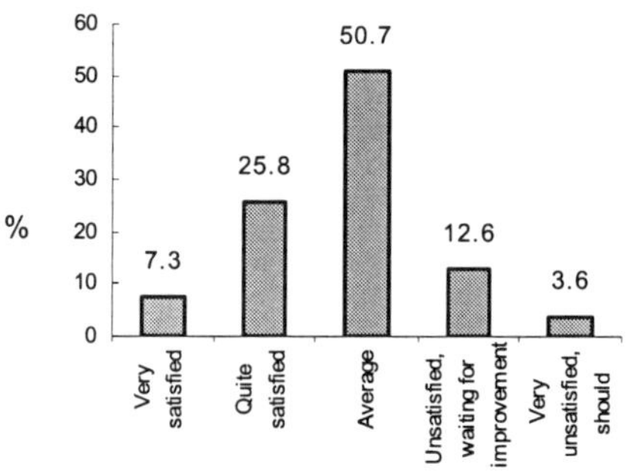

Figure 3. Satisfaction in Courseware (%)

The survey identified adults between the ages of 21 and 35 as the target segment for successful e-learning . Such result is reasonable because e-learning is suitable for working people who are either tied up with work or weighed down with family responsibilities to attend regular classes. Also, students are generally satisfied with e-learning courses.

2.2. ***Collaboration Between Industry and University***

Collaboration between industry and university has a long history. They cooperate from research to student internship. E-learning is becoming a new mode of collaboration recently.

2.2.1. Collaboration in Research

Linking firms to universities to infuse them with new science-based technologies is one form of university-industry relationships. In this approach, the university can start her research that is financially supported by her industrial partner. On the other hand, the industrial partner can launch new technology to market. This approach introduces mutual benefits among the two institutions.

2.2.2. Collaboration in Placement

The industrial placement program, also known as a co-op program in North America, is an agreement to arrange university students to work full-time in companies as "interns" for a short period of time usually between half-year to one year. Such collaboration is a scheme whereby education institutions, industries and other organizations formally coordinate with one another to provide a relevant work experience to students to complement the theoretical knowledge they have obtained in classroom.

2.2.3. *Collaboration in E-learning*

As e-learning is becoming popular in academic institutions, another mode of collaboration between industry and university appeared. Because the infrastructure of e-learning requires relatively large investment, a broad student-base is required to maintain the critical mass required for forming a successful cyber university. The university contributes her academic knowledge whereas the industry contributes its capital and manpower of marketing, management and administration. A company for e-learning with a strong academic background and excellent marketing and management strategies can be formed based on this collaboration. Under this collaboration, both parties can share the risk of running the e-learning business.

2.3. *The Learning Hub*

The MIT Media Lab Future of Learning [12] believes that learning will take place in a globally connected world rich in ubiquitous digital technologies. It released the idea of learning hub as an entry point to 21st century learning. According to the MIT Media Lab about learning hub's organization, each learning hub must take the responsibility for at least one program that models a full alternative to a significant component of traditional education. But in our approach we elaborated the definition of learning hub to match the model of current e-learning institutions. A learning hub is required to fulfill the following three criteria:

1. Provide its own courses to students - the company will support for both course material and administration.

Course *X* offers in *A*	
Courseware	Administration
E-learning institution *A*	

2. Provide courses from other e-learning institutions to students. The company will support for administration only.

Course *Y* offers in *A*	
Courseware	Administration
Institution *B*	Institution *A*

3. Provide own courses to other e-learning institutions. The company will provide support for course materials only.

Course *X* offers in *B*	
Courseware	Administration
Institution *A*	Institution *B*

4. Provide consultancy services to students looking for suitable e-learning courses.

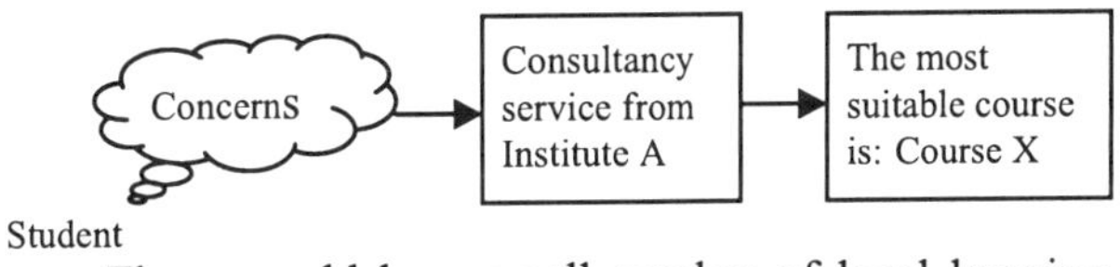

There would be a small number of local learning hubs in each region or country. The aggregation of these would form a global learning hub network providing worldwide e-learning service.

2.4. *Costing Model of Networked Learning*

In general, the costs of any system are driven by a combination of factors, all of which are susceptible to management control:

- Course populations
- The number of courses offered
- The lengths of course
- The media and technologies chosen
- The extent to which cost-inducing actions, e.g. the use of copyrighted materials, are avoided
- The extent to which costs are placed on students, either as tuition, or by moving the system boundaries so that activities the institution might once have paid for are now paid for by students (e.g. access to tutorial and library services)
- The extent to which the institution employs people on contracts *for* service (i.e. salaried posts) to develop courses and teach students, rather than on contracts *of* service (i.e. hired as casual labor)
- The extent to which the institution adopts working practices that reduce the costs of labor by, e.g. designing courses to be wrapped-around existing textbooks rather than developing new materials, and using author-editor models of course design, rather than big course team models
- The use of technology to reduce the student load per academic or administrator
- "Labor for labor" substitution – the replacement of expensive academic labor by student and adjunct labor, in order to reduce staff costs

Particularly, some other costs should be considered for e-learning development:

- Developing e-learning materials: Bates's [3] analysis of the costs of various media concluded that print, audio-cassettes, and pre-recorded Instructional Television are the media that are relatively low cost for courses with populations from under 250 students a year to over 1000 students a year. Although the development costs of even relatively simple online materials may be higher than paper-based print, it is obviously that there are considerable institutional savings on delivery costs. Online delivery could cut inventory, packing and postage costs enormously.
- Teaching and assessing students online
- Accessing the web site
- Administering students online: focus more on Web based, self-service model
- Providing the infrastructure and support within which e-learning can operate
- Planning and managing e-learning at the macro-level

2.4.1. Comparing e-learning costs and traditional face-to-face education

In the following discussion, we consider the case where a conventional course with face-to-face tuition is substituted by computer-mediated communications (CMC) in e-learning mode. A study conducted at the University of Illinois found that unit costs came down on all nine courses in which asynchronous learning networks were substituted for face-to-face instruction [1]. According to Bates [2], we should develop e-learning materials based on existing resources and avoid developing purpose-built materials. Otherwise, the start up costs will be more expensive than face-to-face tuition.

Number of students enrolled is also a factor to determine cost-efficiency. Traditional classroom courses have the limitation of students enrolled due to location, budget, and control of students' discipline within a classroom. However, all these limitations can be ignored in e-learning. The advantages of e-learning include its flexibility in adapting to the educational needs of students, its cost effectiveness in opening educational opportunities to larger number of students, and its convenience in providing access to information [5,8,15]. Bates [2] suggests that a standard Web-based course, with a mix of Web materials, online discussion forums, and printouts of the required texts, is increasingly more cost-effective than face-to-face teaching as numbers per class increase beyond 40 per year over a four-year period. From practitioners' point of view, for situations with less than 20 students, it is not justified for developing courses online. For student numbers between 20 and 40 students per course per year, any cost differences are likely to be less significant than differences in benefits.

The division of labor is necessary in networked learning. It is because on-line courses materials require animations and interactive interface. Therefore in networked learning, we will consider the division of labor between those who design the materials, those who teach the courses, and those who provide administrative support for students.

3. The HKCyberU Model

3.1. *Introduction*

HKCyberU [5] was established in 2000 jointly by the HKPolyU and PCCW with the objective to advancing web-based learning to the workforce by bringing traditional academic programmes to the Internet platform. The strength of HKCyberU was combined by HKPolyU's expertise in professional education, research, consulting and pedagogical development with PCCW's technology expertise to create this multimedia learning environment. HKCyberU is the first and only one of its kind, backed by a major academic institution and an industrial partner with advanced infrastructure to foster quality e-learning.

HKCyberU focuses on delivering postgraduate programmes leading to HKPolyU and non-local awards. At present, HKCyberU has over 10 collaborative partners from countries around the world including Australia, the mainland, Taiwan and UK, which further encourage academic exchange in a global context.

3.2. *The Infrastructure of HKCyberU*

The infrastructure of HKCyberU follows a typical company model. The top of the organization structure is the Board of Directors. The Chief Executive Officer of HKCyberU is taken up by the Vice-President of HKPolyU. Under the Board of Directors, there are different departments responsible for marketing, management, administration, accounting etc. The administrative staff of HKCyberU replaces the role of the Academic Secretary in a university structure. Apart from the company model, which is used for administration and management, the award and academic structure are based on the existing model in HKPolyU.

3.3. *The HKCyberU as a Learning Hub*

HKCyberU is a learning hub because it not only provides its own courses to students and other e-learning institutions, it also provides courses from other e-learning institutions to students. HKCyberU builds up its own courses based on the existing conventional courses from HKPolyU. Besides, HKCyberU provides courses from other e-learning institutions also. For example, the China Academy of Traditional Chinese Medicine (CATCM) in China offers courses to HKCyberU students. HKCyberU provides support for enrollment and CATCM provides course materials. After completion of the course, the qualification will be issued by CATCM. HKCyberU also offers its own courses to other learning institutions. For instance, it offers a MSc in E-Commerce programme to the National Chung Cheng University in Taiwan.

Besides, HKCyberU also provides consultancy services to students who look for suitable e-learning courses. When students seek for academic advice for any specific programmes, HKCyberU will refer the student to the relevant course leaders in HKPolyU.

3.4. *The HKCyberU Financial Model*

HKCyberU is a self-financed company. In order to keep stable income and profit for its operation, marketing and advertising strategies are needed. In HKCyberU, the business activities are monitored by the Board of College of Professional and Continuing Education.

At the initial stage, HKCyberU acquired capital through PCCW and HKPolyU. This capital is used to recruit administrative staff and produce online courses. The pay back period is expected to be 3 to 6 years. Previous studies [11] show that converting existing course materials to e-learning materials is worthwhile. The investments for HKCyberU set up include: web-based courseware development in the Department of Computing, Department of Accounting, and the Department of Building and Real Estate, technical system and infrastructure setup, and the set up for the administrative units in HKCyberU. As of 2004/05, HKCyberU has a cumulative student enrolment of over 5,000, including both part-time and visiting students [6]. With the new developments, HKCyberU is bringing in profits for the University. This shows that the Financial Model of HKCyberU is commercially viable.

3.5. *Converting Existing Courses On-line*

HKCyberU mainly offer courses at master's level. A pre-requisite for course development is that existing Master course running in conventional mode must already exist in HKPolyU. The university has existing staff who teach that course and existing course materials. The course structure and individual subjects in HKCyberU are the same as conventional courses in HKPolyU. This implies that the standard of courses can be assured and the award provided by e-learning mode and conventional mode are of the same standard.

A web-based subject implemented using WebCT [14] consists of around 10 units. The basic structure of a Web-based unit consists of course materials, cyber lectures and online exercises. In order to evaluate students' performance and build interaction between course leader/tutor and students, various facilities such as bulletin board, online tutorial system, and assignment drop box have been used.

Before the e-learning courses are launched to students, it will pass through a validation process. Each online subject is validated by a group of senior staff in HKPolyU from different departments. They are responsible to ensure that the course materials are up to standard required by HKPolyU, and also to ensure that the content is suitable for online delivery.

3.6. *HKCyberU Collaborations*

Several collaborations have been established between HKCyberU and other institutions. The collaboration partners include CATCM, East China Normal University, University of International Business and Economics, and Chinese Academy of Sciences in China; National Chung Cheng University in Taiwan; Edith Cowan University in Australia; Sheffield Hallam University and Heriot-Watt University in UK.

4. Evaluation

To evaluate the teaching effectiveness of the HKCyberU programme, the University conducts teaching evaluations regularly at the end of each semester, through student feedback questionnaires. In general, students are satisfied with the HKCyberU mode of teaching. Since the way the courses are being delivered via HKCyberU is different from the conventional mode of teaching, it is quite difficult to use surveys to conclude whether a HKCyberU course is fully compatible with a conventional one. Instead of drawing conclusions from survey, we compare the examination results of two groups of students. The target population of the study consists of the postgraduate students at HKCyberU who have enrolled in five subjects of the master's programme and that the subjects are delivered in both conventional and e-learning modes. These five subjects are offered by the Department of Computing. One group of students attended the courses online through HKCyberU. The two different groups of students are supervised by the same lecturers, and they attended a formal written examination with the same examination paper. The following are the results of the examination scores of both groups of students up to the year 2003 for five subjects. Consider one of the subjects COMP 5006:

		COMP515	COMP542	COMP564	COMP575
Cyber U	N	128	59	146	127
	$\bar{x}_1$	2.863	2.475	3.096	2.874
	S_1	0.675	0.812	0.585	0.660
HKPolyU	M	79	37	41	50
	$\bar{x}_2$	2.943	2.622	3.098	2.98
	S_2	0.772	0.582	0.450	0.525
	$S_{\bar{x}_1-\bar{x}_2}$	0.105	0.143	0.085	0.095
	Z	-0.757	-1.031	-0.020	-1.121
	Reject H_0	No	No	No	No

	HKCyberU	HKPolyU
Sample Size	146	59
Mean GPA	3.027	2.932
Standard Deviation	0.635	0.660

We want to test whether there is a difference in the examination scores of the two groups of students. Let μ_1 and μ_2 represent the population mean score of HKCyberU students and conventional class students, respectively. We want to test $H_0: \mu_1 - \mu_2 = 0$ against $H_1: \mu_1 - \mu_2 \neq 0$ at the significance level $\alpha = 0.05$. Since the population standard deviation of the mean scores for both populations for HKCyberU and conventional class students σ_1 and σ_2 are both unknown, we use $S_{\bar{x}_1-\bar{x}_2}$ in the formula for the test statistics. The value n refers to the sample size for HKCyberU and the value m refers to the sample size for conventional class, the estimated standard deviation is given by:

$$S_{\bar{x}_1-\bar{x}_2} = \sqrt{\frac{S_1^2}{n}+\frac{S_2^2}{m}} = \sqrt{\frac{(0.635)^2}{146}+\frac{(0.660)^2}{59}} = 0.101$$

The value of the test statistic z for $\bar{x}_1 - \bar{x}_2$ is computed as follows

$$z = \frac{(\bar{x}_1-\bar{x}_2)-(\mu_1-\mu_2)}{S_{\bar{x}_1-\bar{x}_2}} = \frac{(3.027-2.932)-0}{0.101} = 0.943$$

Since the value of the test statistics z = 0.943 falls in the non-rejection region (between –1.96 to 1.96 since significance level $\alpha = 0.05$), we cannot reject the null hypothesis H_0 at 0.05 significance level. Therefore, we conclude that at significance level 0.05, the mean GPA of HKCyberU and PolyU students cannot be considered as different.

Similarly for the other four subjects, the mean examination scores for HKCyberU and HKPolyU students cannot be considered as different at 0.05 level of significance. The results show that HKCyberU multi-institutional collaboration model is academically viable because the offering institution provides a reliable quality assurance system. The results of the analysis and the resulting statistics are described in the following: here n = the size of sample drawn from HKCyberU, m = the size of sample drawn from HKPolyU, $\bar{x}_1$ = the mean of the sample drawn from HKCyberU, $\bar{x}_2$ = the mean of the sample drawn from HKPolyU, S_1 = the standard deviation of the sample drawn from HKCyberU, S_2 = the standard deviation of the sample drawn from HKPolyU, $S_{\bar{x}_1-\bar{x}_2}$ = estimate of the standard deviation of $\bar{x}_1 - \bar{x}_2$, and z = the value of the test statistic.

5. Conclusion

We anticipate that the trend in e-learning would be the collaboration between industry and university to form e-learning institutions (learning hub) from small scale to a global network. Firstly, as we can observe that such collaboration allows e-learning institutions to collect enough capital in a short period of time. Most courses can be implemented in a short period of time, since most of the required resources already existed in HKPolyU. Secondly, industrial collaboration can also enhance the effectiveness of the e-learning institutions by combining existing management and administration manpower from the industry and academia. Thirdly, the concept of learning hub brings different area of courses together, thus increase the competitive power. Lastly, the support of "life-long learning" from the government encourages working citizens to enroll in part-time courses. E-learning is specially designed for students who need flexibility in course schedule. We have testified the results in HKCyberU as an initial take off. We can conclude that the performance of HKCyberU students is compatible with the performance of students studying in the conventional mode.

References

1. L. Arvan, J. C. Ory, C. D. Bullock, K. K. Burnaska and M. Hanson, The SCALE Efficiency Projects, *Journal of Asynchronous Learning Networks* **2(2)**, 33-60 (1998).
2. A. W. Bates, Managing technological change. Strategies for college and university leaders, San Francisco, Jossey-Bass Publishers, 126-129 (2000).
3. A. W. Bates, Technology, Open Learning and Distance Education, London: Routledge, (1995).
4. China Education Online website http://www.eol.cn/.
5. HKCyberU Website www.hkcyberu.com .
6. Hong Kong Polytechnic University Annual Report for the year of 2004/05.
7. M.Q. Huynh, U.N. Umesh and J.S. Valacich, E-learning as an Emerging Entrepreneurial Enterprise in Universities and Firms, *Communications of the Association for Information Systems* **12**, 48-68 (2003).
8. iResearch Report http://www.iresearch.com.cn/ .
9. H. A. Latchman, C. Saltzmann, D. Gillet and H. Bouzekri, Information technology enhanced learning in distance and conventional education, *IEEE Trans. Educ.* **42**, 247-255 (1999).
10. J. Liu, Advanced Distance Learning (ADL), *China Education Daily*, 30 Aug (2001).
11. Qiping Shen, J.K.H. Chung, D. Challis and Ronnie C.T. Cheung, A Comparative Study of Learning Modes for Postgraduate Students In Computing – A Case Study In Hong Kong, To be appeared in *Journal of Computer Application in Engineering Education*, (2007).
12. S. Papert and D. Cavallo, The Learning Hub – Entry Point to Twenty First Century Learning – A Call for Action at the Local and Global Level, MIT Media Lab Future of Learning, (2001).
13. E.D. Wagner, Emerging Learning Trends and the World Wide Web, Web-Based Training (Khan, B.H. ed.), Educational Technology Publications, Englewood Cliffs, 33-49 (2001).
14. WebCT Homepages, Available at http://www.webct.com.

SUPPORTING UML ACTIVITY DIAGRAMS USING ORGANIZATIONAL MODELS

MOSHIUR BHUIYAN
School of Computer Science & Software Engineering, University of Wollongong
Northfields Avenue, NSW 2522, Australia

MM ZAHIDUL ISLAM
School of Computer Science & Software Engineering, University of Wollongong
Northfields Avenue, NSW 2522, Australia

GEORGE KOLIADIS
School of Computer Science & Software Engineering, University of Wollongong
Northfields Avenue, NSW 2522, Australia

ANEESH KRISHNA
School of Computer Science & Software Engineering, University of Wollongong
Northfields Avenue, NSW 2522, Australia

ADITYA GHOSE
School of Computer Science & Software Engineering, University of Wollongong
Northfields Avenue, NSW 2522, Australia

Agent–oriented conceptual modeling notations such as *i** represents an interesting approach for modeling early phase requirements which includes organizational contexts, stakeholder intentions and rationale. On the other hand, Unified Modeling Language (UML) is suitable for later phases of requirement capture which usually focus on completeness, consistency, and automated verification of functional requirements for the new system. In this paper, we propose a methodology to facilitate and support the combined use of notation for modeling requirement engineering process in a synergistic fashion. For organizational modeling/early phase requirements capturing we use the *i** modeling framework that describes the organizational relationships among various actors and their rationales. For late (functional) requirements specification, we rely on UML Activity Diagram.

1. Introduction

Modeling and building effective computer system depends on understanding the organizational environment as well as the reasoning and rationale underlying requirements, design and process formulation decisions. Conceptual modeling notations employing knowledge representation techniques have been developed to support such an understanding [14]. Many modeling techniques tend to address "late phase" requirements while the vast majority of critical modeling is arguably taken in early phase requirements engineering. Agent-Oriented Conceptual Modeling (AOCM) offers an interesting approach in modeling the early phase requirements. The *i** modeling framework [14] is a semi-formal notation built on agent-oriented conceptual modeling.

A number of proposals have been made for combining *i** modeling with late phase requirements analysis and the downstream stages of the software lifecycle. The TROPOS project [2] uses the *i** notation to represent early and late phase requirements, architectures and detailed designs. However, the *i** notation itself is not expressive enough to represent late phase requirements, architectures and designs. To address this problem, a custom designed formal language called FormalTropos [6] has been proposed. Proposals to integrate *i** with formal agent programming languages and formal methods have also been reported in the literature [8] [12] [13]. This paper has similar objectives, but takes a somewhat different approach. We believe that the value of conceptual modeling in the *i** framework lies in its use as a notation complementary to existing specification languages, i.e., the expressive power of *i** complements that of existing notations. The use of *i** in this fashion requires that we define methodologies that support the mapping of *i** models with more traditional specifications. In the current instance, we examine how this might be done with Unified Modeling Language (UML) [1]. Our aim, then, is to support the modeling of organizational contexts, intentions and rationale in *i**, while traditional specifications of functionality and design proceeds in the UML Activity Diagram. More generally, this research suggests how diagrammatic notations for modeling early phase requirements, organization contexts and rationale can be used in a complementary manner with more traditional specification notations that lead towards system modeling.

In this chapter, we propose some guidelines to facilitate and support the combined use of notations for modeling requirement engineering process in a synergistic fashion. For organizational modeling early phase requirements capturing we use the *i** modeling framework that describes the organizational relationships among various actors and their rationales. For late (functional) requirements specification, we rely on a UML Activity Diagram. The heuristics described in this paper helps the system modeler to develop activity diagram based on *i** models.

2. The *i** Modeling Framework

The *i** framework for agent-oriented conceptual modeling was designed primarily for early phase requirements engineering. The central concept in *i** is that of the intentional actor (agent). Intentional properties of an agent such as goals, beliefs, abilities and commitments are used in modeling requirements. The *i** framework consists of two main modeling components: the Strategic Dependency (SD) Model and the Strategic Rationale (SR) Model [14].

The SD model consists of a set of nodes and links. Each node represents an "actor", and each link between the two actors indicates that one actor depends on the other for something in order that the former may attain some goal. The depending actor is known as *depender*, while the actor depended upon is known as the *dependee*. The object around which the dependency relationship centres is called the *dependum*. In the *i** framework, the SR model provides a more detailed level of modeling by looking "inside" actors to model internal intentional relationships. Intentional elements (goals, tasks, resources, and softgoals) appear in the SR model not only as external dependencies, but also as internal elements linked by task decomposition and means-ends relationships.

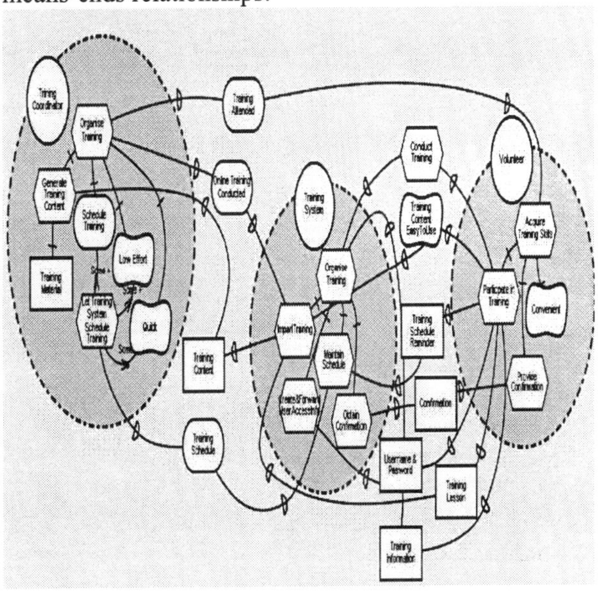

Figure 1. Strategic Rationale (SR) model for computer based training system

For example, the *TrainingCoordinator* has an internal task to *OrganizeTraining*. This task can be performed by sub-tasks *ScheduleTraining* and *GenerateTrainingContent* (these are related to the parent task via task decomposition links). The task *OrganizeTraining* is related to the *LowEffort*, *Quick* softgoals via a task decomposition link.

3. Activity Diagram in UML

An activity diagram is an uncomplicated and perceptive illustration that depicts the actions, parallel activities and any possible alternative ways through the workflow. Activity diagrams defined in the Unified Modeling Language [11] are consequential from various methods to pictorially express sequence of activities or sub-activities and conditions taken within a process. Activity Diagrams explain the operational flow from an initiating point to the terminating point specifying many decision paths that exist in the development of proceedings contained in the activity [1] [9] [10]. They are also used to explain states where parallel processing may occur in carrying out of some activities.

4. Benefits of Mapping *i** Model into Activity Diagram

Some benefits of integrating *i** and Activity Diagrams are given below.

• We feel that the usefulness and effectiveness of *i** can be increased manifold by using it with UML activity diagram. Mapping rules provide a semantics to *i** framework. Our view is that the *i** modeling framework and UML activity diagram can function in a complementary and synergistic way.

• There is a need to map both SD and SR models into late phase requirements specification. Activity diagram can be used effectively to realize the actions and states in the late phase which cannot be represented in the *i** diagram.

• For translating informal specifications provided in *i** into Activity diagram, there is no need to add more details into the corresponding *i** model. The mapping from *i** models into Activity diagram does not result in any information loss.

• Using Activity diagram, we are in a position to express properties that are not restricted to the current state of the system, but also to its past and future history.

5. Methodology Supporting the Integration of *i** and UML Activity Diagram

Our proposed methodology uses the notion of cumulative effect annotation to determine whether the *i** models and UML Activity Diagrams are consistent with each other.

5.1. *Consistency Evaluation*

We introduce consistency rules to provide a mechanism for ensuring consistency between *i** model and UML Activity Diagram. The rules are developed with consideration to [7].

Rule 1: Every actor in an *i** model required as a participant in the Activity Diagram must be represented in the model. Required participants are identified via the associated dependencies among the actors.

Rule 2: Every 'primitively workable' task decomposed (or required by decomposition where a dependency exists) from the chosen routine within the *i** model, must be represented as an action or activity under the control of the appropriate actor in the process model.

Rule 3: There must exist a coordinated transition in the Activity Diagram, whereby the operational objective (as encoded in the fulfillment conditions or effect annotations) of the routine is achieved, and the sequence of activities is consistent with the requirements specified in the routine. There must exist a coordination of activities in the activity diagram that satisfy the requirements of the routine further outlined below.

Rule 3.1: The fulfillment conditions of the operational goal at the root of the routine and all its sub-elements must be achieved through the accumulation of effects during forward traversal of the transition.

Rule 3.2: The fulfillment conditions of a task in the chosen routine must not be fulfilled prior to all tasks that decompose it, upon accumulation of effects during forward traversal of the transition.

Rule 3.3: The fulfillment of a task on the depender side of a dependency must not be realized before the fulfillment of the dependency, upon the accumulation of effects during forward traversal of the transition.

5.2. *Phase-1: Effect Annotations*

The concept of effect annotation denotes the potential outcomes of activities and fulfilment conditions that are required to meet dependencies by achieving certain results. An effect generally defines that a result or consequence of an activity has generated because of its being accomplished by an agent or some previous phenomenon. As an example, effects can be annotated to activity/task nodes or even complete sub-processes in graphical notations. In *i**, we annotate effects to tasks assigned to actors which indicate the realization of a certain conditions aimed in the direction of (i.e. and perhaps required for) some higher order goal. The effect annotations is intended to provide a notation free methodology rather than limited to a specific notation.

An effect annotation is a testimonial to the outcome of an activity related to a state that alters construction of a given model. An effect annotation includes: a label that generalizes the effect (e.g. *'CustomerDetailsStored'*); a designation specifying whether the effect is a normal (i.e. desired) outcome for an activity (e.g. *'RegistrationValidated'*), or an abnormal (i.e. undesired) outcome for the activity that may require the application of some mitigation strategy; an optional informal definition describing the effect in relation to the result achieved in its environment (e.g. 'The details relating to the current customer have been stored within the system.'); an optional formal definition may be used to define achieved states in a chosen formalism.

Fulfillment conditions are annotated to intentional actor elements and dependencies in an *i** model (i.e. not including soft-goals as these are used during assessment of alternatives and describe non-functional properties to be addressed). A fulfillment condition [7] is a statement specifying the outcomes required to satisfy a given goal or dependency. Fulfillment conditions recognize the required effects on a business process model. For example, a fulfillment condition for a task dependency to *'ConductTraining'*, may be the *'TrainingArranged'* effect (subsequently required by the task assigned to a dependee actor).

Intuitively, for a dependency to be fulfilled, explicit assignment of responsibility is made to a dependee actor who possesses an intentional element that can satisfy the dependency. Therefore, one guiding rule during the annotation of fulfillment conditions to an *i** model is that all fulfillment conditions annotated to a dependency must be annotated to the intentional element the dependency is linked to on the dependee.

In this case we are only concerned with the fact that the dependee has the knowledge to achieve the dependency, not the ability (e.g. where another dependency may be required with another actor). We introduce two steps to derive the effect annotations from the CBT *i** diagram. Step 1, Annotate the *i** model with effects and then derive the annotations of dependencies with fulfilment conditions. Step 2, define fulfilment conditions to the tasks that Realizes/Requires the fulfilment conditions.

Step 1: Annotate model with effects and/or fulfilment condition

The tasks assigned to the actors in the CBT model are initially annotated with effects.

Table 1. Sample annotation of tasks with effects.

Actor	Task	Effect Annotation
TC	Let Training System Schedule Training	Training System Schedule Training
TC	Generate Training Content	Training Material Generated
TC	Organize Training	Training Organized

The second segment of the model annotation involves annotating dependencies with fulfilment conditions that relate to required effects in the *i** model.

Table 2. Sample annotation of dependencies with fulfilment conditions Annotation of tasks with effects.

Dependency	Fulfilment Condition
Training Content	TC: Training Content Generated
Training Schedule	TS: Scheduled Training
Confirmation	Vol: Confirmation Provided
Username & Password	TS: Username & Password Created

Step 2: Propagate fulfilment conditions in *i** models to task assigned to dependee and depender actors

The analysis of dependency proliferate effect annotations of dependencies into tasks that realise/require the fulfilment conditions. The task that realizes the dependency obtains the effect annotation as a required post and task requiring the dependency obtains the effect annotations as a required pre-condition. The following table illustrates some dependencies with the fulfilment conditions and tasks that realize/require condition.

Table 3. Tasks that Realizes/Requires the fulfilment conditions.

Dependency	Fulfilment Condition	Task Realizes Fulfilment Condition	Task Requires Fulfilment Condition
Training Content	TC: Training Content Generated	TC: Generate Training Content	TS: Impart Training
Training Scheduled	TS: Schedule Training	TS: Maintain Schedule	TC: Let Training System Schedule Training
Confirmatio n	Vol: Confirmatio n Provided	Vol: Provide Confirmatio n	TS: Obtain Confirmatio n

Now we have the effect annotations for the intentional elements such as goals, resources and tasks. The dependency analysis will recognize the pre/post conditions of the elements.

Table 4. : Sample propagation of Fulfilment conditions to respective tasks.

Task	Effect Annotation	Required Pre
TC: LetTraining SystemSchedule Training	TrainingSystem ScheduleTrainin g	*TC:* Organize Training Schedule
TC: Generate TrainingContent	TrainingMaterial Generated	*TC:* Conduct computer based training

5.3. *Effect Annotations*

Rule-1: Discover the actors and represent them in activity diagram

This step can be completed by looking at either SD model or SR models. Once the actors are found they will be placed as the names of the swimlanes of the activity diagram. We prefer using swimlanes pattern of the activity diagram as they are used to organize responsibilities for the actions.

For example, we get three actors from the SR model in figure-1, *TrainingCoordinator*, *TrainingSystem* and *Volunteer*. When we map the *i** model into UML activity diagram, these actors are represented in the swimlanes to show the responsibilities of each actor (for each actions) associated with the overall system

Rule -2: Discover task/ actions

SR model of the *i** diagram shows the internal tasks and their rationales. For each actor, the SR model will be analyzed to discover the tasks. In our methodology identification of tasks/actions and their effects is analyzed in the effect annotation part. We write all the tasks as shown in table-1 and then categorize them according to the actors.

Tasks in *i** model are regarded as actions in activity diagram. Thus *TrainingCoordinator* has *GenerateTrainingContent* and so on.

Rule -3: Identify the Initiating Actor

Initiating actor is responsible for the initial action in the activity diagram. The initiating actor is identified through their ability to satisfy the pre-condition with an action that realizes the required effect. The initial actor is represented in the first swimlane of the activity diagram. To find the initiating actor, we need to analyze the actions, their effect annotations, required pre-condition and fulfilment conditions. We find that *TrainingCoordinator* is the initiating actor with the ability to satisfy the pre-condition of conducting a computer based training by triggering the action *LetTrainingSystemScheduleTraining*.

Rule -4: Sequence actions by analyzing pre/post conditions derived during annotation

Tasks required for the fulfilment of the trigger condition for the course of action are chosen initially and placed as action within the initiating actor's swimlane in UML activity diagram. After the fulfilment of the pre-condition, the post-condition must be satisfied through the interaction of multiple actors, and the execution of their assigned tasks. These tasks are mapped to activity diagram as actions and placed in the respective swimlanes that represents the controlling actors. The sequencing for actions is a guided task by identifying the required actions and dependencies in order to achieve the operational goal.

The initiating action is *LetTrainingSystemScheduleTraining*, so it is placed in the *TrainingCoordinator's* swimlane. After fulfilment of the pre-condition of this action, the post-conditions are satisfied through the execution of one or more actions with the interaction of other actors. Thus, we get *GenerateTrainingContent* and *MaintainSchedule* actions and so on.

Rule -5: Discover dependencies and represent them in activity diagram

We get the dependencies from SD or SR models. We then represent goal, task and resource dependencies as objects in the activity diagram. The actions will specify which objects perform its operation and their states. Actions within a swimlane can be handled by the same objects or multiple objects.

Softgoal dependency in *i** model is considered as a non-functional requirement of the system, which has a positive or negative contribution for achieving, accomplishing a goal, task, resource. For this reason, softgoal dependency will not represent an object. Thus we have a total of ten dependencies in CBT system including one softgoal dependency. For example the resource dependency *TrainingContent* is the object for *GenerateTrainingContent* and *ObtainConfirmation*. The state of the object *TrainingContent* in this case is [Generated].

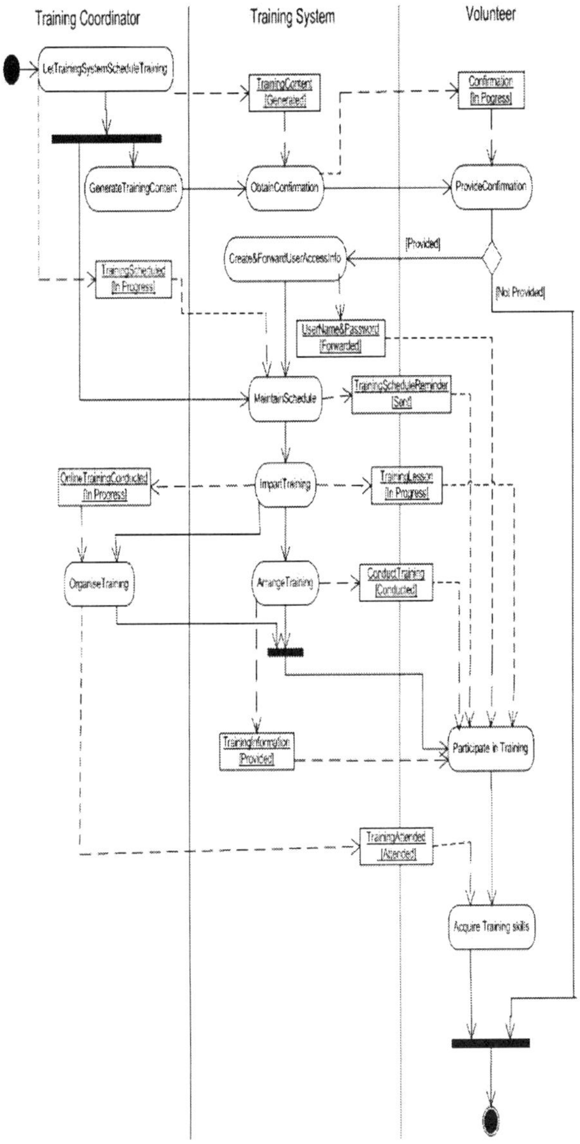

Figure 2. Activity Diagram derived from mapping

Rule -6: Introduce required actions and object flow links between swimlanes

This step includes introducing required actions and objects flow links between actions. Actions are linked according to their sequence and then flow links are represented among them which include the objects and their states.

6. Conclusion

In this chapter we have presented a consistent methodology to support the mapping of early phase requirement modeling notation *i** into UML activity diagram. The methodology supports the mapping of these two otherwise disparate approaches in a synergistic fashion. We can now analyze the system's behavior and explain the workflow from an initiating point to the terminating point which is otherwise not possible by only looking at the *i** model and activity diagram separately. Effect annotations and mapping rules can be viewed as providing informal semantics to the *i** diagrams while mapping into activity diagram of UML specifications, a language which already has one. We believe that these semantics are largely consistent with the somewhat implicit semantics for *i**. The proposed set of mapping rules constrains the modeler to map the elements of the *i** model to appropriate activity diagram and ensures that the two models are consistent. We have not however investigated the possibility of articulating semantic consistency constraints between *i** models and activity diagrams. We have not focused on the reflection of changes in one model into another. There are sixteen categories of changes that may occur to an *i** model [8]. We need to localize these changes to maintain consistency. Further research is needed to relate non-functional requirements (NFRs) with functional requirements of the system [3] [4].

References

1. G. Booch, I. Jacobson and J. Rumbaugh, The Unified Modeling Language User Guide, Addison Wesley (1999).
2. J. Castro, M. Kolp and J. Mylopoulos, Towards Requirements Driven Information Systems Engineering: The Tropos Project, *Information Systems*, (2002).
3. L. Chung, Representing and Using Non - Functional Requirements for Information System Development: A Process Oriented Approach, PhD Thesis, Graduate Department of Computer Science, University of Toronto (1993).
4. L. Chung, B. Nixon, E. Yu and J. Mylopoulos, Non-Functional Requirements in Software Engineering, Kluwer Academic Publishers, 472 (2000).
5. I. Davis, P. Green, M. Rosemannn and S. Gallo, Conceptual Modeling – What And Why in Current Practice, *Lecture notes in Computer Science, Volume 3288*, 30 – 42 (2004).
6. A. Fuxman, M. Pistore, J. Mylopoulos and P. Traverso, Model checking early requirements specifications in Tropos, *Proceedings of Fifth IEEE*

International Symposium on Requirements Engineering, 174 -181 (2001).

7. A. Fuxman, L. Liu, J. Mylopoulos, M. Pistore, M. Roveri and P. Traverso, Specifying and analyzing early requirements in Tropos, *Requirements Engineering* **9(2)**, 132 – 150 (2004).
8. A. Krishna, A. Ghose and S. Vilkomir, Co-Evolution of Complementary Formal and Informal Requirements, *Proceedings of 7th International Workshop on Principles of Software Evolution (IWPSE'04)*, 159-164 (2004).
9. Crai Larman, Applying UML and Patterns: An Introduction to Object-Oriented Analysis and Design, Prentice Hall, (1998).
10. Martin Fowler, Kendall Scott, UML Distilled, Addison Wesley, (2000).
11. [UML2.0] – OMG UML Specification v. 2.0, available at http://uml.org/ (2004).
12. S. Vilkomir, A. Ghose and A. Krishna, Combining agent-oriented conceptual modeling with formal methods, *Proceedings of 15th Australian Software Engineering Conference*, 147-157 (2004).
13. X. Wang, Y. Lesprance, Agent-Oriented Requirements Engineering Using ConGolog and *i**, *Proceedings of 3rd International Bi-Conference Workshop Agent-Oriented Information Systems (AOIS 2001)*, 59-78 (2001).
14. E. Yu, Modeling Strategic Relationships for Process Reengineering, PhD Thesis, Graduate Department of Computer Science, University of Toronto, 124 (1995).

A CASE STUDY OF STUDENT CENTERED TEACHING SUPPORTED WITH E-LEARNING (SCET)

XIANGQIAN CHENG

Computer Teaching and Experiment Center, ,Xi'an Jiaotong University
Xi'an, Shaanxi, P.R. China

JAMES N. K. LIU

Department of Computing, Hong Kong Polytechnic University
Hong Kong, P.R. China

This paper highlights the situations that in recent years Chinese Higher Education Institutes (HEIs) have sought to improve their quality of education by attracting highly qualified faculty, training younger instructors, and using the new media and the Internet to deliver content. There have been few studies of the progress of these efforts, especially where they combine online and traditional teaching. This study describes students' responses to the introduction and use of an e-Learning platform or Course Management System (CMS) in an IT course in a Chinese HEI. The results suggest that e-Learning had no effect on the computer literacy of the participant students and that students who liked the blended instruction or Student Centered Teaching supported with e-Learning (SCeT) spent more time on their work and improved their IT skills.

1. Introduction

In line with global trends, the higher education system in China faces the need to provide quality education to an ever-increasing number of students in a context of limited resources. A vivid illustration of these limitations is provided in Figure-1.

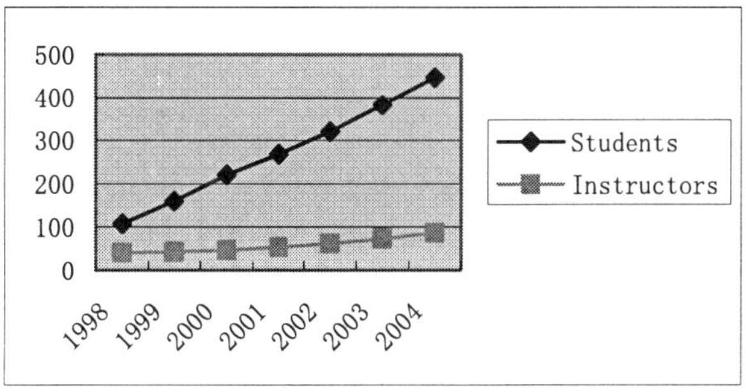

Figure-1 Instructor to student ratios in Chinese HEIs

Which shows the dramatic increase in the student: instructor ratio over the period 1998-2004. In this period, student numbers more than tripled yet instructor numbers remained basically static [15]. It can be no surprise to learn that research has found that this has had a direct negative impact on the quality of the education being provided in local institutes of higher education. Indeed, in a study of graduates of Chinese HEIs, McKinsey (2005) reported that in the nine occupations under study fewer than 10 percent of candidates would be suitable for work in a foreign company.

Around the world, one recent widely advocated and applied approach to this problem of a mismatch between huge demand for higher education and the resources to satisfy it has been the application of new educational technologies [3, 9]. In particular, there has been the attempt to save time and money by replacing face-to-face educational scenarios with e-Learning and IT applications [1]. Superficially, this means that paper- and blackboard-based materials have migrated to new Internet and intranet-supported media. More substantially, the new methods of delivery have created a wide variety of new and potentially highly enabling learner-centered learning paradigms [12] such as Course Management Systems (CMS) which are used to manage web-learning in instructor-led environments. These technologies and paradigms still have some novelty wherever they are applied but in China they are particularly new and their successful integration with established educational practices and institutions may require sometimes painful adjustments for students, teachers and administrators.

The purpose of our research is to primarily investigate if e-Learning and the related pedagogies improve the quality of teaching and learning in IT courses and secondarily to explore the potential of a CMS in the teaching process. More specifically we pose two questions:

1. How do on-campus students at Xi'an Jiaotong University respond to and use this particular e-learning environment?
2. Are more computer-literate students more involved in e-Learning?

To answer these questions, we conducted a mid-semester, online poll among students of the MIS course teaching by the new platform. Of the students who were sampled, 80% agreed that "e-learning is important in the MIS course learning process". As to the second question, a correlation analysis did not show a positive correlation between computer literacy and students' involvement in e-learning. But, by the analysis of the data form the online poll, we realize that students who liked the blended instruction or Student Centered Teaching supported with e-Learning (SCeT) spent more time on their work and improved their IT skills.

2. Literature Review

While e-Learning has already been broadly used to supplement either traditional contact education or print-based distance education and in some cases has even completely replaced traditional modes of teaching and learning [5], at this still relatively early stage of the development of e-learning-based pedagogies it remains legitimate to ask whether current e-learning technologies can effectively replace traditional teaching and learning practices and, if so, what this implies for teachers, learners, and administrators, what related tools and strategies are preferable, what resources are required, and a myriad other questions. To even begin to answer these questions, however, requires that we have some theory of what learning might be.

Academic learning has been said to be a process that emphasizes broad foundational knowledge, theory, and analytical skills. [5]. A student who has had a good learning experience will have "master new knowledge and skills, critically examine assumptions and beliefs, and engage in an invigorating, collaborative quest for wisdom and personal, holistic development" [11]. Perhaps this is beyond being a "good" learning experience. It sounds more like a "great" one. Certainly, one may wonder how this experience comes about. As these same authors go on to point out, "the most valuable activity in a classroom of any kind is the opportunity for learners to work and interact together and to build and become part of a community of scholars and practitioners" [11].

In this vision of learning the crucial element would appear to be interaction, however, semiotically, it may be enacted: visually, graphically, in writing, speech, performance, or in some other way. Early e-learning models, however, did not focus on interaction. Their primary focus was on providing convenient, 24-hour-a-day remote access and little attention was given to the learning design (content development) or the training of educators and learners for online teaching and learning. Ultimately, many educators and technology vendors made the naive and (lowest-cost) assumption that the learning part of e-learning would be automatically achieved merely by delivering traditional learning content through the Internet [6].

More recently, e-learning models have begun to move from being largely technology-driven to taking a more pedagogically-informed approach, that is to say, an approach that is cognizant of the place of interaction in learning. Educators and software designers are trying to satisfy this pedagogical need by using and designing Internet- and intranet-based tools that allows interaction. One widespread class of such tools is CMS which are used to manage web-learning in instructor-led environments. Some typical CMS are eCollege, WebCT, Blackboard, Sakai, and Moodle. CMS offer a number of functionalities to support various e-teaching and administrative activities as well as interactive e-learning.

A further important issue for educational stakeholders in the process of migration to e-learning is that of what we may call cost and future management. One motive for going over to e-learning is economic, the problem of abundant demand and limited supply. The assumption is that e-learning is cheaper than the traditional teaching technologies. This is true, however, only as long as the technologies that we invest in today are upgradeable, renewable, and effective and remain so at some sustainable or economic level of cost. This explains the trend of recent years for higher education institutions to seek out or favor open source rather than proprietary e-learning applications. Open source applications promise HEIs the ability to easily and freely audit their systems and to create systems that are relatively open, transparent, and flexible and less vulnerable to vendor lock-in. Other advantages claimed for the open source model are that it promotes freedom to choose, increases user access/control, encourages links to a global community, promotes quality, and enhances innovation in teaching and learning .

As a last word in this brief background to the circumstances of the test-run implementation of e-learning at Xi'an Jiaotong University we shall briefly comment on the pedagogical model that was applied. Recent e-learning models have focuses on pedagogical issues such as online instructional design and the creation of online learning communities [17]. The Student-Centered approach is based on the finding [2] that students achieve superior academic results and even personal growth in terms of higher self-confidence and openness to experience if they learn in an atmosphere or climate that can be characterized by three basic attitudinal conditions: realness, acceptance, and empathic understanding. Briefly, Student-Centered Teaching requires particular personal attitudes from the facilitator and a certain degree of openness from the students. From personal experience we would like to add the requirement on, or at least the benefit of social skills and techniques such as moderation [7]. These help to make group processes more transparent, to converge faster and these effects are held to improve student satisfaction [4].

3. Research Setting

In this section we provide some background to our research, beginning with an introduction to the course and students which we selected for study. We then describe the requirements and setup of the new MIS course environment -- the CMS system under evaluation in this paper and its related pedagogical model. Finally, we consider how SCeT differs from the more traditional lab teaching in our IT courses.

3.1. *Course and Students*

The course we elected for study was Management Information Systems (MIS). This course is made up of 32 hours of lectures and 32 hours of labs. We regarded the large number of lab hours as being a positive as it would provide enough time for students to practice using SCeT in a lab teaching context. A class of administration management majors (2003) from the public management school in Xi'an Jiaotong University was selected to participate. At the time of the course they were second year students. Their previous IT studies included Computer Literacy, Computer Networks and Visual Basic. The samples in the study are same from the class. There were a total of 40 students per class but only 36 answered the survey, which was taken online.

3.2. *SCeT*

The new CMS-enabled teaching and learning practices at Xi'an Jiaotong University used a student centered learning approach on the e-learning platform which we called SCeT. SCeT has three minimum operating requirements: suitable lab resources, open lab environments, and an effective means of communication. Each of these is characterized in the following.

Suitable lab resources

- Up-to-date. All the application software we used in the course had been published within the past 2 years;
- Available to and easily accessed by all the students. Most of the software we used was open source software which can be found at http://www.sourceforge.org. Being open source, students could even take part in its development;
- Provide sufficient techniques or space for students to explore by themselves;
- Do not violate user conditions or give rise to copyright problems
- Knowledgeable instructors

Open lab environment

An open lab is an online learning environment that is available to students all the time and which can be accessed on or off-campus. Students are encouraged to freely access the lab resources. The lab environment should also be available to students who wish to carry out research or do additional independent study outside normal course or term times.

The construction of the e-Learning platform and its functionalities

It is hoped that interaction between teachers, students, and classmates would be optimized by making easily available multiple communication modes that allow the use of various systems with different communication means, including spoken, written, graphical, multi-modal, and single-user and multiple user collaborative systems. These would minimally include e-mail, ICQ, and websites. The course management system (CMS) was used as a portal for IT courses. The CMS register, access logs, course forum, lecture notes announcement, assignment delivery and feedback, quiz management and grade book functions are all available through the system while it is also possible to link to the platform or display the lab resources and the lab outcomes. All of this system content can be easily retrieved, backed up or recovered, and consequently can be continuously evaluated, reused, and shared.

Xian Jiaotong University's Computer Teaching and Experiment Center (CTEC) has developed the various network resources (including applications for lab work, various lab guides, Internet based experiment and websites for exhibiting student projects). Primarily, this has been integrated using an Open Source Software (OSS) course management system (Moodle) as the course portal.

Jansen et al (2002) suggest an e-Learning application should offer a learning environment, a development environment, and a management environment. In our e-Learning environment, both the Moodle and the CTEC lab resources combine to form a supplementary learning environment where learning materials are delivered and participants can communicate. The Lab server platform acts as the development environment, where students can complete their lab assignments or group projects. The course management system—in our case, the Moodle is used—is the management environment for monitoring, stimulating, and adjusting the learning process by means of various testing, registration, administration and communication functionalities [10].

The Learning communities and the community of inquiry model

The community of inquiry model developed by Garrison and Anderson (2003) is an attempt to give educators an in-depth understanding of the characteristics of e-Learning and direction and guidance to achieving higher-order learning through the use of e-Learning.

The community of inquiry model has three key elements that must be considered when planning and delivering an e-Learning experience. They are cognitive presence, social presence and teaching presence. The following describes how each of these elements was realized in the SCeT system:

- Cognitive presence: Learners provided with paper-based materials such as textbooks and with on-line materials in the form of lecture notes, lab guides, technical manuals, and software.
- Social presence: Students must do lab work in project groups and to communicate in their groups and between groups.
- Teaching presence: Teaching presence is defined as "the design, facilitation and direction of cognitive and social processes for the purpose of realizing personally meaningful and educationally worthwhile learning outcomes"[8].

The course is in two parts, lectures and labs. The lectures are in Chinese but make use of an English-language textbook [13] that emphasizes a framework of analysis that considers technology, management, and organizational assets, and their interactions. The labs involve regular experiments and projects. The experiments address networking skills, including webpage design, web publishing, web programming, and related platform and software technology. The projects are selected by the student groups and involve WWW-based content management system and other MIS course-related information system practices, depending on student career expectations and interest. The students are encouraged to establish their own technical web support. The course provides the following:

- Textbook. The textbook that we use may not be the newest version but it may be the only suitable English textbook available in the Chinese domestic market.

- Supplemental material. Instructors describe best practice in China as supplemental illustrations of the MIS principles in the textbook or to emphasize the specialties of the local situation.
- The e-Learning or CMS platform. This is used to distribute on-line material, deliver assignments and feedbacks and it is used as a course forum.
- The experiment related software is mainly open source software or shareware obtained by either instructors or students. These include WWW-base Content Management software—Postnuke, sugarCRM, osCommerce and the like.

SCeL vs. SCeT

Group projects and other kinds of teamwork education or training are generally regarded as a student-centered e-learning (SCeL) approaches and as such are popular educational tools in many western educational systems [16, 18] but such approaches are rarely applied in Chinese HEIs. The reasons for this are undoubtedly complex and we may like to attribute it to a wide variety of phenomena and pseudo-phenomena, whether it is the one-child policy, traditional approaches to education, or some other concept or practice. It is a commonplace to say that students lack of the spirit of independence or of cooperation, For example, "The Chinese e-learner may feel that they are subservient to a teacher and this could prove problematic when no physical tutor exists." Student-centered teaching (SCT) takes this view into account and makes the instructor take much more responsibility for the student's learning.

The same as the student-centered approach, in our practice, the student-centered approach is more embodied in the group project exercise, IT skill developing and technical supporting, all the students are trusted to take part in the project group for some specific work depending on their interests and skills background; every student could develop some specific skill such as webpage designing, flash making, or content collecting; the IT supports could be from the instructor, but most often might be from internal of the project group or other groups.

The e-Learning platform compliments both the class room teaching and lab experiments. It provides greater opportunities for students to interact with the instructor and with other students. It is why we refer our teaching experiment student-centered teaching with e-Learning support (SCeT).

4. Differences between SCeT and the usual IT Course Lab teaching mode

Central to the SCeT experiment was a thorough redesign of the MIS course lab contents and method. Originally, the laboratory course contents were strictly defined and scheduled: students learnt systems analysis applications and tools such as UML or Rational ROSE, and the processes of the laboratory course were in accordance with an invariant curriculum. In contrast, the SCeT e-learning platform provided students with many more choices, allowing them to select websites design, explore applications such as MS Project and Imagine Extend or practice using web-based Content Management Systems. The SCeT approach to lab teaching is, in terms of content delivery and task completion, very different from the old lab teaching approach. Table-1 tabulates these differences.

The network-based lab platform

Because most of the experiments and projects are related to the Internet, we use servers based on Linux for web publishing with dynamic document and database support. We also establish accounts for every student on the Linux server. Students publish their own content and develop their group project on the Internet.

Table 1 A comparison of the lab teaching approaches

	The superseded lab teaching approach	**The SCeT approach**
Scheduling of Lab/project time	Mainly arranged by teacher	The basic labs arranged by the teacher. The group project mainly arranged by students.
Selection of Lab/Project	Selected by the teacher	The basic labs are elective subject to IT course requirements. The project is developed through teacher-student consultations
Project process control	None	Student control with periodic teacher inspection
Lab resources	Provided by the teacher	In part provided by teacher and in part by students

Summative evaluation	Teacher evaluation	Teacher and peer students evaluation
Content selection	Selected by the teacher	By the teacher and students
Motivation	The students are passive	The students select the content and work as they see fit
Arranged lab time	Teacher directs the students to complete the planned content	The teacher monitors student project progress, advises and helps students
Lab form	Individual learning	Learning activities done in groups
Methods of Evaluation	Final exam 70%, lab and assignment 30%	Final exam 50%, lab and assignment 50%
Infrastructure	The Internet as a resource and assignment delivery platform	Electronic delivery via a CMS, Moodle and Lab platform.

5. Methodology

This research used online questionnaires to collect the responses of a thirty-six student sample to twenty-one questions on factors assumed to affect student performance in courses under the direction of the university's Computer Teaching and Experiment Center. Fifteen of these questions used a five-point Likert scale, suggesting responses "strongly disagree" to "strongly agree". The questionnaires also asked the students to express their opinions on the effect of e-Learning and SCeT. The questions include 9 groups:

1. My computer literacy/Computer and network Accessibility is ___________ (very good/good/fair/poor/very poor) ?
2. The lecture/Lab/ e-Learning/ Peer communication/ The Internet is _______ (very important/important/fair/not too important/not important) to my learning?
3. In my view, selecting project by myself to the learning/ teamwork is ________(very necessary/necessary/Fair/ confused/ Hard to choice)?
4. In the e-Learning platform, mainly I ________ (post question/ browse the forum/ download lecture Notes/browse once a week)?
5. In the SCeT, my time devoting is _________(one time more than usual way/50% more than usual way/same/ over 20% less than usual way/ over 50% less than usual way)?
6. After SCeT, my computer skill is ___________(improved greatly/improved/fair/no improvement/lag behind)?
7. After the SCeT, my confidence on IT self-learning is _________(improved greatly/improved/fair/no improvement/ total give up)?
8. As to the Teamwork output, I am _________(very satisfied/satisfied/fair/not very satisfied /not satisfied)?
9. In my view, the SCeT is _________ (Much better/better/same/not as good as old way/hard to adapting)than usual lab teaching?

They sought to elicit information in six groupings:

Group 1: These sought to identify the students' computer skill and previous access to computers.

Group 2: These sought to identify the student learning styles or preferences.

Group 3: These sought to identify the degree of student understanding of the lab project and teamwork.

Group 4&5: These sought to identify student involvement in e-Learning and how much time they spent using SCeT.

Group 6～8: These sought to identify student gains, if any, in three areas: IT improvement, Confidence in IT self-learning, and Teamwork output.

Group 9: This invited students to compare SCeT with the superseded approach to lab teaching in IT courses

In general, Question groups 1-5 reflect a present set of conditions, learning styles, or attitudes. Question groups 6-9 concern a result set from the SCeT course. Of central interest are items in the present set which are correlated with those in the result set. Simple correlation (Pearson) analysis was used to determine if there were any significant correlations between the items under investigation. A Windows version of the statistical package, SPSS 10.0 package was used.

5.1. *Experimental Results and Analysis*

In this research, we focused on two hypotheses:

H1: Students with good computer literacy background will be more involved in e-Learning.

H2: Students who appreciate e-Learning and SCeT have got IT skill improved greater.

Testing of Hypothesis 1

The student computer literacy is measured in terms of the student's self-estimation. The e-Learning involvement is rated on the activities. For example, an activity such as "send post and ask question" was rated as 5, and "not used basically" was rated 1. The correlation result is shown in Table 2:

Table-2 Statistical test for computer literacy and e-Learning involvement

Correlations

		Computer literacy	Lecture	Lab	e-Learning	e-Learning involve	IT Improvement
Computer literacy	Pearson Correlation	1.000	-.020	-.144	-.276	.034	.233
	Sig. (2-tailed)	.	.906	.403	.104	.842	.172
	N	36	36	36	36	36	36
Lecture	Pearson Correlation	-.020	1.000	.529**	.436**	.310	.206
	Sig. (2-tailed)	.906	.	.001	.008	.066	.229
	N	36	36	36	36	36	36
Lab	Pearson Correlation	-.144	.529**	1.000	.488**	.160	-.051
	Sig. (2-tailed)	.403	.001	.	.003	.351	.768
	N	36	36	36	36	36	36
e-Learning	Pearson Correlation	-.276	.436**	.488**	1.000	.164	-.110
	Sig. (2-tailed)	.104	.008	.003	.	.341	.523
	N	36	36	36	36	36	36
e-Learning involve	Pearson Correlation	.034	.310	.160	.164	1.000	.108
	Sig. (2-tailed)	.842	.066	.351	.341	.	.532
	N	36	36	36	36	36	36
IT improvement	Pearson Correlation	.233	.206	-.051	-.110	.108	1.000
	Sig. (2-tailed)	.172	.229	.768	.523	.532	.
	N	36	36	36	36	36	36

**. Correlation is significant at the 0.01 level (2-tailed).

Correlation analysis shows that there is no significant correlation between computer literacy and e-Learning involvement as defined here. However, there are some points that are worth noting.

1) **There is no significant correlation between computer literacy and the e-Learning involvement**. A good student's computer literacy background seems to have little positive impact on the IT course learning. There is a negative but not significant correlation with face-to-face lectures, arranged labs and e-Learning although those students may be often absent from class and lab. There is also no significant correlation between computer literacy and their opinions on their IT skill improvement.
2) **There is a close correlation between those who appreciate face-to-face lectures and those who appreciate arranged labs and e-Learning.** No significant correlation was found between either the traditional teaching or e-Learning methods and IT skill improvement. This indicated that any single means of learning would not directly affect the SCeT's result, e.g. the introduction of e-Learning won't automatically improve the quality of teaching and learning
3) **There is a close correlation between those who appreciate the arranged lab and e-Learning.** This may be because most of the students who used the Moodle in the lab time did a lot of assigned work, such as downloading files, completing quizzes, delivering assignments and browsing the course forum.

Testing of Hypothesis 2

To determine the impact of e-Learning in the SCeT as a whole, students were asked about their learning style to see if they accepted the SCeT pedagogy as a new way of learning. The factors considered include:

1) Acceptance of SCeT as basic learning concept
2) Acceptance of e-Learning as a new communication platform
3) Acceptance of peer communication as an important approach to "whole person" learning
4) Students' plans for their future profession. (Students selected projects which they believe may have career implications.)
5) Students knowing the importance of teamwork skills in their future profession
6) Student's time devoted to their selected project when compared with the usual IT course labs.

Table 3 shows a correlation analysis of the impact of e-Learning on the SCeT as a whole. There is no significant correlation between confirmation on SCeT, e-Learning and IT improvement. But, those students who appreciate SCeT may spend more time on their course project. Time spent correlates highly with improvements in IT skills. This implies that students will get the greatest improvements in their IT skills if they have a sound understanding of SCeT, select projects with career implications, communication by peer or e-Learning freely, and spend extra time in the lab.

Table 3 Correlation analysis of the impact of e-Learning on the SCeT as a whole

Correlations

		SCeT comfirmation	e-Learning	Peer communication	Select Project	Teamwork necessity	Time Invest	e-Learning involve	IT improvement
SCeT comfirmation	Pearson Correlation	1.000	.110	-.188	.519**	.300	.433**	-.052	.213
	Sig. (2-tailed)	.	.523	.272	.001	.075	.008	.762	.211
	N	36	36	36	36	36	36	36	36
e-Learning	Pearson Correlation	.110	1.000	.384*	-.074	.170	.166	.164	-.110
	Sig. (2-tailed)	.523	.	.021	.668	.322	.332	.341	.523
	N	36	36	36	36	36	36	36	36
Peer communication	Pearson Correlation	-.188	.384*	1.000	-.190	.555**	-.111	-.073	-.007
	Sig. (2-tailed)	.272	.021	.	.267	.000	.518	.671	.967
	N	36	36	36	36	36	36	36	36
Select Project	Pearson Correlation	.519**	-.074	-.190	1.000	.096	.335*	.103	.320
	Sig. (2-tailed)	.001	.668	.267	.	.579	.046	.550	.057
	N	36	36	36	36	36	36	36	36
Teamwork necessity	Pearson Correlation	.300	.170	.555**	.096	1.000	.293	-.194	.110
	Sig. (2-tailed)	.075	.322	.000	.579	.	.083	.256	.523
	N	36	36	36	36	36	36	36	36
Time Invest	Pearson Correlation	.433**	.166	-.111	.335*	.293	1.000	.024	.411*
	Sig. (2-tailed)	.008	.332	.518	.046	.083	.	.891	.013
	N	36	36	36	36	36	36	36	36
e-Learning involve	Pearson Correlation	-.052	.164	-.073	.103	-.194	.024	1.000	.108
	Sig. (2-tailed)	.762	.341	.671	.550	.256	.891	.	.532
	N	36	36	36	36	36	36	36	36
IT improvement	Pearson Correlation	.213	-.110	-.007	.320	.110	.411*	.108	1.000
	Sig. (2-tailed)	.211	.523	.967	.057	.523	.013	.532	.
	N	36	36	36	36	36	36	36	36

**. Correlation is significant at the 0.01 level (2-tailed).

*. Correlation is significant at the 0.05 level (2-tailed).

6. Conclusion

In this paper we present the design and implementation of a teaching reform experiment our MIS Course. The e-Learning platform was implemented for undergraduate IT courses in networking and web applications. The implementation combined Student-Centered Teaching with the use of the Internet and sought in particular to help in assessing whether a customized and Internet-enabled version of Student-Centered Teaching would fit into the traditional university curriculum and grading system.

The integration of e-learning with traditional approaches should be carefully planned based on learner characteristics, course content, and the learning context. As implied by our SCeT study, because e-Learning provides an efficient way to evaluate the student learning characteristics, the instructor could divide the students into different categories and encourage students to complement and learn from each other in their learning groups.

Acknowledgments

The authors would like to acknowledge the partial support of the Teaching and Learning grant of The Hong Kong Polytechnic University.

References

1. C. Anderson, eLearning in Practice Blended Solutions in Action, *IDC White Paper* sponsored by Mentergy Inc., (Ed.) (2000).
2. D. N. Aspy, Toward a Technology for Humanizing Education, Research Press Company, (1972).
3. T. W. Bates, Managing Technological Change: Strategies for College and University Leaders, Jossey Bass, (2000).
4. K. A. Bruffee, Collaborative Learning. Higher education, interdependence, and the authority of knowledge, Johns Hopkins University Press, (1999).
5. E. Elmarie, A look at e-Learning models: investigating their value for developing an e-Learning strategy, *Bureau for Learning Development*, Unisa, *Progressio* **25(2)**, (2003).
6. E. Engelbrecht, A look at e-learning models: investigating their value for developing an e-learning strategy, *Bureau for Learning Development*, Unisa, *Progressio* **25(2)**, 38-47 (2003)
7. J. Freimuth, Moderation in der Hochschule: Konzepte und Erfahrungen in der Hochschullehre und Hochschulentwicklung, Windm, (2000).
8. D. R. Garrison and T. Anderson, E-Learning in the 21st century: a framework for research and practice, RoutledgeFalmer, (2003).
9. R. Hazemi, St. Hailes and. S. Wilbur. The Digital University: Reinventing the Academy, Springer Publishing, (1998).
10. Van Den Jansen, Jägers Hooven and Steenbakkers, The Added Value of E-learning, *Informing Science*, (2002).
11. D. H. Jonassen, M. Davidson, M. Dollins, J. Campbell and Haag, B Bannan, Constructivism and computer-mediated communication in distance education, *The American Journal of Distance Education*, (1995).
12. G. Julia and M. Peter, Competing in the E-Learning Environment – Strategies for Universities, *Proceedings of the 35th Hawaii International Conference on System Sciences*, (2002).
13. K. C. Laudon and J. P. Laudon, Management Information System --Organization and Technology in the Networked Enterprise, 6th Edition, Prentice Hall & Higher Education Press, (2001).
14. McKinsey, China's looming talent shortage, by Diana Farrell & Andrew J. Grant, McKinsey Global Institute (MGI), (2005).
15. MoE,[1998-2004], *National education developing statistics reports*, from: http://www.moe.edu.cn/edoas/website18/level2.jsp ?tablename=1068.
16. R. Motschnig-Pitrik and A. Holzinger, Student-Centered Teaching Meets New Media: Concept and Case Study, *Educational Technology & Society* **5(4)**, 436-4522 (2002).
17. R. Motschnig-Pitrik and K. Mallich, Effects of Person-Centered Attitudes on Professional and Social Competence in a Blended Learning Paradigm, *Educational Technology & Society* **7(4)**, 176-192 (2004).
18. Karl L Smart, Cappel and J. James, Students' Perceptions of Online Learning: A Comparative Study, *Journal of Information Technology Education* **5**, 201-219 (2006).

EVALUATION INFORMATION SYSTEM USING FUZZY NEURAL NETWORKS

WEIMIN MA[1,2]

[1]School of Economics and Management, Beihang University, 37 Xueyuan Rd.
Beijing 100083, China
[2]School of Economics and Management, Zhong Yuan University of Technology, 41 Zhongyuanzhong Rd.
Zhengzhou 450007, China

XIUJUAN MA

School of Economics and Management, Beihang University, 37 Xueyuan Rd.
Beijing 100083, China

Information systems Information systems (IS) are widely used but are rarely objectively evaluated. Further, there are difficulties associated with choosing the indices upon which an evaluation of IS should be made and with the numerical representation of human knowledge. This paper propose a novel IS evaluation system that uses Fuzzy Neural Networks (FNN) and provides a comprehensive assessment that draws data from every layer of the IS.

1. Introduction

Information systems (IS) are widely used but are rarely objectively evaluated. [1~3] indices. One reason for this has been the multi-subjective, multi-objective and multi-layered [4] nature of evaluation, where numerical representation can be simplistic or give a false impression of precision while linguistic representations come with the difficulties of interpreting ambiguity. In general, each of these two representations is associated with a different data source; and, linguistic information with human experts.

There are further difficulties associated with choosing the indices upon which an evaluation of IS should be made. Suggested indices have included practical, economic, and scientific [11], technology and economic factors [12], and technology, economics, and social and environment effects [9].

This paper proposes an approach to the evaluation of information makes use of fuzzy neural networks (FNN). It does this by establishing a multi-layered index system that parallels the application layers of an enterprise IS, from bottom to top, operational layer, knowledge layer, tactical layer and strategic layer. The proposed approach uses both linguistic and numerical representations Through the use of fuzzy logic for linguistic rules [5, 6] and neural networks for numerical data pairs (i.e., desired input-output pairs) [7, 8]. The method takes use of the self-learn ability of neural network and makes decision on the basis of weighted indices and membership rules.

The rest of the paper is organized as follows. Section 2, the index system of the evaluation will be established. Section 3 will construct the evaluation system based on the FNN. In section 4, some discussion concerning the realization of the evaluation will be given.

2. The indices of evaluation

The purpose for evaluating a system is to estimate, examine, test, analyze and assess the whole function of a system. In this section, we describe the principles upon which we construct our indices of evaluation and then describe the construction of the index itself.

2.1. *The principles for constructing the indices of evaluation*

Our proposed system will evaluate an IS against four criteria. An IS should be:

1. Comprehensive: IS is intricate and covers many fields. The evaluation should reflect the overall condition and all characters of IS. Thus IS should be evaluated systematically.

2. Feasible: Data should be convenient to acquire.

3. Situated: The indices should take account of the needs of the user of the IS, the enterprise, in its own situation.

4. Profitable: The IS should provide an acceptable return on investment.

2.2. *The construction of the index system*

An IS in an enterprise is multi-layered and made up of many sub-systems, such as, for example, an Inventory Management System, Office Automation System, or Decision Support System, which may function both independently and in coordination. IS in enterprises can be divided into four levels: operational level, knowledge level, tactical level, and strategic level, with information flowing up. As the logistics, and capital and information flows vary with enterprises, the exact nature of what parts of this information would be used as indices would be chosen by users.

2.3.1 Operational level

The operational level is the lowest level of the system. Here the IS collects, examines and records data which describe the daily accounts of a company, and help line managers manage daily activities of the company, such as accounts receivable or accounts payable. Evaluation of the IS at this level will focus on the ability to deal with the basic data, with the adequacy or performance of operating functions, and system reliability. Suitable indices would include mean time between failures (MTBF), the rate of processing, the ability to examine and correct input data, and elements of human computer interactions (HCI) such as the interface.

2.3.2 Knowledge level

The knowledge level is used by the knowledge and data processing personnel. It helps the enterprise to identify new knowledge, use it, and integrate it with the business processes, as well as to control the work flow. A representative system at this level is Office Automation System, which can support group work. At this level, evaluation focuses on fluency of the work flow and the quality of the information from the system. The precise indices are the response latency of online work, the standardization of input and output, the timeliness and completeness of the information, and the fluency of communication between personnel.

2.3.3 Tactical level

The tactical level is used by middle managers to help them supervise and to control and make decision about administrative issues within the enterprise. This part of the system functions in a longer time frame than the two levels below, for example in producing periodic reports such as sales reports broken down by product, district, or staff. The focus is on analysis so the precise indices at this level include the system processing rate, capacity to analyze, and the correctness and the accuracy of the information.

2.3.4 Strategic level

The strategic level helps senior managers with the longer range strategic issues inside or outside the enterprise. It is concerned with the relations between the environment and the enterprise. It synthesizes information from within the enterprise received from the operational and the tactical levels and external information, such as information about the market, technology, competitors, customers and policies. Managers use this information to formulate long term goals and policies. Evaluation of IS at this level refer to its ability to support enterprise strategic decision making. Specific indices include user satisfaction, the coverage of management

The IS in strategic level is to help the top managers to deal with the long period strategic problems inside or outside the enterprise. The system with strategic level are mainly concerned with the relation between the environment outside the enterprise and the enterprise's own ability. Its function is to synthesize the inside information, from the operational level and the tactical level, and the outside information, such as the marketing changes, the technology progress, the competitors' actions, the demands of customers and the policy information, and then to aid the top managers to make decision on the long developing goal of the enterprise, marketing position, product structure and so on. As a result, the essential point of the evaluation of IS in this level is to see whether the system can provide the support to fulfill the enterprise's strategy. The indexes are: user satisfaction, the coverage of management and the decision making reference to the leader.

The multi-level index system (Figure 1) proposed here parallels combine the results of lower level evaluations with its own indices, giving the final at the top level.

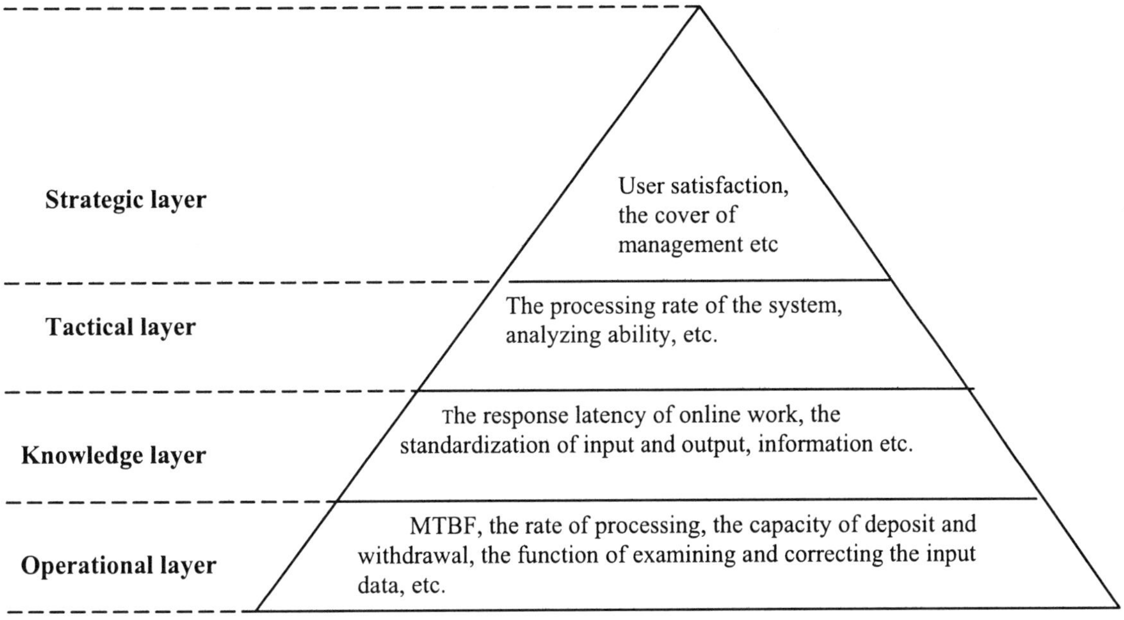

Figure 1 The index system

3. Evaluation based on the fuzzy neural network

3.1. *The principle of FNN*

In recent years, fuzzy logic has been applied in many fields [8~11] as a way of capturing expert knowledge. Fuzzy logic is suitable for usefully capturing the ambiguity of linguistically represented expert knowledge. Even so, the membership function of fuzzy sets also encodes ambiguity. Therefore, this paper also presents a learning algorithm for fuzzy logic, a fuzzy neural network (FNN), which can learn fuzzy if-then rules.

The proposed (FNN) is integrated with Artificial Neural Network (ANN) and Fuzzy Inference System (FIS). ANN is a system derived from neurophysiologic models. In general, it consists of a collection of simple nonlinear computing elements whose inputs and outputs are tied together to form a network. The learning algorithms of ANN can generally be divided into three different types: supervised, unsupervised, and hybrid learning.

ANN has a strong ability to learn but it is hard to receive human knowledge. In contrast, FIS makes use of fuzzy sets to represent fuzzy knowledge numerically. It also uses fuzzy logic in inference. The drawback of FIS is that it has no capacity for learning.

It is possible to combine ANN and FIS, either by fusing or integrating them. In the first one, the traditional fuzzy system mentioned above is based on experts' knowledge. However, it is not very objective. It is also difficult to acquire robust knowledge and human experts are not always available. The ANN learning algorithm has been applied to enhance the performance of a fuzzy system. Also, fuzzy if-then rules were generated and adjusted by learning methods using numerical data.

3.2. *Architecture of the FNN*

The FNN designed in this paper is based on the model of TSK (Takagi-Sugeno-Kang) [12], [13] using a Back Propagation (BP) learning scheme to adjust the weights and the variables of the membership function (MF). The architecture of this network is shown in Figure 2. The FNN consists of five layers, input layer, an output layer, and three hidden layers. The following will describe the five layers in detail.

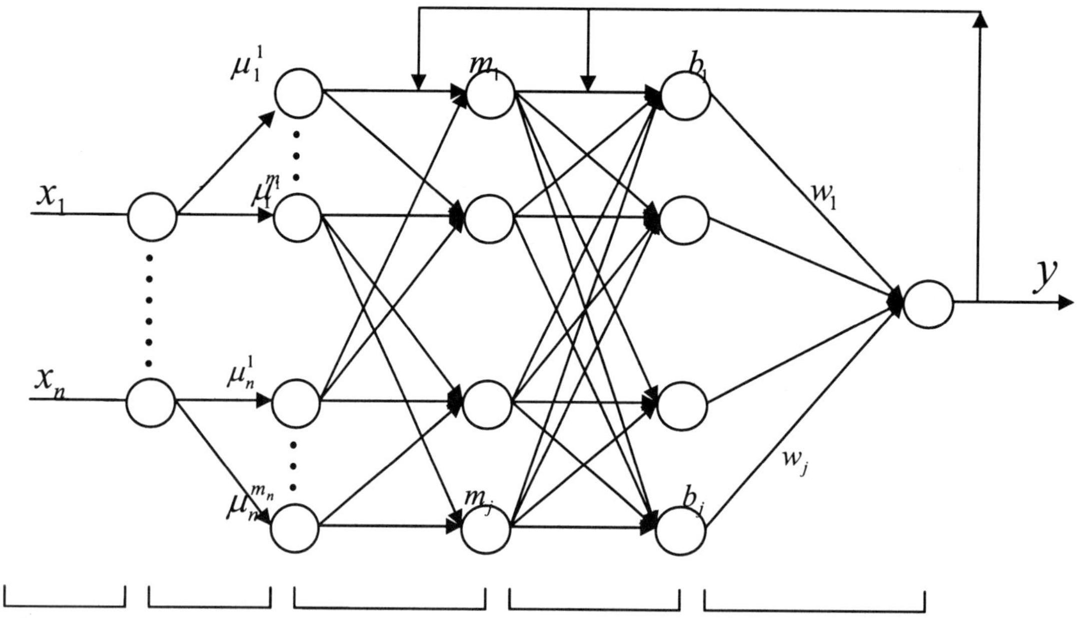

Figure 2 The architecture of the FNN

3.2.1. Layer1: input layer

$X^T = \{x_1, x_2 ... x_n\}$ is the input of the network, which is the evaluated objectives. n denotes there are n indices. Some indices, such as MTBF, the rate of processing, the deposit and withdrawal capacity, and the function for examining and correcting the input data, all come from immediately available data. Some indices such as the convenience of operation and user-friendliness of the interface are based on expert assessments.

3.2.2. Layer2: vague layer

Each neuron denotes a linguistic variable, e.g., that the processing rate is "fast", "middle", or "slow". Here there are three linguistic variables. The number of variables is represent by the vague divided number, m_i, so this layer has a total of $\sum_i^n m_i$ neurons.

This layer is used to calculate each input's membership which shows to what extent this input vector belongs to the linguistic variable. This paper uses *Gaussian MF* (1)

$$\mu_i^j(x) = \exp[-(\frac{x_i - c_{ij}}{\sigma_{ij}})^2], i = 1,2..n, j = 1,2..m_i \quad (1)$$

as the membership function. c_{ij} denotes *Gaussian MF*'s central value and σ_{ij} denotes *Gaussian MF*'s width corresponding to the ith input vector and the jth vague linguistic variable. The weights connecting layer1 and layer2 determine the vague variable, that is c_{ij} and σ_{ij}.

3.2.3. Layer3: rule layer

Definition R: IF x_1 is A_1^i and x_2 is A_2^i and$\cdots$ x_n is A_n^i, THEN y is B_j, $A_1^i, A_2^i, \cdots A_n^i, B_j$ are fuzzy sets [14].

Every neuron in this layer presents the *IF* part of the rule. In fuzzy logic, "*and*" can present three calculations, minimum, multiplication and addition. However, a research shows that multiplication is superior to the other two [15]. So this paper employs multiplication. The output of this layer is as follows:

$$a_j = \mu_1^{i_1} \times \mu_2^{i_2} \times \cdots \times \mu_n^{i_n}, \quad (2)$$

where $i_t \in \{1,2,\cdots m_t\}$, t=1,2,...n, and *j=1,2,...,m*

3.2.4. *Layer4: fuzzy inference layer*

This layer includes *m* neurons. Each neuron implements the rule *R* , the *THEN* part of the rule. The conclusion of the rule is this layer's output.

$$b_j = \frac{a_j}{\sum_{i=1}^{m} a_i} \qquad (3)$$

where *j=1,2,...,m.* It realizes regression calculation.

3.2.5. *Layer5: output layer*

This layer realizes defuzzification calculation that is

$$y = \sum_{j=1}^{m} w_j \cdot b_j \qquad (4)$$

where w_j represents the central value of the jth fuzzy set membership of y. y is the result of the evaluation.

3.3. *Back Propagation (BP) learning scheme*

In the network, *Gaussian MF*'s central value c_{ij} and width σ_{ij} , and the weights of the last layer w_j must be learnt.

Definition error function:

$$E = \frac{1}{2}\sum_j (t_j - y_j)^2 \qquad (5)$$

where t_j is the expected output and y_j is the actual output.

According to the BP learning scheme, we need to know how to adjust the weights and how to compute the value of $\frac{\partial E}{\partial w_j}, \frac{\partial E}{\partial c_{ij}}, \frac{\partial E}{\partial \sigma_{ij}}$. In the following formulas, $f_i^{(q)}$ denotes the function with *i* as its variable of the *q*th layer and $\beta > 0$ is the rate of learning.

$$\sigma_{ij}(k+1) = \sigma_{ij}(k) - \beta \frac{\partial E}{\partial \sigma_{ij}} \qquad (6)$$

$$\frac{\partial E}{\partial c_{ij}} = \frac{\partial E}{\partial f_{ij}^{(2)}} \frac{\partial f_{ij}^{(2)}}{\partial c_{ij}} = -\sigma_{ij}^{(2)} \frac{2(x_i - c_{ij})}{\sigma_{ij}^2} \qquad (7)$$

$$\frac{\partial E}{\partial \sigma_{ij}} = \frac{\partial E}{\partial f_{ij}^{(2)}} \frac{\partial f_{ij}^{(2)}}{\partial \sigma_{ij}} = -\sigma_{ij}^{(2)} \frac{2(x_i - c_{ij})^2}{\sigma_{ij}^3} \qquad (8)$$

$$w_j(k+1) = w_j(k) - \beta \frac{\partial E}{\partial w_j} \qquad (9)$$

$$c_{ij}(k+1) = c_{ij}(k) - \beta \frac{\partial E}{\partial c_{ij}} \qquad (10)$$

$$\sigma_{ij}(k+1) = \sigma_{ij}(k) - \beta \frac{\partial E}{\partial \sigma_{ij}} \qquad (11)$$

4. The implementation of the evaluation

According to the index system discussed in Session 2, the evaluation uses four FNN [16]: FNN1, FNN2, FNN3, FNN4, used separately in four levels (Figure 3). The architectures of the four FNN are similar. The differences are the number of the indices and the vague divided number, which lead to the difference of number of the nodes.

The evaluating process is from bottom level to top level. At first, input the operational level's indices and get out the result of the first level. Secondly, input the result of the first level and the five indices of the knowledge level to FNN2 and reach the result of the second level, and so on. At last, combine the result of the third level with the indices of the fourth level and put them into FNN4 to reach the ultimate result of the evaluation.

The operating stage of IS in every enterprise will differ different enterprises use them according to their own situations. In condition, we can also analyze the quality of systems in each level according to the result of every FNN, which is convenient for improving.

5. Conclusion

This paper has proposed an approach to the evaluation of information systems that makes use of fuzzy neural networks (FNN)The model is currently admittedly slow and complex, but it is also thorough, as it deals with and every layer of a system, computationally economical, we believe that it is a positive step towards evaluations of IS systems that are not just automatic, but are also measurably consistent and comparable. The FNN IS evaluation model proposed here combines the merits of Neural Network self-learning while integrating difficult-to-quantify expert knowledge by using Fuzzy Systems. Suggested future work would include: Confirming fuzzy rules with experts and periodic reviews and updates of such situated knowledge.

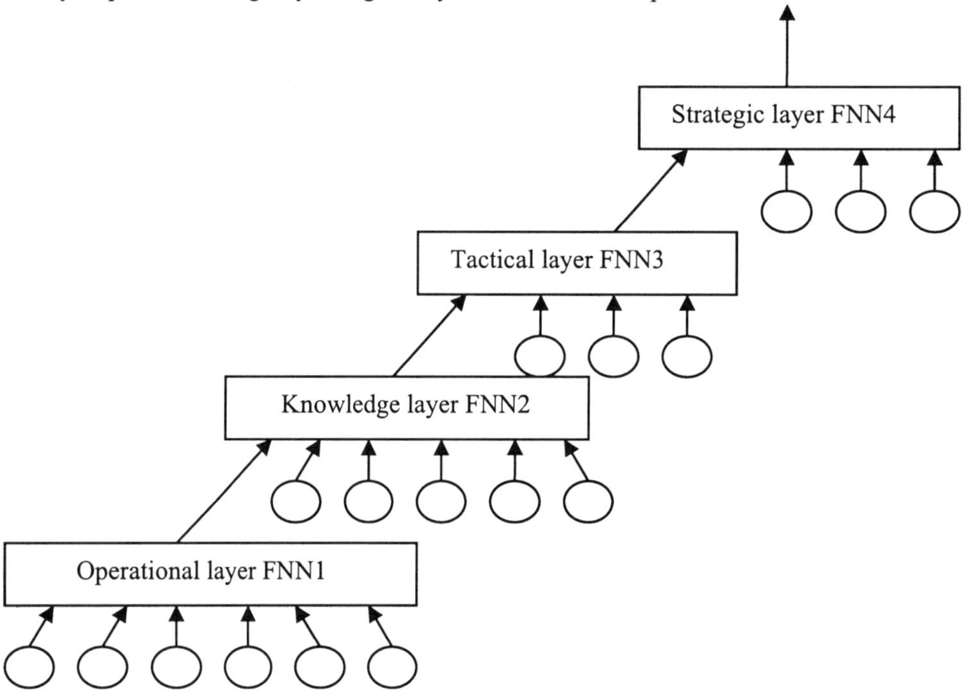

Figure 3 Multi-layer evaluation of IS

Acknowledgments

The work was partly supported by the National Natural Science Foundation of China (70671004, 70401006, 70521001), Beijing Natural Science Foundation (9073018) Program for New Century Excellent Talents in University (NCET-06-0172) and A Foundation for the Author of National Excellent Doctoral Dissertation of PR China (200782).

References

1. L Ball and R Harris, SMIS member: a membership analysis, *MIS Quarterly*, 6(1), 19-38 (1982).
2. G W Dickson, R L Leitheiser, J C. Wetherbe and M. Nechis, Key information system issues for the 1980's, *MIS Quarterly*, **8(3)**, 135-159 (1984).
3. J C Brancheau and J C Wetherbe, Key issues in information systems management, *MIS Quarterly*, 23 – 45 (1987).
4. Qiuyan Zhong and Mudan Lu, Research of the complication of the evaluation of information system, *Science and Technology Management Research* 1, 67-69 (2004).
5. C.C. Lee, Fuzzy Logic in Control Systems: Fuzzy Logic Controller, Part Ⅰ, *IEEE Trans. Syst., Man, Cybern.* **20(2)**, 404-418 (1990).
6. C.C. Lee, Fuzzy Logic in Control Systems: Fuzzy Logic Controller, Part Ⅱ, *IEEE Trans. Syst., Man, Cybern.* **20(2)**, 419-435 (1990).
7. K. S. Narendra and K. Parthasarathy, Identification and Control of Dynamical Systems Using Neural Network, *IEEE Trans. on Neural Network* **1(1)**, 4-27 (1990).
8. K. S. Narendra and K. Parthasarathy, Gradient Methods for the Optimization of Dyamical Systems Containing Neural Network, *IEEE Trans. on Neural Network* **2(2)**, 252-262 (1991).
9. Wenjie Min, Jianming Chen and Zhongyi Zhang, The research of the appraise index system and method of information systems, *Journal of the China railway society* **22(5)**, 37-41 (2000).
10. Xiaojian Chen, The methodology and application of the evaluation of system, China Science and Technology Univ. Publishers, (1993).
11. Raymond McLeod, Management Information System,Prentice Hall.Inc., (2002).

12. Tiyun Huang, Management Information System, Higher Education Press, (1999).
13. Zhong An and Xiaobo Wu, Management Information System, China Railway Publishers, Beijing, (1998).
14. S K Pal, R K De and J Basak, Unsupervised feature evaluation: A neuro-fuzzy approach, *IEEE Transactions on Neural Networks* **11(2)**, 366-376, (2000).
15. B. Bhattacharya and D.P. Solomatine, Neural network and M5 model trees in modeling water level–discharge relationship, *Journal of Neurocomputing* **63**, 381–396 (2005).
16. P Deka and V Chandramouli, A fuzzy neural network model for deriving the river stage–discharge relationship, *Hydrological Science Journal* **48(2)**, 197–209 (2003).
17. Liang-Chih Huang, Ren-Jieh Kuo, Pci-Tsang Wu, and Han-Chun Huang, A Neural Network Modeling on Human Resource Talent Selection, *International Journal of Human Resources Development and Management* **1**, 206-219 (2001).
18. T Takagi and M Sugeno, Fuzzy identification of systems and it's application to modeling and control, *IEEE Trans. Syst., Man, Cybern.* **15**, 116-132 (1985).
19. M Sugeno and G T Kang, Structure identification of fuzzy model, *Fuzzy Sets Syst.* **28**, 329-349 (1986).
20. H. Ishibuchi, H. Okada, R. Fujioka and H. Tanaka, Neural Networks that learn from Fuzzy if-then Rules, *IEEE Trans. Fuzzy Systems* **1(2)**, 85-97 (1993).
21. X J Zeng and M G Singh, Approximation accuracy algorithm, *IEEE Trans. Syst., Man, Cybern.* **15(4)**, 580-585 (1985).
22. Zhongtuo Wang and Lili Rong, Learning evaluation system based on knowledge and fuzzy neural networks, *Journal of Management Sciences in China* **6(3)**, (2003).

IMMUNOLOGY-BASED SUBSPACE DETECTORS FOR ANOMALY DETECTION[1]

XIAOSHU HANG

School of Engineering and Information Technology Deakin University, 221Burwood Highway, Burwood Melbourne, Vic 3125, Australia

HONGHUA DAI

School of Engineering and Information Technology Deakin University, 221Burwood Highway, Burwood Melbourne, Vic 3125, Australia

A key problem in high dimensional anomaly detection is that the time spent in constructing detectors by the means of generate-and-test is intolerable. In fact, due to the high sparsity of the data, it is ineffective to construct detectors in the whole data space. Previous investigations have shown that most essential patterns can be discovered in different subspaces. This inspires us to construct detectors in significant subspaces only for anomaly detection. We first use ENCLUS-based method to discover all significant subspaces and then use a greedy-growth algorithm to construct detectors in each subspace. The elements used to constitute a detector are grids instead of data points, which makes the time-consumption irrelevant to the size of the normal data. We test the effectiveness and efficiency of our method on both synthetic and benchmark datasets. The results reveal that our method is particularly useful in anomaly detection in high dimensional data spaces.

1. Introduction

Detecting rare events via learning has drawn great attention in recent years, especially in the areas of network intrusion detection and fraud identification. There are a number of other terms, such as novelty detection [6], surprising detection [7], fault detection [8] and outlier detection [9], which deal with the problem in different ways. The methods mainly fall into two categories: signature-based and anomaly-based. The advantages of anomaly-based detection approaches are that they do not require any prior knowledge about anomalies and focus on detecting innovative anomalies. Such approaches first construct a large number of detectors, and then use them to monitor the system for detecting anomalies. The performance of such an anomaly detection system is mainly dependent on how well the detectors are yielded.

One of the anomaly detection approaches is the immunology-inspired approach. The natural immune system protects biologic bodies from disease-causing pathogens through pattern recognition, reinforcement learning and adaptive response [1]. It consists of a large number of immune cells which conduct in a variety of ways to detect and eliminate antigens. The basic immune model in artificial immune systems is negative selection algorithm which aims at distinguishing the normal data from the abnormal ones. The algorithm is briefly described as follows. (1) A given normal data set S to be protected is called self-data set. (2) Randomly generate a detector d and match d against each element in S. If d does not match any element in S then store d in R, otherwise ignore d. (3) Repeat step 2 until enough detectors in R are generated to ensure a desirable protection. (4) Match new instances against each detector d in R. if any detector ever matches, then an anomaly is known to have been detected, as the detectors are designed to not match any self data.

This generate-and-test method requires sampling quite a large number of candidate detectors and the computational complexity is exponential to the size of self data set *S* [2]. A challenging problem is how to efficiently construct enough valid detectors in a huge data space. The problem is extremely important when the data with dozens of dimensions. The following factors must be considered when anomaly detection is performed in a high dimensional data space:

The density of data points in a high dimensional data space is so low that it is ineffective to construct detectors.

The scalability of an algorithm on dimensionality becomes the predominant problem. An algorithm with low scalability will result in a very high time cost when constructing a repertoire of detectors in the full dimensional space.

As it is difficult to construct a complete repertoire of detectors in the whole dimensional data space, consequently,

* This research project is partially supported by Deakin Central Research grant.

neither detection rate nor false alarm rate in this case could be satisfying.

A detector, which actually is a detection rule, in a high dimensional space is too long to understand.

A good example of anomaly detection problem in a high dimensional data space is the network intrusion dataset published in KDD Cup 1999 competition, which consists of 42 attributes. As we have neither the knowledge about how many detectors are ideally required for a given problem, nor the knowledge about the coverage of the generated detectors in the data space, we are inclined to generate a very large number of detectors in order to acquire a satisfying detection rate. This strategy, however, is infeasible when the data space is of high dimensional. In recent years, investigations on high dimensional data spaces have revealed that data often hide their essential patterns in subspaces. Based on this consideration, we are motivated to find out those significant subspaces in which normal data can be well partitioned into patterns, and then construct an appropriate number of detectors in these significant subspaces to protect normal data from intrusion or fraud.

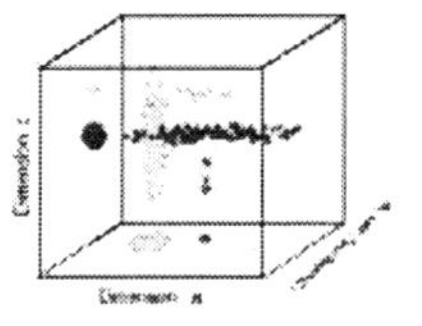

Fig 1. An example of data forming patterns in subspaces

2. Problem Formulation

Anomaly detection, from immunology point of view, aims at identifying whether a new element in a problem space is non-self (abnormal) or not when self (normal) is known.

Suppose that a problem space $S=x_1\times x_2\times\cdots\times x_n$ is an n-dimensional numeric vector space, where x_j is the jth numeric attribute. An element $e^*\in S$, where $*\in\{$normal, abnormal$\}$ is an n-dimensional numeric vector. Those elements that belong to *normal* form a subspace donated as *NS*, and the abnormal subspace *AS* is defined as the complementary space of *NS*. Each attribute is normalized into [0, 1], so we have:

$S\subseteq [0,1]^n \subseteq R^n$

$NS\cup AS=S$ and $NS\cap AS=\varnothing$.

Given a problem space S for anomaly detection, the characteristic function χ_{self} for differentiating self and non-self is defined as follows:

$$\chi_{self}(e_j) = \begin{cases} 1, & if\ e_j \in NS \\ 0, & if\ e_j \in AS \end{cases}$$

A detector is actually a detection rule, which is a hyper-rectangle in the data space and represented in CNF (conjunctive normal form) as follows:

$$if\ \ x_1 \in [low_1^i, high_1^i] \wedge \ldots \wedge x_n \in [low_n^i, high_n^i]\ \ then\ \ abnormal$$

The condition part of the rule defines a hypercube in the complementary subspace of normal data.

The performance of an anomaly detection system is generally evaluated by two measures: detection rate and false alarm rate. Let TP denote anomalous instances identified as anomalous; TN, normal instances identified as normal; FP, normal instances identified as anomalous; FN, anomalous instances identified as normal. The two measures are calculated as follows:

$$Detection\_rate = \frac{TP}{TP + FN}$$

$$False\ alarm\_rate = \frac{FP}{TN + FP}$$

3. Mining Significant Subspace

3.1. *Related Work*

In a high dimensional data space, as the average density of points anywhere in the data space is likely to be quite low, it is not meaningful to look for clusters in such a high dimensional space [3]. Patterns are more likely hidden in different subspaces, which makes conventional feature selection approaches invalid. As many dimensions or combination of dimensions in a high dimensional data space have values that are uniformly distributed, they are not important and thus pruned in the mining process, resulting in clusters in significant subspaces. CLIQUE is the first subspace clustering algorithm. It is a grid-density based clustering approach and uses an APRIORI style search technique to find out subspaces with dense grids. CLIQUE assumes that if a k-dimensional region is dense, all its (k-1)-dimensional regions containing it should also be dense. ENCLUS uses the similar approach by CLIQUE but measures entropy rather than density or coverage to find the subspaces. Its basic idea is that a subspace with clusters typically has lower entropy than those without clusters. In this paper, we combine the merits of CLIQUE and ENCLUS by firstly using entropy and mutual information to mine significant subspaces and then identify each cluster based on grid density.

3.2. *Definitions and Algorithm Description*

Let $S=A_1\times A_2\times\ldots\times A_n$ be a n-dimensional numeric vectorspace. A_1, A_2,…,A_n are the n numeric attributes of S

and, the domain of each attribute is normalized into [0,1]. A point $v=\langle v_1, v_2, \ldots, v_n \rangle$ in S is a n-dimensional numeric vector, where $v_i \in Domain(A_i)$. Each attribute is equally divided into η intervals, where η is an input parameter. Hence, we have the following terms:

Grid(cell): A grid or cell is the intersection of one interval from each dimension. A k-grid is the intersection of k intervals from k-dimensions, respectively.

Density: The density of a grid equals the ratio of the number of points it contains to the total number of points in the subspace. A grid with density greater than a given threshold is called dense grid.

Neighbour: Given a k-grid g, its neighbors are those k-grids that each has (k-1) common dimensional faces with g. Therefore, a 2-grid (k=2) has 4 neighbors and a 3-grid (k=3) has 6 neighboring grids. A k-grid has $\binom{k-1}{k}$ neighbors.

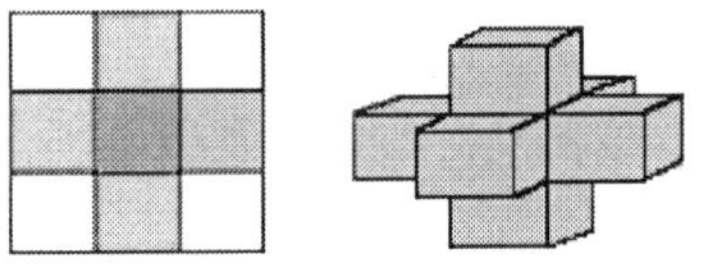

k=2 k=3

Fig. 2. A grid and its neighbors in two and three dimensions

Cluster: A cluster in a k-dimensional space is the maximal set of connected dense grids.

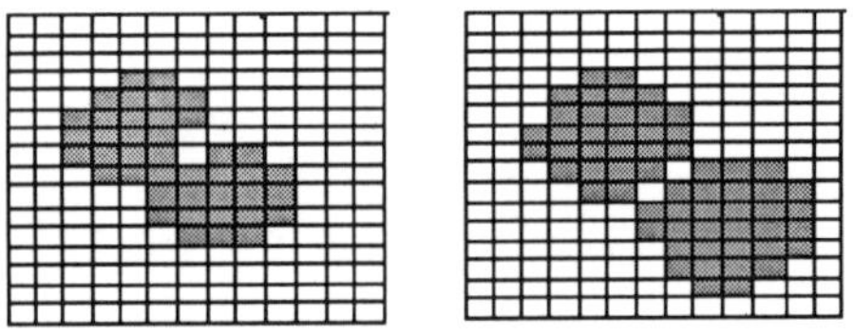

a) b)

Fig. 3. Examples of clusters in two dimensional spaces

A cluster in our work can be any shape although we are not concerned with it. In Fig.3 a), all the dense grids form a cluster which is concave in shape, whereas in Fig.3 b) two separate convex clusters are formed in a subspace. A subspace with fewer clusters is more ideal than one with more clusters.

Significant subspace: Given a clustering criterion, those subspaces satisfying the criterion are called significant subspaces.

We consider that, in a high dimensional data space, data may form clusters in more than one subspace. Hence, we have to seek for a method which can mine all significant subspaces rather than a single subspace. Having built up the above basic concepts, we are ready to describe the subspace clustering algorithm that was first introduced in [4]. As pointed in [4], entropy meets all the three clustering criterions: high coverage, high density and high correlation of dimensions. We use **entropy** to measure the uncertainty of a subspace, and **mutual information** to measure the correlation between dimensions. Suppose all the points in the entire data space is projected onto a single dimension x which is divided into η intervals of the same length, then the entropy of dimension x is

$$H(x) = -\sum d(c_i)\log_2 d(c_i) \qquad (1)$$

where $d(c_i)$ denotes the density of cell c_i, η is a input parameter, which determines the length of each interval and the density of each cell, and consequently affects the accuracy and efficiency of a subspace clustering algorithm.

Example: This example illustrates how to calculate the entropy value of a subspace. In Fig.4, the points, when projected on axis x, are uniformly distributed, but show a high-skewed distribution on axis y. The entropy values: $H(x)$, $H(y)$ and their joint value $H(x,y)$ are calculated as follows:

$$H(x) = -2/16\log_2(2/16)\times 8 = 3\,bit$$

$$H(y) = -3/16\log_2(3/16) - 5/16\log_2(5/16) - 8/16\log_2(8/16)$$
$$= 1.4772\,bit$$

$$H(x,y) = -1/16\log_2(1/16)\times 16 = 4\,bit$$

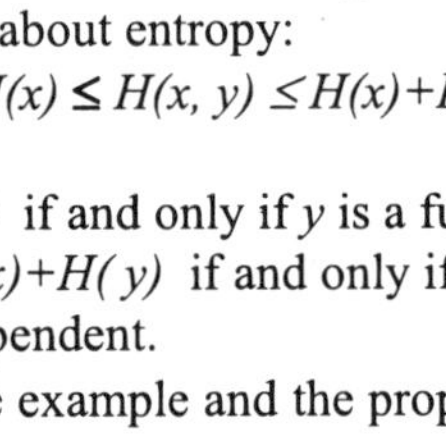

Fig. 4. An example of calculating entropy in subspaces

Suppose x, y are two variables, generally we have the following property about entropy:

$$H(x) \le H(x,y) \le H(x)+H(y).$$

and:

$H(x) = H(x,y)$ if and only if y is a function of x.

$H(x,y) = H(x)+H(y)$ if and only if x, y are independent.

Both the above example and the property imply that the original n-dimensional data space has the highest entropy value, while all 1-dimensional subspaces have the lowest entropy values. The algorithm of mining subspaces with clusters uses bottom-up searching strategy which is similar to Apriori algorithm used in mining association rules. It starts with mining 1-dimensional significant subspaces, proceeding towards k-dimensional subspaces. This is an entropy-increasing process. Therefore, if entropy is selected as the sole criterion, a subspace with entropy value smaller than a specified threshold ω is considered to be significant because our goal is to seek for subspaces with low entropy values. The threshold value is determined by trail and error, and different from dataset to dataset. A lower threshold ω will result in quite a lot of low dimensional subspaces, while a higher threshold ω will lead to fewer relatively high dimensional subspaces. An improper ω may not even produce correct result. This can be illustrated in Fig. 5, where a 2-dimenional subspace is found to be pregnant of two clusters after the second pass over the data set, but if we just stop there, we would miss a better result of four clusters in a 3-dimensional subspace. With regard to the problems of anomaly detection, it is reasonable to choose a little high threshold ω so that more detectors can be constructed.

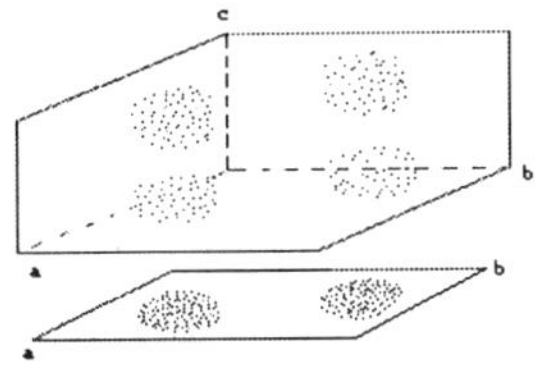

Fig. 5. An example of clusters formed in different subspaces

Considering the above situation in Fig.5, we think it is difficult to obtain an ideal result by using entropy as the unique subspace-pruning criterion, so we consider another information measure: mutual information.

In information theory, mutual information is used to measure the correlation between two variables. Here, a higher value of mutual information means stronger correlation between the dimensions. The definition of mutual information is given as follows:

$$I(x_1,x_2,\ldots,x_n)=\sum_{i=1}^{n}H(x_i)-H(x_1,x_2,\ldots,x_n) \qquad (2)$$

Mutual information has the following properties:

1) $I(x)=0$;
2) $I(x,y)=0$ if and only if x, y are independent;
3) If x,y are correlated, then for any z, $I(x,y,z) \geq I(x,y)$;

The last property indicates if the dimensions of subspace S are correlated, then the dimensions of any super-space of S are correlated.

A combination of entropy and mutual information is used to prune search spaces. This strategy guarantees that we can mine those significant subspaces with lower entropy values and higher mutual information values. The pruning strategy is as follows: In the kth iteration, we obtain a set of candidates, each of which is a k-dimensional subspace. We prefer those k-dimensional subspaces that, on the one hand, their entropy values are smaller than a specified threshold ρ, on the other hand, their mutual information are greater than a specified threshold σ. All other k-dimensional subspaces that have higher entropies and lower mutual information will be pruned.

Lemma 1. If a k-dimensional space S_k contains a set of good clusters C, then any (k-1)-dimensional subspace S_{k-1} of S_k contains good clusters and, for any cluster $c_i \in C$, there must exist a cluster c_i' in S_{k-1} such that $c_i \subseteq c_i'$

Proof: Suppose that a subspace made up of attributes: $x_1,x_2,\ldots, x_k$ contains good clusters, which means, for a given threshold ω for clustering criterion, we have

$$H(x_1,x_2,\ldots, x_k) < \omega$$

We only need to proof that $H(x_1,x_2,\ldots, x_{k-1}) < \omega$ is satisfied as well. The existence of the set of clusters C in the subspace S_k implies that $x_1,x_2,\ldots, x_k$ are correlated to each other, so we have $H(x_k \mid x_1,x_2,\ldots,x_{k-1}) > 0$.

$$H(x_1,x_2,\ldots,x_{k-1}) < H(x_1,x_2,\ldots,x_{k-1}) + H(x_k \mid x_1,x_2,\ldots,x_{k-1})$$
$$=H(x_1,x_2,\ldots, x_k) < \omega$$

Therefore, any (k-1)-dimensional subspace has good clusters. And $H(x_1,x_2,\ldots,x_{k-1}) < H(x_1,x_2,\ldots,x_k)$ means that there are fewer clusters in the subspace S_{k-1} than in the subspace S_k. The reason for this is that some clusters in the space S_k forms one cluster when the points are projected onto the (k-1)–dimensional subspace. Therefore, for any cluster $c_i \in C$, there exists a cluster c_i' in S_{k-1} such that $c_i \subseteq c_i'$
□

The bottom-up algorithm first partitions all dimensions into equivalent intervals according to the given threshold η, and calculates the density of each interval and the entropy of each dimension, then starts with mining 1-dimensional significant subspaces. Having found (k-1)-dimensional important subspaces, the candidates of k-dimensional subspaces are generated by procedure *Candidate_gen()*. Each candidate of k-dimensional subspace is calculated for entropy and mutual information, and then pruned based on the thresholds ω and ε. This process repeats until no candidate is generated. The algorithm was first introduced in [4] .

Algorithm_1: Mining Subspaces with Clusters

```
Input : dataset and parameter: η, ρ and σ
Output: A set of significant subspaces
divide each dimension into η intervals
k=1, Sk=∅, NSk=∅;
let Ck be all k-dimensional subspaces
for each subspace c ∈ Ck
    D(c) =Density_cal (c);
    H(c) =Entropy_cal (D(c ));
    if H(c) <ρ then
        I(c)=Mutual_Info(c);
        if I(c) > σ then
            Sk=Sk ∪ c;
        else
            NSk=NSk ∪ c;
        end if
```

```
14    end if
15  end for
16  C_{k+1}= Candidate_gen(NS_k);
17  if C_{k+1} = ∅ then goto 19
18  k=k+1; goto 4 ;
19  Output  ∪_{∀k} S_k
```

The candidate generation function *Candidate_gen(NS_k) can* be found in data mining books[6][10].

3.3. *Cluster Identification*

The output of Algorithm_1 is a set of subspaces which are significant according to the clustering criteria. The next step is to circumscribe each cluster in each significant subspace. We now make a little non-essential change to the definition of density. The density here refers to the number of points within a grid and is used as a criterion to circumscribe a cluster. A threshold ε is used to judge whether a grid is dense or not. A cluster is removed when it is identified. The method for circumscribing a cluster in a significant subspace is straightforward. We randomly select a dense grid and insert it into a queue, and then we remove the first grid in the queue and check if this gird has any dense neighbors. All its dense neighboring grids are inserted into the queue at rear. This process repeats until the queue is empty, resulting in a cluster being identified and removed. A significant subspace is processed in this way until it has no dense grids. The algorithm is described as follows:

Algorithm_2: Identification of Clusters in Subspaces

```
Input:  a set S of significant subspaces and parameter ε
Output:  a set S with all dense grids removed
1.   NE=φ;  /* initialize a set of neighbors*/
2.   for each significant subspace s ∈S_k
3.       randomly select a grid g_i with density ≥ ε
4.       Insert_queue (Q, g_i );  /* insert at real */
5.       g_1=Remove_grid(Q);
6.       NE=Neighbor(g_1);
7.       for each neighbor ne_i ∈NE
8.           Insert_queue (Q, ne_i );
9.       endfor
10.      if Q is not empty goto 5
11.      if s has dense girds goto 3;
12.  endfor
13.  Output  S_k
```

We now discuss the selection of threshold ε, which determines whether a grid is dense or not. Parameter ε affects the shape of a cluster, and consequently, affects the anomaly detection performance.

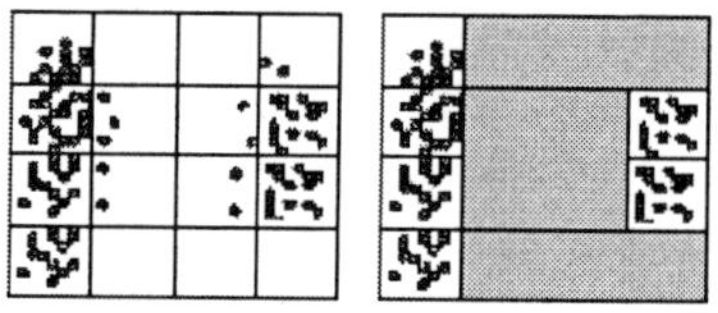

a b

Fig. 6. Illustration of cluster identification & detector construction with ε=4.

Given a η, which means the length of each gird and the total number of grids in each significant subspace are known, the problem then becomes to select a proper ε so that clusters are properly circumscribed, consequently leading to a good coverage of the non-self data space by detectors. In Fig. 8, a number of grids with points less than 4 are excluded by clusters, 3 detectors are constructed to cover the whole non-self data space. A lower ε means fewer points are excluded by clusters and, accordingly, results in more holes in the non-self data space; whereas a higher ε means more points are excluded by clusters and, consequentially, leads to a high false alarm rate. In Fig.9, when ε decreases to 2, only 2 detectors can be constructed and accordingly, holes appear.

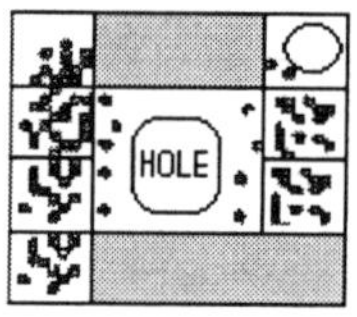

Fig. 7. Holes appear in the non-self space when ε=2

3.4. *Constructing detectors in subspaces*

Once the patterns of normal data are removed from significant subspaces, the work on generating detectors in pattern complementary subspace becomes straightforward.

We present a novel algorithm which constructs detectors in pattern complementary subspaces without need of any matching between detectors and normal data. The detectors are generated in order to cover the entire complementary subspaces. A detector is actually a hyper-rectangle and can be represented by a CNF. Given a pattern complementary subspace, to find out an optimal cover is a NP-hard problem. The so called optimal cover is to find out a minimal number of detectors which cover the entire complementary subspace. The output is a set of detection rules. The algorithm starts with randomly selecting a vacant grid *g* and greedily grows *g* as much as possible in the first dimension, resulting in a narrow rectangle *d* (see the blue rectangle in Fig.8 left and middle). Then *d* grows in the same way along the second dimension to form a maximal region (see the blue rectangle in Fig.8 right). This process proceeds in all the *k* dimensions, yielding a hyper-rectangle which can be represented in a CNF. Then all the vacant grids contained in detector *d* are removed. We repeat this procedure until the subspace has no vacant girds.

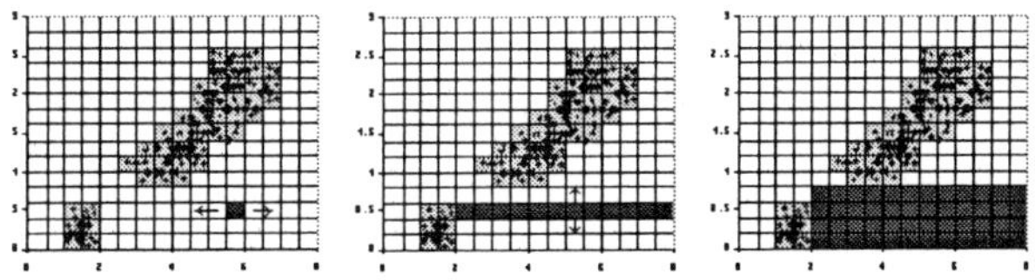

Fig. 8. Constructing detectors in abnormal data subspace

The algorithm is as follows:

Algorithm_3: Constructing Detectors in Subspaces

Input: A set S of significant subspaces
Output: A set D of detectors

1. D=∅; / * store the number of detectors */
2. for S_i=1 to | S |
3. while S_i has vacant grids
4. randomly select a vacant grid g_i
5. d_i = Detector_generation(g_i);
6. $S_i = S_i - d_i$;
7. $D = D \cup d_i$;
8. end while
9. endfor
10. output D

Detector_generation(*g*)

11. d=g; g_1=g_2=g; count =0;
12. j=1; // the first dimension
13. while g_1 has a vacant left neighbour g_l
14. $d = d \cup g_l$; g_1=g_l ; count++;
15. while g_2 has a vacant right neighbour g_r
16. $d = d \cup g_r$ g_2=g_r ; count++;
17. j++; // from the second dimension on
18. d_1=d; d_2=d; count′=count;
19. while d_1 has a vacant left neighbour d_l
20. $d = d \cup d_l$; d_1=d_l; count=count +count′;
21. while d_2 has a vacant right neighbour d_r
22. $d = d \cup d_r$; d_2 = d_r ; count=count +count′;
23. if j < k then goto 15
24. return d ;

The shape of each detector is determined by the first randomly selected vacant grid, which is called a seed grid. Once the seed grid is selected, the algorithm tries to find out a maximal hyper-rectangle consisting of connected vacant grids. Essentially all the detectors are randomly generated, but there is an essential difference between this method and the *generate-and-test* method and those based on genetic algorithms or evolutionary algorithms. In those algorithms, after we generate a set of detectors, we still have no knowledge about how well the abnormal data space is covered by the detectors, and we are not sure how many detectors would be enough for an ideal detection rate. In the above description, once a detector is generated, all the grids within the detector are removed, which guarantees that all the detectors do not overlap. In addition, the condition of *while* loop in the algorithm guarantees that there is no *hole* in the pattern complementary subspace. The most important feature in this phase is that detectors are made up of grids instead of data points, which implies the time consumed is irrelevant to the size of normal data.

4. Experiments

4.1. *Experiments on Mining Subspaces*

To test the effectiveness and efficiency of our method, we conduct the experiments on both synthetic and benchmark datasets. First, we generate a number of synthetic datasets. Each of them is specified with significant subspaces so that we can test the effectiveness of Algorithm_1. Then we test the accuracy and efficiency of Algorithm_3 on a group of benchmark datasets. Finally we evaluate the performances of different sets of detectors based on ROC curve analysis.

The benchmark datasets are obtained from UCI dataset repertory. We choose 8 of them with numeric attributes. If a dataset is multi-class, we map it into two-class by labeling the instances of some classes as "abnormal" and the rests as "normal" (see Table 1). We use the method to mine significant subspaces in KDD'99 Cup dataset (after removing all discrete attributes) with setting ρ=5.0 and σ=1.5, we obtained 5 significant subspaces and each subspace with 5 dimensions (see Table 2).

Table 1. Five subspaces mined in KDD'99 Cup dataset

Subspace	Entropy	Mutual info.
1 13 14 21 24	4.9324	1.6169
1 22 23 24 26	4.7417	1.5111
13 14 21 23 24	4.3755	1.5918
13 14 21 24 26	4.6477	1.5127
13 14 23 24 26	4.6544	1.5216

However, it is easy to see from Table 3 that the last 3 subspaces have a common subspace"13,14,24". This implies that some significant subspaces mined might not be the real ones we want and could be pruned manually.

Table 2. Self/non-self data and significant subspaces mined from UCI datasets

Dataset	Dimen-Sionality	Normal Sample size	abnormal sample size	Number of Subspaces	Dim. of Subspace	Parameters: ρ and σ
Bupa	6	200	147	2	3	ρ=3.5, σ=0.5
Iris	4	100	50	3	2	ρ=3.0, σ=0.5
Pima	8	500	268	1	5	ρ=5.5, σ=2.0
Shuttle	9	10,594	2,700	4	5	ρ=4.0, σ=1.8
Yeast	8	1,227	44	4	5	ρ=6.0, σ=2.0
KDD99Cup	33	200,000	200,000	5	5	ρ=5.0, σ=1.5

Note: * refers to class label "ME1", "ME2" and "ME3" in yeast

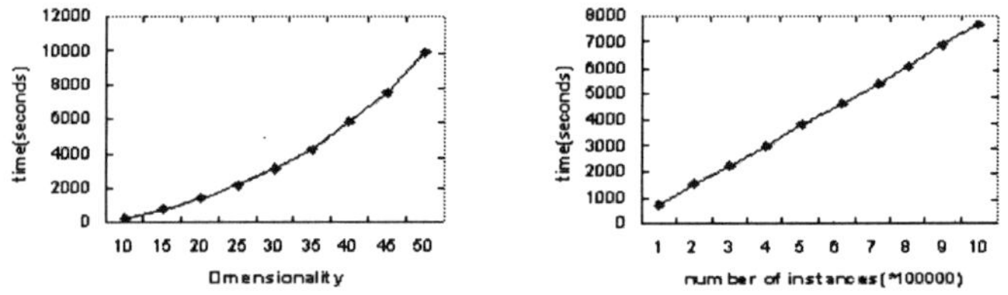

Fig.9 Scalability of Algorithm_1 on dimensionality and sample size

4.2. *Experiments on Detection Performance*

Table 3 shows the test results, where Num is the number of detectors, D.R. refers to detection rate and FA.R. denotes false alarm rate. The D.R and FAR are calculated according to the following regulations: (1) *For a non-self data, it is considered to be correctly detected if it is identified as non-self in one of the significant subspaces.* (2) *For a self data, it is considered to be correctly detected if and only if is identified as self in all subspaces.* The experimental results seem to fall into two groups: high detection rate with low false alarm rate (*KDD99Cup* and *shuttle*) and high detection rate with high false alarm rate (the rest). If we look back at Table 2, we may easily get the point that a properly large size of self data is crucial to obtaining both ideal D.R and FAR. Most of the UCI datasets have a few hundreds of self instances, and 20% of them are taken away for testing FAR. The number of instances in each of these cases is too small to characterize the normal data, resulting in a high FAR. The experimental results clearly show that any increase in D.R is always accompanied by an increase in FAR. The number of detectors, D.R and FAR are fairly affected by parameter η and ε. The number of detectors generated increases with η, but decreases with ε. As ε increases, more and more grids with density $<\varepsilon$ are excluded by clusters and become a part of detectors, consequentially the system will produce high D.R as well as high FAR. The lowest FAR is always obtained at $\eta=1$ and $\varepsilon=1$ for each dataset.

Table 3. Experimental results

Dataset		$\eta=10$			$\eta=20$			$\eta=30$		
		Num.	D.R.	FA.R.	Num.	D.R.	FA.R.	Num.	D.R.	FA.R.
bupa	$\varepsilon=1$	72	0.8027	0.0888	173	0.9455	0.3211	177	0.9932	0.4222
	$\varepsilon=3$	19	0.8503	0.2666	29	1.0000	0.6222	33	1.0000	0.8888
	$\varepsilon=5$	16	0.9728	0.3555	20	1.0000	0.7777	28	1.0000	0.9555
iris	$\varepsilon=1$	24	0.5600	0.0000	68	0.9400	0.0000	121	0.9600	0.2500
	$\varepsilon=3$	18	0.9200	0.0000	31	1.0000	0.1500	25	1.0000	0.6000
	$\varepsilon=5$	24	0.9600	0.2000	18	1.0000	0.5000	12	1.0000	0.7500
yeast	$\varepsilon=1$	6091	1.0000	0.4185	30538	1.0000	0.9222	68924	1.0000	0.9851
	$\varepsilon=3$	1195	1.0000	0.6629	1809	1.0000	0.9962	2552	1.0000	1.0000
	$\varepsilon=5$	569	1.0000	0.7926	897	1.0000	1.0000	1844	1.0000	1.0000
KDD99 Cup	$\varepsilon=1$	7455	0.9865	0.0000	81231	1.0000	0.0015	327126	1.0000	0.0039
	$\varepsilon=3$	5812	0.9865	0.0002	30537	1.0000	0.0027	62730	1.0000	0.0099
	$\varepsilon=5$	4791	0.9865	0.0006	16616	1.0000	0.0051	28088	1.0000	0.0151

The scalability of Algorithm_3 is tested on dimensionality. The experiments have shown that the time consumed in this phase is irrelevant to the number of instances in the dataset. The reason is that the elements for constructing detectors are grids instead of data points. Hence, the time consumed is mainly dependent on the number of grids in the subspace, which, in turn, is determined by the dimensionality and the parameter η. The scalability with dimensionality is tested on synthetic datasets because we can easily generate a dataset with specified dimensionality of the significant subspaces. However, the time consumed varies from subspace to subspace even if they have the same dimensionality. For a given subspace and η, the time-consumption is then determined by the number of clusters that normal data are partitioned into. If normal data are well partitioned into clusters, then fewer detectors are generated and less time is consumed in the process of construction. Hence, it may be more reasonable for us to concern with the relationship between time-consumption and the number of detectors constructed in a subspace. The relationship between time-consumption and dimensionality is non-linear.

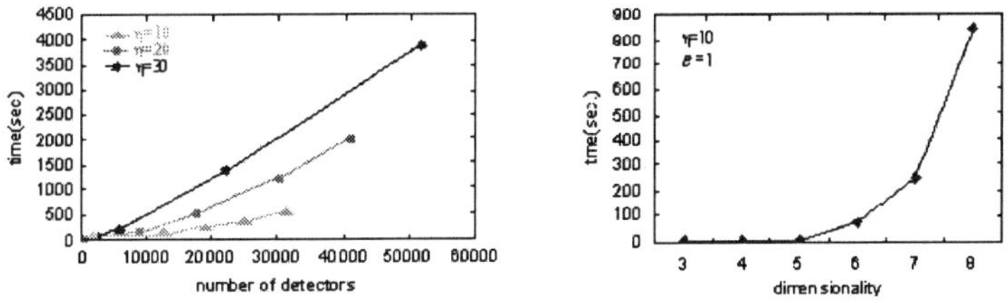

Fig. 10 Scalability of Algorithm_3 on the number of detector(left) and dimensionality(right)

The performance of different sets of detectors is evaluated with ROC(receiver operating characteristic) curve, which is used to make a tradeoff between the detection rate and false alarm rate of a detection system. The diagrams in Fig.10 show that the best curve is obtained with η*=20* for the dataset: *bupa, iris,* and *KDD99Cup,* and with η*=10* for the rest. In most of the cases, the shape of ROC curve changes apparently from sharp to flat when η increases from *10 to 30.* This implies that, on the one hand, a proper increase in η will cause detection rate to rise a lot while keeping false alarm rate under control, on the other hand, an over high η may not only increases greatly the computational cost, but also decreases the detection performance. The ROC curves on *KDD'99 Cup* and *shuttle* datasets show very good performance of the detectors, but the ROC curve on *pima* is close to the diagonal line from (0,0) to (1,1), representing a very poor performance.

5. Conclusions

In this paper, we investigated anomaly detection in high dimensional data spaces. Our solution to the problem is to construct detectors in different subspaces instead of the whole high dimensional space. Some key points are as follows: *a). In a high dimensional space, it is ineffective to construct detectors in the whole dimension because of the sparsity of data points everywhere in the space. However, normal data likely hide essential patterns in subspaces. b). Some significant subspaces mined are not as significant as the others, therefore, the two parameters* ρ *and* σ *play important role in the selection of significant subspaces. c). In the phase of constructing detectors, the elements constituting detects are grids instead of data points, which determines that the time consumed is irrelevant to the size of self data. The time consumed in this phase is closely related to the number of detectors constructed, which, in turn, is determined by how well normal data are clustered in subspaces. d). A bigger* η *leads to both higher detect rate and false alarm rate, so does* ε*. Hence, the best thresholds for* η *and* ε *vary from dataset to dataset. e). A properly large size of data is essential to characterize the normal data and accordingly essential to acquire both satisfying detection rate and false alarm rate.*

Our feature work will mainly focus on investigating more efficient methods for mining significant subspaces.

References

1. S. Hofmeyr and S. Forrest, Intrusion Detection: Architecture for an Artificial Immune System, *Evolutionary Comp Journal* **8(4)**, 443-473(2000).
2. S.Forrest, A.Oerelson, L.Allen, and R.cherukuri. "Slef-nonself discrimination in a computer", *In: proc of IEEE symp on res in security and privacy*, (1994).
3. C Cheng, A Fu and Y Zhang, Entropy-based subspace clustering for mining numerical data, *Proc. of ACM SIGKDD*, (1999).
4. R Ng and J Han, CLARANS: a method for clustering spatial data mining, *IEEE Trans on Knowledge and data engineering* **14(5)**, (2002).
5. J Han and M Kamber, *Data Mining: Concepts and Techniques*, Morgan Kaufmann Publishers, (2000).
6. M. Markou and S. Singh, Novelty Detection: A Review, http://www.dcs.ex.ac.uk/research/pann/pdf/pann_SS_086.PDF.

7. E. Keogh, S. Lonardi and B. Chiu, Finding surprising patterns in a time series database in linear time and space, in *Proc of the 8th ACM SIGKDD*, (2002).
8. M. L. Visinsky, J. R. Cavallaro and I. D. Walker, Robotic fault detection and fault tolerance: A survey, *Reliability Eng & Sys Safety* **46**, 139–158 (1994).
9. Yukio Ohsawa, Introduction to Chance Discovery and Chance Management: What we did, what we should, what we can, *AAAI Fall 2002 Symp on Chance discovery*, (2002).
10. I. Witten and E Frank, Data mining: Practical Machine Learning Tools & Tech with Java Impl., Acad Pres.

AUTHOR INDEX